ZX Spectrum
Assembly

Let´s make a game?

Juan Antonio Rubio García

Let's learn together how to make ZX Spectrum games in assembly language
for the Z80 microprocessor.

1st edition: november 2023
ISBN: 9798856087207

Text: © Juan Antonio Rubio García
Web: https://espamatica.com
Twitter: @juanantonio1072
Telegram: https://t.me/EnsambladorZXSpectrum

Arts and translation: © Felipe Monge Corbalán
Web: https://playonretro.com/
Twitter: @PlayOnRetro

Let´s make a game?

Index

*Forewords*_____*9*

   Emilio Serrano García _____*9*

   Javier Serrano García _____*11*

   Javier García Navarro _____*13*

*Why this book?*_____*16*

Acknowledgements _____*19*

Introduction _____*21*

Tools we will use _____*23*

   Text editor _____*23*

   ZX Spectrum Emulator _____*23*

   Assembly compiler _____*23*

   Source code control _____*23*

   Visual Studio Code Extensions _____*24*

   Useful links _____*24*

*Hello World*_____*26*

   What is the Z80? _____*26*

   Z80 registers _____*27*

     8-bit registers _____27

     Alternative registers _____27

     16-bit registers _____27

     Record operation codes (opcodes) _____28

     Registration F _____28

   ZX Spectrum Memory _____*29*

   Decimal, binary, hexadecimal_____*30*

   Labels, variables and constants _____*31*

   ORG and END_____*31*

   Loading instructions _____*32*

   RST Instructions_____*33*

Increases and decreases _____33

Logical operations _____34

Programme flow changes _____35

Subroutines _____37

Ports of entry and exit _____39

*ZX-Pong*_____42

Step 1: Drawing on the screen _____42

Step 2: Control keys _____50

Step 3: paddles and centre line _____56
   Change border colour_____56
   Assign the colour attributes to the screen _____57
   Draw the centre line of the field _____59
   Draw the paddles of both players _____62
   Move the paddles up and down_____64

Step 4: we start moving the ball_____71

Step 5: We move the ball around the screen_____79

Step 6: Field, paddle, ball and timing_____88

Step 7: Collision detection _____102

Step 8: Two players game and change ball speed _____110

Step 9: Change of direction and ball speed _____128

Step 10: Optimisation _____139
   Optimisation of ScanKeys_____147
   Optimisation of Cls _____147
   Optimisation of MoveBall_____148
   ReprintLine optimisation _____149
   Optimisation of GetPointSprite _____150
   Optimising PrintPoints and ReprintPoints _____152
   Ball strike bug at the bottom of the paddle _____155

Step 11: Sound and 16K _____157

Step 12: Optimisation part 2_____164
   Optimising PlaySound_____164
   Optimisation of ReprintPoints _____165

Step 13: Loading screen _____169

We implement the loader _____169
We add the loading screen_____170
Including ZX-Pong _____171

Space Battle _____174

Introduction_____174

Step 1: Definition of graphics _____175
Hexadecimal/binary conversion_____175
Practising hexadecimal/binary conversion _____176

Step 2: Painting UDG _____188
Where are the UDG? _____188
We paint our UDGs_____188
We load the enemies' UDGs_____190

Step 3: Play area _____195
Changing the active display _____195
We paint text strings _____195
We paint the game screen _____198
We clean and colour the screen_____201
We paint the information of the game _____203

Step 4: Ship _____207
On-screen positioning _____207
We paint the ship _____208
We move the ship_____212

Step 5: Interruptions and shot _____219
Interruptions_____219
We compile into multiple files _____220
We slow down the ship _____221
We implement the shot _____223

Step 6: Enemies _____227
We define enemies_____227
We paint the enemies _____230
We move the enemies _____233

Step 7: Collisions and level change_____241
Enemy collisions with the shot_____241
Level change _____244
Collisions between enemies and the ship _____248

Step 8: Transition between levels and scoreboard _____253
Level change transition_____253
Scoreboard _____257

Step 9: Start the game _____**271**

PrintString routine _____271

Start and end of the game _____276

Step 10: Joystick and extra life _____**286**

Delay _____286

Joystick _____286

Extra life _____292

Change of shot _____296

Step 11: Enemy behaviour _____**298**

Changes of direction_____298

Colour change_____302

Enemy shots _____303

Difficulty setting _____317

Step 12: Sound_____**319**

Testing, testing _____319

Rhythm and beat _____326

Different rhythms _____329

Step 13: Music _____**333**

Constants _____333

Variables _____333

Reproduction _____335

Music control by interruptions_____342

Sound effects _____344

Step 14: Difficulty, mute and loading screen _____**347**

Difficulty _____347

Muting _____356

Loading screen _____357

Tic-tac-toe_____***361***

Introduction _____**361**

Step 1: Game board_____**362**

Sprites _____362

ROM routines and variables _____363

Variables _____364

Screen _____365

Main _____371

Step 2: scoreboards and a two player game _____**373**

Information_____373

Two-player game _____376

Step 3: Sound _____392

Step 4: Options and end of game _____397
Menu_____397
Start of game _____401
Shift time _____405
End of game _____411

Step 5: Me versus the Spectrum _____414

Step 6: Final adjustments _____426
Tables menu _____426
Table detection_____427
We save bytes and clock cycles _____430
Spectrum movement _____438
Difficulty _____439
Loading screen _____441

Appendix 1: Frequencies and notes_____446

Appendix 2: ZEsarUX _____452

Personalisation _____452

Debugging _____455

Bibliography _____461

Let´s make a game?

Forewords

Emilio Serrano García

We had already seen "War Games", "Tron" and "Star Wars" more than once... the world of the mid-eighties was far from what it is today and computers and other technological gadgets were something almost exclusively relegated to the science fiction of these films. My brother Javi and I were only two years apart, we had a simple life in a small town near Madrid, where all our friends lived in the same neighbourhood, we went out to play together, we went to school and sometimes to the cinema when it was possible... there wasn't much else to do, to be honest. It is not surprising that when we saw and experienced a Spectrum for the first time, at the house of a cousin who was already working and could afford it, it affected us the way it did, and from that moment on, a strange mixture of illusion, passion, dedication and, of course, a lot of luck, changed us forever, determining our lives and our future to this day.

"Juanan, as we called him, was part of this group of friends from the neighbourhood and, of course, the author of this book. We lived in the same street, went to the same school, did the same things after school and, of course, shared something close to an obsession with the Spectrum. Every week we would check the Microhobby, we would compete to see Ponce's signature on the cover, and then we would fantasise about creating games and doing a thousand things with it... childhood dreams that fade with time and harsh reality in most cases, but not in ours.

As it happened, Juanan was the first lucky one to get it: a wonderful 48k with a rubber keyboard! I still remember going to his house and trying it out, especially the Panama Joe games that came as a gift.

Ours arrived a little later. After a lot of saving and nagging from our parents, we finally got them to buy it for my birthday. We went to the famous "decomisos" in Arenal Street in Madrid and got a Spectrum +. As expected, our lives changed from that day on and we dedicated ourselves almost exclusively to the Spectrum, spending most of our time playing with it, especially at the beginning. Somehow our room became our social headquarters, and it was not uncommon for us to gather at least five or six friends there and spend the afternoon playing whatever games we had available. It was also in the same room, some years later and after a lot of work and countless attempts, that we completed our first and only Spectrum game: "The Prayer of the Warrior. Both Juanan and most of our friends were direct witnesses to how we started playing and how, with little information or resources available, we were able to develop games at a level close to what we were playing. That's how we grew as people and, unconsciously, as professionals: me as an artist and my brother as a programmer.

A little later, as teenagers, we started hanging out with a new group of friends, "Juanan" became "Yuyu" and we shared another new passion:

music. We played in a rock/heavy band for many years, while I continued to study and work with the illusion of becoming a video game artist one day. In the meantime, the Spectrum had become almost a thing of the past, "obsolete" and replaced mainly by today's personal computers.

Juanan, on the other hand, had already left school to work with his father and brother as a plasterer. The opposite of computer science and game development, right? Our paths were very different: I started as a professional artist/animator at Dynamic Multimedia in 1994, and Juanan continued as a bricklayer for a long time, until years later he made a radical change and decided to leave the building site and dedicate himself to programming, which was his true vocation. Soon after, he began to take an interest in retro, getting back into everything he hadn't been able to do at the time, Spectrum, Amstrad, hardware, creating his own games, tutorials and helping others get into retro and preserving the memory of what was the beginning of all this and a good part of our lives: the ZX Spectrum.

I take it for granted that when you hold this book or digital device in your hands, you know what you are accessing and why... I also know that you will not be disappointed. For me, however, this book and this prologue are a tribute to our lifelong friendship, sometimes shaken by unforgiving factors that force you to adapt, to search, to improve or "simply" to reinvent yourself, and finally, how important it is to believe in yourself so that, at least sometimes, dreams come true; Juanan's life and this book prove it.

Enjoy it.

Javier Serrano García

I have always remembered my beginnings in the Z80 microprocessor language of the ZX Spectrum with great enthusiasm, although many details have been forgotten over the years. I miss everything I experienced and from time to time I try to relive it in my mind to keep as much as possible in my memory. The love at first sight of the ZX Spectrum + given to my cousin Rafa for his birthday, the illusion of buying it and flicking through the Microhobby magazines, the day we went to Madrid's Arenal Street to pick it up, the first projects with my brother, the bittersweet end of Zigurat's interest in our game, or the speculation among friends about who would be the first to have it, what I would do when I had it, and so on.

Against all the odds, Juan Antonio was the first to have it. What a good game of Panama Joe we had at his house.

My brother Emilio and I saved every peseta they gave us as a tip for the ZX Spectrum+ we had fallen in love with. We remember the weeks of waiting as if they were years until we could finally buy it, and that's when it all began. Then there were the afternoons spent playing Match Day with friends, and even though Juan Antonio wasn't very good, he was always very enthusiastic. Those afternoons were a fundamental part of the inspiration for our first 'prototypes' of BASIC games.

Fate and circumstances meant that my brother spent some time in hospital with a broken leg. I imagine he must have read Microhobby a thousand times while he was there. I remember that during one of my visits he told me, as he lay in bed: "We have to learn assembly, that's what makes good games...".

From that moment on, all my motivation and time with the Spectrum was devoted to making the leap into this new universe that was assembly. I started to write lists in hexadecimal, to try out those little examples and curiosities in assembly that I had only looked at in bewilderment. One of the moments I have to thank fate for, and I can't remember how it happened, was when we got our hands on the Gens3.

The goal was to make our games faster, to move "pixel by pixel" on the screen, and all the information helped a little. Chips and machine code, of course, but above all the great article in Microhobby Special nº 6 "Sprite Control" by Pablo Ariza.

How I wish I could have back then the information and examples that Juan Antonio has now published in this book. In it you will be able to learn in a progressive way and with examples the architecture of the Z80, how to start the assembly, how to organise your project with a version control and many other things that you will discover.

I'm glad that there are people like Juan Antonio who keep the Z80 flame alive among 8-bit computers, be it Spectrum, Amstrad, MSX, etc.

It is admirable that he has managed to reinvent himself and dedicate himself professionally to software programming.

I would like to say goodbye and hope that you will enjoy the book and that you will be able to make use of it, thanking Juan Antonio for thinking of me for the prologue of his book, which I am sure he has written with such enthusiasm and passion.

Javier García Navarro

A few decades ago, in an era that now seems distant and perhaps a little magical, a small device with rubber keys and bright colours on the screen appeared. It was the ZX Spectrum. A humble device that arrived in our homes to revolutionise the way we understood entertainment and, in many cases, our vision of what a handful of transistors could do. Some may call it nostalgia, but for others this fascinating universe is still alive, evolving and feeding our thirst for knowledge.

And here we are, immersed in a journey through binary code, registers and interrupts, captained by a character whose life journey may be as surprising as the world he is about to introduce us to. This character, dear readers, is my friend Juan Antonio, whose name you will see on the cover of this book. A man who almost said goodbye to us a year ago, but who, like the ZX Spectrum, resisted, persisted and prevailed.

Stories of near-death often provoke deep reflection, drastic life changes and a re-evaluation of priorities. For my friend Juan Antonio, this experience was a powerful reminder of how precious every moment, every breath, every line of code we can write is. And he has decided to share this knowledge and his passion for the Z80 assembly with us all. Who better than someone who has been to the edge of the abyss to teach us to appreciate and master the intricacies of the language that made the ZX Spectrum beat.

More than just a programming guide, this book is an invitation to delve into the mysteries and wonders of the ZX Spectrum. Not only will you learn the ins and outs of Z80 assembly, but you will also understand how many of the games and programs that defined our childhood and teenage years were created. And maybe, just maybe, it will inspire you to develop your own creations to revive the original spirit of the early days of microcomputing.

To the uninitiated, the Z80 assembly may seem a difficult and challenging terrain. But Juan Antonio, with his experience and his gift for explaining the most complex things in a simple way, will make the path easier for you. I promise you that this book will be the perfect companion for your adventure, a detailed map to the hidden treasure of the Z80 assembly.

As he was about to leave this world, my friend found an amazing clarity: a clarity that comes through in every word he has written in this book. Every chapter, every code example, every diagram flows from his pen (or rather keyboard) with the precision and grace of someone who truly understands what it means to live each moment to the fullest. His work is a constant reminder that every day, every hour, every minute counts. And nothing could be more appropriate for a book about assembly programming, where every bit, every clock cycle, every instruction matters.

The story of the ZX Spectrum is in many ways the story of computing itself. It is a story of overcoming limitations, of ingenuity and boundless creativity, of small miracles achieved with just a few kilobytes of memory and an 8-bit processor. It is also the story of a community of developers and hobbyists, many of whom took their first steps into programming thanks to this marvellous machine.

And this book, written by someone who was and still is part of that community, is imbued with that same passion and spirit. Every page is filled with anecdotes, practical tips and, of course, assembly code. You'll learn not only how the ZX Spectrum works on a hardware level, but also what it's like to program in assembly, with its unique challenges and equally unique rewards.

So, lover of retro computing, curious about programming, fan of the ZX Spectrum, open this book and immerse yourself in its contents. Let its pages carry you away, let the words of my friend guide you on this journey. And remember, every line of code you write is a victory, a testimony that you too, like my friend, can overcome challenges and create miracles.

Because, after all, isn't that what makes life, and programming, so fascinating?

Why this book?

San Martín de la Vega, Madrid

June 2023

Many years ago, in 1985, my brother, who was doing his military service, went on a leave of absence to some seizures near our house and came back with a ZX Spectrum 48K, which became one of the two best gifts of my life, the other being the Amstrad CPC 464 that my parents gave me a year later.

I had only seen this wonderful computer in MicroHobby, the computer magazine of reference at the time (at least for my group of friends), but couldn't stop talking about it at home.

When I opened the box of my brand new computer, the first thing I did was to read the first pages of a slim manual that explained how to connect it, how to turn it on and the most used command in the world, with the permission of "Run":

LOAD ""

I remember the first tape we loaded was Horizons and we spent several hours on it. The next one was Panama Joe. At that moment a new world of possibilities opened up and my path began to lead me to where I am today.

The next thing I did was to open the other, much bigger manual that came with the Spectrum and start learning Basic, and with that came the real concern of what could be done with this beast, that was the moment I started dreaming of making a game, which I didn't manage to do.

Soon I got my hands on an assembly book, which, together with the articles published by MicroHobby, got me interested in this language, although to be honest I understood very little.

In the meantime I enjoyed playing everything I could get my hands on, Sir Fred being the video game I enjoyed the most, and still do.

I wanted to make a video game like the ones I loved to play, but another passion of mine, going out with friends, got in the way.

In between my studies, I was already in high school, and the time I wasn't studying, I studied very little, I was with my friends, the Spectrum took a second place, and although I still played with it, reading manuals and making games was forgotten.

Many years later, in 2018, my great friend Emilio Serrano told me about an event where you could see the ZX Spectrum working and play with it, and so we went, to the 2018 Run ZX held at MediaLab-Prado. I brought my ZX-Uno with me.

It was there that I really got bitten by the bug. Little by little I started to get involved in what is now called retro, and in particular my interest in programming, especially assembly, grew again.

Today we have access to information that we could not even dream of in the 1980s: books, magazines, video games, etc.

A colleague at work told me about some videos from the University of Alicante, by a certain Professor Retroman (Fran Gallego), and I started my journey with Z80 assembly.

Later I found Santiago Romero's Z80 assembly course on one of the sites I discovered, speccy.org, and it all started. Following this course I started to make my first progress. As an exercise, after the chapter on interrupts, Batalla espacial was born.

Some time later, it was suggested that I make a Pong clone for Spectrum, and then make a tutorial to teach it in collaboration with Retro Parla. Due to the pandemic, the tutorial was put on hold and I published it on the website of my friends at AUA.

This is where I got my taste for writing tutorials, and after the Pong tutorial I wrote the Space Battle tutorial and published it on my website.

After reading Club de programación de juegos de ZX Spectrum, I made my third game, Tres en raya, for which I have just written the tutorial to be included in this book.

With the Pong tutorial written and published in AUA, Manuel Iglesias (HobbyRetro) asked me if I hadn't thought about preparing a self-published book. I started to like the idea of publishing my own book and here is the result. Thank you Manu for encouraging me to do it.

The situation of the last few months also had a lot to do with it, so I leave something for posterity.

I hope you enjoy reading it and learn from it.

Let´s make a game?

Acknowledgements

There are many people to thank for the fact that this book is in your hands today, starting with you. Thank you for buying it.

I would like to thank Felipe Monge Corbalán for designing the front and back covers. To Emilio and Javier Serrano García (Retos Soft) for giving me the opportunity to see how a good game is made. To Francisco Gallego Durán (Professor Retroman), whose great videos started me on the path to assembly programming for the Z80. To Javier García Navarro (4MHz) for his advice and talks, almost never about programming. To Enrique Segura Alcalde, he is a role model for me. To Manuel J. Rico Borrego, Jesús Martínez del Vas, Alejandro Ibáñez, Javier Ortiz Carrasco and Juan Francisco Torres Chica, with your wonderful book I remembered what the Spectrum meant to me and started everything that led me here. To S.T.A.R., thanks to him the number of video games on my shelf grew exponentially. To Retro Parla and AUA, associations that I work with and that have allowed me to meet many other people with the same interests as me. To Rafa Pardo (Spirax) and Joaquín Ferrero for their comments. To Santiago Romero for teaching me almost everything I know about assembly with his course.

Of course, thanks to my parents and my brother, they were the ones who introduced computers into my life, they were the ones who started the retro.

And my wife and children. During the preparation of this book I was very busy and sacrificed my time with them to make this project happen, and they still love me.

There are so many people to thank, so many that I would almost have to write a book just to do it; thank you all very much.

Let´s make a game?

Introduction

The aim of this book is to learn the basic concepts that will allow us making our own developments in the Z80 Assembly for the ZX Spectrum later on.

To make the learning process more enjoyable, I propose to develop, step by step, a version of a video game that is perhaps one of the most famous of all time, Pong. We will then develop a simple Martian killer (with in-game music) and a tic-tac-toe game (with one and two player modes).

All these video games will be compatible with 16, 48 and 128K ZX Spectrum computers.

At each stage we will have something new and functional, we will make things and then change them until development is complete.

The code we will develop will in many cases not be the most optimal, the aim is to learn how to do things in different ways, to know many of the Z80 instructions and some of the ZX Spectrum hardware.

As for the source format, instructions are in column one, parameters in column six and comments in column 28.

At the end of each chapter you will find a QR code and a URL to download the chapter code, but readers of the first edition requested that all the source code contained in the book could be downloaded from a single link.

You can download all the source code here:

https://tinyurl.com/2d5v4l3d

Let´s make a game?

Tools we will use

The tools we will use throughout the book are described below.

Text editor

Any text editor will do, no matter how simple, such as Windows Notepad. There are other free editors, more powerful and with syntax highlighting:

- NotePad++
- Visual Studio Code, with the Z80 assembly extension
    imanolea.z80-asm
- Sublime Text, install the z80asm-ti package

ZX Spectrum Emulator

There are many ZX Spectrum emulators, with the free ones being perhaps the best.

I use ZEsarUX, a Spanish-developed emulator available for Linux, MacOS and Windows systems, and a few others.

Assembly compiler

We will use PASMO, a cross-assembler with versions for Linux, MacOS and Windows, which generates executable code for the ZX Spectrum, among other things.

PASMO works from the command line, if you are using Windows you need to add it to the Path system variable to be able to run it from any directory. In this video I explain how to do this.

https://tinyurl.com/2mmgzufn

Source code control

It is good practice to have some form of source control so that if something stops working, you can see how it was in a previous version.

In this case I chose Git, created a local repository and installed the Git Graph extension in Visual Studio Code. This is not essential, but highly recommended.

mhutchie.git-graph

Visual Studio Code Extensions

If you are using Visual Studio Code, you will find it very interesting to install the Z80 Assembly Meter extension, it provides the size and clock cycles of each instruction.

thenestruo.z80-asm-meter

I also installed the Hex Editor to be able to open the contents of the binaries we will generate.

ms-vscode.hexeditor

Useful links

- Notepad++
  https://notepad-plus-plus.org/
- Visual Studio Code
  https://code.visualstudio.com/
- Sublime Text
  https://www.sublimetext.com/
- ZEsarUX
  https://github.com/chernandezba/zesarux
- Pasmo
  https://pasmo.speccy.org/
- Compiler Software Z80 Assembly Course
  https://wiki.speccy.org/cursos/ensamblador/indice
- Professor Retroman (Fran Gallego)
  https://www.youtube.com/@ProfessorRetroman
- Z80 Assembly on Telegram
  https://t.me/EnsambladorZXSpectrum
- Basic ZX Course
  https://t.me/CursoBasicZX

Hello World

Before we start developing our video games, we are going to do what you do when you learn a programming language, we are going to develop a "Hello World".

The creation of our Hello World will help us to acquire the minimum knowledge we will need to develop our programmes.

With "Hello World" we will discover:

- The main features of the Zilog Z80 microprocessor and its registers.
- The memory layout of the ZX Spectrum.
- Numbers in different notations.
- Labels, variables and constants in assembly.
- ORG and END directives.
- Loading instructions.
- RST instructions.
- Increments and decrements.
- Logical operations.
- Programme flow changes.
- Subroutines.
- Entry and exit ports.

You can download this spreadsheet with the Z80 instructions, cycles, bytes, flag assignments, etc.

https://tinyurl.com/27fbuyfb

What is the Z80?

The Z80 is a microprocessor released by Zilog in 1976. It is the microprocessor used in all models of the ZX Spectrum.

The Z80 is a CPU of the "Little Endian" type. A CPU of this type, when storing 16-bit values in memory, stores the least significant byte in the first position and the most significant byte in the next; if the value $CCFF is loaded into memory position $8000, it stores the value $FF in position $8000 and the value $CC in position $8001.

Another feature of the Z80 that we will sometimes not like is that it is not orthogonal, which means that not all operations between registers are allowed.

Z80 registers

The registers are high-speed, low-capacity memory and are integrated into the microprocessor.

The Z80 has 8-bit and 16-bit registers.

8-bit registers

- **A**: accumulator. It is the destination of 8-bit arithmetic, logic and comparison operations. A is the high byte of the 16-bit AF register.
- **F**: flags (indicators). A set of flags that provide information on the operations being performed. F is the low byte of the 16-bit AF register.
- **B**: general purpose register often used in loops; it is used by DJNZ as a counter. B is the high byte of the 16-bit BC register.
- **C**: general purpose register. C is the low byte of the 16-bit BC register.
- **D**: general purpose register. D is the high byte of the 16-bit DE register.
- **E**: general purpose register. E is the low byte of the 16-bit DE register.
- **H**: general purpose register. H is the high byte of the 16-bit HL register.
- **L**: general purpose register. L is the low byte of the 16-bit HL register.
- **I**: Interrupt register. Allows 128 different interrupts to be handled.
- **R**: Memory refresh register. Handled by the Z80, only bits 0 to 6 change. Can be used to generate semi-random numbers between 0 and 127.

Alternative registers

The alternate registers are used to make a temporary copy of the 8-bit registers:

- **A'**: alternative register of A.
- **F'**: alternative register of F.
- **B'**: alternative register of B.
- **C'**: alternative register of C.
- **D'**: alternative register of D.
- **E'**: alternative register of E.
- **H'**: alternative registration of H.
- **L'**: alternative registration of L.

16-bit registers

- **AF**: consisting of register A as the high byte and F as the low byte.
- **BC**: is formed by register B as the high byte and C as the low byte. It is generally used as a counter in operations such as LDIR, LDDR, etc.

- **DE**: consisting of register D as the high byte and E as the low byte. It is generally used for reading and writing in a single operation, and as a target in LDIR, LDDR, etc. operations.
- **HL**: formed by the H register as the high byte and L as the low byte. It is generally used for reading and writing in a single operation, as well as for source operations such as LDIR, LDDR, etc. The HL register acts as an accumulator in 16-bit operations.
- **IX**: indexed memory access, LD (IX + N), where N can be a value between -128 and 127.
- **IY**: indexed memory access, LD (IY + N), where N can be a value between -128 and 127.
- **SP**: Stack pointer. Points to the current position of the stack header.
- **PC**: Programme counter. Address of the current instruction to be executed.

Record operation codes (opcodes)

- **0:** B
- **1:** C
- **2:** D
- **3:** E
- **4:** H
- **5:** L
- **6:** (HL)
- **7:** A

These operation codes are used to calculate the operation code for instructions where the parameter is a register.

LD A, r: 0x78 + rb

LD C, r: 0x48 + rb

Where rb is the operation code of the records to be loaded.

Registration F

Each bit of the F register, flags, has its own meaning which changes automatically according to the result of the operations performed:

- **Bit 0:** C flag (carry). A one if the result of the previous operation needs an extra bit to represent it (I take one). The carry flag is the extra bit needed.
- **Bit 1:** Flag N (subtraction). Set to one if the last operation was a subtraction.
- **Bit 2:** P/V flag (parity/overflow). In operations that change the parity bit, it is set to one when the number of bits to one of the result is even. In operations that change the overflow bit, it is set to one when the result of the operation requires more than eight bits to represent.
- **Bit 3:** not used.

- **Bit 4:** H Flag (BCD carry). A one if there is a carry from bit 3 to bit 4 in BCD operations.
- **Bit 5:** not used.
- **Bit 6:** Z Flag (zero). A one if the previous operation returns zero. Very useful in loops.
- **Bit 7:** S flag (sign). A one if the above two's complement is a negative number.

The F register is not directly accessible, and not all operations affect it.

Record F - indicators/flags

Bit	7	6	5	4	3	2	1	0
Flag	S	Z	F5	H	F3	P/V	N	C

ZX Spectrum Memory

The memory is divided into two blocks of 16 KB (16384 bytes) on 16K models and four blocks of 16 KB (16384 bytes) on 48K models:

- **First block**: from position $4000 to $3FFF (0 to 16383). This block corresponds to the ROM and is read-only.
- **Second block**: from position $4000 to $7FFF (16384 to 32767). This block contains the screen area, printer buffer, system variables, etc., leaving about 9KB for programs on 16K models.

The following memory blocks are only found in 48K models:

- **Third block**: from position $8000 to $BFFF (32768 to 49151). This is general purpose RAM.
- **Fourth block**: from position $C000 to $FFFF (49152 to 65535). This is general purpose RAM.

The distribution of the second block is superficially as follows:

- **$4000 - $57FF (16384 to 22527)**: Screen pixel area. The ZX Spectrum's screen has a resolution of 256 * 192 pixels. Each byte represents eight pixels (256 * 192 / 8 = 6144 bytes).
- **$5800 - $5AFF (22528 to 23295)**: Colour attribute area of the display. In this case a resolution of 32 * 24 characters is available. Each byte specifies the colour of an 8 * 8 pixel area, where bits 0 to 2 define the ink colour (0 to 7), bits 3 to 5 the background colour (0 to 7), bit 6 the brightness (0 to 1) and bit 7 the flicker (0 to 1). This area occupies a total of 768 bytes (32 * 24).
- **$5B00 to $5BFF (23296 to 23551)**: Printer buffer. 256 bytes that can be used if you don't have a printer or if it is not used by the program.
- **$5C00 - $5CB5 (23552 to 23733)**: System variables.
- **$5CB0 - $5CB1 (23728 to 23729)**: Unused memory that can be used for data exchange.

- **$7FFF**: Stack pointer. Normally points to this address and decrements as data is fed into it.

Decimal, binary, hexadecimal

Decimal notation is the way we are used to seeing numbers, as a series of digits with values between 0 and 9. This is also known as base 10 notation.

In computing, it is different because computers work with two values: 0 and 1. These numbers are known as binary, in base 2.

In assembly, the most common way of representing numbers is in base 16 (hexadecimal notation), where each digit represents values from 0 to 15:

- A = 10
- B = 11
- C = 12
- D = 13
- E = 14
- F = 15

A hexadecimal digit represents 4 bits, so we know at a glance how many bits it is made up of. It is common to speak of multiples of 8 (8, 16, 32, 64...).

Without a calculator at hand, converting numbers between the different bases can be very tedious. It is helpful to know the value of each bit; in the case of the Z80, 8-bit and 16-bit numbers.

We will use the following table. It shows the values of each bit to help us with the conversions:

15	14	13	12	11	10	9	8
32728	16384	8192	4096	2048	1024	512	256
7	**6**	**5**	**4**	**3**	**2**	**1**	**0**
128	64	32	16	8	4	2	1

As you can see, we only need to add to convert numbers from one base to another, as shown in the example below:

```
5FA0h
0101 1111 1010 0000
32 + 128 + 256 + 512 + 1024 + 2048 + 4096 + 16384 = 24480
```

Hexadecimal to binary conversion is straightforward, with four bits making up each digit.

```
F0h = 1111 0000     3Ah = 0011 1010
CCh = 1100 1100     78h = 0111 1000
0001 0000 = 10h     0100 0101 = 45h
1010 1010 = AAh     0010 0011 = 23h
```

Labels, variables and constants

Tags allow us to refer to memory locations without having to calculate them. The assembler program is responsible for replacing the labels with the correct memory addresses; this process is done when the object code is created.

If we could not use labels, each time we modified any part of the code, the memory addresses would have to be recalculated for use in each JR, JP or CALL. The assembler replaces the labels with the memory addresses of the following instructions.

Labels are used to define routines and data; in the case of data, it can be numeric or text, constants or variables.

The data is defined by the following instructions:

- **EQU**: define constants

    name EQU value

- **DB/DEFB**: define bytes

    name DB 1, $FF, %10101010

- **DM/DEFM**: define message

    name DEFM "Hello World"

- **DW/DEFW**: define word

    name DW $0040

- **DS/DEFS**: define space

    name DEFS $08

DB, DEFB, DM, DEFM, DW, DEFW, DS and DEFS are not assembled, so it is recommended to put them at the end of the code, otherwise they will be executed as if they were Z80 instructions. If we start the code with:

```
DB $CD, $00, $00
```

Since the DB directive is not assembled, this line would do a reset; DB $CD, $00, $00 is CALL $0000.

ORG and END

ORG and END are two of the most important directives we will use. With ORG we specify the memory address where the code will be loaded. Multiple ORGs can be set so that code can be loaded into different memory addresses.

END indicates where the programme ends, also an autostart address for PASMO.

With what we have seen so far, we can now develop the first programme; open the text editor to write these lines:

```
org    $8000
```

```
ret
end   $8000
```

We save the file as "helloworld.asm" and compile with PASMO:

```
pasmo --name HelloWorld --tapbas helloworld.asm helloworld.tap --log
```

This command (pasmo...) will always be used to compile our programs.

Now we can open the holamundo.tap file with a ZX Spectrum emulator and see that it runs, even though it just exits and we haven't broken anything.

Loading instructions

We use these instructions to load literal values into a register, the value of a register into another register, a value into memory, the value of a register into memory and a memory value into a register.

The syntax of the load instructions is as follows:

```
LD    destination, origin
```

The destination can be a register or a memory location, the source can be a register, a memory location or an 8-bit or 16-bit value.

These instructions do not affect the F register, except for **LD A, I** and **LD A, R**.

This is the moment to return to our first programme, where we will add the following lines just below ORG:

```
ld    hl, $4000
ld    (hl), $ff
```

With these lines we activate the 8 bits of the first memory address of the screen, hereafter called VideoRAM. Compile with PASMO and load into the emulator:

```
pasmo --name HelloWorld --tapbas helloworld.asm helloworld.tap --log
```

RST Instructions

These instructions are used to jump to a specific address with a single opcode instruction.

There are several RST instructions, but we will only use RST $10 (RST 16), which prints the ASCII corresponding to the value in register A.

We get the file helloworld.asm, remove the two lines we added and write the following:

```
ld    a, 'H'
rst   $10
```

We compile and load it into the emulator. The letter H appears on the screen.

Increases and decreases

They are used to increment (INC) or decrement (DEC) the contents of certain registers or memory locations (pointed to by the HL, IX or IY registers) by one unit.

The permitted operations are:

INC r	DEC r
INC rr	DEC rr
INC (HL)	DEC (HL)
INC (IX + n)	DEC (IX + n)
INC (IY + n)	DEC (IY + n)

These operations, when performed on 16-bit registers, do not affect the F register, but when performed on 8-bit registers, they affect it in different ways:

	Flags					
Instruction	S	Z	H	P/V	N	C
INC r	*	*	*	V	0	-
INC (HL)	*	*	*	V	0	-

INC (ri + n)	*	*	*	V	0	-
INC rr	-	-	-	-	-	-
DEC r	*	*	*	V	1	-
DEC (HL)	*	*	*	V	1	-
DEC (ri + n)	*	*	*	V	1	-
DEC rr	-	-	-	-	-	-

- = no impact, * = impact, 0 = set to 0, 1 = set to 1, V = overflow

We edit the helloworld.asm file and leave it as it is:

```
org   $8000              ; Address where you load the programme

ld    hl, msg            ; HL = message memory address
ld    a, (hl)            ; A = first character
rst   $10                ; Prints the character
inc   hl                 ; HL = address next character
ld    a, (hl)            ; A = next character
rst   $10                ; Prints the character

ret

msg:  defm 'Hello ZX Spectrum Assembly'

end   $8000
```

Compile and load into the emulator. Now we see "He" on the screen.

Logical operations

Logical operations are performed at bit level by comparing two bits. There are three kinds of logical operations:

- **AND**: Logical multiplication. The result is only one if both bits are set to one.
- **OR**: Logical addition. If either bit is one, the result is one, otherwise the result is zero.

34

- **XOR**: Exclusive OR. If both bits are equal, the result is zero, otherwise the result is one.

The following table shows the possible results of the logic operations:

Bit 1	Bit 2	AND	OR	XOR
1	1	1	1	0
1	0	0	1	1
0	1	0	1	1
0	0	0	0	0

The format of the logical operations is as follows:

```
AND   origin
OR    origin
XOR   origin
```

For logical operations, the source can be any of the 8-bit registers (except F), a value, a memory location pointed to by (HL) or by the index registers, (IX + n) or (IY + n). The target is always register A; logical operations are performed on the value contained in register A and the result is left in the same register.

Logical operations affect register F in this way:

Instruction	S	Z	H	P/V	N	C
				Flags		
AND s	*	*	*	P	0	0
OR s	*	*	*	P	0	0
XOR s	*	*	*	P	0	0

- = does not affect, * = affects, 0 = set to 0, 1 = set to 1, P = parity

Programme flow changes

They modify the programme flow (jumps), with or without conditions, absolute (JP) or relative (JR). These instructions do not affect the F register.

Absolute jumps are possible:

- **JP nn**: Jumps to memory address **nn**, which can be a label (in the following cases as well).
- **JP (HL)**: Jumps to the memory address of the value held by HL; to the value of HL (16 bits), not to the value of the address pointed to by HL (8 bits).

- **JP (index register)**: jumps to the memory address of the value that has IX or IY.
- **JP NZ, nn**: Jumps to address **nn**, if the Z flag is zero; the result of the last operation is not zero.
- **JP Z, nn**: Jumps to memory address **nn** if the Z flag is set to one; the result of the last operation is zero.
- **JP NC, nn**: Jumps to memory address **nn** if the C flag is set to zero; no carry.
- **JP C, nn**: Jumps to memory address **nn** if the C flag is set to one; there is carry.
- **JP PO, nn**: Jumps to memory address **nn** if the P/V flag is zero; no parity/overflow.
- **JP PE, nn**: Jumps to memory address **nn** if the P/V flag is set to one; there is parity/overflow.
- **JP P, nn**: Jumps to memory address **nn** if the S flag is zero; the result of the last operation is positive.
- **JP M, nn**: Jumps to memory address **nn** if the S flag is set to one; the result of the last operation is negative.

Relative jumps are relative to the current instruction and jump a number of bytes from -128 to 127. Routines with relative jumps are relocatable as they do not affect the memory location in which they are loaded.

Relative jumps can be:

- **JR n**: Jumps to the memory address that is **n** bytes away; **n** can be a label (in the following cases also).
- **JR NZ, n**: Jumps to the memory address that is **n** bytes away if the Z flag is zero; the result of the last operation is non-zero.
- **JR Z, n**: Jumps to the memory address that is **n** bytes away if the Z flag is set to one; the result of the last operation is zero.
- **JR NC, n**: Jumps to the memory address that is **n** bytes away if the C flag is set to zero; no carry.
- **JR C, n**: Jumps to the memory address that is **n** bytes away if the C flag is set to one; there is a carry.

We open the file helloworld.asm; we use logical operations and flow changes to print the whole message:

```
org  $8000              ; Address where the programme is loaded

ld   hl, msg            ; HL = message memory address

Loop:
ld   a, (hl)            ; Loads a character from the string
or   a                  ; ¿A = 0? A or A = 0 only if A = 0
jr   z, Exit            ; If A = 0, jump to the Exit label.
rst  $10                ; Paints the character
inc  hl                 ; HL = next character
jr   Loop               ; Returns to the beginning of the loop

Exit:
ret                     ; Exits the programme
```

```
msg: defm 'Hello ZX Spectrum Assembly', $00
; String ending in 0 = null

end  $8000
```

We compile with PASMO, load in the emulator and see the results:

Subroutines

Subroutines are blocks of code that perform a specific action and can be called multiple times; CALL is used to jump to a subroutine and RET is used to exit and return to where it was called from.

CALL is similar to JP, but before jumping it does a PC PUSH to store where the programme is going. When RET is finished, PC POP is finished and the program returns to where it was.

PUSH and POP put and remove values on the stack. The values are always 16-bit registers.

Conditional CALLs and RETs are possible, as seen with JP and JR:

```
CALL nn                              RET
CALL NZ, nn                          RET NZ
CALL Z, nn                           RET Z
CALL NC, nn                          RET NC
CALL C, nn                           RET C
CALL PO, nn                          RET PO
CALL PE, nn                          RET PE
CALL P, nn                           RET P
CALL M, nn                           RET M
```

We edit helloworld.asm and call ROM routines with CALL; we want the results to be more attractive:

```
org  $8000                  ; Address where the programme is loaded

; System variable: permanent display attributes.
; Format: FLASH, BRIGHT, PAPER, INK (FBPPPIII).
ATTR_S: equ $5c8d

; System variable: current attribute (FBPPPIII).
ATTR_T: equ $5c8f

;----------------------------------------------------------------
```

```
; ROM Routine similar to Basic AT
; Position the cursor at the specified coordinates.
; Input: B -> Y-coordinate.
;        C -> X-coordinate.
; In this routine, the top left-hand corner of the screen
; it is (24, 33).
; Alters the value of the A, DE and HL registers.
; -----------------------------------------------------------------
LOCATE: equ $0dd9

; -----------------------------------------------------------------
; ROM routine similar to Basic's CLS.
; Clears the display using the attributes loaded in the
; system variable ATTR_S.
; Alters the value of the AF, BC, DE and HL registers.
; -----------------------------------------------------------------
CLS: equ $0daf

Main:
ld    a, $0e              ; A = colour attributes
ld    hl, ATTR_T          ; HL = address current attributes
ld    (hl), a             ; Load into memory
ld    hl, ATTR_S          ; HL = address permanent attributes
ld    (hl), a             ; Load into memory

call CLS                  ; Clear screen: use ATTR_S

ld    b, $18-$0a          ; B = Y coordinate
ld    c, $21-$03          ; C = X-coordinate
call LOCATE               ; Position cursor

ld    hl, msg             ; HL = message address

Loop:
ld    a, (hl)             ; A = string character
or    a                   ; ¿A = 0?
jr    z , Exit            ; If A = 0, skip
rst   $10                 ; Prints character
inc   hl                  ; HL = address next character
jr    Loop                ; Loop until A = 0

Exit:
jr    Exit                ; Infinite loop

msg: defm 'Hello ZX Spectrum Assemby', $00
; String ending in 0 = null

end   $8000
```

We compile with PASMO, load in the emulator and see the results:

Ports of entry and exit

The input and output ports are used for reading the keyboard, joystick, etc.

In our case, we will only use it to change the colour of the screen border, using the OUT command and the $FE port.

Write a small program to see how to change the border:

```
org   $8000          ; Address where the programme is loaded
ld    a, $01         ; A = border color
out   ($fe), a       ; Border = blue
ret
end   $8000
```

We compile with PASMO, load in the emulator and see the result:

With this we can finish our first ZX Spectrum program in assembly. We restore the helloworld.asm file and add the lines to change the border colour before the CLS call:

```
ld    a, $01         ; Load the border colour in A
out   ($fe), a       ; Change border colour
```

We compile with PASMO, load in the emulator and see the results:

We had already developed our first assembly program for the ZX Spectrum; we started the development of ZX-Pong.

Download the source code from here

https://tinyurl.com/2bxez7yn

ZX-Pong

Step 1: Drawing on the screen

The ZX Spectrum's screen, the pixel area, is located from memory address $4000 to $57FF, both inclusive, for a total of 6144 bytes, or 256 * 192 pixels, 32 columns and 24 lines.

The ZX Spectrum divides the screen into three thirds of eight lines each, with eight scanlines (one pixel high horizontal line of the screen) per line. The memory addresses that refer to each screen byte (pixel area) are coded in this way:

```
010T TSSS LLLC CCCC
```

Where TT is the third (0 to 2), SSS is the scanline (0 to 7), LLL is the line (0 to 7) and CCCCCC is the column (0 to 31).

In this first step we will learn how to draw on the screen and see two routines that we will use in our ZX-Pong and possibly in our next developments.

The first thing we are going to do is create a folder called Pong, and inside it we are going to create another folder called Step01. Inside this last folder we will create the files main.asm and video.asm.

The two routines we are going to implement in video.asm, NextScan and PreviousScan, are taken from Santiago Romero's Compiler Software Z80 Assembly Course, which can be found on the speccy.org wiki, and calculate the next and previous scanlines to a given position.

Both routines get the position in the VideoRAM from which the next or previous scanline is to be calculated in HL and return this position in the same register. They also change the AF value.

Let's have a look at the NextScan routine:

```
NextScan:
inc  h
ld   a, h
and  $07
ret  nz
```

In the first instruction we increment the scanline, **INC H**, which is in bits 0 to 2 of H. We then load the value of H into A, **LD A, H**, and we are left with only the value of the bits of the scanline, **AND $07.**

If the value of the previous operation is not zero, the scanline has a value between 1 and 7, no further calculation is necessary and we exit the routine, **RET NZ.**

If the value is zero, the scanline was 7 before incrementing H:

```
0100 0111
```

Adding one sets the bits of the scanline to zero and increments the bits of the third line by one:

```
0100 1000
```

The next thing the routine does is:

```
ld    a, l
add   a, $20
ld    l, a
ret   c
```

We load the value of L into A, **LD A, L**, which contains the row and column. We add one to the row, **ADD A, $20**:

```
$20 = 0010 0000 = LLLC CCCC
```

We load the result into L, **LD L, A**, and if there is a carry we exit, **RET C**.

If there's a carry, the line before adding $20 was 7. Adding one makes the line go to zero and we have to increment the third, but since it's already been incremented by incrementing the scanline, we don't do anything.

Finally, if we continue, it is because we are still in the same third, so we have to decrement it and leave it as it was. At this point, increasing the scanline has changed the line and increasing the line has not changed the third.

```
ld    a, h
sub   $08
ld    h, a
ret
```

We load the value of H in A, **LD A, H**, third and scanline. We subtract $08 from this value to decrease the third by one, **SUB $08**, and leave it as it was:

```
$08 = 0000 1000 = 010T TSSS
```

We load the result of the operation into H, **LD H, A**, and exit the routine with **RET**.

The full code of the routine is:

```
;-------------------------------------------------------------
; NextScan
; https://wiki.speccy.org/cursos/ensamblador/gfx2_direccionamiento
; Gets the memory location corresponding to the scanline.
; The next to the one indicated.
;     010T TSSS LLLC CCCC
; Input:  HL -> current scanline.
; Output: HL -> scanline next.
; Alters the value of the AF and HL registers.
;-------------------------------------------------------------
NextScan:
inc   h                     ; Increment H to increase the scanline
ld    a, h                  ; Load the value in A
and   $07                   ; Keeps the bits of the scanline
```

```
ret  nz                       ; If the value is not 0, end of routine

; Calculate the following line
ld   a, l                     ; Load the value in A
add  a, $20                   ; Add one to the line (%0010 0000)
ld   l, a                     ; Load the value in L
ret  c                        ; If there is a carry-over, it has changed
                              ; its position, the top is already adjusted
                              ; from above. End of routine.

; If you get here, you haven't changed your mind and you have to adjust
; as the first inc h increased it.
ld   a, h                     ; Load the value in A
sub  $08                      ; Subtract one third (%0000 1000)
ld   h, a                     ; Load the value in H
ret
```

At this point we will edit the main.asm file to test the NextScan routine.

The first step is to specify where to load the program, in our case at address $8000 (32768):

```
org  $8000
```

The next thing to do is to point HL in the direction of the screen where we want to start drawing, the top left corner:

```
ld   hl, $4000
```

Let us recall how a VideoRAM memory address is encoded:

```
                    010T TSSS LLLC CCCC
```

And we put $4000 in binary:

```
                    0100 0000 0000 0000
```

We can see that $4000 refers to third 0, row 0, scanline 0 and column 0.

We are going to draw a vertical column, from top to bottom, that fills the entire screen, so we need to loop 192 iterations, the number of scanlines the screen has, and we will load this value into B:

```
ld   b, $c0
```

Once we have reached this point, we can make the loop. To do this we will set a label to refer to. We load the pattern 00111100 ($3C) at the screen address pointed to by HL, get the location of the next scanline and go back to the start of the loop until B equals 0:

```
loop:
ld   (hl), $3c
call NextScan
djnz loop
```

As we can see, HL is in parentheses, but previously when we loaded $4000 in HL, it was not in parentheses. What is the difference?

When we write **LD HL, $4000**, we load the value $4000 into HL, i.e. HL = $4000. Conversely, when we write **LD (HL), $3C**, we load $3C into the memory location to which HL points, i.e. ($4000) = $3C.

After loading $3C into the location pointed to by HL, we get the address of the next scanline by calling the NextScan routine, **CALL NextScan**.

The last instruction, **DJNZ loop**, is the reason for choosing the B register to control the loop iterations. If we chose another 8-bit register, we would have to decrement it and then check that it has not reached zero, in which case we would jump to the loop:

```
dec   a
jr    nz, loop
```

DJNZ does all this in a single instruction using the B register, using one byte and 8 or 13 clock cycles depending on whether the condition is met or not. Using **DEC** and **JR** takes three bytes and 11 or 17 clock cycles.

All that remains is to tell the program the output, include the file containing the NextScan routine and tell PASMO the address to call when the program is loaded.

```
ret

include "video.asm"

end   $8000
```

Compile the programme with PASMO. From the command line, change to the directory containing the .asm files and type the following.

```
pasmo --name ZX-Pong --tapbas main.asm pong.tap --pong.log
```

Now we can load our programme into the ZX Spectrum emulator and see something like this:

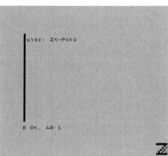

As we can see, it has drawn a vertical column, but it's so fast that we can't see how it's drawn. To see it, we can add the **HALT** instruction before **DJNZ**. **HALT** waits for an interrupt to occur, which in the case of the ZX Spectrum is triggered by the ULA.

The resulting code is:

```
org   $8000
```

```
ld   hl, $4000          ; HL = first scanline of the first line
                        ; of the first third and column one of the
                        ; display (Column 0 to 31)
ld   b, $c0             ; B = 192. Number of scanlines on the screen

loop:
ld   (hl), $3c          ; Paint on screen 001111000
call NextScan           ; Goes to the next scanline
; halt                  ;   Uncomment line to see what it looks like
djnz loop               ; until B = 0

ret

include "video.asm"
end  $8000
```

We compile again and now we can see how it looks from scanline to scanline. If we want it to be fast again, we comment out the HALT statement.

In video.asm we now implement the routine that gets the memory address of the previous scanline:

```
PreviousScan:
ld   a, h
dec  h
and  $07
ret  nz
```

First we load the value of H, **LD A, H, H**, third and scanline into A, and then decrement H, **DEC H**. Then we keep the bits of the original scanline, **AND $07**, that we have in A, and if it was not in scanline 0 we exit the routine, **RET NZ**. A has the original value of H.

If it was on scanline 0, decrementing H moved us to scanline 7 of the previous line, and the third was decremented.

Now the line needs to be calculated:

```
ld   a, l
sub  $20
ld   l, a
ret  c
```

We load L, **LD A, L**, row and column in A, subtract $20, **SUB $20**, to decrement the row, and reload the value in L, **LD L, A**. We exit if there is a carry, **RET C**, since there is a change of a third, which occurred when the scanline was decremented.

If there is no carry, it is necessary to leave the third as it was:

```
ld   a, h
add  a, $08
ld   h, a
ret
```

We load the value of H (which contains the third and the scanline) into A, **LD A, H**, add $08 to increment the third, **ADD A, $08**, load the value into H, **LD H, A**, and exit the routine, **RET**.

The final code of the routine is as follows:

```
; ------------------------------------------------------------------
; PreviousScan
; https://wiki.speccy.org/cursos/ensamblador/gfx2_direccionamiento
; Gets the memory location corresponding to the scanline.
; The following is the first time this has been done; prior
; to that indicated.
;     010T TSSS LLLC CCCC
; Input:  HL -> current scanline.
; Output: HL -> previous scanline.
; Alters the value of the AF, BC and HL registers.
;-------------------------------------------------------------------
PreviousScan:
ld    a, h              ; Load the value in A
dec   h                 ; Decrements H to decrement the scanline
and   $07               ; Keeps the bits of the original scanline
ret   nz                ; If not at 0, end of routine

; Calculate the previous line
ld    a, l              ; Load the value of L into A
sub   $20               ; Subtract one line
ld    l, a              ; Load the value in L
ret   c                 ; If there is carry-over, end of routine

; If you arrive here, you have moved to scanline 7 of the previous line
; and subtracted a third, which we add up again
ld    a, h              ; Load the value of H into A
add   a, $08            ; Returns the third to the way it was
ld    h, a              ; Load the value in h
ret
```

Finally, we go back to main.asm to implement the PreviousScan test. Let's add the new code after the **DJNZ loop** statement.

The first thing to do is to load into HL the address of the VideoRAM where we want to draw, in this case the bottom right corner:

```
ld    hl, $57ff
```

If we put $57FF into binary:

```
0101 0111 1111 1111
```

Reference is made to third 2, line 7, scanline 7 and column 31.

The loop goes back 192 iterations to draw to the top right corner. We load the value into B:

```
ld    b, $c0
```

And then we do the loop:

```
loopUp:
ld    (hl), $3c
call PreviousScan
halt
```

```
djnz loopUp
```

The only difference with the loop is in the **CALL**, which this time is made to PreviousScan instead of NextScan. **HALT** is uncommented so that you can see how it looks.

The full main.asm code is:

```
; Draw two vertical lines, one from bottom to top
; and one from top to bottom.
; Top to bottom to test the NextScan and PreviousScan routines.
org  $8000

ld   hl, $4000            ; HL = scanline 0, line 0, third 0
                         ; and column 0 (column from 0 to 31)
ld   b, $c0              ; B = 192. Scanlines that the display has

loop:
ld   (hl), $3c          ; Paint on screen 001111000
call NextScan           ; Goes to the next scanline
; halt                   ; Uncomment to see the painting process
djnz loop               ; Until B = 0
ld   hl, $57ff           ; HL = last scanline, line, third
                         ; and column 31
ld   b, $c0              ; B = 192. Scanlines that the display has

loopUp:
ld   (hl), $3c          ; Paint on screen 001111000
call PreviousScan       ; Goes to the previous scanline
; halt                   ; Uncomment to see the painting process
djnz loopUp             ; Until B = 0
ret

include "video.asm"

end  $8000
```

We compile again and see the result by loading the generated programme into the ZX Spectrum emulator:

```
pasmo --name ZX-Pong --tapbas main.asm pong.tap --pong.log
```

This time we paint two lines: the left one from top to bottom and the right one from bottom to top. If you remove the comment on the HALT lines, you will not be able to see in which direction the lines are painted.

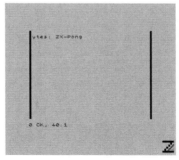

Download the source code from here

https://tinyurl.com/2bzz8axp

Step 2: Control keys

In this step we will develop the routine that checks if the control keys of our game have been pressed, and returns which keys have been pressed.

The keyboard of the ZX Spectrum is divided into eight half rows, each containing five keys.

When evaluating whether a key in a half-row has been pressed, the values come in one byte, in bits 0 to 4, whose values are one if it has not been pressed and zero if it has been pressed. Bit 0 is the key furthest from the centre (Caps Shift, A, Q, 1, 0, P, Enter, Space) and 4 is the key closest to the centre (V, G, T, 5, 6, Y, H and B).

Each half row is identified by a number:

Half-row	Hexadecimal value	Binary Value
Caps Shift-V	$FE	1111 1110
A-G	$FD	1111 1101
Q-T	$FB	1111 1011
1-5	$F7	1111 0111
0-6	$EF	1110 1111
P-Y	$DF	1101 1111
Enter-H	$BF	1011 1111
Space-B	$7F	0111 1111

Note that to calculate the value of a half row, the one before or the one after, only circular bit rotations (RLC, RRC) are needed.

Inside the Pong folder we create the Step02 folder, and inside it the main.asm and controls.asm files.

The routine we are going to use to check the controls can be found in Santiago Romero's course: Compiler Software's Z80 Assembly Course. You can find this course on the speccy.org wiki.

The controls we will use are A-Z for player one and 0-O for player two.

We will develop in controls.asm a routine to check if any of the control keys have been pressed, which will return the keys pressed in the D register, using bit 0 for the A key, bit 1 for the Z key, bit 2 for the 0 key and bit 3 for the O key. The value of these bits is one if the key was pressed and zero otherwise.

The routine first resets the D register to zero:

```
ScanKeys:
ld    d, $00
```

It then checks that the A button has been pressed:

```
scanKeys_A:
ld    a, $fd
in    a, ($fe)
```

```
bit  $00, a
jr   nz, scanKeys_Z
set  $00, d
```

With **LD A, $FD** we load the identifier of the half row A-G ($FD = 11111101) into A.

Next, with **IN A, ($FE)** we read the input port $FE (254) and leave the value at A. The input port $FE is the port from which we read the keyboard status.

The next step is to check whether key A has been pressed; we use the instruction **BIT $00, A**, which evaluates the status of bit 0 of register A. If the bit is zero, the Z flag is set, otherwise it is disabled.

With the following instruction, **JR NZ, scanKeys_Z**, if the bit becomes one, it jumps to evaluate the Z key press.

If the bit is zero, we set bit 0 of register D, **SET $00, D**, to indicate that key A has been pressed.

The next step is to check that the Z key has been pressed:

```
scanKeys_Z:
ld   a, $fe
in   a, ($fe)
bit  $01, a
jr   nz, scanKeys_0
set  $01, d
```

The difference with the A key check is that we load the Caps Shift-V half stack, **LD A, $FE**, into A, check the status of bit 1 corresponding to the Z key, **BIT $01, A**, if the key was pressed we jump to checking the 0 key press, **JR NZ, scanKeys_0**, and finally, we set bit 1 of D, **SET $01, D,** if the Z key was pressed.

It is possible to press the A and Z buttons at the same time. In this case, we deactivate the indicators to indicate that neither key has been pressed. The other option would be to leave the indicators of both keys pressed and move the character up and then down, leaving it where it was.

Let's check that the two keys have been pressed and, if so, deactivate the corresponding bits:

```
ld   a, d
sub  $03
jr   nz, scanKeys_0
ld   d, a
```

First we load the value of D in A, **LD A, D**, and check if the value is three, **SUB $03**, in which case both keys would have been pressed. If the result is not zero, the two keys have not been pressed and we jump to check the 0 key press, **JR NZ, scanKeys_0**. If it is zero, we set D to zero, **LD D, A**; A is already zero.

We could have used the **CP** instruction to evaluate the value of A with another register, a number or a value in memory pointed to by (HL), (IX + N) or (IY + N). CP subtracts one of these values from the value of register A; although it does not modify A, it does modify the pointers (register F), as follows:

Flag value	Meaning
Z	A = Value
NZ	A <> Value
C	A < Value
NC	A >= Value

If we use **CP**, we must set A to zero before **LD D, A**, e.g. with **XOR A**.

The **AND**, **OR** and **XOR** instructions have A as their target and the result they give at bit level is as follows:

Operation	Bit 1	Bit 2	Result
AND	1	1	1
	1	0	0
	0	1	0
	0	0	0
OR	1	1	1
	1	0	1
	0	1	1
	0	0	0
XOR	1	1	0
	1	0	1
	0	1	1
	0	0	0

The list would look like this:

```
ld    a, d
cp    $03
jr    nz, scanKeys_0
xor   a
ld    d, a
```

We would use one byte and seven clock cycles with **XOR A**.

Finally, we need to check that the 0 and O keys have been pressed, and that both keys have been pressed at the same time. The code is almost the same as we have seen so far, let's see the complete code of the routine:

```
;-----------------------------------------------------------------
; ScanKeys
; Scans the control keys and returns the pressed keys.
; Output: D -> Keys pressed.
;         Bit 0 -> A pressed 0/1.
;         Bit 1 -> Z pressed 0/1.
;         Bit 2 -> 0 pressed 0/1.
;         Bit 3 -> O pressed 0/1.
; Alters the value of the AF and D registers.
;-----------------------------------------------------------------
ScanKeys:
ld    d, $00                 ; Sets the D register to 0
```

```
scanKeys_A:
ld   a, $fd              ; Load in A the A-G half-stack
in   a, ($fe)            ; Read status of the semi-stack
bit  $00, a              ; Checks if the A has been pressed
jr   nz, scanKeys_Z      ; If not clicked, skips
set  $00, d              ; Set the bit corresponding to A to one

scanKeys_Z:
ld   a, $fe              ; Load in A the CS-V half-stack
in   a, ($fe)            ; Read status of the half-stack
bit  $01, a              ; Checks whether Z has been pressed
jr   nz, scanKeys_0      ; If not clicked, skips
set  $01, d              ; Sets the bit corresponding to Z to one

; Check that the two arrow keys have not been pressed
ld   a, d                ; Load the value of D into A
sub  $03                 ; Checks whether A and Z have been pressed
                         ; at the same time
jr   nz, scanKeys_0      ; If not pressed, skips
ld   d, a                ; Sets D to zero

scanKeys_0:
ld   a, $ef              ; Load the half-stack 0-6
in   a, ($fe)            ; Read status of the semi-stack
bit  $00, a              ; Checks if 0 has been pressed
jr   nz, scanKeys_O      ; If not pressed, skip
set  $02, d              ; Set the bit corresponding to 0 to a one

scanKeys_O:
ld   a, $cf              ; Load the P-Y half-stack
in   a, ($fe)            ; Read status of the semi-stack
bit  $01, a              ; Checks if the O has been pressed
ret  nz                  ; If not pressed, jumps to
set  $03, d              ; Sets the bit corresponding to O to one

; Check that the two arrow keys have not been pressed
ld   a, d                ; Load the value of D into A
and  $0c                 ; Keeps the 0 and O bits
cp   $0c                 ; Check if the two keys have been pressed
ret  nz                  ; If they have not been pressed, it exits
ld   a, d                ; Pressed, loads the value of D in A
and  $03                 ; Takes the bits of A and Z
ld   d, a                ; Load the value in D

ret
```

The main difference from the A-Z keystroke check is that it checks whether the two keys were pressed at the same time.

Before checking that the bits of register D corresponding to 0 and O ($0C = 0000 1100) are active, it is necessary to maintain only these bits, otherwise, if A or Z were pressed, **CP $0C** would never return zero, so **AND $0C** was inserted before this instruction to maintain the value of bits 2 and 3.

The second difference is the way we reset bits 2 and 3 when 0 and O are pressed at the same time.

To check if A and Z were pressed at the same time, we put **SUB $03** and **LD D, A**, because in A we only had these keystrokes, but now, in addition to whether 0 and O were pressed, we also have the keystrokes of A and Z, and if we were to **LD D, A** directly, we would destroy this information.

To avoid destroying this information, we load the value of register D into A, **LD A, D**, then we keep only the value of bits 0 and 1, **AND $03**, and we load the value back into D, **LD D, A**. In this way we have set the value of bits 2 and 3 to 0, but without destroying the value of bits 0 and 1.

We can optimise by replacing **LD A, D** and **AND $03** with **XOR D**, which has the same effect as the other two lines, but uses four clock cycles and one byte.

```
If the value of A is 00001100 and the value of D is 00001101
after XOR D, the value of A is 00000001.
```

All that's left now is to test the routine. We will paint the value of D in the upper left corner when it returns from the keystroke check routine. We will write the code in the main.asm file.

Specify the address where the program is loaded:

```
org   $8000
```

We point HL at the top left corner of the screen:

```
ld    hl, $4000
```

We make an infinite loop that calls ScanKeys and loads the value of the D register into the upper left corner of the window:

```
Loop:
call ScanKeys
ld   (hl), d
jr   Loop
```

Finally, we include the controls.asm file and tell PASMO the address to call when the programme is loaded.

```
include "controls.asm"

end   $8000
```

At this point we will compile the programme and load it into the emulator to see the result.

```
pasmo --name ZX-Pong --tapbas main.asm pong.tap pong.log
```

The result of the programme will be something like this:

54

The final code of the main.asm file will look like this:

```
; Checks the operation of the A-Z and 0-O controls.
; Paints the representation of the keys pressed.
org  $8000
ld   hl, $4000               ; HL = first screen position

Loop:
call ScanKeys                ; Scan for keystrokes
ld   (hl), d                 ; Paints the keystroke display
jr   Loop                    ; Infinite loop

include "controls.asm"

end  $8000
```

We have left one optimisation, which we will see in the last chapter of ZX-Pong's development, which will save one clock cycle in checking each keystroke, for a total of four clock cycles of savings in the ScanKeys routine.

Download the source code from here

https://tinyurl.com/26g2ek2u

Step 3: paddles and centre line

We have already acquired enough knowledge to start the development of our ZX-Pong, we have implemented a good part of the basics of the programme.

In this step we will:

- Change the border colour.
- Assign the colour attributes to the screen.
- Draw the centre line of the board.
- Draw the paddles of both players.
- Move the paddles up and down.

We create a folder called Step03 and inside it we create the files main.asm and sprite.asm.

This time we are not going to start from scratch, as in the previous steps we developed the code, controls.asm and video.asm files that we are going to use in this step, so we are going to copy these two files into the new directory.

Change border colour

First step. Although the colour of the final border will be the same as the rest of the screen, for these first steps we will make it red to visualise the borders of the screen.

We are going to edit the main.asm file, and the first thing to do, as always, is to specify the memory address where we are going to load the program:

```
org   $8000
```

The next step is to set the border to red:

```
ld    a, $02
out   ($fe), a
```

We load the value of the red colour into A, **LD A, $02**, and write this value to port $FE (254), **OUT ($FE), A**. We already know this port, we have used it to read the keyboard status.

Finally, we quit the programme and tell PASMO where to call it when it is loaded.

```
ret

end   $8000
```

We compile with PASMO and see the end result:

The main.asm code looks like this:

```
org  $8000

ld   a, $02                ; A = 2
out  ($fe), a              ; Turns the border red
ret

end  $8000
```

Assign the colour attributes to the screen

In our case, the attributes are white ink and black background.

We will implement a routine, Cls, which will clear the screen and set the background to black and the ink to white.

The screen attributes are contiguous with the area in which the pixels are drawn; it starts at address $5800 and is $300 (768) bytes long, 32 columns by 24 lines. On the Sinclair ZX Spectrum, the colour attributes are at the character level, one attribute affects an area of 8x8 pixels, hence the attribute clash.

The attributes of a character are defined in one byte:

Bit 7	Bit 6	Bits 5, 4 & 3	Bits 2, 1 & 0
Blink (0/1)	Brightness (0/1)	Background (0 to 7)	Ink (0 to 7)

The Cls routine has two parts:

- Clean the screen.
- Assigning the colour and background.

Let's edit the video.asm file and implement the routine:

```
Cls:
ld   hl, $4000
ld   (hl), $00
ld   de, $4001
ld   bc, $17ff
ldir
ret
```

The first thing our routine does is point HL to the start of VideoRAM, **LD HL, $4000**, and erase that byte from the screen, **LD (HL), $00**.

The next step is to point DE to the position next to HL, **LD DE, $4001**, load the number of bytes to erase into BC, **LD BC, $17FF**, which is the entire VideoRAM area ($1800) minus one, the position where HL points and which is already erased.

LDIR, **LoadData, Increment and Repeat**, loads the value into the memory location pointed to by HL, pointed to by DE. When this is done, increment HL and DE. This is repeated in a loop until BC reaches zero. Finally, we exit the routine.

In the main.asm file, we add the call to Cls before **RET**:

```
call Cls
```

Before **END $8000**, we add the line to include the video.asm file:

```
include "video.asm"
```

Compile with PASMO and load into the emulator:

As you can see in the picture, the **Bytes: ZX-Pong** line is no longer displayed; it shows that we have cleared the screen.

To implement the second part of the routine, the assignment of the colour attributes, we will write the following lines just before the **RET** instruction of the Cls routine:

```
ld    hl, $5800
ld    (hl), $07
ld    de, $5801
ld    bc, $2ff
ldir
```

The first thing this part does is set HL to the beginning of the attribute area, **LD HL, $5800**, sets this area to flicker-free, matte, black background and white ink, **LD (HL), $07**.

```
$07 = 0000 0111 = 0 (flicker) 0 (brightness) 000 (background) 111 (ink)
```

The next step is to point DE to the position next to HL, **LD DE, $5801**, and load into BC the number of bytes to load, **LD BC, $2FF**, which is the entire attribute area ($300) minus one, which is the position where HL points, and already has the attributes. **LDIR** is executed, and the colour is assigned to the whole screen.

The full code of the routine is:

```
;--------------------------------------------------------------
; Clean screen, ink 7, background 0.
; Alters the value of the AF, BC, DE and HL registers.
;--------------------------------------------------------------
Cls:
; Clean the pixels on the screen
ld   hl, $4000            ; HL = start of VideoRAM
ld   (hl), $00            ; Clears the pixels of that address
ld   de, $4001            ; DE = next VideoRAM position
ld   bc, $17ff            ; 6143 repetitions
ldir                      ; Clears all pixels from VideoRAM

; Sets the ink to white and the background to black.
ld   hl, $5800            ; HL = start of attribute area
ld   (hl),$07             ; White ink and black background
ld   de, $5801            ; DE = next attribute position
ld   bc, $2ff             ; 767 repetitions
ldir                      ; Assigns the value to attributes

ret
```

At this point, we compile and see the result:

We notice that, in addition to cleaning the screen, he has set the background to black and the ink to white, but as he has not drawn anything on the screen, we cannot see if the ink is really white.

To see different effects, change the values loaded in (HL).

This routine can be modified, saving us eight clock cycles and four bytes. We leave it up to you to find out how to do this; we will give the solution in the last chapter. Don't worry, it's not a critical routine, so it won't affect the development of our game.

Draw the centre line of the field

The centre line of the field consists of a blank scanline, six scanlines with bit 7 set to one, and a final blank scanline:

```
00000000
10000000
10000000
10000000
10000000
10000000
```

```
10000000
00000000
```

In this case, we will only define the empty part and the part that draws the line. In the sprite.asm file, we add the following lines:

```
ZERO: EQU $00
LINE: EQU $80
```

The EQU directive defines constant values which are not compiled; on the contrary, the compiler replaces all references in the code to these tags with the value assigned to them.

```
Example: ld a, ZERO → Compiler → ld a, $00
```

Once we have the line sprite, let's implement the routine to draw it. Go back to the video.asm file:

```
PrintLine:
ld    b, $18
ld    hl, $4010
```

We will paint our line sprite on twenty-four lines (all of them), **LD B, $18**, starting at scanline 0, line 0, third 0 and column 16, **LD HL, $4010**.

```
printLine_loop:
ld    (hl), ZERO
inc   h
push bc
```

We will draw the first scanline blank, **LD (HL), ZERO**, move to the next scanline, **INC H**, and finally keep the value of BC on the stack as we will be using B in the loop that will draw the visible part of the line, **PUSH BC**.

To change the scanline, instead of calling A NextScan, we will increment H. Why? Quite simply. Since we are going to paint the eight scanlines of the same character, we are not going to change the line or the third, so incrementing the scanline is enough, saving bytes and processing time.

We also put a value on the stack, namely BC. It is very important to remember that each PUSH must have a POP, and even if there are multiple PUSHs, there must be the same number of POPs, but in reverse order:

```
push af
push bc
pop   bc
pop   af
```

Now let's make the loop that paints the visible part of the line:

```
ld    b, $06
printLine_loop2:
ld    (hl), LINE
inc   h
djnz printLine_loop2
pop   bc
```

First we indicate the number of iterations of the new loop, **LD B, $06**, draw the scanline with the visible part of the line, **LD (HL), LINE**, move to the next scanline, **INC H**, and repeat until B is zero, **DJNZ printLine_loop2**. When B is zero, we take the value of BC from the stack to continue the loop of the twenty-four lines of the screen, **POP BC**.

This brings us to the final part of the routine:

```
ld   (hl), ZERO
call NextScan
djnz printLine_loop
ret
```

Now we draw the last scanline, **LD (HL), ZERO**, get the next one, **CALL NextScan**, repeat until B is zero and we draw all twenty-four lines of the screen, **DJNZ printLine_loop**. This time we call NextScan as we change lines.

The final aspect of the routine is as follows:

```
;------------------------------------------------------------------
; Paints the centre line.
; Alters the value of the AF, B and HL registers.
;------------------------------------------------------------------
PrintLine:
ld   b, $18              ; Paints on all 24 lines of the screen
ld   hl, $4010          ; Starts on line 0, column 16

printLine_loop:
ld   (hl), ZERO         ; In the first scanline it paints blank
inc  h                  ; Go to the next scanline

push bc                 ; Preserves BC value for second loop
ld   b, $06             ; Paints six times
printLine_loop2:
ld   (hl), LINE         ; Paint byte the line, $10, b00010000
inc  h                  ; Go to the next scanline
djnz printLine_loop2    ; Loop until B = 0
pop  bc                 ; Retrieves value BC
ld   (hl), ZERO         ; Paint last byte of the line
call NextScan           ; Goes to the next scanline
djnz printLine_loop     ; Loop until B = 0 = 24 lines
ret
```

The only thing left to do is to test it. We open the file main.asm, add the call to PrintLine after the call to Cls and include the file sprite.asm as we did with the file video.asm:

```
call PrintLine
include "sprite.asm"
```

We compile and see the result in the emulator:

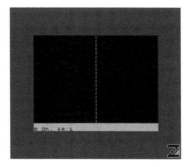

Now we can see that we have put the ink in white.

Draw the paddles of both players

In this step we are going to draw the paddles of both players, which occupy 1x3 characters, one byte (eight pixels) and twenty-four scanlines.

We are going to use the definition type we used for the horizontal line definition, and we are going to do it in the sprite.asm file:

```
PADDLE: EQU $3c
```

This would be the visible part of the paddle, 00111100, as we are going to paint an empty scanline, twenty-two scanlines with this definition and the last empty scanline.

The paddles will be movable elements, so in addition to their sprite we need to know where they are and what the top and bottom margins are to which we can move them.

We continue with the sprite.asm file:

```
PADDLE_BOTTOM: EQU $a8      ; TTLLLSSS
PADDLE_TOP:    EQU $00      ; TTLLLSSS
paddle1pos:    dw  $4861    ; 010T TSSS LLLC CCCC
paddle2pos:    dw  $487e    ; 010T TSSS LLLC CCCC
```

In the first two constants, which are the limits to which we can move the paddles, we specify the Y coordinate expressed in third, line and scanline. While PADDLE_TOP points to the upper limit of the screen (third 0, line 0, scanline 0), PADDLE_BOTTOM does not point to the lower limit of the screen (third 2, line 7, scanline 7), but to third 2, line 5, scanline 0, the result of subtracting twenty-three scanlines from the lower limit ($BF) to paint the twenty-four scanlines of the paddle sprite without invading the attributes area of the screen.

paddle1pos and paddle2pos are not constant, as these values change in response to control key presses.

The initial position of the paddles is:

	Paddle 1	Paddle 2
Third	1	1
Line	3	3
Scanline	0	0

<u>**Column**</u>   1   30

Once this is defined, in the video.asm file we implement the routine that draws the paddles, which has as an input parameter the position of the paddle that it receives in HL; this is necessary because we have two paddles to print, the other alternative would be to duplicate the routine and have each one print one paddle.

```
PrintPaddle:
ld   (hl), ZERO
call NextScan
```

The first thing it does is to paint the first scanline of the paddle, **LD (HL), ZERO**, blank, and then it gets the next scanline, **CALL NextScan**.

Contrary to what happened when painting the centre line, in this routine the calls to NextScan are necessary. The movement of the paddle will be pixel by pixel, this in vertical is scanline by scanline, which means that we do not know in advance when we are going to change lines (we could know, but we are not going to).

The next step is to paint the visible part of the paddle:

```
ld   b, $16
printPaddle_loop:
ld   (hl), PADDLE
call NextScan
djnz printPaddle_loop
```

The visible part of the paddle is painted in twenty-two scanlines, **LD B, $16**, loading the paddle sprite at the position indicated by HL, **LD (HL), PADDLE**, and getting the next scanline, **CALL NextScan**, until B is zero, **DJNZ printPaddle_loop**.

Finally we paint the last scanline of the paddle in white:

```
ld   (hl), ZERO
ret
```

It is useful to paint the first and last scanline in white, so that when the paddle is moved it erases itself and leaves no trace.

The final aspect of the routine is as follows:

```
;--------------------------------------------------------------------
; Paint the paddle.
; Input: HL -> paddle position.
;
; Alters the value of the B and HL registers.
;--------------------------------------------------------------------
PrintPaddle:
ld   (hl), ZERO          ; Paints first byte of blank paddle
call NextScan            ; Goes to the next scanline
ld   b, $16              ; Paints visible byte of paddle 22 times
printPaddle_loop:
ld   (hl), PADDLE        ; Paints the paddle byte
call NextScan            ; Goes to the next scanline

djnz printPaddle_loop    ; Loop until B = 0
```

```
ld    (hl), ZERO              ; Paints last byte of blank paddle

ret
```

Finally, we need to test that the routine works. We open the main.asm file and add after the PrintLine call:

```
ld   hl, (paddle1pos)
call PrintPaddle
ld   hl, (paddle2pos)
call PrintPaddle
```

With **LD HL, (paddle1pos)** we load the position of paddle one in HL and with **CALL PrintPaddle we print it**. The same with paddle two.

We compile and look at the results:

Move the paddles up and down

We tackle the last part of step 3.

We have declared constants with lower and upper limits. Now we implement the check whether a memory location on the screen has reached or is outside a certain limit.

The set of routines to be implemented receives the limit in TTLLLSSS format in A, and the current position in 010TTSSS LLLCCCCC format in HL. These routines return Z if the limit has been reached and NZ otherwise (we continue in video.asm):

```
CheckBottom:
call checkVerticalLimit
ret  c
```

We call the checkVerticalLimit routine, **CALL checkVerticalLimit**, and if there is a carry it exits, **RET C**, with NZ. If there is a carry, the memory location is above (on the screen) the lower limit.

```
checkBottom_bottom:
xor   a
ret
```

If it gets this far, it is because it has reached the lower limit, activate the Z flag, **XOR A**, and exit, **RET**.

This routine doesn't do much, so we can assume that most of the logic is in checkVerticalLimit.

Let's implement the upper limit routine:

```
CheckTop:
call checkVerticalLimit
ret
```

As in the previous routine, checkVerticalLimit is called. In this case the limit has not been reached if the result of checkVerticalLimit is not zero, so we leave with the correct result, **RET**.

Most of the upper and lower limit detection is done in the checkVerticalLimit routine, which receives the vertical limit in A (TTLLLSSS) and the current position (010TTSSS LLLCCCCC) or position to compare with in HL.

Because of the different format we have in HL and A, the first step is to convert the content in HL to the same format as the content in A.

```
checkVerticalLimit:
ld    b, a
ld    a, h
and   $18
rlca
rlca
rlca
ld    c, a
```

First we keep the value of A, **LD B, A**, and then we load the value of H into A, **LD A, H**, and keep the third, **AND $18**. We rotate register A to the left three times, **RLCA**, to put the third in bits 6 and 7, and load the value into C, **LD C, A**. Now C contains the third of the position we received in HL.

```
ld    a, h
and   $07
or    c
ld    c, a
```

We load the value of H again into A, **LD A, H**, but this time we keep the scanline, **AND $07**. Now we have in A the scanline that comes in HL, and we add the third that we have stored in C, **OR C**, and we load the result in C, **LD C, A**. Now C has the third and the scanline that we received in HL, but with the same format as the value that we received in A (TT000SSS).

```
ld    a, l
and   $e0
rrca
rrca
or    c
```

Now we are going to put the value of the line where it belongs, loading the value of L into A, **LD A, L**, keeping the bits where the line came from, **AND $E0**, and rotating the bits twice to put the line in bits 3, 4 and 5, **RRCA**. Finally, we add the third and the scanline that we have stored in

C, **OR C**, so that in A we now have the third, the line and the scanline that came in HL, with the format we need (TTLLLLLSSS).

```
cp   b
ret
```

The last step is to compare what we now have in A with what we have in B, which is the original value of A (vertical limit), **CP B**.

This last operation will, among other things, change the carry and zero flags:

Result	Z	C
A = B	1 - Z	0 - NC
A < B	0 - NZ	1 - C
A > B	0 - NZ	0 - NC

Depending on the flags and whether we are evaluating the lower or upper limit, we will know whether the limit has been reached or exceeded.

The full code for this set of routines is as follows:

```
;-----------------------------------------------------------------
; Evaluates whether the lower limit has been reached.
; Input:  A  -> Upper limit (TTLLLSSS).
;         HL -> Current position (010TTSSS LLLCCCCC).
; Output: Z  =  Reached.
;         NZ =  Not reached.
;
; Alters the value of the AF and BC registers.
;-----------------------------------------------------------------
CheckBottom:
call checkVerticalLimit    ; Compare current position with limit
; If Z or NC has reached the ceiling, Z is set, otherwise NZ is set.
ret c
checkBottom_bottom:
xor a                      ; Active Z
ret


;-----------------------------------------------------------------
; Evaluates whether the upper limit has been reached.
; Input:  A  -> Upper margin (TTLLLSSS).
;         HL -> Current position (010TTSSS LLLCCCCC).
; Output: Z  =  Reached.
;         NZ =  Not reached.
;
; Alters the value of the AF and BC registers.
;-----------------------------------------------------------------
CheckTop:
call checkVerticalLimit    ; Compare current position with limit
ret                        ; checkVerticalLimit is enough


;-----------------------------------------------------------------
; Evaluates whether the vertical limit has been reached.
; Input: A  -> Vertical limit (TTLLLSSS).
;        HL -> Current position (010TTSSS LLLCCCCC).
;
; Alters the value of the AF and BC registers.
;-----------------------------------------------------------------
```

```
checkVerticalLimit:
ld    b, a              ; Stores the value of A in B
ld    a, h              ; A = value of H (010TTSSS)
and   $18               ; Keeps the third
rlca
rlca
rlca                    ; Sets the value of the third in bits 6 and 7
ld    c, a              ; Load the value in C
ld    a, h              ; A = value of H (010TTSSS)
and   $07               ; Keeps the scanline
or    c                 ; Add the third
ld    c, a              ; Load the value in C
ld    a, l              ; A = value of L (LLLCCCCC)
and   $e0               ; Keeps the line
rrca
rrca                    ; Puts the line on bits 3, 4 and 5
or    c                 ; Adds third and scanline. A = TTLLLSSS
cp    b                 ; Compare with B = original value
                        ; A = boundary
ret
```

Using these routines, we can now implement the movement of the paddles and prevent them from leaving the screen.

We will edit main.asm and include controls.asm:

```
include "controls.asm"
```

We are going to implement an infinite loop in which we evaluate whether any control key has been pressed, in which case we move the corresponding paddle. The loop is implemented immediately after the PrintLine call:

```
loop:
call ScanKeys
```

The first thing the loop does is to check whether any of the control keys, **CALL ScanKeys**, have been pressed.

```
MovePaddle1Up:
bit   $00, d
jr    z, MovePaddle1Down
ld    hl, (paddle1pos)
ld    a, PADDLE_TOP
call CheckTop
jr    z, MovePaddle2Up
call PreviousScan
ld    (paddle1pos), hl
jr    MovePaddle2Up
```

After evaluating the controls, we check if the control key was pressed to move paddle one up, **BIT $00**, D, and if not, we jump to the next check, **JR Z, MovePaddle1Down**.

To move the paddle up, we need to see if the paddle leaves the upper limit, for which we need to know the current position of the paddle, **LD HL, (paddle1pos)**, we need to get the upper limit, **LD A, PADDLE_TOP**, and check if it has been reached, **CALL CheckTop**.

When CheckTop triggers the Z flag, we have reached the limit, so we jump to check paddle two, **JR Z, MovePaddle2Up.**

If the Z flag is not set, we get the position to paint the paddle, **CALL PreviousScan**, load into memory, **LD (paddle1pos), HL,** and jump to check paddle two, **JR MovePaddle2Up.**

If the control key above paddle one has not been pressed, a check is made to see if the control key below has been pressed:

```
MovePaddle1Down:
bit   $01, d
jr    z, MovePaddle2Up
ld    hl, (paddle1pos)
ld    a, PADDLE_BOTTOM
call CheckBottom
jr    z, MovePaddle2Up
call NextScan
ld    (paddle1pos), hl
```

Evaluates whether the control key was pressed to move paddle one down, **BIT $01, D**, and if not, **JR Z, MovePaddle2Up**, jumps.

To move the paddle downwards, before moving it, we must check that it does not leave the lower limit, for which we must know the current position, **LD HL, (paddle1pos)**, get the lower limit, **LD A, PADDLE_BOTTOM**, and check that we have not already reached it, **CALL CheckBottom**.

When CheckBottom triggers the Z flag it means we have reached the limit, so we jump to check the movement of paddle two, **JR Z, MovePaddle2Up**.

If the Z flag is not activated, we get the position where the paddle is to be painted, **CALL NextScan**, and load it into memory, **LD (paddle1pos), HL**. This time we don't jump, the next instruction starts to check the movement of paddle two.

As to the fact that the checking of the movement of paddle two is very similar to that of paddle one, the memory positions change to obtain the position of paddle two and the jump positions, we do not detail it:

```
MovePaddle2Up:
bit  $02, d
jr   z, MovePaddle2Down
ld   hl, (paddle2pos)
ld   a, PADDLE_TOP
call CheckTop
jr    z, MovePaddleEnd
call PreviousScan
ld   (paddle2pos), hl
jr   MovePaddleEnd

MovePaddle2Down:
bit  $03, d
jr   z, MovePaddleEnd
ld   hl, (paddle2pos)
ld   a, PADDLE_BOTTOM
```

```
call CheckBottom
jr   z, MovePaddleEnd
call NextScan
ld   (paddle2pos), hl

MovePaddleEnd:
```

The last line, **MovePaddleEnd**, is a tag to jump to the area where the paddles will be painted.

Finally, after painting the paddles, we will replace **RET** with **JR loop** to stay in an infinite loop.

The final code in the main.asm file is as follows:

```
; Draw the two paddles and the centre line.
; Moves the paddles up and down in response to pulsation
; the control keys.
org $8000

ld   a, $02                 ; A = 2
out  ($fe), a               ; Turns the border red

call Cls                    ; Clear the screen
call PrintLine              ; Paints the centre line

loop:
call ScanKeys               ; Scan for keystrokes

MovePaddle1Up:
bit  $00, d                 ; Evaluates whether A has been pressed
jr   z, MovePaddle1Down     ; If not pressed, it skips
ld   hl, (paddle1pos)       ; HL = position of paddle one
ld   a, PADDLE_TOP          ; A = top margin
call CheckTop               ; Evaluates whether the margin
                            ; has been reached
jr   z, MovePaddle2Up       ; If reached, skip
call PreviousScan           ; Gets scanline before paddle
ld   (paddle1pos), hl       ; Loads new paddle position into memory
jr   MovePaddle2Up          ; Jump

MovePaddle1Down:
bit  $01, d                 ; Evaluates if the Z has been pressed
jr   z, MovePaddle2Up       ; If not pressed it skips
ld   hl, (paddle1pos)       ; HL = position of paddle one
ld   a, PADDLE_BOTTOM       ; A = bottom margin
call CheckBottom            ; Evaluates whether the margin
                            ; has been reached
jr   z, MovePaddle2Up       ; If reached, skip
call NextScan               ; Gets scanline next to the paddle
ld   (paddle1pos), hl       ; Loads new paddle position into memory

MovePaddle2Up:
bit  $02, d                 ; Evaluates if 0 has been pressed
jr   z, MovePaddle2Down     ; If not pressed, it skips
ld   hl, (paddle2pos)       ; HL = paddle two position
ld   a, PADDLE_TOP          ; A = top margin
call CheckTop               ; Evaluates whether the margin
                            ; has been reached
```

```
jr   z, MovePaddleEnd        ; If reached, skip
call PreviousScan            ; Gets scanline prior to the paddle
ld   (paddle2pos), hl        ; Loads new paddle position into memory
jr   MovePaddleEnd           ; Jump

MovePaddle2Down:
bit  $03, d                  ; Evaluates whether the O has been pressed
jr   z, MovePaddleEnd        ; If not clicked, skips
ld   hl, (paddle2pos)        ; HL = paddle two position
ld   a, PADDLE_BOTTOM        ; A = bottom margin
call CheckBottom             ; Evaluates whether the margin
                             ; has been reached
jr   z, MovePaddleEnd        ; If reached, skip
call NextScan                ; Gets scanline next to the paddle
ld   (paddle2pos), hl        ; Loads new paddle position into memory

MovePaddleEnd:
ld   hl, (paddle1pos)        ; HL = position of paddle one
call PrintPaddle             ; Paint the paddle
ld   hl, (paddle2pos)        ; HL = paddle two position
call PrintPaddle             ; Paint the paddle
jr   loop                    ; Infinite loop

include "controls.asm"
include "sprite.asm"
include "video.asm"

end  $8000
```

We compile and see the results in the emulator:

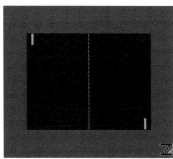

Download the source code from here

https://tinyurl.com/2azoaevf

Step 4: we start moving the ball

Create a folder called Step04, create a file called main.asm in it and copy sprite.asm and video.asm from Step03.

We start by editing the sprite.asm file to define the necessary ball data:

```
BALL_BOTTOM:     EQU $ba
BALL_TOP:        EQU $00
```

As with the paddles, we define lower and upper limits for the ball, in the format TTLLLSSS.

```
ballPos:        dw $4870
ballSetting:    db $00
ballRotation:   db $f8
```

As with the paddles, we will use a variable to hold the position of the ball at each moment, **ballPos**.

In **ballSetting** we store the X-speed in bits 0 to 3, the Y-speed in bits 4 and 5, the X-direction (0 right / 1 left) in bit 6 and the Y-direction (0 up / 1 down) in bit 7.

We store the rotation of the ball in **ballRotation**, where rotation to the right is represented by positive values and rotation to the left by negative values.

The rotation is necessary because of the way we are going to do the horizontal movement.

The ball will consist of one empty scanline, four scanlines with the visible part and another empty scanline. The blank scanlines ensure that the ball leaves no trace when it moves.

We will define two bytes to paint the ball and define each movement pixel by pixel:

```
; Ball sprite:  1 line at 0, 4 lines visible, 1 line at 0
ballRight:      ; Right          Sprite          Left
db $3c, $00     ; +0/$00 00111100      00000000 -8/$f8
db $1e, $00     ; +1/$01 00011110      00000000 -7/$f9
db $0f, $00     ; +2/$02 00001111      00000000 -6/$fa
db $07, $80     ; +3/$03 00000111      10000000 -5/$fb
db $03, $c0     ; +4/$04 00000011      11000000 -4/$fc
db $01, $e0     ; +5/$05 00000001      11100000 -3/$fd
db $00, $f0     ; +6/$06 00000000      11110000 -2/$fe
db $00, $78     ; +7/$07 00000000      01111000 -1/$ff
ballLeft:
db $00, $3c     ; +8/$08 00000000      00111100 +0/$00
```

Each line defines the visible part of the sphere, depending on how the pixels are positioned. We define two bytes per position. In the comment you can see the rotation when the ball goes to the right, the bytes we are going to paint, and the rotation when the ball goes to the left.

The start ball is drawn as shown in the first sprite:

```
00111100 00000000
```

If it moves one pixel to the right, we don't change the position of the ball, we change the rotation and draw the second sprite:

```
00011110 00000000
```

When we reach the last rotation, we change the position of the ball, specifically the column. The last aspect of the code is:

```
; Limits of the objects on the screen
BALL_BOTTOM:    EQU $ba      ; TTLLLSSS
BALL_TOP:       EQU $00      ; TTLLLSSS

; Ball sprite:
;      1 line at 0, 4 lines 3c, 1 line at 0
ballRight:      ; Right          Sprite          Left
db $3c, $00   ; +0/$00 00111100    00000000 -8/$f8
db $1e, $00   ; +1/$01 00011110    00000000 -7/$f9
db $0f, $00   ; +2/$02 00001111    00000000 -6/$fa
db $07, $80   ; +3/$03 00000111    10000000 -5/$fb
db $03, $c0   ; +4/$04 00000011    11000000 -4/$fc
db $01, $e0   ; +5/$05 00000001    11100000 -3/$fd
db $00, $f0   ; +6/$06 00000000    11110000 -2/$fe
db $00, $78   ; +7/$07 00000000    01111000 -1/$ff
ballLeft:
db $00, $3c   ; +8/$08 00000000    00111100 +0/$00

; Ball position
ballPos:      dw $4870      ; 010T TSSS LLLC CCCC

; Ball speed and direction.
; bits 0 to 3: speed X: 1 to 4
; bits 4 to 5: speed Y: 0 to 3
; bit 6:       X direction: 0 right / 1 left
; bit 7:       Y direction: 0 up / 1 down
ballSetting:  db $00
; Ball rotation
; Positive values right, negative values left
ballRotation: db $f8
```

Now we are going to implement the routine that paints the ball in video.asm; we are going to put it after the PreviousScan routine:

```
PrintBall:
ld    b, $00
ld    a, (ballRotation)
ld    c, a
cp    $00
ld    a, $00
jp    p, printBall_right
```

First we find out the horizontal direction of the ball. Then we add or subtract the rotation to the base sprite of the ball to get the sprite to paint. The base direction of the sprite is stored in HL and we subtract or add the rotation that we will have in BC, so the first thing to do is set B to zero, **LD B, $00**.

72

The next step is to load the rotation of the ball into A, **LD A, (ballRotation)**, and from there into C, **LD C, A**. We could load the value directly into C, after passing through HL, but depending on the value we get, it will go to the right or to the left. To get this, we compare the value with zero, and since the comparisons are always made against the A register, it is necessary to load the rotation into this register.

We compare the value of A with zero, **CP A, $00**, if the result is positive, the ball moves to the right and we jump, **JP P, printBall_right**. Before, we set A = 0 for the following calculations, **LD A, $00**.

We continue to implement the movement to the left:

```
printBall_left:
ld    hl, ballLeft
sub   c
add   a, a
ld    c, a
sbc   hl, bc
jr    printBall_continue
```

If the ball moves to the left, we have to load the direction of the left base sprite in HL, **LD HL, ballLeft**.

At this point A is zero, so we subtract the rotation we have in C to get the value we need to subtract to get the correct sprite, **SUB C**:

```
Example: C = $FF, A = $00    A - C = $01
```

As each sprite occupies two bytes, we have to duplicate the value to subtract from HL, **ADD A, A**, and then load it into C, **LD C, A**.

Now we can calculate the address of the sprite to print, **SBC HL, BC**, and print the ball, **JR printBall_continue**.

We implement the movement to the right:

```
printBall_right:
ld    hl, ballRight
add   a, c
add   a, a
ld    c, a
add   hl, bc
```

If the ball moves to the right, the routine is slightly different. We again load the direction of the base sprite into HL, **LD HL, ballRight**, in this case it goes to the right, we add the rotation to A, **ADD A, C**, multiply by two, **ADD A, A**, and load the result into C, **LD C, A**, and then add it to HL, **ADD HL, BC**, to get the direction of the sprite to print.

And now we print the ball:

```
printBall_continue:
ex    de, hl
ld    hl, (ballPos)
```

Since the NextScan routine receives the current address in HL and returns, also in HL, the new address, the first thing to do is to load the value of HL in DE, **EX DE, HL**. With EX we exchange the value of the registers and save four clock cycles and one byte compared to LD (**LD D, H** and **LD E, L**). We load the position of the ball in HL, **LD HL, (ballPos)**.

```
ld   (hl), ZERO
inc  l
ld   (hl), ZERO
dec  l
call NextScan
```

We paint the first byte of the first scanline empty, **LD (HL), ZERO**, increment the column to go to the next byte, **INC L**, paint the second byte, **LD (HL), ZERO**, leave the column as it was, **DEC L**, and get the next scanline, **CALL NextScan**.

The next step is to draw the four scanlines that are actually visible on the ball:

```
ld    b, $04
printBall_loop:
ld    a, (de)
ld    (hl), a
inc   de
inc   l
ld    a, (de)
ld    (hl), a
dec   de
dec   l
call  NextScan
djnz  printBall_loop
```

We load the scanlines to be painted into B, **LD B, $04**, the first byte of the sprite into A, **LD A, (DE)**, and paint it, **LD (HL), A**.

We point DE to the next byte of the sprite, **INC DE**, point HL to the next column, **INC L**, load the sprite into A, **LD A, (DE)**, and paint it, **LD (HL), A**.

We repoint DE to the first byte of the sprite, **DEC DE, HL**, to the previous column, **DEC L**, and calculate the next scanline, **CALL NextScan**.

Repeat all operations until B is zero, **DJNZ printBall_loop**.

```
ld   (hl), ZERO
inc  l
ld   (hl), ZERO

ret
```

We draw the first byte of the last empty ball scanline, **LD (HL), ZERO**, increment L to point to the next column, **INC L**, and draw the second byte, **LD (HL), ZERO**.

The final code of the routine is as follows:

```
;--------------------------------------------------------------
; Paint the ball.
; Alters the value of the AF, BC, DE and HL registers.
;--------------------------------------------------------------
PrintBall:
ld    b, $00                 ; B = 0
```

```
ld   a, (ballRotation)     ; A = ball rotation, what to paint?
ld   c, a                  ; C = A
cp   $00                   ; Compare with 0, see where it rotates to
ld   a, $00                ; A = 0
jp   p, printBall_right    ; If positive jumps, rotates to right

printBall_left:
; The rotation of the ball is to the left
ld   hl, ballLeft          ; HL = address bytes ball
sub  c                     ; A = A-C, ball rotation
add  a, a                  ; A = A+A, ball = two bytes
ld   c, a                  ; C = A
sbc  hl, bc                ; HL = HL-BC (ball offset)
jr   printBall_continue

printBall_right:
; Ball rotation is clockwise
ld   hl, ballRight         ; HL = address bytes ball
add  a, c                  ; A = A+C, ball rotation
add  a, a                  ; A = A+A, ball = two bytes
ld   c, a                  ; C = A
add  hl, bc                ; HL = HL+BC (ball offset)

printBall_continue:
; The address of the ball definition is loaded in DE.
ex   de, hl
ld   hl, (ballPos)         ; HL = ball position

; Paint the first line in white
ld   (hl), ZERO            ; Moves target to screen position
inc  l                     ; L = next column
ld   (hl), ZERO            ; Moves target to screen position
dec  l                     ; L = previous column
call NextScan              ; Next scanline

ld   b, $04                ; Paint ball in next 4 scanlines
printBall_loop:
ld   a, (de)               ; A = byte 1 definition ball
ld   (hl), a               ; Load ball definition on screen
inc  de                    ; DE = next byte definition ball
inc  l                     ; L = next column
ld   a, (de)               ; A = byte 2 definition ball
ld   (hl), a               ; Load ball definition on screen
dec  de                    ; DE = first byte definition ball
dec  l                     ; L = previous column
call NextScan              ; Next scanline
djnz printBall_loop        ; Until B = 0

; Paint the last blank line
ld   (hl), ZERO            ; Moves target to screen position
inc  l                     ; L = next column
ld   (hl), ZERO            ; Moves target to screen position

ret
```

Now we just need to see if everything we implemented works, for which we will edit main.asm:

```
org  $8000
```

```
ld    a, $02
out   ($fe), a

ld    a, $00
ld    (ballRotation), a
```

We specify the address to load the program, **ORG $8000**, set A = 2, **LD A, $02**, to set the border to red, **OUT ($FE), A**, and then set A = 0, **LD A, $00**, to initialise the ball rotation, **LD (ballRotation), A**.

We implement an infinite loop so that the ball moves indefinitely:

```
Loop:
call PrintBall
```

We are going to print the ball, **CALL PrintBall**, in the home position:

```
loop_cont:
ld    b, $08
loopRight:
exx
ld    a, (ballRotation)
inc   a
ld    (ballRotation), a
call PrintBall
exx
halt
djnz loopRight
```

Let's move, rotate, the ball eight pixels to the right, **LD B, $08**, swapping the values with the alternate registers to preserve the value of B, **EXX**.

EXX swaps the value of the general purpose registers with the value of the alternate registers:

```
BC <-> 'BC
DE <-> 'DE
HL <-> 'HL
```

We have chosen EXX in this case because it takes four clock cycles and occupies one byte, while PUSH BC takes eleven clock cycles and the value of the registers, except for B, is not critical for any operation to be performed in the loop, and we see this instruction.

We load the rotation of the ball into A, **LD A, (ballRotation)**, increment the rotation, **INC A**, and load the resulting value into memory, **LD (ballRotation), A**.

We paint the ball, **CALL PrintBall**, exchange the values of the registers, **EXX**, and retrieve the value of B and pause to see how the ball moves, **HALT**.

Repeat until B is zero, **DJNZ loopRight**.

We set the rotation of the ball to zero, this time without painting it, to start rotating the pixels to the left (see the definition of the ball sprite):

```
ld   a, $00
ld   (ballRotation), a
```

We are going to move the ball eight pixels to the left. Only one instruction and one label change in relation to the shift to the right, so the routine will not be explained, we will mark the changes in bold so you can see the difference:

```
ld   b, $08
loopLeft:
exx
ld   a, (ballRotation)
dec  a
ld   (ballRotation), a
call PrintBall
exx
halt
djnz loopLeft
```

To finish, we reset the rotation to zero. We load the value into memory and repeat the loop:

```
ld   a, $00
ld   (ballRotation), a

jr   loop_cont
```

Don't forget to include the files sprite.asm and video.asm. Tell PASMO where to call them when loading the program:

```
include "sprite.asm"
include "video.asm"
end  $8000
```

The ball does not move, on the contrary, we always draw it in the same two columns, moving the pixels eight times to the right and then eight times to the left, and we repeat this over and over again.

The final appearance of the main.asm file is as follows:

```
; Move the ball from left to right between two columns.
org  $8000

ld   a, $02            ; A = 2
out  ($fe), a          ; Red border
ld   a, $00            ; A = 0
ld   (ballRotation), a  ; Rotation ball = 0

Loop:
call PrintBall          ; Print ball

loop_cont:
ld   b, $08            ; Move ball 8 pixels to the right
loopRight:
exx                     ; Exchanges records, preserves B
ld   a, (ballRotation)  ; A = ball rotation
inc  a                  ; Increases turnover
ld   (ballRotation), a  ; Store rotation value
call PrintBall          ; Print ball
```

```
exx                        ; Exchanges records, retrieves B
halt                       ; Synchronise with screen refresh
djnz loopRight             ; Until B = 0

ld   a, $00                ; A = 0
ld   (ballRotation), a     ; Rotation ball = 0

ld   b, $08                ; Move ball 8 pixels to the right
loopLeft:
exx                        ; Exchanges records, preserves B
ld   a, (ballRotation)     ; A = ball rotation
dec  a                     ; Decreases the rotation
ld   (ballRotation), a     ; Store rotation value
call PrintBall             ; Print ball
exx                        ; Exchanges records, retrieves B
halt                       ; Synchronise with screen refresh
djnz loopLeft              ; Until B = 0

ld   a, $00                ; A = 0
ld   (ballRotation), a     ; Rotation ball = 0

jr   loop_cont             ; Infinite loop

include "sprite.asm"
include "video.asm"

end  $8000
```

All that's left is to compile and see the results in the emulator:

Download the source code from here

https://tinyurl.com/24z8a2d3

Step 5: We move the ball around the screen

Create the folder Step05, create main.asm and game.asm, and copy sprite.asm and video.asm from the folder Step04.

We edit sprite.asm to add the two counters we need to move the ball around the screen:

```
MARGIN_LEFT:   EQU $00
MARGIN_RIGHT:  EQU $1e
```

Just as we have vertical and horizontal boundaries, we need right and left boundaries to keep the ball within them.

The next step is to implement the logic of the ball movement, which we will do in game.asm:

```
MoveBall:
ld    a, (ballSetting)
and   $80
jr    nz, moveBall_down
```

First we load the current ball configuration into A, **LD A, (ballSetting)**, and hold bit 7, **AND $80**, which tells us whether the ball is moving up or down. If the bit is not set to zero, the ball moves down and jumps, **JR NZ, moveBall_down**.

If the bit is set to zero, the ball moves up:

```
moveBall_up:
ld    hl, (ballPos)
ld    a, BALL_TOP
call CheckTop
jr    z, moveBall_upChg
call PreviousScan
ld    (ballPos), hl
jr    moveBall_x
```

We load the current position of the ball in HL, **LD HL, (ballPos)**, the vertical limit in A, **LD A, BALL_TOP** and check if the limit has been reached, **CALL CheckTop**. If the Z flag is set, the limit has been reached and a jump is made to change the vertical direction of the ball, **JR Z, moveBall_upChg**.

If we have not reached the vertical limit, we must get the previous scanline, **CALL PreviousScan**, load it into memory, **LD (ballPos), HL**, and jump to check the horizontal offset, **JR moveBall_x**.

If it reaches the limit, we change the vertical direction of the ball:

```
moveBall_upChg:
ld    a, (ballSetting)
or    $80
ld    (ballSetting), a
call NextScan
ld    (ballPos), hl
jr    moveBall_x
```

We load the ball setting into A, **LD A, (ballSetting)**, set bit 7, **OR $80**, to indicate that the ball should go down, and load the value into memory, **LD (ballSetting), A**. We need to calculate the new vertical position of the ball, **CALL NextScan**, load the value into memory, **LD (ballPos), HL**, and jump to check for horizontal displacement, **JR moveBall_x**.

To activate bit 7, we have done an OR with $80 (10000000). It is useful to remember the result of the OR operation depending on the value of the bits:

Bit 1	Bit 2	Result
0	0	0
1	0	1
0	1	1
1	1	1

As you can see in the table, using OR $80 sets bit 7 to 1 and leaves the rest as they are.

If the ball went down at the start of the routine, do something similar to what we have seen above:

```
moveBall_down:
ld    hl, (ballPos)
ld    a, BALL_BOTTOM
call CheckBottom
jr    z, moveBall_downChg
call NextScan
ld    (ballPos), hl
jr    moveBall_x
```

We load the position of the ball in HL, **LD HL, (ballPos)**, and the lower limit in A, **LD A, BALL_BOTTOM**, check if we have reached it, **CALL CheckBottom**, in which case we jump to change the direction of the ball, **JR Z, moveBall_downChg**.

If we have not reached the bottom, we must calculate the new position of the ball, **CALL NextScan**, load it into memory, **LD (ballPos), HL**, and jump to check the horizontal displacement, **JR moveBall_x**.

If the lower limit is reached, the vertical direction of the ball must be changed:

```
moveBall_downChg:
ld    a, (ballSetting)
and   $7f
ld    (ballSetting), a
call PreviousScan
ld    (ballPos), hl
```

We load the ball setting into A, **LD A, (ballSetting)**, disable bit 7, **AND $7F**, to indicate that the ball should now go up, and load this value into memory, **LD (ballSetting), A**. We calculate the new vertical position of the ball, **CALL PreviousScan**, and load the value into memory, **LD (ballPos), HL**.

To disable bit 7 we have done an AND with $7F, in binary it is 01111111. It is useful to remember the result of the AND operation depending on the value of the bits:

Bit 1	Bit 2	Result
0	0	0
1	0	0
0	1	0
1	1	1

As you can see in the table, applying AND $7F sets bit 7 to zero and leaves the rest as they are.

We start to calculate the horizontal shift:

```
moveBall_x:
ld    a, (ballSetting)
and   $40
jr    nz, moveBall_left
```

We load the ball configuration in A, **LD A, (ballSetting)**, check the status of bit 6, **AND $40**, and if it is not zero, the ball moves to the left and jumps, **JR NZ, moveBall_left**.

If bit 6 is zero, the ball moves to the right:

```
moveBall_right:
ld    a, (ballRotation)
cp    $08
jr    z, moveBall_rightLast
inc   a
ld    (ballRotation), a
jr    moveBall_end
```

We load the rotation of the ball into A, **LD A, (ballRotation)**, and check if it is the last, **CP $08**, in which case we must jump, **JR Z, moveBall_rightLast**.

If it is not in the last rotation, we increment it, **INC A**, load it into memory, **LD (ballRotation), A**, and jump to the end of the routine, **JR moveBall_end**.

If it is on the last rotation and not on the right border, we move the ball to the next column:

```
moveBall_rightLast:
ld    a, (ballPos)
and   $1f
cp    MARGIN_RIGHT
jr    z, moveBall_rightChg
ld    hl, ballPos
inc   (hl)
ld    a, $01
ld    (ballRotation), a
jr    moveBall_end
```

We load the row and column in A, **LD A, (ballPos)**, leave the column, **AND $1F**, and check if we have reached the right margin, **CP**

MARGIN_RIGHT, in which case we jump to change the direction of the ball, **JR Z, moveBall_rightChg**.

If the right limit is not reached, we move the ball to the next column. We load the address where the ball is in HL, **LD HL, ballPos**, and increment the column, **INC (HL)**.

We set the ball rotation to one, **LD A, $01**, load it into memory, **LD (ballRotation), A**, and jump to the end of the routine, **JR moveBall_end**.

As you can see, to load the column into A, the instruction used was **LD A, (ballPos)** and to increment the column, **LD HL, ballPos** and **INC (HL)**.

Given that the memory locations on the screen are coded as 010TTSSS LLLCCCCC, do we load and modify the scanline? No, because the Z80 is a Little Endian microcontroller.

A Little Endian microcontroller, when loading 16-bit values into memory, loads the least significant byte into the first memory location and the most significant byte into the next, so if memory location $C000 loads the value $4000, $C000 loads $00 and $C001 loads $40. Therefore, when loading the value from (ballPos) into A, the least significant byte is loaded, which is where the row and column are. Incrementing (HL) increments the column.

If the load is done on a 16-bit register, it loads the low byte into the low part of the register and the high byte into the high part. That's why when ballPos is loaded in HL, it loads the high byte of the memory address in H and the low byte in L.

When it has reached the right limit, the direction of the ball must be changed:

```
moveBall_rightChg:
ld    a, (ballSetting)
or    $40
ld    (ballSetting), a
ld    a, $ff
ld    (ballRotation), a
jr    moveBall_end
```

We load the ball setting into A, **LD A, (ballSetting)**, set bit 6 to change the direction to the left, **OR $40**, and load the value into memory, **LD (ballSetting), A**.

We set the rotation to minus one, **LD A, $FF**, load it into memory, **LD (ballRotation), A**, and jump to the end, **JR moveBall_end**.

If the ball moves to the left, you need to do something similar to what we saw above:

```
moveBall_left:
ld    a, (ballRotation)
cp    $f8
jr    z, moveBall_leftLast
dec   a
ld    (ballRotation), a
```

```
jr    moveBall_end
```

We load the rotation into the A register, **LD A, (ballRotation)**, check if it is the last, **CP $F8**, and jump if it is, **JR Z, moveBall_leftLast**.

If we are not at the last rotation, we decrement it, **DEC A**, load the value into memory, **LD (ballRotation), A**, and jump to the end, **JR moveBall_end**.

If we have reached the last rotation but not the left border, we move the ball to the previous column:

```
moveBall_leftLast:
ld    a, (ballPos)
and   $1f
cp    MARGIN_LEFT
jr    z, moveBall_leftChg
ld    hl, ballPos
dec   (hl)
ld    a, $ff
ld    (ballRotation), a
jr    moveBall_end
```

We load the row and column in A, **LD A, (ballPos)**, keep the column, **AND $1F**, and check if it has reached the left margin, **CP MARGIN_LEFT**, in which case we must jump, **JR Z, moveBall_leftChg**.

If it has not reached the left margin, we load the address where the ball position is in HL, **LD HL, ballPos**, and decrement the column, **DEC (HL)**.

We set the rotation to minus one, **LD A, $FF**, load the value into memory, **LD (ballRotation), A**, and jump to the end, **JR moveBall_end**.

Finally, we change direction when the left boundary is reached:

```
moveBall_leftChg:
ld    a, $01
ld    (ballRotation), a
ld    a, (ballSetting)
and   $bf
ld    (ballSetting), a

moveBall_end:
ret
```

We set the ball rotation to one, **LD A, $01**, and load it into memory, **LD (ballRotation), A**. We load the ball setting into A, **LD A, (ballSetting)**, set the direction to right by turning off bit 6, **AND $BF**, and load the value we have obtained into memory, **LD (ballSetting), A**.

We can save two clock cycles and five bytes by making a small modification. It's up to you; we'll see how to do it in step 10.

The final aspect of the routine is as follows:

```
;--------------------------------------------------------------------
; Calculates the position, rotation and direction of the ball
; to paint it.
; Alters the value of the AF and HL registers.
```

```
;---------------------------------------------------------------------
MoveBall:
ld   a, (ballSetting)      ; A = ball direction and ball speed
and  $80                   ; Check vertical direction
jr   nz, moveBall_down     ; bit 7 = 1?, goes down

moveBall_up:
; Ball goes up
ld   hl, (ballPos)         ; HL = ball position
ld   a, BALL_TOP           ; A = upper margin
call CheckTop              ; Reached top margin?
jr   z, moveBall_upChg     ; If reached, jumps
call PreviousScan          ; Scanline previous to ball position
ld   (ballPos), hl         ; Loads new ball position into memory
jr   moveBall_x            ; Jump

moveBall_upChg:
; Ball goes up, has reached the stop and changes direction
ld   a, (ballSetting)      ; A = ball direction and velocity
or   $80                   ; Vertical direction = down
ld   (ballSetting), a      ; Load new address ball into memory
call NextScan              ; Scanline next to ball position
ld   (ballPos), hl         ; Loads new ball position into memory
jr   moveBall_x            ; Jump

moveBall_down:
; Ball goes down
ld   hl, (ballPos)         ; HL = ball position
ld   a, BALL_BOTTOM        ; A = upper margin
call CheckBottom           ; Reached upper margin?
jr   z, moveBall_downChg   ; If reached jumps
call NextScan              ; Scanline next to ball position
ld   (ballPos), hl         ; Loads new ball position into memory
jr   moveBall_x            ; Jump

moveBall_downChg:
; Ball goes down, has reached the stop and changes direction
ld   a, (ballSetting)      ; A = ball direction and ball velocity
and  $7f                   ; Vertical direction = up
ld   (ballSetting), a      ; Load new address ball into memory
call PreviousScan          ; Scanline previous to ball position
ld   (ballPos), hl         ; Loads new ball position into memory

moveBall_x:
ld   a, (ballSetting)      ; A = ball direction and ball velocity
and  $40                   ; Check horizontal direction
jr   nz, moveBall_left     ; bit 6 = one? goes to the left

moveBall_right:
; Ball goes to the right
ld   a, (ballRotation)     ; A = ball rotation
cp   $08                   ; Last rotation?
jr   z, moveBall_rightLast ; If last rotation skip
inc  a                     ; Increases turnover
ld   (ballRotation), a     ; Loading into memory
jr   moveBall_end          ; End of routine

moveBall_rightLast:
; He is in the last rotation
```

```
; If you have not reached the right limit, set the rotation to 1
; and puts the ball in the next column
ld   a, (ballPos)          ; A = line and column ball
and  $1f                   ; Remains with column
cp   MARGIN_RIGHT          ; Buy with right boundary
jr   z, moveBall_rightChg  ; Reached, skip
ld   hl, ballPos           ; HL = ball position
inc  (hl)                  ; Increments column
ld   a, $01                ; Set rotation to 1
ld   (ballRotation), a     ; Load value into memory
jr   moveBall_end          ; End of routine

moveBall_rightChg:
; You have reached the right limit
; Set rotation to -1 and change horizontal direction of ball
ld   a, (ballSetting)      ; A = ball direction and ball speed
or   $40                   ; Horizontal direction = left
ld   (ballSetting), a      ; Loads new ball address into memory
ld   a, $ff                ; A = -1
ld   (ballRotation), a     ; Loads it into memory Rotation = -1
jr   moveBall_end          ; End of routine

moveBall_left:
; Ball goes to the left
ld   a, (ballRotation)     ; A = current ball rotation
cp   $f8                   ; Last rotation?
jr   z, moveBall_leftLast  ; If last rotation skip
dec  a                     ; Decreasing rotation
ld   (ballRotation), a     ; Loading into memory
jr   moveBall_end          ; End of routine

moveBall_leftLast:
; He is in the last rotation
; If you have not reached the left limit, set the rotation to -1
; and puts the ball in the previous column
ld   a, (ballPos)          ; A = row and column
and  $1f                   ; It remains only with column
cp   MARGIN_LEFT           ; Left boundary?
jr   z, moveBall_leftChg   ; If it has reached it, it jumps
ld   hl, ballPos           ; HL = ball position address
dec  (hl)                  ; Goes to previous column
ld   a, $ff                ; Set rotation to -1
ld   (ballRotation), a     ; Load value into memory
jr   moveBall_end          ; End of routine

moveBall_leftChg:
; You have reached the left limit
; Set rotation to 1 and change direction
ld   a, $01                ; HL = ball position
ld   (ballRotation), a     ; Load value into memory Rotation = 1
ld   a, (ballSetting)      ; A = ball direction and ball velocity
and  $bf                   ; Sets horizontal right direction
ld   (ballSetting), a      ; Load new memory ball address

moveBall_end:
ret
```

Now it's time to test the implementation. We edit main.asm; the implementation is very simple:

```
org  $8000

ld   a, $02
out  ($fe), a
call PrintBall
```

We specify the address where the programme is to be loaded, set the border to red and draw the ball in its initial position.

```
Loop:
call MoveBall
call PrintBall
halt
jr   Loop
```

We implement an infinite loop in which we move the ball, paint it, wait for the screen to refresh, and repeat these three operations indefinitely.

```
include "game.asm"
include "sprite.asm"
include "video.asm"

end  $8000
```

We include the necessary files and tell PASMO where to call them when loading the programme.

The final appearance of main.asm is as follows:

```
; Move the ball around the screen by tracing diagonals.
org  $8000

ld   a, $02              ; A = 2
out  ($fe), a            ; Turns border red
call PrintBall           ; Prints the ball

Loop:
call MoveBall            ; Move the ball
call PrintBall           ; Paint the ball
halt                     ; Wait for screen refresh
jr   Loop                ; Infinite loop

include "game.asm"
include "sprite.asm"
include "video.asm"

end  $8000
```

The big moment is here, we compile and have a look at the result in the emulator:

Does the ball seem slow to you? Comment on the HALT.

Download the source code from here

https://tinyurl.com/26924ftp

Step 6: Field, paddle, ball and timing

We create the folder Step06 and copy the files game.asm, sprite.asm and video.asm from the folder Step05, copy controls.asm from the folder Step03 and create the file main.asm.

We will start by editing the main.asm file to set the loading position, set the border to black, clean the screen, paint the centre line and make an infinite loop to avoid returning to Basic.

We will also include the rest of the files and tell PASMO where to call when loading the program:

```
org  $8000

Main:
ld   a, $00
out  ($fe), a
call Cls
call PrintLine

Loop:
jr   Loop

include "controls.asm"
include "game.asm"
include "sprite.asm"
include "video.asm"

end  $8000
```

We compile and have a look at the result in the emulator.

The next step is to paint the border of the field. In sprite.asm we add a new constant at the beginning:

```
FILL:           EQU $ff
```

The routine that paints the border is implemented before the PrintLine routine, in the video.asm file:

```
PrintBorder:
ld   hl, $4100
ld   de, $56e0
ld   b, $20
```

```
ld   a, FILL
```

We load into HL the address of third 0, line 0, scanline 1, **LD HL, $4100**, we load into DE the address of third 2, line 7, scanline 6, **LD DE, $56E0**, and into B the thirty-two columns in which we will draw the border, **LD B, $20**. We load the border sprite into A, **LD A, FILL**.

We implement the loop to draw the border:

```
printBorder_loop:
ld   (hl), a
ld   (de), a
inc  l
inc  e
djnz printBorder_loop
ret
```

We paint the border sprite in the direction that HL, **LD (HL), A**, points to, and do the same with the direction that DE, **LD (DE), A**, points to.

We point HL to the next column, **INC L**, the same with DE, **INC E**. We repeat until B is zero, **DJNZ printBorder_loop**, after which we exit the routine, **RET**.

The final appearance of the PrintBorder routine is as follows:

```
;-----------------------------------------------------------------
; Paint the edge of the field.
; Alters the value of AD, B, DE and HL registers.
;-----------------------------------------------------------------
PrintBorder:
ld   hl, $4100           ; HL = third 0, line 0, scanline 1
ld   de, $56e0           ; DE = third 2, line 7, scanline 6
ld   b, $20              ; B = 32 to be painted
ld   a, FILL             ; Load the byte to be painted into A

printBorder_loop:
ld   (hl), a             ; Paints direction pointed by HL
ld   (de), a             ; Paints address pointed by DE
inc  l                   ; HL = next column
inc  e                   ; DE = next column
djnz printBorder_loop    ; Loop until B reaches 0
ret
```

To test this routine, we go back to main.asm and after the call to PrintLine, we insert the call to the new routine:

```
call PrintBorder
```

We compile and see the results in the emulator. We can see that we have drawn the field where the action will take place.

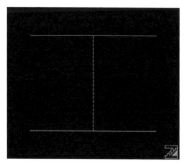

We are going to introduce the ball into our field. As we will be moving and painting it all the time, we will place the calls inside the loop, between Loop and JR Loop:

```
call MoveBall
call PrintBall
```

We compile and see the results in the emulator:

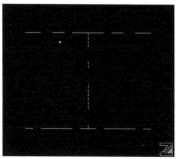

If we look at the result, we can see two problems: the ball is blurring the centre line and the edge, and it is moving at a devilish speed.

The first thing we are going to address is the speed of the ball.

In the previous step we set a HALT to wait for the screen to refresh, but this makes it move too slowly. To slow down the speed of the ball, we are going to make it not move every time it goes through the loop; it will move one out of every N times.

We continue in main.asm and, before END $8000, we declare the variable in which we will keep track of the number of times through the loop:

```
countLoopBall: db $00
```

And now let's implement the part after the Loop tag where it checks if the ball has passed enough times for us to move it:

```
ld   a, (countLoopBall)
inc  a
ld   (countLoopBall), a
cp   $0f
jr   nz, loop_continue
```

We load into A the counter of the number of times we have passed through the loop without moving the ball, **LD A, (countLoopBall)**, increment it, **INC A**, and store it in memory, **LD (countLoopBall), A**.

We compare if the counter has passed the number of times necessary to move the ball, **CP $0F**, and if not, **JR NZ, loop_continue**, we jump.

The **loop_continue** tag is new and we put it just above the PrintBall call:

```
loop_continue:
```

There is one last thing to do. If the counter has reached the number of times needed to move the ball, we need to reset the counter to zero after moving the ball, otherwise we would have to wait another 255 times instead of the number of times we set.

We add the following lines after the MoveBall call and before the loop_continue tag:

```
ld   a, ZERO
ld   (countLoopBall), a
```

Implementing main.asm would look like the following:

```
org  $8000
Main:
ld   a, $00
out  ($fe), a            ; Black border

call Cls                 ; Clean screen
call PrintLine           ; Paint centre line
call PrintBorder         ; Paint border

Loop:
ld   a, (countLoopBall)  ; A = count ball
inc  a                   ; Increases counter
ld   (countLoopBall), a  ; Loads value into memory
cp   $0f                 ; Counter = 15?
jr   nz, loop_continue   ; No, skip
call MoveBall            ; Move ball position
ld   a, ZERO             ; A = 0
ld   (countLoopBall), a  ; Load memory value

loop_continue:
call PrintBall           ; Paint ball
jr   Loop                ; Infinite loop

include "game.asm"
include "controls.asm"
include "sprite.asm"
include "video.asm"

countLoopBall: db $00     ; Counter to move ball

end  $8000
```

We compile, load into the emulator and watch the ball move at a more acceptable speed.

We have not defined a constant to compare with the ball counter as the speed will be variable in the future.

Next, we will tackle the problem of the parts that the ball erases as it passes, starting with the centre line.

As a first technique, we will repaint the part of the line that coincides with the Y-coordinate of the ball, whether the ball passes over it or not; this is unnecessary, but it helps us to time it.

We open the video.asm file and implement it after the PrintLine routine:

```
ReprintLine:
ld    hl, (ballPos)
ld    a, l
and   $e0
or    $10
ld    l, a
```

We load the position of the ball into HL, **LD HL, (ballPos)**, the line and the column into A, **LD A, L**, we keep the line, **AND $E0**, set the column to sixteen, where the vertical line is, **OR $10**, and load the value into L, **LD L, A**.

We are going to repaint six scanlines, which are the same as the ones on the sphere:

```
ld    b, $06
reprintLine_loop:
ld    a, h
```

We load the number of scanlines to be painted in B, **LD B, $06**, and the third and final scanline in A, **LD A, H**.

To paint the line, we painted in white in scanlines 0 and 7, and the visible part of the line in the rest:

```
and   $07
cp    $01
jr    c, reprintLine_00
cp    $07
jr    z, reprintLine_00
```

We keep the scanline, **AND $07**, and check if it is one, **CP $01**. If it is less than one we jump, **JR C, reprintLine_00**, otherwise we check if it is seven, **CP $07**. If the scanline is equals to seven, we jump, **JR Z, reprintLine_00**.

If we have not jumped, the scanline is between one and six:

```
ld    c, LINE
jr    reprintLine_loopCont
```

We load the line sprite in C, **LD C, LINE**, and jump, **JR reprintLine_loopCont**.

If we jumped before, the scanline is zero or seven:

```
reprintLine_00:
ld   c, ZERO
```

We load the empty sprite in C, **LD C, ZERO**, and paint accordingly:

```
reprintLine_loopCont:
ld   a, (hl)
or   c
ld   (hl), a
call NextScan
djnz reprintLine_loop

ret
```

We load the address value of the byte to be repainted into A, **LD A, (HL)**, add the pixels of the line to be repainted, **OR C**, and paint it on the screen, **LD (HL), A**. We calculate the address of the next scanline, **CALL NextScan**, repeat the operation until B is zero, **DJNZ reprintLine_loop** and exit, **RET**.

The final aspect of the routine is as follows:

```
;------------------------------------------------------------------
; Repaint the centre line.
; Alters the value of the AF, BC and HL registers.
;------------------------------------------------------------------
ReprintLine:
ld   hl, (ballPos)         ; HL = ball position
ld   a, l                  ; A = row and column
and  $e0                   ; A = line
or   $10                   ; A = row and column 16 ($10)
ld   l, a                  ; HL = initial position repaint

ld   b, $06                ; Repaints 6 scanlines
reprintLine_loop:
ld   a, h                  ; A = third and scanline
and  $07                   ; A = scanline
; If it is on scanline 0 or 7 it paints ZERO
; If you are on scanline 1 to 6 paint LINE
cp   $01                   ; Scanline = 1?
jr   c, reprintLine_00     ; Scanline < 1, paint $00
cp   $07                   ; Scanline = 7?
jr   z, reprintLine_00     ; Scanline = 7, paints ZERO

ld   c, LINE               ; Scanline from 1 to 6, paint LINE
jr   reprintLine_loopCont  ; Skip
reprintLine_00:
ld   c, ZERO               ; Scanline 0 or 7, paints ZERO
reprintLine_loopCont:
ld   a, (hl)               ; A = pixels current position
or   c                     ; A = A OR C (adds pixels from C)
ld   (hl), a               ; Paints current position result
call NextScan              ; Next Scanline
djnz reprintLine_loop      ; Until B = 0

ret
```

We save four bytes and nineteen clock cycles by modifying six lines of the routine. It's up to you, and we'll see how to do it in step 10.

Now we just need to test what we have implemented by opening Main.asm and after the call to PrintBall we add the call to ReprintLine:

```
call ReprintLine
```

We compile and see the results in the emulator:

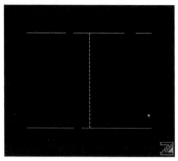

The centre line is no longer blurred, but we notice that the speed of the ball has decreased. We must remember that we are now performing many more operations than before. As we go on, we will adjust the speed of the ball.

We now want to prevent the border from being erased, so we will change the upper and lower limits of the ball; they are in sprite.asm:

```
BALL_BOTTOM:    EQU $b8
BALL_TOP:       EQU $02
```

Compile, load in the emulator and check that the border is no longer erased.

Now let's start with the paddles. Go back to main.asm and add the following lines between **CALL ReprintLine** and **JR Loop**:

```
ld   hl, (paddle1pos)
call PrintPaddle
ld   hl, (paddle2pos)
call PrintPaddle
```

We load the position of the first paddle, paddle one, in HL, **LD HL, (paddle1pos)**, and print it, **CALL PrintPaddle**. We do the same with paddle two.

Notice that the paddles are painted in all iterations of the loop, as well as the ball and the line repainting.

We compile and see the results in the emulator:

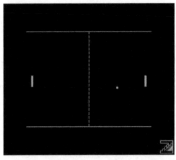

The paddles are drawn and the ball does not erase them as it passes. You can also see that the ball is now much slower, because we are doing more operations in each iteration of the loop.

To make the ball move faster again, let's change the value in main.asm that the counter had to reach for the ball to move:

```
ld   (countLoopBall), a
cp   $06
jr   nz, loop_continue
```

We compile, load the emulator and check that the ball is moving faster again.

Let's implement the routine to move the paddles; we already saw how to do this in step three. We edit the file game.asm and go to the end of it.

The routine we are going to implement receives the control keystrokes in D:

```
MovePaddle:
bit  $00, d
jr   z, movePaddle_1Down
```

We check if player one's up key was pressed, **BIT $00, D**. If not, we jump, **JR Z, movePaddle_1Down**, to check if the down key was pressed.

If not, player one's up key has been pressed:

```
ld   hl, (paddle1pos)
ld   a, PADDLE_TOP
call CheckTop
jr   z, movePaddle_2Up
```

Next we load the position of paddle one in HL, **LD HL, (paddle1pos)**, the upper limit for paddles in register A, **LD A, PADDLE_TOP**, and check if it has been reached, **CALL CheckTop**. If the limit has been reached, we move on to check the controls for player two, **JR Z, movePaddle_2Up**.

If the upper limit has not been reached, we move paddle one:

```
call PreviousScan
ld   (paddle1pos), hl
```

```
jr    movePaddle_2Up
```

Now we need to calculate the new position of paddle one, **CALL PreviousScan**, load it into memory, **LD (paddle1pos), HL**, and jump to check the keystrokes of player two's controls, **JR movePaddle_2Up**.

If player one's up button has not been pressed, we check that the down button has been pressed:

```
movePaddle_1Down:
bit   $01, d
jr    z, movePaddle_2Up
```

We check whether player one's down key, **BIT $01, D**, has been pressed. If it has not been pressed, we jump to check the keystrokes of player two's controls, **JR Z, movePaddle_2Up**.

If it does not jump, player two's down key has been pressed:

```
ld    hl, (paddle1pos)
ld    a, PADDLE_BOTTOM
call  CheckBottom
jr    z, movePaddle_2Up
```

We load the position of paddle one into the HL register, **LD HL, (paddle1pos)**, the lower limit for the paddles into the A register, **LD A, PADDLE_BOTTOM**, and check if the limit has been reached, **CALL CheckBottom**. If it has been reached, we jump to checking the controls for player two, **JR Z, movePaddle_2Up**.

If the lower limit has not been reached, move paddle one:

```
call NextScan
ld   (paddle1pos), hl
```

We calculate the new position for paddle one, **CALL NextScan**, and load it into memory, **LD (paddle1pos), HL**.

We make the checks using the controls for player two. Given the similarity, we simply mark the changes in bold with respect to player one's check:

```
movePaddle_2Up:
bit   $02, d
jr    z, movePaddle_2Down
ld    hl, (paddle2pos)
ld    a, PADDLE_TOP
call CheckTop
jr    z, movePaddle_End
call PreviousScan
ld    (paddle2pos), hl
jr    movePaddle_End

movePaddle_2Down:
bit   $03, d
jr    z, movePaddle_End
ld    hl, (paddle2pos)
ld    a, PADDLE_BOTTOM
call CheckBottom
```

```
jr    z, movePaddle_End
call NextScan
ld    (paddle2pos), hl

movePaddle_End:
ret
```

The final aspect of the routine is as follows:

```
;-------------------------------------------------------------------
; Calculate the position of the paddles to move them.
; Input: D -> Controls keystrokes
; Alters the value of the AF and HL registers.
;-------------------------------------------------------------------
MovePaddle:
bit  $00, d               ; A pressed?
jr   z, movePaddle_1Down  ; Not pressed, skip
ld   hl, (paddle1pos)     ; HL = paddle position 1
ld   a, PADDLE_TOP        ; A = top margin
call CheckTop             ; Reached top margin?
jr   z, movePaddle_2Up    ; Reached, skip
call PreviousScan         ; Scanline previous to position paddle 1
ld   (paddle1pos), hl     ; Load new position paddle 1 into memory
jr   movePaddle_2Up       ; Jump

movePaddle_1Down:
bit  $01, d               ; Z pressed?
jr   z, movePaddle_2Up    ; Not pressed, skip
ld   hl, (paddle1pos)     ; HL = paddle position 1
ld   a, PADDLE_BOTTOM     ; A = bottom margin
call CheckBottom          ; Reached bottom margin?
jr   z, movePaddle_2Up    ; Reached, skip
call NextScan             ; Scanline next to position paddle 1
ld   (paddle1pos), hl     ; Load new position paddle 1 into memory

movePaddle_2Up:
bit  $02, d               ; 0 pressed?
jr   z, movePaddle_2Down  ; Not pressed, skip
ld   hl, (paddle2pos)     ; HL = paddle position 2
ld   a, PADDLE_TOP        ; A = top margin
call CheckTop             ; Reached top margin?
jr   z, movePaddle_End    ; Reached, skip
call PreviousScan         ; Scanline previous to position paddle 2
ld   (paddle2pos), hl     ; Loads new paddle position 2 to memory
jr   movePaddle_End       ; Jump

movePaddle_2Down:
bit  $03, d               ; O pressed?
jr   z, movePaddle_End    ; Not pressed, skip
ld   hl, (paddle2pos)     ; HL = paddle position 2
ld   a, PADDLE_BOTTOM     ; A = bottom margin
call CheckBottom          ; Reached bottom margin?
jr   z, movePaddle_End    ; Reached, skip
call NextScan             ; Scanline next to position paddle 2
ld   (paddle2pos), hl     ; Loads new paddle position 2 to memory

movePaddle_End:
ret
```

We can save two bytes and two clock cycles, in the same way as in the previous chapter. This time we will not give the solution, as it is similar to the one in the previous chapter.

Finally, let's implement the calls to this routine in main.asm, inside our infinite loop, just above the loop_continue tag:

```
loop_paddle:
call ScanKeys
call MovePaddle
```

First we check which keys have been pressed, **CALL ScanKeys**, and then we move the paddles, **CALL MovePaddle**.

We also need to change the label to the one that jumps when the ball does not move, four lines above:

```
cp    $06
jr    nz, loop_paddle
call MoveBall
```

We compile and test in the emulator:

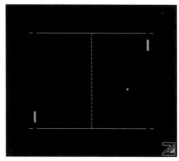

We noticed two problems:

- The paddles erase the edge.
- The paddles move very fast and are difficult to control.

To solve the first problem, we are going to modify the constants that mark the upper and lower limits of the paddles, which are in sprite.asm:

```
PADDLE_BOTTOM: EQU $a6
PADDLE_TOP:    EQU $02
```

Compile, load into the emulator and check that the border is no longer erased:

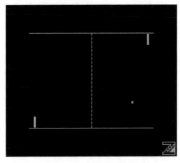

To slow down the speed of the paddle movement, we are going to use the same technique we used with the ball, we are not going to move the paddles in every iteration of the loop.

The first thing we need to do is declare the variable we are going to use as a counter, which we do in main.asm before END $8000:

```
countLoopPaddle: db $00
```

Now, just below the loop_paddle tag, we implement the counter check:

```
ld   a, (countLoopPaddle)
inc  a
ld   (countLoopPaddle), a
cp   $02
jr   nz, loop_continue
```

We load the counter into A, **LD A, (countLoopPaddle)**, increment it, **INC A**, and load the value of the result into memory, **LD (countLoopPaddle), A**. We evaluate if the number of times we defined to move the paddles has passed, **CP $02**, and if not we jump, **JR NZ, loop_continue**.

If not, we check that no key has been pressed, **CALL ScanKeys**, and we move the paddles, **CALL MovePaddle**, and as with the ball, we must reset the counter to zero. Finally, we add the following lines before the loop_continue tag:

```
ld   a, ZERO
ld   (countLoopPaddle), a
```

We load zero into A, **LD A, ZERO**, and load it into memory, **LD (countLoopPaddle), A**, setting the counter to zero.

Compile and load into the emulator. Now the paddle control is less fast and more precise.

The final main.asm code is as follows:

```
; Field painting, paddle and ball movement and timing
org  $8000

;------------------------------------------------------------------
; Programme entry
;------------------------------------------------------------------
```

```
Main:
ld    a, $00              ; A = 0
out   ($fe), a            ; Black border

call Cls                  ; Clean screen
call PrintLine            ; Prints centre line
call PrintBorder          ; Print field border

Loop:
ld    a, (countLoopBall)  ; A = countLoopsBall
inc   a                   ; It increases it
ld    (countLoopBall), a  ; Load to memory
cp    $06                 ; Counter = 6?
jr    nz, loop_paddle     ; Counter != 6, skip
call MoveBall             ; Move ball
ld    a, ZERO             ; A = 0
ld    (countLoopBall), a  ; Counter = 0

loop_paddle:
ld    a, (countLoopPaddle) ; A = count number of paddle turns
inc   a                   ; It increases it
ld    (countLoopPaddle), a ; Load To memory
cp    $02                 ; Counter = 2?
jr    nz, loop_continue   ; Counter != 2, skip
call ScanKeys             ; Scan for keystrokes
call MovePaddle           ; Move paddles
ld    a, ZERO             ; A = 0
ld    (countLoopPaddle), a ; Counter = 0

loop_continue:
call PrintBall            ; Paint ball
call ReprintLine          ; Reprint line
ld    hl, (paddle1pos)    ; HL = paddle position 1
call PrintPaddle          ; Paint Paddle 1
ld    hl, (paddle2pos)    ; HL = paddle position 2
call PrintPaddle          ; Paint Paddle 2
jr    Loop                ; Infinite loop

include "game.asm"
include "controls.asm"
include "sprite.asm"
include "video.asm"

countLoopBall:   db $00   ; Counter turns ball
countLoopPaddle: db $00   ; Counter turns paddles

end  $8000
```

Download the source code from here

https://tinyurl.com/29nxnrrd

Step 7: Collision detection

Create the folder Step07 and copy from the folder Step06 controls.asm, game.asm, main.asm, sprite.asm and video.asm.

From now on we will use everything we have implemented and develop it further.

We are going to implement the collision detection of the ball with the paddles. To do this we need to define the column in which the collision occurs, which we will do in sprite.asm:

```
CROSS_LEFT:     EQU $01
CROSS_RIGHT:    EQU $1d
```

To check for collision in the X coordinate, we will use the column. To check for collision on the Y coordinate we will use the third, the line and the scanline.

As we have seen above, the Y-coordinate is in two different bytes (010T TSSS LLLC CCCC), so we implement a routine that takes a memory location from the screen and returns the Y-coordinate (TTLLLSSS).

The routine is implemented in video.asm, after the Cls routine, and receives the screen location in HL and returns the Y coordinate obtained in A:

```
GetPtrY:
ld    a, h
and   $18
rlca
rlca
rlca
ld    e, a
```

We load the third and the scanline into A, **LD A, H**, keep the third, **AND $18**, pass it to bits 6 and 7, **RLCA, RLCA, RLCA**, and load the result into E, **LD E, A**.

```
ld    a, h
and   $07
or    e
ld    e, a
```

We load the third and the scanline in A, **LD A, H**, we keep the scanline, **AND $07**, we add the third that we have already placed correctly in E, **OR E**, and we load the result in E, **LD E, A**.

```
ld    a, l
and   $e0
rrca
rrca
or    e
ret
```

We load the row and column in A, **LD A, L**, keep the row, **AND $E0**, put the value in bits 3 to 5, **RRCA, RRCA**, and add the third and scanline, **OR E**.

The final aspect of the routine is:

```
;------------------------------------------------------------------
; Gets third, line and scanline of a memory location.
; Input:  HL -> Memory location.
; Output: A  -> Third, line and scanline obtained.
; Alters the value of the AF and E registers.
;------------------------------------------------------------------
GetPtrY:
ld    a, h                    ; A = H (third and scanline)
and   $18                     ; A = third
rlca
rlca
rlca                          ; Passes value of third to bits 6 and 7
ld    e, a                    ; E = A
ld    a, h                    ; A = H (third and scanline)
and   $07                     ; A = scanline
or    e                       ; A OR E = Tercio and scanline
ld    e, a                    ; E = A = TT000SSS
ld    a, l                    ; A = L (row and column)
and   $e0                     ; A = line
rrca
rrca                          ; Passes line value to bits 3 to 5
or    e                       ; A OR E = TTLLLSSS

ret
```

This type of conversion was previously done in the checkVerticalLimit routine, but as it is needed in more than one routine, we have implemented it as a separate routine.

To test it, let's modify the checkVerticalLimit routine by replacing almost all of it with a call to GetPtrY, as follows:

```
;------------------------------------------------------------------
; Evaluates whether the vertical limit has been reached.
; Input: A  -> Vertical limit (TTLLLSSS).
;        HL -> Current position (010TTSSS LLLCCCCC).
; Alters the value of the AF and BC registers.
;------------------------------------------------------------------
checkVerticalLimit:
ld    b, a                    ; B = A
call GetPtrY                  ; Y-coordinate (TTLLLSSS)
                              ; of the current position
cp    b                       ; A = B? B = value A = vertical limit
ret
```

We compile, load in the emulator and check that nothing is broken.

We now implement the collision detection in the game.asm file.

We start with the routine that checks if there is a collision on the X axis. This routine gets the column in C where the collision occurs and activates the Z flag if it has occurred:

```
CheckCrossX:
ld    a, (ballPos)
and   $1f
cp    c
ret
```

We load the position of the ball into A, **LD A, (ballPos)**, leave the column, **AND $1F**, and compare the resulting value with the collision column, **CP C**.

The next step is to implement the routine that evaluates if there is a collision on the Y axis; it receives the position of the paddle in HL and triggers the Z flag if there is a collision:

```
CheckCrossY:
call GetPtrY
inc  a
ld   c, a
```

We get the Y coordinate of the paddle, **CALL GetPtrY**. As the first scanline of the paddle is white, we don't take it into account for collisions, so we move on to the next one, **INC A**, and load the value into C, **LD C, A**.

```
ld   hl, (ballPos)
call GetPtrY
ld   b, a
```

We load the position of the ball into HL, **LD HL, (ballPos)**, then get the Y coordinate, **CALL GetPtrY**, and load the value into B, **LD B, A**.

```
add  a, $04
sub  c
ret  c
```

In A we have the Y-coordinate of the ball, we make it point to the penultimate scanline of the ball, which is the last one that is not a target, **ADD A, $04**, we subtract the Y-coordinate of the paddle, **SUB C**, and if there is a carry we exit, **RET C**, since the ball passes over it.

If we are not out, we must check if the ball goes under the paddle:

```
ld   a, c
add  a, $16
ld   c, a
ld   a, b
inc  a
sub  c
ret  nc
xor  a
ret
```

We load the Y-coordinate of the paddle into A, **LD A, C**, add $16 (22) to position ourselves on the penultimate scanline, the last one not equal to zero, **ADD A, $16**, and load the value into C, **LD C, A**.

We load the Y-coordinate of the ball into A, **LD A, B**, point to scanline 1, the first non-zero one, **INC A**, and subtract the Y-coordinate of the paddle, **SUB C**.

If there is no carry after the subtraction, we exit, **RET NC**, because either the ball passes underneath or it collides with the last scanline of the paddle, which is in the same Y-coordinate as the first scanline of the ball, and during the subtraction the Z-flag is activated.

If there is a carry, the ball collides with the rest of the paddle, so we activate the Z flag, **XOR A**, and exit, **RET**.

The next step is to implement the main routine, which we will call to check for collision, and in this case perform the necessary actions:

```
CheckBallCross:
ld   a, (ballSetting)
and  $40
jr   nz, checkBallCross_left
```

We load the ball configuration into A, **LD A, (ballSetting)**, and hold bit 6, **AND $40**, which indicates whether the ball goes right or left. If bit 6 is set to one, the ball goes left and we jump to check for a collision with player one's paddle, **JR NZ, checkBallCross_left**.

If it does not jump, the ball goes right and we check for a collision with player two's paddle:

```
checkBallCross_right:
ld   c, CROSS_RIGHT
call CheckCrossX
ret  nz
ld   hl, (paddle2pos)
call CheckCrossY
ret  nz
```

We load the collision column in C, **LD C, CROSS_RIGHT**, check if there is a collision on the X axis, **CALL CheckCrossX**. If there is no collision, we exit the routine, **RET NZ**.

If there is a collision on the X axis, we load the position of paddle two in HL, **LD HL, (paddle2pos)**, and check if there is a collision on the Y axis, **CALL CheckCrossY**. If there is no collision, we exit the routine, **RET NZ**.

If we have not exited the routine, there has been a collision:

```
ld   a, (ballSetting)
or   $40
ld   (ballSetting), a
ld   a, $ff
ld   (ballRotation), a
ret
```

We load the ball setting into A, **LD A, (ballSetting)**, set bit 6 to one by shifting the ball address to the left, **OR $40**, and load the value into memory, **LD (ballSetting), A**.

We load minus one into A, **LD A, $FF**, change the ball rotation, **LD (ballRotation), A**, and exit the routine, **RET**.

Checking if there is a collision with player one's paddle is similar to what we have seen before, we will copy the code and mark the differences without going into detail:

```
checkBallCross_left:
ld   c, CROSS_LEFT
call CheckCrossX
```

```
ret  nz
ld   hl, (paddle1pos)
call CheckCrossY
ret nz

ld   a, (ballSetting)
and  $bf
ld   (ballSetting), a
ld   a, $01
ld   (ballRotation), a
ret
```

The final aspect of the routines that check for collisions between the paddles and the ball is as follows:

```
;---------------------------------------------------------------
; Assesses whether there is a collision between the ball
; and the paddles.
; Alters the value of the AF, C and HL registers.
;---------------------------------------------------------------
CheckBallCross:
ld   a, (ballSetting)      ; A = ball direction/speed
and  $40                   ; A = bit 6 (left/right)
jr   nz, checkBallCross_left ; Bit 6 = 1 goes left, skip

checkBallCross_right:
ld   c, CROSS_RIGHT        ; C = collision column
call CheckCrossX           ; Collide X-axis?
ret  nz                    ; No collision, exits
ld   hl, (paddle2pos)      ; HL = paddle position 2
call CheckCrossY           ; Y-axis collision?
ret  nz                    ; No collision, exits

; If it gets here there is a collision
ld   a, (ballSetting)      ; A = ball direction/speed
or   $40                   ; Change direction, left
ld   (ballSetting), a      ; Load to memory
ld   a, $ff                ; Change ball rotation
ld   (ballRotation), a     ; Load to memory
ret                        ; Sale

checkBallCross_left:
; Ball goes to the left
ld   c, CROSS_LEFT         ; C = collision column
call CheckCrossX           ; Collide X-axis?
ret  nz                    ; No collision, exits
ld   hl, (paddle1pos)      ; HL = paddle position 1
call CheckCrossY           ; Y-axis collision?
ret  nz                    ; No collision, exits

; If it gets here there is a collision
ld   a, (ballSetting)      ; A = ball direction/speed
and  $bf                   ; Change direction, right
ld   (ballSetting), a      ; Load to memory
ld   a, $01                ; Change ball rotation
ld   (ballRotation), a     ; Load to memory
ret                        ; Exits

;---------------------------------------------------------------
```

```
; Evaluates whether the ball collides on the X-axis with the paddle.
; Input:       C -> Column where the collision occurs.
; Exit: Z -> Collide.
;             NZ -> No collision.
; Alters the value of the AF registers.
;--------------------------------------------------------------------
CheckCrossX:
ld    a, (ballPos)         ; A = line and column ball
and   $1f                  ; A = column
cp    c                    ; Is there a collision?

ret                        ; Exits


;--------------------------------------------------------------------
; Evaluates whether the ball collides in the Y-axis with the paddle.
; Input:  HL -> Paddle position.
; Output: Z   -> Collide.
;             NZ -> No collision.
; Alters the value of the AF, BC and HL registers.
;--------------------------------------------------------------------
CheckCrossY:
call GetPtrY               ; Vertical position paddle (TTLLLSSS)
; Position returned points to the first scanline of the paddle that is 0
inc   a                    ; A = second scanline paddle
ld    c, a                 ; C = A
ld    hl, (ballPos)        ; HL = ball position
call GetPtrY               ; Vertical ball position (TTLLLSSS)
ld    b, a                 ; B = vertical ball position
; Check if the ball goes over the paddle.
; The ball is composed of 1 scanline at 0, 4 at $3c and another at 0.
; The position points to the 1st scanline, and checks the collision
; with 5º.
add   a, $04               ; A = ball position to 5th scanline
sub   c                    ; A = A - C (paddle position)
ret   c                    ; If carry, ball goes over the top
; Check if the ball passes under the paddle.
ld    a, c                 ; A = vertical position paddle
add   a, $16               ; A = penultimate scanline paddle
ld    c, a                 ; C = A
ld    a, b                 ; A = vertical position ball
inc   a                    ; A = scanline 1 ball
sub   c                    ; A = A - C (paddle position)
ret   nc                   ; If no carry, ball passes underneath
                           ; or the last scanline collides, in which
                           ; case the Z flag is activated with SUB C
                           ; in this case the Z flag is activated
                           ; with SUB C
; There is a collision
xor   a                    ; Active flag Z
ret
```

Now we just need to see if what we have implemented does what we want it to do.

Open main.asm and add the following line just below the loop_continue tag:

```
call CheckBallCross
```

We compile and load the emulator to see the results. If everything goes well, the ball hits the paddles, the collisions work.

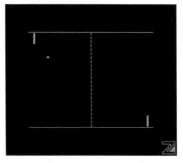

The final appearance of the main.asm file is as follows:

```
; Collision detection
org  $8000

;--------------------------------------------------------------
; Programme entry
;--------------------------------------------------------------
Main:
ld    a, $00              ; A = 0
out   ($fe), a            ; Black border

call Cls                  ; Clear screen
call PrintLine            ; Print centre line
call PrintBorder          ; Print field border

Loop:
ld    a, (countLoopBall)  ; A = countLoopsBall
inc   a                   ; It increases it
ld    (countLoopBall), a  ; Load to memory
cp    $06                 ; Counter = 6?
jr    nz, loop_paddle     ; Counter != 6, skip
call MoveBall             ; Move ball
ld    a, ZERO             ; A = 0
ld    (countLoopBall), a  ; Counter = 0

loop_paddle:
ld    a, (countLoopPaddle) ; A = count number of paddle turns
inc   a                   ; It increases it
ld    (countLoopPaddle), a ; Load to memory
cp    $02                 ; Counter = 2?
jr    nz, loop_continue   ; Counter != 2, skip
call ScanKeys             ; Scan for keystrokes
call MovePaddle           ; Move paddles
ld    a, ZERO             ; A = 0
ld    (countLoopPaddle), a ; Counter = 0

loop_continue:
call CheckBallCross       ; Checks for collision between ball
                          ; and paddles
call PrintBall            ; Paint ball
call ReprintLine          ; Reprint line
ld    hl, (paddle1pos)    ; HL = paddle 1 position
```

```
call PrintPaddle          ; Paint paddle 1
ld   hl, (paddle2pos)     ; HL = paddle 2 position
call PrintPaddle          ; Paint paddle 2
jr  Loop                  ; Infinite loop

include "game.asm"
include "controls.asm"
include "sprite.asm"
include "video.asm"

countLoopBall:   db $00   ; Count turns ball
countLoopPaddle: db $00   ; Count turns paddles

end  $8000
```

Download the source code from here

https://tinyurl.com/2a8h3rh8

Step 8: Two players game and change ball speed

In this step we will implement the two player game with a scoreboard and the ability to change the speed of the ball.

Create the folder Step08 and copy the files controls.asm, game.asm, main.asm, sprite.asm and video.asm from the folder Step07.

We start by defining the position where we want to draw the score and the sprites we need in the sprite.asm file:

```
POINTS_P1:      EQU $450d
POINTS_P2:      EQU $4511
```

Each digit in the markers occupies 8x16 pixels, one character wide by two characters high (1 byte x 16 bytes/scanlines):

```
White_sprite:
ds $10  ; 16 spaces = 16 bytes at $00

Zero_sprite:
db $00, $7e, $7e, $66, $66, $66, $66, $66
db $66, $66, $66, $66, $66, $7e, $7e, $00

One_sprite:
db $00, $18, $18, $18, $18, $18, $18, $18
db $18, $18, $18, $18, $18, $18, $18, $00

Two_sprite:
db $00, $7e, $7e, $06, $06, $06, $06, $7e
db $7e, $60, $60, $60, $60, $7e, $7e, $00

Three_sprite:
db $00, $7e, $7e, $06, $06, $06, $06, $3e
db $3e, $06, $06, $06, $06, $7e, $7e, $00

Four_sprite:
db $00, $66, $66, $66, $66, $66, $66, $7e
db $7e, $06, $06, $06, $06, $06, $06, $00

Five_sprite:
db $00, $7e, $7e, $60, $60, $60, $60, $7e
db $7e, $06, $06, $06, $06, $7e, $7e, $00

Six_sprite:
db $00, $7e, $7e, $60, $60, $60, $60, $7e
db $7e, $66, $66, $66, $66, $7e, $7e, $00

Seven_sprite:
db $00, $7e, $7e, $06, $06, $06, $06, $06
db $06, $06, $06, $06, $06, $06, $06, $00

Eight_sprite:
db $00, $7e, $7e, $66, $66, $66, $66, $7e
db $7e, $66, $66, $66, $66, $7e, $7e, $00

Nine_sprite:
db $00, $7e, $7e, $66, $66, $66, $66, $7e
```

```
db $7e, $06, $06, $06, $06, $7e, $7e, $00
```

With the sprites ready, we define the numbers so that they refer to the sprite labels:

```
Zero:
dw White_sprite, Zero_sprite

One:
dw White_sprite, One_sprite

Two:
dw White_sprite, Two_sprite

Three:
dw White_sprite, Three_sprite

Four:
dw White_sprite, Four_sprite

Five:
dw White_sprite, Five_sprite

Six:
dw White_sprite, Six_sprite

Seven:
dw White_sprite, Seven_sprite

Eight:
dw White_sprite, Eight_sprite

Nine:
dw White_sprite, Nine_sprite

Ten:
dw One_sprite, Zero_sprite

Eleven:
dw One_sprite, One_sprite

Twelve:
dw One_sprite, Two_sprite

Thirteen:
dw One_sprite, Three_sprite

Fourteen:
dw One_sprite, Four_sprite

Fifteen:
dw One_sprite, Five_sprite
```

We need to define where the players' scores will be stored. We open main.asm and add two tags before END $8000:

```
p1points:        db $00
p2points:        db $00
```

We are now ready to start implementing the scoreboard.

We need to know which sprite to paint depending on the score. To know this, we will implement a routine that receives the score in A and returns the address of the sprite to paint in HL.

We open video.asm to implement the routine just before the NextScan routine:

```
GetPointSprite:
ld   hl, Zero
ld   bc, $04
inc  a
```

We load the address of the zero sprite into HL, **LD HL, Zero**. As each sprite is four bytes away from the previous one, we load this offset into BC, **LD BC, $04**, and increment A so that the loop does not start at zero, **INC A**, to prevent it from malfunctioning if the points are zero.

Now we loop HL to point to the correct sprite:

```
getPointSprite_loop:
dec  a
ret  z
add  hl, bc
jr   getPointSprite_loop
```

We decrement A, **DEC A**, and if we have reached zero, HL already points to the correct sprite and we exit, **RET Z**. If we have not yet reached zero, we add the offset to HL, **ADD HL, BC**, and repeat the loop, **JR getPointSprite_loop**.

This is the final aspect of the routine:

```
;-------------------------------------------------------------
; Gets the corresponding sprite to paint on the marker.
; Input:  A  -> score.
; Output: HL -> address of the sprite to be painted.
; Alters the value of the AF, BC and HL registers.
;-------------------------------------------------------------
GetPointSprite:
ld   hl, Zero              ; HL = address sprite 0
ld   bc, $04              ; Sprite is 4 bytes away from
                          ; the previous one
inc  a                    ; Increment A, loop start != 0
getPointSprite_loop:
dec  a                    ; Decreasing A
ret  z                    ; A = 0, end of routine
add  hl, bc              ; Add 4 to sprite address
jr   getPointSprite_loop  ; Loop until A = 0
```

Now let's implement the routine that draws the markers at the end of the video.asm file:

```
PrintPoints:
ld   a, (p1points)
call GetPointSprite
```

We load the points of player one into A, **LD A, (p1points)** and get the memory address of the sprite definition corresponding to this score, **CALL GetPointSprite**.

GetPointSprite returns in HL the address where the sprite was defined. If the score is zero, HL will give us the memory address where the zero tag is defined, i.e:

```
Zero:
dw White_sprite, Zero_sprite
```

As we can see, zero is defined by two other memory addresses: the first is the address where the empty sprite used to justify two digits is defined, and the second is the address where the zero sprite is defined.

If the memory addresses were as follows:

```
$9000 White_sprite
$9020 Zero_sprite
$9040 Zero
```

The definition of the Zero tag, after replacing the White_sprite and Zero_sprite tags with the memory addresses where they are defined, would be as follows:

```
Zero:
Dw $9000, $9020
```

The value of HL after calling GetPointSprite when the marker is zero would be $9040, i.e. the memory address defining the zero marker.

As the Z80 is little-endian, the memory address values would be from $9040 onwards:

$9040	$00
$9041	$90
$9042	$20
$9043	$90

In other words, the memory addresses where the sprites for White_sprite and Zero_sprite are defined.

This explanation is necessary to understand how the rest of the routine works:

```
push hl
ld    e, (hl)
inc   hl
ld    d, (hl)
ld    hl, POINTS_P1
call printPoint_print
```

We are going to paint the first digit of the first player's marker. We keep the value of HL that points to the sprite of the number we are going to paint, **PUSH HL**, load into E the low byte of the address of the sprite of the first digit, **LD E, (HL)**, point to HL the high byte of the address, **INC HL**, and load it into D, **LD D, (HL)**.

We load into HL the screen address where the first digit of player one's marker will be printed, **LD HL, POINTS_P1**, and call to paint, **CALL printPointPrint**.

Now we paint the second digit of player one's marker:

```
pop   hl
inc   hl
inc   hl
```

We get the value of HL, **POP HL**, and point it to the bottom of the address where the second digit sprite is defined, **INC HL, INC HL**.

```
ld    e, (hl)
inc   hl
ld    d, (hl)
```

We load the low part of this address into E, **LD E, (HL)**, point HL to the high part of the address, **INC HL**, and load it into D, **LD D, (HL)**.

```
ld    hl, POINTS_P1
inc   l
call  printPoint_print
```

We load into HL the screen location where player one's marker is painted, **LD HL, POINTS_P1**. As each digit is one byte wide, we place HL in the column where the second digit, **INC L**, is painted and paint it, **CALL printPoint_print**.

The way player two's marker is painted is almost the same as player one's, so we show the code by bolding the changes without going into detail:

```
ld    a, (p2points)
call  GetPointSprite
push  hl
; 1st digit
ld    e, (hl)
inc   hl
ld    d, (hl)
ld    hl, POINTS_P2
call  printPoint_print

pop   hl
; 2nd digit
inc   hl
inc   hl
ld    e, (hl)
inc   hl
ld    d, (hl)
ld    hl, POINTS_P2
inc   l
```

As you can see, the changes are few. The last line has been removed because it is not necessary to call it to draw the second digit of player two, we will implement it after the last INC L.

Remember that each digit occupies 8 x 16 pixels (one column and sixteen scanlines):

```
printPoint_print:
ld   b, $10
push de
push hl
```

We load into B the number of scanlines to be painted, **LD B, $10**, and keep the value of the DE register, **PUSH DE**, and of HL, **PUSH HL**.

```
printPoint_printLoop:
ld   a, (de)
ld   (hl), a
inc  de
call NextScan
djnz printPoint_printLoop
```

We load into A the byte to paint, **LD A, (DE)**, and paint it, **LD (HL), A**. We point DE to the next byte, **INC DE**, get the address of the next scanline, **CALL NextScan**, and repeat the operation until B is 0 and we have painted all the scanlines, **DJNZ printPoint_printLoop**.

Finally, we recover the values of HL and DE and exit:

```
pop  hl
pop  de
ret
```

This is the final aspect of the marker painting routine:

```
;--------------------------------------------------------------
; Paint the scoreboard.
; Each number is 1 byte wide by 16 bytes high.
; Alters the value of the AF, BC, DE and HL registers.
;--------------------------------------------------------------
PrintPoints:
ld   a, (p1points)        ; A = points player 1
call GetPointSprite       ; Gets sprite to be painted in marker
push hl                   ; Preserves the value of HL
; 1st digit of player 1
ld   e, (hl)              ; HL = low part 1st digit address
                          ; E = (HL)
inc  hl                   ; HL = high side address 1st digit
ld   d, (hl)              ; D = (HL)
ld   hl, POINTS_P1        ; HL = memory address where to paint
                          ; points player 1
call printPoint_print     ; Paint 1st digit marker player 1

pop  hl                   ; Retrieves the value of HL
; 2nd digit of player 1
inc  hl
inc  hl                   ; HL = low part 2nd digit address
ld   e, (hl)              ; E = (HL)
inc  hl                   ; HL = high side address 2nd digit
ld   d, (hl)              ; D = (HL)
ld   hl, POINTS_P1        ; HL = memory address where to paint
                          ; points player 1
inc  l                    ; HL = address where to paint 2nd digit
call printPoint_print     ; Paint 2nd digit marker player 1

ld   a, (p2points)        ; A = points player 2
call GetPointSprite       ; Gets sprite to be painted in marker
```

```
push hl                        ; Preserves value of HL
; 1st digit of player 2
ld    e, (hl)                  ; HL = low part 1st digit address
                               ; E = (HL)
inc   hl                       ; HL = high side address 1st digit
ld    d, (hl)                  ; D = (HL)
ld    hl, POINTS_P2            ; HL = memory address where to paint
                               ; points player 2
call printPoint_print          ; Paint 1st digit marker player 2

pop   hl                       ; Retrieves the value of HL
; 2nd digit of player 2
inc   hl
inc   hl                       ; HL = low part 2nd digit address
ld    e, (hl)                  ; E = (HL)
inc   hl                       ; HL = high side address 2nd digit
ld    d, (hl)                  ; D = (HL)
ld    hl, POINTS_P2            ; HL = memory address where to paint
                               ; points player 2
inc   l                        ; HL = address where 2nd digit paints
; Paint the second digit of player 2's marker.

printPoint_print:
ld    b, $10                   ; Each digit: 1 byte x 16 (scanlines)
push de                        ; Preserves the value of DE
push hl                        ; Preserves the value of HL
printPoint_printLoop:
ld    a, (de)                  ; A = byte to be painted
ld    (hl), a                  ; Paints the byte
inc   de                       ; DE = next byte
call NextScan                  ; HL = next scanline
djnz printPoint_printLoop      ; Until B = 0

pop   hl                       ; Retrieves the value of HL
pop   de                       ; Retrieves the value of DE

ret
```

In the routine, it is easy to save twelve clock cycles and two bytes. This is done by moving two instructions around, which allows us to remove two more: we will see this in step 10.

All that remains is to see if what we have implemented works.

Open main.asm and under the call to PrintBorder, just before Loop, add the following line:

```
call PrintPoints
```

We compile and load into the emulator to see the results.

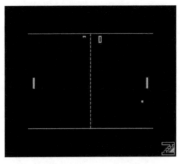

At first everything goes well, but as the ball moves we see that we have a problem, an old acquaintance of ours, and that is that the ball erases the marker as it passes; we are going to solve it below.

To prevent the ball from erasing the marker, we do the same as we did with the centre line, we repaint the marker.

We implement this routine at the end of the video.asm file.

The marker repaint routine is almost the same as the painting routine, except that we change the name of the labels and add a line.

Below we show the final appearance, with the changes to PrintPoints in bold:

```
;--------------------------------------------------------------
; Repaint the scoreboard.
; Each number is 1 byte wide by 16 bytes high.
; Alters the value of the AF, BC, DE and HL registers.
;--------------------------------------------------------------
ReprintPoints:
ld    a, (p1points)       ; A = points player 1
call GetPointSprite       ; Gets sprite to be painted marker
push hl                   ; Preserves value of HL
; 1st digit of player 1
ld    e, (hl)             ; HL = low part 1st digit address
                          ; E = (HL)
inc  hl                   ; HL = high side address 1st digit
ld    d, (hl)             ; D = (HL)
ld    hl, POINTS_P1       ; HL = memory address where to paint
                          ; points player 1
call reprintPoint_print   ; Paint 1st digit marker player 1

pop hl                    ; Retrieves value of HL
; 2nd digit of player 1
inc  hl
inc  hl                   ; HL = low part 2nd digit address
ld    e, (hl)             ; E = (HL)
inc  hl                   ; HL = high side address 2nd digit
ld    d, (hl)             ; D = (HL)
ld    hl, POINTS_P1       ; HL = memory address where to paint
                          ; points player 1
inc  l                    ; HL = address where to paint 2nd digit
call reprintPoint_print   ; Paint 2nd digit marker player 1

ld    a, (p2points)       ; A = points player 2
```

```
call GetPointSprite        ; Gets sprite to be painted on marker
push hl                    ; Preserves value of HL
; 1st digit of player 2
ld   e, (hl)               ; HL = low part 1st digit address
                           ; E = (HL)
inc  hl                    ; HL = high side address 1st digit
ld   d, (hl)               ; D = (HL)
ld   hl, POINTS_P2         ; HL = memory address where to paint
                           ; points player 2
call reprintPoint_print    ; Paint 1st digit marker player 2

pop  hl                    ; Retrieves the value of HL
; 2nd digit of player 2
inc  hl
inc  hl                    ; HL = low part 2nd digit address
ld   e, (hl)               ; E = (HL)
inc  hl                    ; HL = high side address 2nd digit
ld   d, (hl)               ; D = (HL)
ld   hl, POINTS_P2         ; HL = memory address where to paint
                           ; points player 2
inc  l                     ; HL = address where to paint 2nd digit
; Paint the second digit of player 2's marker.

reprintPoint_print:
ld   b, $10                ; Each digit 1 byte by 16 (scanlines)
push de
push hl                    ; Preserves value of DE and HL
reprintPoint_printLoop:
ld   a, (de)               ; A = byte to be painted
or   (hl)                  ; Mixes it with what is on the screen
ld   (hl), a               ; Paints the byte
inc  de                    ; Points DE to the next byte
call NextScan              ; Points HL to the next scanline
djnz reprintPoint_printLoop ; Until B = 0

pop  hl
pop  de                    ; Retrieves the value of HL and DE

ret
```

Let us explain the line we have added:

```
ld   a, (de)
or   (hl)
ld   (hl), a
```

What we do with **OR (HL)** is to add the pixels on the screen to the pixels of the number sprite. This way we repaint the number without erasing the ball.

To see if it works, open main.asm and add the following line after the call to ReprintLine:

```
call ReprintPoints
```

We compile and load in the emulator to see the results.

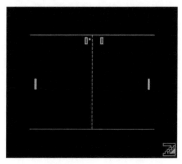

We have solved one problem, but another has arisen. The marker no longer disappears, but the ball is very slow. Fortunately, the solution is simple, as the ball's speed is one of the things we control.

As you may recall, the ball moves one out of every six iterations of the main loop, so all we need to do is reduce that interval in main.asm to, say, two:

```
ld     (countLoopBall), a
cp     $02
jr     nz, loop_paddle
```

We compile, load the emulator and check that the ball speed has increased.

In the ballSetting variable we define the speed of the ball in bits 4 and 5, where one can be the fastest and three the slowest.

We will use this aspect to define and change the speed of the ball. We will go to sprite.asm and change the initial value of ballSetting.

```
ballSetting:   db $20
```

This the initial value:

- Vertical direction: upwards
- Horizontal direction: right
- Speed: two

We will use this value to control the interval at which the ball moves. In main.asm we locate the Loop tag and add it at the bottom:

```
ld     a, (ballSetting)
rrca
rrca
rrca
rrca
and    $03
ld     b, a
```

We load the ball setting in A, **LD A, (ballSetting)**, pass the value of bits 4 and 5 to bits 0 and 1, **RRCA, RRCA, RRCA, RRCA**, leaving only bits 0 and 1 (ball speed), **AND $03**, and load the value in B, **LD B, A**.

Four lines down, we modify the CP $02 line:

```
cp     b
```

We compile and check that everything still works the same. The difference is that now the ball speed is taken from the ball configuration and we can change it.

To change the speed of the ball we will use keys 1 to 3. Open the controls.asm file and start typing after the ScanKeys label:

```
scanKeys_speed:
xor  a
ld   (countLoopBall), a
scanKeys_ctrl:
```

If one of the speed change keys has been pressed, the loop counter must be reset to zero in order to paint the ball, otherwise if the counter is set to two and the speed is set to one, it will take 254 iterations for the ball to move again.

We set A to zero, **XOR A**, and the iteration counter for the ball to zero, **LD (countLoopBall), A**.

The scanKeys_ctrl tag marks the point where the routine as we have it now starts. The new implementation is between the ScanKeys and scanKeys_speed tags:

```
ld   a, $f7
in   a, ($fe)
```

We load the half stack 1-5 into A, **LD A, $F7**, and read from the keyboard port, **IN A, ($FE)**.

```
bit  $00, a
jr   nz, scanKeys_2
```

We check if 1, **BIT $00, A**, has been pressed, and if not, we jump to check if 2, **JR NZ, scanKeys_2**, has been pressed.

If 1 has been pressed, we change the speed of the ball:

```
ld   a, (ballSetting)
and  $cf
or   $10
ld   (ballSetting), a
jr   scanKeys_speed
```

We load the ball configuration into A, **LD A, (ballSetting)**, set the speed bits to zero, **AND $CF**, set the speed to one, **OR $10**, load the configuration into memory, **LD (ballSetting), A**, and set the ball iteration counter to zero, **JR scanKeys_speed**.

Checking for 2 and 3 is similar to checking for 1; we look at the full code and mark the differences in bold:

```
scanKeys_2:
bit  $01, a
jr   nz, scanKeys_3
ld   a, (ballSetting)
and  $cf
or   $20
ld (ballSetting), a
```

```
jr    scanKeys_speed
scanKeys_3:
bit   $02, a
jr    nz, scanKeys_ctrl
ld    a, (ballSetting)
and   $cf
or    $30
ld    (ballSetting), a
```

The routine, once modified, looks like this:

```
;--------------------------------------------------------------------
; ScanKeys
; Scans the control keys and returns the pressed keys.
; Output: D -> Keys pressed.
;          Bit 0 -> A pressed 0/1.
;          Bit 1 -> Z pressed 0/1.
;          Bit 2 -> 0 pressed 0/1.
;          Bit 3 -> O pressed 0/1.
; Alters the value of the AF and D registers.
;--------------------------------------------------------------------
ScanKeys:
ld    a, $f7            ; A = half-row 1-5
in    a, ($fe)          ; Reads half-stack status
bit   $00, a            ; 1 pressed?
jr    nz, scanKeys_2    ; Not pressed, jumps
; Pressed; changes the speed of ball 1 (fast)
ld    a, (ballSetting)  ; A = configuration ball A
and   $cf               ; Set the speed bits to 0
or    $10               ; Sets the speed bits to 1
ld    (ballSetting), a  ; Load value to memory
jr    scanKeys_speed    ; Jump check controls
scanKeys_2:
bit   $01, a            ; 2 pressed?
jr    nz, scanKeys_3    ; Not pressed, skips
; Pressed; changes ball speed 2 (middle)
ld    a, (ballSetting)  ; A = ball configuration
and   $cf               ; Set the speed bits to 0
or    $20               ; Sets the speed bits to 2
ld    (ballSetting), a  ; Load value to memory
jr    scanKeys_speed    ; Jump check controls
scanKeys_3:
bit   $02, a            ; 3 pressed?
jr    nz, scanKeys_ctrl ; Not pressed, skip
; Pressed; changes the speed of the ball 3 (slow)
ld    a, (ballSetting)  ; A configuration = ball
or    $30               ; Sets the speed bits to 3
ld    (ballSetting), a  ; Load value to memory

scanKeys_speed:
xor   a                 ; A = 0
ld    (countLoopBall), a ; CountLoopBall iterations = 0
scanKeys_ctrl:
ld    d, $00            ; D = 0

; Rest of the routine from ScanKeys_A
```

We compile, load in the emulator and see how this modification behaves. If all went well, we can now change the speed of the ball.

Finally, we need to count the points that the players reach, for which we will modify the MoveBall routine inside game.asm, the moveBall_rightChg and moveBall_leftChg parts.

These routines change the direction of the ball when it reaches the left or right boundary. We will implement what is needed to mark the points.

We will place the code below these markers, starting with moveBall_rightChg:

```
moveBall_rightChg:
ld   hl, p1points
inc  (hl)
call PrintPoints
```

We load into HL the memory address where player one's marker is, **LD HL, p1points**, increment it, **INC (HL)**, and print the marker, **CALL PrintPoints**. The rest of the routine stays as it was.

The modifications to the moveBall_leftChg tag are almost the same:

```
moveBall_leftChg:
ld   hl, p2points
inc  (hl)
call PrintPoints
```

We compile and load into the emulator to see the results.

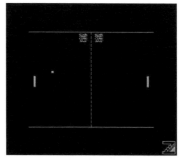

We have a scoreboard, but the game goes on endlessly, and when we go over fifteen points it starts to draw nonsense.

We can also see that it is getting slower and slower, but why? We paint the marker at each iteration, and to find the sprite of the number to be painted we make a loop, and a loop with fifteen iterations at most is not the same as a loop with up to two hundred and fifty-five iterations. Isn't it? In chapter ten we will see how to implement GetPointSprite so that it always takes the same time and we save two bytes and a few clock cycles.

What we need to do now is to stop the game when one of the two players reaches fifteen points; we will also implement a way to start the game, for example by pressing 5.

At the end of controls.asm we will implement the routine that waits for the 5 to be pressed to start the game:

```
WaitStart:
ld   a, $f7
in   a, ($fe)
bit  $04, a
jr   nz, WaitStart
ret
```

We load the half stack 1-5 into A, **LD A, $F7**, read the keyboard, **IN A, ($FE)**, check if 5 has been pressed, **BIT $04, A**, and repeat until it has been pressed, **JR NZ, WaitStart**.

The final aspect of the routine is as follows:

```
;---------------------------------------------------------------
; WaitStart.
; Wait for the 5 key to be pressed to start the game.
; Alters the value of the AF register.
;---------------------------------------------------------------
WaitStart:
ld   a, $f7         ; A = half-row 1-5
in   a, ($fe)       ; Read keyboard
bit  $04, a         ; 5 pressed?
jr   nz, WaitStart  ; Not pressed, loop

ret
```

We go back to main.asm and after the call to PrintPoints we add the following line:

```
call WaitStart
```

We compile it, load it into the emulator and see that the game doesn't start until we press 5.

But this is not enough, because the game does not end when one of the players reaches fifteen points.

We continue in main.asm, at the end of the loop_continue routine, just before the **JR Loop**; this is where we will implement the score control:

```
ld   a, (p1points)
cp   $0f
jr   z, Main
```

We load player 1's score into A, **LD A, (p1points)**, compare it with fifteen, **CP $0F**, and if it is fifteen we jump to the start of the programme, **JR Z, Main**.

We do the same for player 2's score:

```
ld   a, (p2points)
cp   $0f
jr   z, Main
```

We compile, load the emulator and see if any player reaches fifteen points and the game ends:

But what happens if we press 5 again? There is no way to start the game, at no point do we reset the score to zero. If we leave 5 pressed, we will see that it returns to the start and stops at each iteration of the loop.

To fix this, we go back to the beginning of main.asm and set the markers to zero just after the call to WaitStart:

```
ld    a, ZERO
ld    (p1points), a
ld    (p2points), a
call PrintPoints
```

We set A to zero, **LD A, ZERO**, set player one's score to 0, **LD (p1points), A**, and player two's score, **LD (p2points), A**. It's time to print the scoreboard, **CALL PrintPoints**. This way, when we start the game, we set the markers to zero and paint them.

We compile and load into the emulator to see the results. This is starting to take shape.

We still need to make some adjustments. We are going to make it so that when a goal is scored, the ball goes out on the opposite side, i.e. as if the player who scored was serving.

We will implement a routine to delete the ball, another to place it on the right side of the screen and another to place it on the left side of the screen.

The routine that erases the ball will be implemented in the video.asm file, just before the Cls routine:

```
ClearBall:
ld    hl, (ballPos)
ld    a, l
and   $1f
cp    $10
jr    c, clearBall_continue
inc   l
```

We load the position of the ball in HL, **LD HL, (ballPos)**, the row and column in A, **LD A, L**, we keep the column, **AND $1F**, and compare it with the centre of the screen, **CP $10**.

If there is a carry, the ball can only be on the left border. We jump to clear the ball, **JR C, clearBall_continue**. If it does not jump, it is in the right border, but the ball is painted one column to the right (the ball is painted in two bytes/columns); we point HL to the column where the ball is painted, **INC L**.

```
clearBall_continue:
ld   b, $06
clearBall_loop:
ld   (hl), ZERO
call NextScan

djnz clearBall_loop

ret
```

We load the number of scanlines to be deleted into B, **LD B, $06**, delete the position to which HL points, **LD (HL), ZERO**, and point HL to the next scanline, **CALL NextScan**. Repeat until B is equals zero, **DJNZ clearBall_loop**, and exit, **RET**.

The final aspect of the routine is as follows:

```
;-----------------------------------------------------------------
; Delete the ball.
; Alters the value of the AF, B and HL registers.
;-----------------------------------------------------------------
ClearBall:
ld   hl, (ballPos)         ; HL = ball position
ld   a, l                  ; A = row and column
and  $1f                   ; A = column
cp   $10                   ; Compare with centre display
jr   c, clearBall_continue ; If carry, jump, is on left
inc  l                     ; It is in right, increase column
clearBall_continue:
ld   b, $06                ; Loop 6 scanlines
clearBall_loop:
ld   (hl), ZERO            ; Deletes byte pointed to by HL
call NextScan              ; Next scanline
djnz clearBall_loop        ; Until B = 0

ret
```

The other two routines are implemented at the end of game.asm:

```
SetBallLeft:
ld   hl, $4d60
ld   (ballPos), hl
ld   a, $01
ld   (ballRotation), a
ld   a, (ballSetting)
and  $bf
ld   (ballSetting), a
ret
```

We load the new ball position into HL, **LD HL, $4D60**, and load it into memory, **LD (ballPos), HL**.

We load the ball rotation into A, **LD A, $01**, and store it in memory, **LD (ballRotation), A**.

We load the ball configuration into register A, **LD A, (ballSetting)**, set the horizontal address to the right, **AND $BF**, load it into memory, **LD (ballSetting), A**, and exit, **RET**.

The routine for setting the ball to the right is practically the same; we mark the differences in bold without going into detail:

```
SetBallRight:
ld    hl, $4d7f
ld    (ballPos), hl
ld    a, $ff
ld    (ballRotation), a
ld    a, (ballSetting)
or    $40
ld    (ballSetting), a
ret
```

The final appearance of the two routines is as follows:

```
;--------------------------------------------------------------------
; Position the ball to the left.
; Alters the value of the AF and HL registers.
;--------------------------------------------------------------------
SetBallLeft:
ld    hl, $4d60          ; HL = ball position
ld    (ballPos), hl      ; Loads value to memory
ld    a, $01             ; A = 1
ld    (ballRotation), a  ; Rotation = 1
ld    a, (ballSetting)   ; A = ball direction and ball velocity
and   $bf                ; A = Horizontal right direction
ld    (ballSetting), a   ; Horizontal direction = right

ret

;--------------------------------------------------------------------
; Position the ball to the right.
; Alters the value of the AF and HL registers.
;--------------------------------------------------------------------
SetBallRight:
ld    hl, $4d7f          ; HL = ball position
ld    (ballPos), hl      ; Loads value to memory
ld    a, $ff             ; A = -1
ld    (ballRotation), a  ; Rotation = -1
ld    a, (ballSetting)   ; A = ball direction and ball velocity
or    $40                ; A = horizontal direction left
ld    (ballSetting), a   ; Horizontal direction = left

ret
```

To complete this step, we only need to use these routines.

We are going to modify two routines in the game.asm file: moveBall_rightChg and moveBall_leftChg.

In the moveBall_rightChg routine we need to delete the lines between CALL PrintPoints and JR moveBall_end and replace them with:

```
call ClearBall
call SetBallLeft
```

The final aspect of the routine is as follows:

```
moveBall_rightChg:
; You have reached the right limit, POINT!
ld   hl, p1points          ; HL = score address player 1
inc  (hl)                  ; Increases score
call PrintPoints           ; Paint marker
call ClearBall             ; Clears ball
call SetBallLeft           ; Set ball to left
jr   moveBall_end          ; End routine
```

In the moveBall_leftChg routine, we delete the lines between CALL PrintPoints and the moveBall_end tag, and replace them with:

```
call ClearBall
call SetBallRight
```

The final aspect of the routine is as follows:

```
moveBall_leftChg:
; You have reached the left limit, POINT!
ld   hl, p2points          ; HL = address score player 2
inc  (hl)                  ; Increments marker
call PrintPoints           ; Paint marker
call ClearBall             ; Clears ball
call SetBallRight          ; Set ball right
```

We compile, load the emulator and can start playing our first two-player games, although we still have a few things to do.

Download the source code from here

https://tinyurl.com/2yohrv6g

Step 9: Change of direction and ball speed

We are going to dispense with some of what we implemented in the previous step. The speed of the ball will change depending on which part of the paddle it collides with.

Create a folder called Step09. Copy controls.asm, game.asm, main.asm, sprite.asm and video.asm from Step08.

First we will remove the ability to change the speed of the ball with keys 1 to 3.

Open controls.asm and in the ScanKeys routine delete all lines up to the scanKeys_ctrl tag, leaving the beginning of the routine as follows:

```
ScanKeys:
ld    d, $00

scanKeys_A:
```

When we compile and load in the emulator, we notice that the speed of the ball does not change.

We will add constants and variables to sprite.asm to control the inclination of the ball. We will also change the sprites of the paddles, which will draw the four pixels closest to the centre of the screen.

We add the constants that specify the rotation that the ball should have when it collides with the paddle:

```
CROSS_LEFT_ROT:   EQU $ff
CROSS_RIGHT_ROT:  EQU $01
```

We add the initial position of the ball and the cumulative number of moves the ball must make to change the Y position. We will use the latter data to change the tilt of the ball:

```
BALLPOS_INI:   EQU $4850
ballMovCount:  db $00
```

We change the initial configuration of the ball and the documentation (comments) of the ball:

```
; Ball speed and direction.
; bits 0 to 3:   Movements of the ball to change the Y position.
;                Values: f = half-diagonal, 2 = half-diagonal,
;                        1 = diagonal
; bits 4 and 5: Ball speed:  1 very fast, 2 fast, 3 slow
; bit 6:        X-address:   0 right / 1 left
; bit 7:        Y-direction: 0 up / 1 down
ballSetting:   db $31     ; 0011 0001
```

According to the new configuration, the ball initially moves to the right and upwards, at a slow speed, and the Y-position changes with each movement.

We add the paddle sprites and remove the previous one:

```
; PADDLE:          EQU$3c
```

```
PADDLE1:          EQU $0f
PADDLE2:          EQU $f0
```

Finally, we add the initial positions of the paddles:

```
PADDLE1POS_INI:EQU $4861
PADDLE2POS_INI:EQU $487e
```

We have added separate sprites for each paddle and removed the constant we used to paint the paddles; when we compile, we get errors.

We fix these errors by modifying the PrintPaddle routine in video.asm.

The PrintPaddle routine receives the position of the paddle in HL. Now it also gets the sprite of the paddle in C.

We modify the line below the printPaddle_loop tag:

```
ld    (hl), PADDLE
```

We leave it as follows:

```
ld    (hl), c
```

We compile it, it doesn't give an error, but when we load it into the emulator, we see that the results are not what we want.

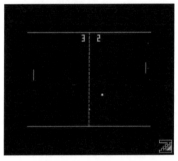

The paddle being painted by the sprite we defined. This is because we have not loaded in C which sprite to paint.

Open main.asm and look for the loop_continue tag. From line five we print the paddles, load the HL with the position of the paddle and call the painting of the paddle. Before calling the painting method we need to specify the sprite to paint.

This is what it looks like after the modification:

```
ld    hl, (paddle1pos)
ld    c, PADDLE1
call PrintPaddle
ld    hl, (paddle2pos)
ld    c, PADDLE2
call PrintPaddle
```

We compile, open in the emulator and see that the paddles are well painted again.

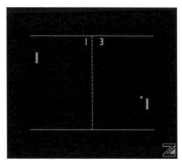

Taking advantage of the fact that we are in main.asm, we are going to change a behaviour that you may not have noticed. At the end of one game, and the start of another, the paddles stay in the same position they were at the end of the game, and the ball goes out of the court of the player who scored the last point.

We add the following lines before the Loop tag:

```
ld    hl, BALLPOS_INI
ld    (ballPos), hl
ld    hl, PADDLE1POS_INI
ld    (paddle1pos), hl
ld    hl, PADDLE2POS_INI
ld    (paddle2pos), hl
```

The ball and the paddles are placed in their initial positions.

When we compile, we get an error:

```
ERROR on line 68 of file main.asm
ERROR: Relative jump out of range
```

This error occurs because when we add lines, we have some JR that is out of range. JR can only jump 127 bytes forwards or 128 bytes backwards, and we have some JR that is jumping to an address outside this range.

Specifically, we have two **JR Z, Main** and one **JR Loop** at the end of the main.asm file. We replace these three **JR** with **JP** and we have solved the problem. JP occupies one byte more than JR, our program has grown by three bytes, but we have reduced six clock cycles.

We compile the game, load it into the emulator and see that when we stop the game and start another one, both the ball and the paddles return to their initial position.

We have implemented the change in speed, inclination and direction of the ball when it collides with the paddles.

Open game.asm and look for the checkBallCross_left tag. We find it three lines above:

```
ld    a, $ff
```

We modify this line and leave it as follows:

```
ld    a, CROSS_LEFT_ROT
```

130

We look for the CheckCrossX tag and three lines above it:

```
ld    a, $01
```

We change this line and leave it as follows:

```
ld    a, CROSS_RIGHT_ROT
```

We have changed the values to constants so that if we need to change the values in the future, we will be able to locate them more easily.

The next step is to change the ball configuration, which depends on the collision zone.

We divide the paddle into five. The behaviour depends on the collision zone:

Strike zone	Vertical direction	Inclination	Speed
1/5	Up	Diagonal	3 (slow)
2/5	Up	Semi-diagonal	2 (normal)
3/5	It does not change	Semi-flat	1 (fast)
4/5	Below	Semi-diagonal	2 (normal)
5/5	Below	Diagonal	3 (slow)

We locate the CheckCrossY tag, go to the penultimate line, **XOR A**, and implement before it:

```
ld    a, c
sub   $15
ld    c, a
ld    a, b
add   a, $04
ld    b, a
```

At this point we have in C the position of the penultimate scanline of the paddle and in B the position of the ball. Both positions are in TTLLLSSS format.

We load into A the position of the penultimate scanline of the paddle, **LD A, C**, we position ourselves in the first scanline, **SUB $15**, and we load the value back into C, **LD C, A**.

We load the position of the ball into A, **LD A, B**, we position ourselves at the bottom of the ball, **ADD A, $04**, and we load the value back into B, **LD B, A**.

From here we implement the change of behaviour depending on the collision position of the ball:

```
checkCrossY_1_5:
ld    a, c
add   a, $04
cp    b
jr    c, checkCrossY_2_5
```

We load the vertical position of the paddle in A, **LD A, C**, position ourselves on the last scanline of the first part, **ADD A, $04**, and compare it with the position of the ball, **CP B**. If there is carry, the ball is lower; we jump to check the next part, **JR C, checkCrossY_2_5**.

If there is no carry, the ball has collided in this part and we must change its configuration:

```
ld    a, (ballSetting)
and   $40
or    $31
jr    checkCrossY_end
```

We load the ball configuration in A, **LD A, (ballSetting)**, leave the horizontal direction (it comes calculated), **AND $40**, and set the vertical direction up, speed three and diagonal tilt, **OR $31**. We jump to the end of the routine, **JR checkCrossY_end**.

If the ball has not collided with the first part, we check if it has collided with the second part:

```
checkCrossY_2_5:
ld    a, c
add   a, $09
cp    b
jr    c, checkCrossY_3_5
```

We load the vertical position of the paddle in A, **LD A, C**, position ourselves on the last scanline of the second part, **ADD A, $09**, and compare it with the position of the ball, **CP B**. If there is carry, the ball is lower and we jump to check the next part, **JR C, checkCrossY_3_5**.

If there is no carry, the ball has collided in this part and we must change its configuration:

```
ld    a, (ballSetting)
and   $40
or    $22
jr    checkCrossY_end
```

We load the ball setting in A, **LD A, (ballSetting)**, we keep the horizontal direction (it comes calculated), **AND $40**, and we set the vertical direction up, speed two and semi-diagonal tilt, **OR $22**. We jump to the end of the routine, **JR checkCrossY_end**.

If the ball has not collided with the second part, we check if it has collided with the third part:

```
checkCrossY_3_5:
ld    a, c
add   a, $0d
cp    b
jr    c, checkCrossY_4_5
```

We load the vertical position of the paddle in A, **LD A, C**, go to the last scanline of the third part, **ADD A, $0D**, and compare it with the position of the ball, **CP B**. If there is a carry, the ball goes lower and we jump to check the next part, **JR C, checkCrossY_4_5**.

If there is no carry, the ball has collided in this part and we need to change its configuration:

```
ld    a, (ballSetting)
and   $c0
or    $1f
jr    checkCrossY_end
```

We load the ball configuration in A, **LD A, (ballSetting)**, keep the horizontal and vertical directions (which are calculated), **AND $C0**, and set the speed to one and semi-flat tilt, **OR $1F**. We jump to the end of the routine, **JR checkCrossY_end**.

If the non-ball collided with the third part, we check if it collided with the fourth part:

```
checkCrossY_4_5:
ld    a, c
add   a, $11
cp    b
jr    c, checkCrossY_5_5
```

We load the vertical position of the paddle in A, **LD A, C**, go to the last scanline of the fourth part, **ADD A, $11**, and compare it with the position of the ball, **CP B**. If there is carry, the ball is lower and we jump to check the next part, **JR C, checkCrossY_5_5**.

If there is no carry, the ball has collided in this part and we need to change its configuration:

```
ld    a, (ballSetting)
and   $40
or    $a2
jr    checkCrossY_end
```

We load the ball configuration in A, **LD A, (ballSetting)**, we keep the horizontal direction (it comes calculated), **AND $40**, and we set the vertical direction down, speed two and semi-diagonal tilt, **OR $A2**. We jump to the end of the routine, **JR checkCrossY_end**.

If the ball has not collided with the fourth part of the paddle, it has collided with the fifth part:

```
checkCrossY_5_5:
ld    a, (ballSetting)
and   $40
or    $b1
```

We load the ball configuration in A, **LD A, (ballSetting)**, we keep the horizontal direction (it is calculated), **AND $40**, and we set the vertical direction, speed three and the diagonal inclination, **OR $B1**.

Finally, just above **XOR A**, we add the end-of-function tag we mentioned and load the new ball configuration into memory:

```
checkCrossY_end:
ld    (ballSetting), a
```

After XOR A, let's set the ball movement counter to 0:

```
ld    (ballMovCount), a
```

The final aspect of the routine is as follows:

```
; ------------------------------------------------------------------
; Evaluates whether the ball collides in the Y-axis with the paddle.
; In the event of a collision, update the ball configuration.
; Input:  HL -> Paddle position
; Output: Z  -> Collide.
;         NZ -> No collision.
; Alters the value of the AF, BC and HL registers.
; ------------------------------------------------------------------
CheckCrossY:
call GetPtrY               ; Vertical position paddle (TTLLLSSS)
; The position points to the first scanline of the paddle which is at 0
inc  a                     ; A = next scanline
ld   c, a                  ; C = A
ld   hl, (ballPos)         ; HL = ball position
call GetPtrY               ; Vertical position ball (TTLLLSSS)
ld   b, a                  ; B = A
; Check if the ball goes over the paddle
; The ball is composed of 1 scanline at 0, 4 at $3c and another at 0
; Position points to 1st scanline, check for collision with 5th scanline
add  a, $04                ; A = 5th scanline
sub  c                     ; A = ball position - paddle position
ret  c                     ; Carry? Out, ball passes over
; Check if the ball passes under the paddle
ld   a, c                  ; A = vertical position paddle
add  a, $16                ; A = penultimate scanline, last != 0
ld   c, a                  ; C = A
ld   a, b                  ; A = vertical position ball
inc  a                     ; A = 1st scanline, first != 0
sub  c                     ; A = ball position - paddle position
ret  nc                    ; Carry? No, ball passes underneath
                           ; or collide in the last scanline
                           ; The latter case activates flag Z

; Depending on collision location, inclination and speed
ld   a, c                  ; A = penultimate scanline of paddle
sub  $15                   ; A = first scanline
ld   c, a                  ; C = A

ld   a, b                  ; A = ball position
add  a, $04                ; A = lower ball
ld   b, a                  ; B = A

checkCrossY_1_5:
ld   a, c                  ; A = vertical position paddle
add  a, $04                ; A = last scanline of 1/5
cp   b                     ; Compare with ball position
jr   c, checkCrossY_2_5    ; Carry? Ball is lower, jump
ld   a, (ballSetting)      ; A = ball configuration
and  $40                   ; A = horizontal direction
or   $31                   ; up, speed 3 and diagonal
jr   checkCrossY_end       ; End of routine

checkCrossY_2_5:
ld   a, c                  ; A = vertical position paddel
add  a, $09                ; A = last scanline of 2/5
```

```
cp   b                       ; Compare with ball position
jr   c, checkCrossY_3_5      ; Carry? Ball is lower, jump
ld   a, (ballSetting)        ; A = ball setting
and  $40                     ; A = horizontal direction
or   $22                     ; up, speed 2 and semi-diagonal
jr   checkCrossY_end         ; End of routine

checkCrossY_3_5:
ld   a, c                    ; A = vertical position paddle
add  a, $0d                  ; A = last scanline of 3/5
cp   b                       ; Compare with ball position
jr   c, checkCrossY_4_5      ; Carry? Ball is lower, jump
ld   a, (ballSetting)        ; A = ball configuration
and  $c0                     ; A = horizontal and vertical direction
or   $1f                     ; speed 1 and semi flat
jr   checkCrossY_end         ; End of routine

checkCrossY_4_5:
ld   a, c                    ; A = vertical position paddle
add  a, $11                  ; A = last scanline of 4/5
cp   b                       ; Compare with ball position
jr   c, checkCrossY_5_5      ; Carry? Ball is lower, jump
ld   a, (ballSetting)        ; A = ball configuration
and  $40                     ; A = horizontal and vertical direction
or   $a2                     ; down, speed 2 and semi-diagonal
jr   checkCrossY_end         ; End of routine

checkCrossY_5_5:
ld   a, (ballSetting)        ; A = ball configuration
and  $40                     ; A = horizontal direction
or   $b1                     ; down, speed 3 and diagonal

; There is a collision
checkCrossY_end:
ld   (ballSetting), a        ; Load into memory ball configuration
xor  a                       ; Flag Z = 1, A = 0
ld   (ballMovCount), a       ; Ball movement counter = 0
ret
```

We compile, load into the emulator and look at the results.

We see that the speed changes depending on the collision zone of the ball, but not the inclination. Also, when a goal is scored, the speed is not reset, which makes it very difficult to continue playing when the ball is at maximum speed.

Why does the speed change but not the slope?

If we think back, in the previous step we implemented the possibility of changing the speed of the ball with keys 1 to 3. In fact, we started this step by warning that we were going to abandon this implementation, but what we did not abandon is the change we made in Main.asm to take into account the speed of the ball in the configuration; that is why the speed changes.

What is missing is the implementation to take into account the tilt, so that when a point is scored, the ball speed and tilt are reset.

We will start by changing the tilt. We continue in the file game.asm and implement the routine that changes the Y-position of the ball; we implement it after the RET of the moveBall_end tag:

```
MoveBallY:
ld   a, (ballSetting)
and  $0f
ld   d, a
```

We load the ball setting into A, **LD A, (ballSetting)**, keep the slope, **AND $0F**, and load the value into D, **LD A, D**.

```
ld   a, (ballMovCount)
inc  a
ld   (ballMovCount), a
cp   d
ret  nz
```

We load the number of moves the ball makes into A, **LD A, (ballMovCount)**, increment it, **INC A**, load the value into memory, **LD (ballMovCount), A**, and compare it with D, which contains the number of moves needed to change the Y position, **CP D**. If they are not equal, it has not been reached and we exit, **RET NZ**.

```
xor  a
ld   (ballMovCount), a
ret
```

When we have reached the value, we set A = 0 and activate the Z flag, **XOR A**, zero the accumulated movements of the ball, **LD (ballMovCount), A**, and exit, **RET**. Activating the Z flag indicates to the caller that the Y position of the ball needs to be changed.

The final aspect of the routine is as follows:

```
; ------------------------------------------------------------------
; Changes the Y position of the ball
; Alters the value of the AF and D registers.
; ------------------------------------------------------------------
MoveBallY:
ld   a, (ballSetting)    ; A = ball configuration
and  $0f                 ; A = inclination
ld   d, a                ; D = A

ld   a, (ballMovCount)   ; A = accumulated ball movements
inc  a                   ; A = A + 1
ld   (ballMovCount), a   ; Loads value into memory
cp   d                   ; Compare with inclination
ret  nz                  ; Different? Exit, no change of position

; The position must change
xor  a                   ; A = 0, flag Z = 1
ld   (ballMovCount), a   ; Accumulated ball movements = 0

ret
```

Locate the moveBall_up tag and add the following between the JR Z, moveBall_upChg and CALL PreviousScan lines:

```
call MoveBallY
jr   nz, moveBall_x
```

We check if the Y position of the ball needs to be changed, **CALL MoveBallY**, and if not it jumps, **JR NZ, moveBall_x**.

Locate the moveBall_down tag and add the following between the lines JR Z, moveBall_downChg and CALL NextScan:

```
call MoveBallY
jr   nz, moveBall_x
```

We check if the Y-position of the ball needs to be changed, **CALL MoveBallY**, and if not it jumps, **JR NZ, moveBall_x**.

We compile, load the emulator and check that the tilt and speed change.

Finally, we will make it so that when a point is scored, the speed and inclination of the ball are reset.

We locate the SetBallLeft routine, remove the **AND $BF** line and replace it with the following:

```
and   $bf
and   $80
or    $31
```

We keep the Y direction, **AND $80**, set the horizontal direction to the right, speed three and diagonal tilt, **OR $31**.

Before the **RET** command, we add the following lines:

```
ld   a, $00
ld   (ballMovCount), a
```

We set A to zero, **LD A, $00**, and the movements of the ball, **LD (ballMovCount), A**.

We locate the SetBallRight routine, remove the **OR $40** line and replace it with the following:

```
or    $40
and   $80
or    $71
```

We keep the Y direction, **AND $80**, set the horizontal direction to the left, the speed to three and the diagonal tilt, **OR $11**.

Before the **RET** command, we add the following lines:

```
ld   a, $00
ld   (ballMovCount), a
```

We set A to zero, **LD A, $00**, and the movements of the ball, **LD (ballMovCount), A**.

The final appearance of both routines is as follows:

```
; ------------------------------------------------------------------
; Position the ball to the left.
; Alters the value of the AF and HL registers.
```

```
; ------------------------------------------------------------------
SetBallLeft:
ld   hl, $4d60          ; HL = ball position
ld   (ballPos), hl      ; Load value into memory
ld   a, $01             ; A = 1
ld   (ballRotation), a  ; Rotation = 1
ld   a, (ballSetting)   ; A direction and velocity ball
and  $80                ; A = Y-direction
or   $31                ; X right, speed 3 and diagonal
ld   (ballSetting), a   ; New ball address in memory
ld   a, $00             ; A = 0
ld   (ballMovCount), a  ; Ball movement counter = 0

ret

; ------------------------------------------------------------------
; Position the ball to the right.
; Alters the value of the AF and HL registers.
; ------------------------------------------------------------------
SetBallRight:
ld   hl, $4d7f          ; HL = ball position
ld   (ballPos), hl      ; Load value into memory
ld   a, $ff             ; A = -1
ld   (ballRotation), a  ; Rotation = -1
ld   a, (ballSetting)   ; A = ball direction and velocity
and  $80                ; A = Y-direction
or   $71                ; X left, speed 3 and diagonal
ld   (ballSetting), a   ; New ball address in memory
ld   a, $00             ; A = 0
ld   (ballMovCount), a  ; Ball movement counter = 0

ret
```

We compile, load the emulator and see the results, which should be as expected, although the ball is a bit slow, isn't it?

Have you noticed that when the ball hits the bottom of the paddle it doesn't change its vertical direction, pitch or speed? In step ten we will see why.

Download the source code from here

https://tinyurl.com/27lbawqf

Step 10: Optimisation

Yes, the ball is a bit slow. This is largely because the marker is repainted on every iteration of the main loop, which is not necessary.

The marker should only be repainted when it is erased by the ball. By changing this aspect, we will gain speed in the sphere by reducing the processing time in each iteration of the main loop.

As usual, we create the folder Step10 and copy the files controls.asm, game.asm, main.asm, sprite.asm and video.asm from the folder Step09.

The first thing to do is to locate the area of the screen where the ball clears the marker by defining a series of constants in sprite.asm, under the constant POINTS_P2:

```
POINTS_X1_L:    EQU $0c
POINTS_X1_R:    EQU $0f
POINTS_X2_L:    EQU $10
POINTS_X2_R:    EQU $13
POINTS_Y_B:     EQU $14
```

The meaning of these constants, in order of appearance, is as follows

- **POINTS_X1_L**: column in which the ball starts to leave player one's marker from the left.
- **POINTS_X1_R**: column in which the ball starts to leave the marker of the first player from the right.
- **POINTS_X2_L**: column in which the ball starts to leave player two's marker from the left.
- **POINTS_X2_R**: column in which the ball starts to leave player two's marker from the right.
- **POINTS_Y_B**: third row and scanline where the ball starts to leave the marker at the bottom.

Once the constants have been defined, we will modify the PrintPoints and ReprintPoints routines in video.asm, starting by locating the printPoint_print tag, which we will replace with PrintPoint.

Within the PrintPoints routine we find that there are three calls to printPoint_print, which we will replace with PrintPoint.

Compile, load in the emulator and check that we haven't broken anything.

Next, we will delete the ReprintPoints routine as we will be reimplementing it from start to finish.

```
ReprintPoints:
ld    hl, (ballPos)
call GetPtrY
cp    POINTS_Y_B
ret   nc
```

We load the position of the ball in HL, **LD HL, (ballPos)**, then get the third, line and scanline of the ball position, **CALL GetPtrY**, and compare it with the position where the marker starts to be erased by the ball from below, **CP POINTS_Y_B**. No carry, the ball passes under the marker and exits, **RET NC**.

If we have carry, depending on the X coordinate of the ball, it could erase the marker.

```
ld    a, l
and   $1f
cp    POINTS_X1_L
ret   c
jr    z, reprintPoint_1_print
```

We load the row and column of the ball's position in A, **LD A, L**, keep the column, **AND $1F**, and compare it with the X coordinate where player one's marker starts to be erased from the left, **CP POINTS_X1_L**. If there is a carry, the ball passes to the left of the marker and exits, **RET C**. If the two coordinates match, the ball will erase player one's marker and jump to reprint it, **JR Z, reprintPoint_1_print**.

If we don't go out or jump, we continue with the checks:

```
cp    POINTS_X2_R
jr    z, reprintPoint_2_print
ret   nc
```

We compare the X coordinate of the ball with the coordinate where player two's marker starts to be erased from the right, **CP POINT_X2_R**. If they are the same, it jumps to reprint player two's marker, **JR Z, reprintPoint_2_print**. If it does not jump and there is no carry, the ball passes to the right and goes out, **RET NC**.

If we don't jump or go out, we continue with the checks:

```
reprintPoint_1:
cp    POINTS_X1_R
jr    c, reprintPoint_1_print
jr    nz, reprintPoint_2
```

We compare the X-coordinate of the ball with the coordinate where the ball starts to erase the marker of player two from the right, **CP POINTS_X1_R**. If there is a carry, it erases the marker and jumps to reprint it, **JR C, reprintPoint_1_print**. If they are not the same coordinates, it passes to the right of player one's marker and jumps to check if it erases player two's marker, **JR NZ, reprintPoint_2**.

If it erases player one's marker, repaint it:

```
reprintPoint_1_print:
ld   a, (p1points)
call GetPointSprite
push hl
```

We load the points of player one into A, **LD A, (p1points)**, get the address of the sprite, **CALL GetPointSprite**, and keep the value, **PUSH HL**.

We start by painting the first digit, the tens:

```
ld    e, (hl)
inc   hl
ld    d, (hl)
ld    hl, POINTS_P1
call  PrintPoint
pop   hl
```

We load the low part of the address of the first digit sprite into E, **LD E, (HL)**, point HL to the high part of the address, **INC HL**, load it into D, **LD D, (HL)**, load the address where player one's marker will be painted into HL, **LD HL, POINTS_P1**, paint the first digit, **CALL PrintPoint**, and get the value of HL, **POP HL**.

Finally we paint the second digit:

```
inc   hl
inc   hl
ld    e, (hl)
inc   hl
ld    d, (hl)
ld    hl, POINTS_P1
inc   l
jr    PrintPoint
```

We point HL to the address of the second digit sprite, **INC HL, INC HL**, load the low part into E, **LD E, (HL)**, point HL to the high part, **INC HL**, load it into D, **LD D, (HL)**, load the address to paint player one's marker into HL, **LD HL, POINTS_P1**, point HL to the address where the second digit will be painted, **INC L**, and paint the digit and exit, **JR PrintPoint**.

You might ask, how do we get out? There is no RET!

You might think that instead of JR PrintPoint we should have written JR PrintPoint:

```
call PrintPoint
ret
```

And it does work, but it is not necessary. Besides, the way we have implemented it saves time and bytes.

PrintPoint's last instruction is a RET, and since this is the RET we want to leave, that's why we use JR instead of CALL and RET. That, and the fact that we don't have anything to retrieve from the stack. If we did, the results would be unpredictable.

Below we see the difference in time and bytes between one way and the other:

Instruction	Clock cycles	Bytes
CALL PrintPoint	17	3
RET	10	1

JR PrintPoint	12	2

We have saved fifteen clock cycles and two bytes.

We have also changed the way we repaint. We used to repaint the markers by doing OR with whatever we had painted in that area, and now we paint the marker directly. The result is that when we paint the marker, we erase the ball, which can cause some flickering. As this flickering is also present in the original arcade, we will leave it as it is, or you can change it.

Let's see how we repaint player 2's marker:

```
reprintPoint_2:
cp    POINTS_X2_L
ret   c
```

At this point we just need to check that the ball does not pass between the markers without clearing them. We compare with the left boundary of player two's marker, **CP POINTS_X2_L**, and if there is a carry, it goes out, it passes to the left, **RET C**.

If it doesn't, we have to repaint player two's marker, which is almost identical to what we do with player one's marker, so we'll mark the differences without going into detail:

```
reprintPoint_2_print:
ld    a, (p2points)
call GetPointSprite
push hl
; 1st digit
ld    e, (hl)
inc   hl
ld    d, (hl)
ld    hl, POINTS_P2
callPrintPoint
pop   hl
; 2nd digit
inc   hl
inc   hl
ld    e, (hl)
inc   hl
ld    d, (hl)
ld    hl, POINTS_P2
inc   l
jr    PrintPoint
```

The final aspect of the routine is as follows:

```
; ------------------------------------------------------------------
; Repaint the scoreboard.
; Each number is 1 byte wide by 16 bytes high.
; Alters the value of the AF, BC, DE and HL registers.
; ------------------------------------------------------------------
ReprintPoints:
ld    hl, (ballPos)         ; HL = ball position
call GetPtrY                ; Third, line and scanline
cp    POINTS_Y_B            ; Compare with position Y where starts
                            ; deleting marker
ret   nc                    ; No carry? Passes underneath
```

```
; If the ball arrives here it could erase marker,
; depending on Y position.
ld   a, l                 ; A = line and ball column
and  $1f                  ; A = column
cp   POINTS_X1_L          ; Compare with the position where deletes
                          ; marker player 1 from the left
ret  c                    ; Carry? pass left
jr   z, reprintPoint_1_print ; Same? Delete, repaint
; Continue with the checks
cp   POINTS_X2_R          ; Compare X ball coordinate with position
                          ; where the marker is deleted 2 on the right
jr   z, reprintPoint_2_print ; Equal? Repaint marker
ret  nc                   ; No carry? pass right
; Remaining checks to find out if it clears marker 1
reprintPoint_1:
cp   POINTS_X1_R          ; Compare X ball coordinate with position
                          ; where the marker is deleted 1 on the right
jr   c, reprintPoint_1_print ; Carry? Delete, repaint
jr   nz, reprintPoint_2   ; != 0? passes through right
; Repaint player 1's marker
reprintPoint_1_print:
ld   a, (p1points)        ; A = score player 1
call GetPointSprite       ; Address of sprite to paint
push hl                   ; Preserves HL
ld   e, (hl)              ; E = lower part of direction
inc  hl                   ; HL = upper part
ld   d, (hl)              ; D = upper part
ld   hl, POINTS_P1        ; HL = address where to paint
call PrintPoint           ; Paint first digit
pop  hl                   ; Retrieve HL
inc  hl
inc  hl                   ; HL = sprite second digit
ld   e, (hl)              ; E = lower part direction
inc  hl                   ; HL = upper part
ld   d, (hl)              ; D = upper part
ld   hl, POINTS_P1        ; HL = address where to paint marker 1
inc  l                    ; HL = direction where to paint second digit
jr   PrintPoint           ; Paint digit and it comes out
; Other checks to find out if it deletes the marker 2
reprintPoint_2:
cp   POINTS_X2_L          ; Compare X ball coordinate with position
                          ; where the marker is deleted 2 on the left
ret  c                    ; Carry? Pass left
; Repaint player 2's marker
reprintPoint_2_print:
ld   a, (p2points)        ; A = player score 2
call GetPointSprite       ; Address of the sprite to be painted
push hl                   ; Preserves HL
ld   e, (hl)              ; E = lower part direction
inc  hl                   ; HL = upper part
ld   d, (hl)              ; D = upper part
ld   hl, POINTS_P2        ; HL = address where to paint marker 2
call PrintPoint           ; Paints first digit
pop  hl                   ; Retrieve HL
inc  hl
inc  hl                   ; HL = sprite second digit
ld   e, (hl)              ; E = lower part direction
inc  hl                   ; HL = upper part
ld   d, (hl)              ; D = upper part
```

```
ld    hl, POINTS_P2    ; HL = address where to paint marker 2
inc   l                ; HL = direction where to paint second digit
jr    PrintPoint       ; Paints digit, it comes out over there
```

We compile, load the emulator and see the result.

We can see that the ball is now moving faster, even when it should be moving slower. If you look closely, when player two scores and the ball has to go out to the right, you can see part of the ball on the left of the screen for a moment.

If we remember, when we score a point, the ball leaves the court of the player who scored the point. This leads us to the conclusion that the problem lies in the SetBallRight routine, and more specifically in the first line:

```
ld    hl, $4d7f
```

According to this line, we position the ball at third 1, scanline 5, line 3, column 31.

In addition, two lines below, we change the rotation of the ball, setting it to minus one:

```
ld    a, $ff
ld    (ballRotation), a
```

If we look for the sprite that corresponds to this rotation, we see that it is the following:

```
db $00, $78    ; +7/$07 00000000 01111000 -1/$ff
```

So we paint column 31 empty, and in column 32 we paint $78. But column 32 does not exist: there are 32 columns in total, but they go from 0 to 31. If we paint there, we paint in column 0 of the next row.

Having seen this, the solution is simple. We change the first line of the SetBallRight routine to position the ball in column 30:

```
ld    hl, $4d7e
```

We compile it, load it into the emulator and see how it solves the problem.

And now we're going to change the speed of the ball so that it doesn't run so fast.

The ball configuration is stored in ballSetting, in the sprite.asm file:

```
; Ball speed and direction.
; bits 0 to 3:  movements of the ball to change the Y position.
;               Values f = half-diagonal, 2 = half-diagonal,
;                      1 = diagonal
; bits 4 and 5: ball speed:  1 very fast, 2 fast, 3 slow
; bit 6:        X direction: 0 right / 1 left
; bit 7:        Y direction: 0 up / 1 down
ballSetting:    db $31       ; 0011 0001
```

As we can see in the comments, the speed of the ball is configured in bits 4 and 5. It would be as simple as speed 2 being very fast, 3 being fast, and so on. In two bits we can only specify values from 0 to 3, the rest of the bits are occupied.

We will borrow a bit for the pitch of the ball. This will allow us to reduce the speed of the ball. In return, when the ball goes flat, it will go a little steeper:

```
; Ball speed and direction.
; bits 0 to 2:  Ball movements to change the Y position.
;               Values 7 = half-plane, 2 = half-diagonal, 1 = diagonal
; bits 3 to 5:  ball speed: 2 very fast, 3 fast, 4 slow
; bit 6:        X direction: 0 right / 1 left
; bit 7:        Y direction: 0 up / 1 down
ballSetting:    db $21       ; 0010 0001
```

And now there are five routines we need to change:

- **CheckCrossY in game.asm**: here we assign the inclination and speed of the ball depending on which part of the paddle it hits.
- **MoveBallY in game.asm**: here we check if the accumulated ball movements are the ones we need to change the Y-coordinate.
- **SetBallLeft and SetBallRight in game.asm**: here we reset the ball configuration.
- **Loop in main.asm**: at the start of this routine we check if we have reached the number of loop iterations we need to move the ball.

We start with CheckCrossY found in game.asm. We locate the checkCrossY_1_5 tag and then the OR $31 line:

```
or    $31                   ; Up, speed 3, diagonal
```

According to the new definition, we set speed 4 and diagonal tilt:

00 100 001

Bits three to five specify the speed, bits zero to two specify the pitch. The OR $31 line should look like this:

```
or    $21
```

Locate the checkCrossY_2_5 tag and set speed 3, semi-diagonal tilt:

00 011 010

We modify the line:

```
or    $22                   ; Top, speed 2, half-diagonal
```

And we leave it as:

```
or    $1a
```

Locate tag checkCrossY_3_5 and set speed 2, semi-flat tilt:

00 010 111

We modify the line:

```
or    $1f                   ; Up/Down, speed 1, half-flat
```

And we keep it that way:

```
or    $17
```

Locate the checkCrossY_4_5 tag and set speed 3, semi-diagonal tilt:

10 011 010

We modify the line:

```
or    $a2                    ; Down, speed 2, semi diagonal
```

And we keep it that way:

```
or    $9a
```

Find the checkCrossY_5_5 tag and set speed 4, diagonal tilt:

10 100 001

We modify the line:

```
or    $b1                    ; Down, speed 3, diagonal
```

And we keep it that way:

```
or    $a1
```

This brings us to the most tedious part of the modification.

From the MoveBallY routine, modify the second line:

```
and   $0f
```

And we keep it that way:

```
and   $07
```

With $0f we would get the tilt and the first bit of velocity. With $07 we only get the tilt.

We modify the reset of the ball configuration, which is in the SetBallLeft and SetBallRight routines.

In SetBallLeft we change the line:

```
or    $31                    ; Direction X right, speed 3, diagonal
```

And we keep it that way:

```
or    $21
```

In SetBallRight we change the line:

```
or    $71                    ; Direction X left, speed 3, diagonal
```

And we keep it that way:

```
or    $61
```

Finally, let's modify the code of the Loop tag of main.asm.

On the second line we find 4 RRCA instructions. We remove one, rotate it three times and leave the ball speed in bits 0 to 2.

```
rrca
rrca
```

```
rrca
rrca
```

As we now have three bits for the speed instead of the previous two, we modify the following line, which reads:

```
and   $03
```

And we keep it that way:

```
and   $07
```

We compile, load into the emulator and find that the ball speed is now more tolerable, at the expense of the slope.

Optimisation of ScanKeys

Now it is time to optimise the ScanKeys routine, as announced in step 2.

In ScanKeys we have several BIT instructions, two **BIT $00, A** and two **BIT $01, A**. With BIT instructions we evaluate the state of a particular BIT in a register without changing its value; the BIT instruction occupies 2 bytes and takes 8 clock cycles.

Let's replace the BIT instructions with AND instructions, saving one clock cycle each. We replace the instructions **BIT $00, A** with **AND $01** and the instructions **BIT $01, A** with **AND $02**. With this change we save four clock cycles, even though we are changing the value of register A, which is not important in this case.

Optimisation of Cls

In step 3 we commented that the Cls routine could be optimised by saving eight clock cycles and 4 bytes.

Let's remember what the routine currently looks like:

```
; ------------------------------------------------------------------
; Clean screen, ink 7, background 0.
; Alters the value of the AF, BC, DE and HL registers.
; ------------------------------------------------------------------
Cls:
; Clean the pixels on the screen
ld    hl, $4000          ; HL = start VideoRAM
ld    (hl), $00          ; Clear pixels from that address
ld    de, $4001          ; DE = next VideoRAM address
ld    bc, $17ff          ; 6143 repetitions
ldir                     ; Clears VideoRAM pixels

; Sets the ink to white and the background to black.
ld    hl, $5800          ; HL = start area attributes
ld    (hl), $07          ; White ink, black background
ld    de, $5801          ; DE = next address area attributes
ld    bc, $2ff           ; 767 repetitions
ldir                     ; Assigns value to attribute area

ret
```

The first part of the routine cleans the pixels, while the second part assigns the colours to the screen. It is in this second part that we do the optimisation.

Once the first LDIR has been executed, HL is worth $57FF, while DE is worth $5800. Loading a 16-bit value into a register takes ten clock cycles and 3 bytes, so with **LD HL, $5800** and **LD DE, $5801**, we consume twenty clock cycles and 6 bytes.

As we can see, HL and DE are worth one less than the value we need to assign the attributes to the screen, so all we need to do is increment their value by one, and that's where we get the optimisation; we replace **LD HL, $5800** and **LD DE, $5801** with **INC HL** and **INC DE**. Incrementing a 16-bit register takes six clock cycles and occupies one byte, so the total cost will be twelve clock cycles and 2 bytes, as opposed to the current twenty clock cycles and 6 bytes, saving eight clock cycles and 4 bytes.

The last aspect of the routine is:

```
; ------------------------------------------------------------------
; Clean screen, ink 7, background 0.
; Alters the value of the AF, BC, DE and HL registers.
; ------------------------------------------------------------------
Cls:
; Clean the pixels on the screen
ld   hl, $4000            ; HL = start VideoRAM
ld   (hl), $00            ; Clear pixels from that address
ld   de, $4001            ; DE = next VideoRAM address
ld   bc, $17ff            ; 6143 repetitions
ldir                      ; Clears VideoRAM pixels

; Sets the ink to white and the background to black
inc  hl                   ; HL = start attribute area
ld   (hl), $07            ; White ink, black background
inc  de                   ; DE = next address attribute area
ld   bc, $2ff             ; 767 repetitions
ldir                      ; Assigns value to attribute area

ret
```

Optimisation of MoveBall

In step 5 we said that we could save 5 bytes and two clock cycles, which we will do by modifying five lines of the MoveBall routine set found in game.asm. Let's replace the five **JR moveBall_end** lines with **RET**; JR takes 2 bytes and twelve clock cycles, while RET takes ten clock cycles and one byte.

As we can see, there is only one instruction in the MoveBall_end tag, RET, so we can replace the JR moveBall_end with RET.

We have said that we save two clock cycles, this is because each time MoveBall is called only one of the JR is executed, so we only save two cycles and not ten, although we do save 5 bytes.

The JR to be replaced are found as the last line of the labels:

- moveBall_right.
- moveBall_rightLast.
- moveBall_rightChg.
- moveBall_left.
- moveBall_leftLast.

The movelBall_end tag can be removed, but not the RET that follows it, even though the tag takes up nothing.

ReprintLine optimisation

In step 6 we said that we could save 5 bytes and twenty-two clock cycles, which we will achieve by modifying eight lines of the ReprintLine routine in the video.asm file.

Locate the **reprintLine_loopCont** tag and move it three lines down, just above the **CALL NextScan** line.

Locate the line **LD C, LINE** and delete the following three lines:

```
jr    ReprintLine_loopCont
ReprintLine_00:
ld    c, ZERO
```

Locate **JR C, reprintLine_00** and **JR Z, reprintLine_00** and replace **reprintLine_00** with **reprintLine_loopCont**.

Find the position of the **reprintLine_loopCont** tag and delete **LD C, LINE** four lines above it. Two lines below the deleted line we replace **OR C** with **OR LINE**.

What have we done?

The final objective of the routine is to repaint the deleted central line without deleting the area of the ball where it is to be repainted, for which we obtain the pixels on the screen and mix them with the part of the line to be painted, and that is the point; if the part of the line to be repainted is the part that goes to ZERO (white), it is not necessary to repaint it.

The final aspect of the routine is as follows:

```
; -----------------------------------------------------------------
; Repaint the centre line.
; Alters the value of the AF, B and HL registers.
; -----------------------------------------------------------------
ReprintLine:
ld    hl, (ballPos)        ; HL = ball position
ld    a, l                 ; A = row and column
and   $e0                  ; A = line
or    $10                  ; A = row and column 16 ($10)
ld    l, a                 ; L = A. HL = Initial position

ld    b, $06               ; Repaints 6 scanlines
reprintLine_loop:
ld    a, h                 ; A = third and scanline
and   $07                  ; A = scanline
; If it is on scanlines 0 or 7, it paints ZERO.
```

```
; If you are on scanlines 1, 2, 3, 4, 5 or 6, paint LINE.
cp    $01                    ; Scanline 1?
jr    c, reprintLine_loopCont ; Scanline < 1, skip
cp    $07                    ; Scanline 7?
jr    z, reprintLine_loopCont ; Scanline = 7, skip

ld    a, (hl)                ; A = pixels current position
or    LINE                   ; Add LINE
ld    (hl), a                ; Paints current position
reprintLine_loopCont:
call NextScan                ; Get next scanline
djnz reprintLine_loop        ; Until B = 0

ret
```

Optimisation of GetPointSprite

In step 8 we commented that we could save 2 bytes and a few clock cycles by implementing GetPointSprite in a different way; we will do this without using a loop.

Currently this routine takes longer the higher the score of the players. As long as the maximum score is fifteen, there is no problem, but if it is ninety-nine or two hundred and fifty-five, we have a problem; we saw this in the tests when the game did not stop at fifteen points.

As we can see in the definition of the sprites, each one is 4 bytes away from the other, so we make a loop starting from the address of Cero and adding 4 bytes for each point of the player we are going to paint the marker for. This is the same as multiplying the player's points by 4 and adding the result to the address of the Zero sprite. This way we would always take the same time whether the points were zero or ninety-nine; we save 2 bytes and a few clock cycles.

In GetPointSprite we get the score in A and return the address of the sprite to paint in HL.

How do we multiply by four, since the Z80 does not have a multiply instruction?

Multiplying is nothing more than adding a number as many times as the multiplier says, or in other words, multiplying a number by 4 would be equal to

$$2*4 = 2+2+2+2 = 8$$

We could do this with a loop, but we are going to make it even simpler, because to multiply a number by 4 we only need to do two additions:

$$3*4 = 3+3 = 6 \text{ y } 6+6 = 12$$

That is, we add the number to itself, do the same with the result, and we already have a multiplication by 4. If we added this result to itself, we would already have a multiplication by 8. We continue in this way to multiply by 16, 32, 64, etc., or in other words, $n*2n$.

There are two ways to implement GetPointSprite without further modification: with a scoreboard of up to sixty-one points or with a scoreboard of up to ninety-nine points.

Let's take the first one, with a scoreboard of up to sixty-one points (61 * 4 = 244 = 1 byte).

```
; --------------------------------------------------------------------
; Gets the corresponding sprite to paint on the marker.
; Input:  A  -> score.
; Output: HL -> address of the sprite to be painted.
; Alters the value of the AF, BC and HL registers.
; --------------------------------------------------------------------
GetPointSprite:
; UP TO 61 POINTS
ld   hl, Zero              ; HL = address sprite Zero
; Each sprite is 4 bytes from the previous one
add  a, a                 ; A = A * 2
add  a, a                 ; A = A * 2 ( A * 4)
ld   b, ZERO
ld   c, a                 ; BC = A
add  hl, bc               ; HL = HL + BC = sprite to be painted
ret
```

In this case, the maximum score would be sixty-one, which multiplied by 4 gives two hundred and forty-four, a result that occupies only one byte, so we can use register A to multiply by 4. This routine occupies 10 bytes and takes fifty clock cycles.

If a game of ZX-Pong is too short at sixty-one points, we can do it at ninety-nine. The routine would take the same time as the previous one, but it would take sixty-four clock cycles because we use a 16-bit register for the additions (99 * 4 = 396 = 2 bytes).

```
; --------------------------------------------------------------------
; Gets the corresponding sprite to paint on the marker.
; Input:  A  -> score.
; Output: HL -> Address of the sprite to be painted.
; Alters the value of the AF, BC and HL registers.
; --------------------------------------------------------------------
GetPointSprite:
; UP TO 99 WITHOUT CHANGING MARKER PRINT ROUTINE
ld   h, ZERO
ld   l, a                 ; HL = points
; Each sprite is 4 bytes from the previous one.
add  hl, hl               ; HL = HL * 2
add  hl, hl               ; HL = HL * 2 (HL * 4)
ld   bc, Zero             ; BC = sprite address Zero
add  hl, bc               ; HL = HL + BC (sprite to be painted)
ret
```

If we want a score higher than ninety-nine, we have to modify the marker printing routine, they only print two digits, and take into account that the GetPointSprite implementations would not be valid (we would have to rethink everything, even the way we declare the sprites).

Optimising PrintPoints and ReprintPoints

But hey, we just implemented ReprintPoints at the beginning of this chapter!

Well, we've actually added a part to repaint the marker only when necessary, but we've inherited some things from the original implementation.

In step 8 we said that we could save 2 bytes and twelve clock cycles by modifying the PrintPoints routine. Well, we are in luck, because we will actually save 33 bytes and one hundred and seventy-eight clock cycles; the changes to be made in PrintPoints are also made in ReprintPoints.

On the third line of PrintPoints we find **PUSH HL**, and this is the first line we are going to move, preserving the value of the HL register in advance. We cut this line and paste it three lines down, just before loading the memory address where player one's dots are painted in HL, **LD HL, POINTS_P1**; this is the instruction that motivates us to preserve HL.

After calling paint the dot, we retrieve the value of HL, POP HL, and increment HL twice to point to the lower part of the address where the second digit is. Since we have already preserved HL after positioning it on the high part of the address of the first digit, we remove one of these two **INC HL**, saving 1 byte and six clock cycles.

The same modification is made when we paint player two's marker and in the ReprintPoints routine. We save 4 bytes and twenty-four clock cycles.

Spirax told me about another optimisation we could do, where we could remove four **INC L** instructions, saving 4 bytes and sixteen clock cycles.

In both PrintPoints and ReprintPoints, when we draw the second digit of the markers, we do the following.

```
ld    hl, POINTS_P1
inc   l

ld    hl, POINTS_P2
inc   l
```

As we do in both PrintPoints and ReprintPoints, we actually do four INC L, and we can avoid it this way:

```
ld    hl, POINTS_P1 + 1

ld    hl, POINTS_P2 + 1
```

In this way we point HL directly to the position where the second digit is drawn and store **INC L**.

And now we are going to save 25 bytes and one hundred and thirty-eight more clock cycles, thanks again to Spirax.

At the end of ReprintPoints is the **reprintPoint2_print tag**, and just above it is the **RET C** instruction. Well, let's delete the **reprintPoint2_print** tag and everything below it until the end of the routine. After **RET C** we'll insert **JR printPoint2_print**.

In the previous implementation, **PrintPoints** and **ReprintPoints** painted differently, **ReprintPoints** did an **OR** with the pixels on the screen, but this is no longer the case, we are going to use the code that paints the marker for player two to repaint it, and we are going to save 25 bytes and one hundred and thirty-eight clock cycles.

The **printPoint2_print** tag does not exist, so we include it. We look for the **PrintPoints** tag and see how it first paints the marker for player one, and when it is finished it paints the marker for player two, which starts just below the second **CALL PrintPoint**. So it is there, just below the second **CALL PrintPoint**, that we will add the **printPoint_2_print** tag.

Locate **reprintPoint_1**, two lines above it is the **JR Z line, reprintPoint_2_print**. We replace it with:

```
jr   z, printPoint_2_print
```

Thank you very much Spirax!

The final look and feel of the routines is as follows:

```
; --------------------------------------------------------------------
; Paint the scoreboard.
; Each number is 1 byte wide by 16 bytes high.
; Alters the value of the AF, BC, DE and HL registers.
; --------------------------------------------------------------------
PrintPoints:
ld   a, (p1points)        ; A = points player 1
call GetPointSprite       ; Sprite to be painted on marker
; 1st digit of player 1
ld   e, (hl)              ; E = low part 1st digit address
inc  hl                   ; HL = top management
ld   d, (hl)              ; D = top management
push hl                   ; Preserves HL
ld   hl, POINTS_P1        ; HL = address where to paint points player 1

call PrintPoint           ; Paint 1st digit marker player 1
pop  hl                   ; Retrieves HL
; 2nd digit of player 1
inc  hl                   ; HL = low part 2nd digit address
ld   e, (hl)              ; E = lower part 2nd digit address
inc  hl                   ; HL = top management
ld   d, (hl)              ; D = top management

; Spirax
ld   hl, POINTS_P1 + 1    ; HL = address where to paint
; 2nd digit points player 1
call PrintPoint           ; Paint 2nd digit marker player 1

printPoint_2_print:
; 1st digit of player 2
ld   a, (p2points)        ; A = points player 2
```

```
call GetPointSprite      ; Sprite to be painted on marker
ld   e, (hl)             ; E = low part 1st digit address
inc  hl                  ; HL = high side
ld   d, (hl)             ; D = upper part
push hl                  ; Preserves HL
ld   hl, POINTS_P2       ; HL = address where to paint points player 2
call PrintPoint          ; 1st digit of marker player 2
pop  hl                  ; Retrieves HL
; 2nd digit of player 2
inc  hl                  ; HL = low part 2nd digit address
ld   e, (hl)             ; E = lower part
inc  hl                  ; HL = high part
ld   d, (hl)             ; D = upper part
; Spirax
ld   hl, POINTS_P2 + 1   ; HL = address where to paint 2nd digit
; Paint the second digit of player 2's marker.

PrintPoint:
ld   b, $10              ; Each digit 1 byte by 16 (scanlines)
printPoint_printLoop:
ld   a, (de)             ; A = byte to be painted
ld   (hl), a             ; Paints the byte
inc  de                  ; DE = next byte
call NextScan            ; HL = next scanline
djnz printPoint_printLoop ; Until B = 0

ret

; ------------------------------------------------------------------
; Repaint the scoreboard.
; Each number is 1 byte wide by 16 bytes high.
; Alters the value of the AF, BC, DE and HL registers.
; ------------------------------------------------------------------
ReprintPoints:
ld   hl, (ballPos)       ; HL = ball position
call GetPtrY             ; Third, line and scanline of ball position
cp   POINTS_Y_B          ; Compare lower limit marker
ret  nc                  ; No carry? Pass underneath
ld   a, l                ; A = line and column ball position
and  $1f                 ; A = column
cp   POINTS_X1_L         ; Compare left boundary marker 1
ret  c                   ; Carry? Pass on the left
jr   z, reprintPoint_1_print ; 0?, Is in left margin jumps to paint

cp   POINTS_X2_R         ; Compare right boundary marker 2
jr   z, printPoint_2_print ; 0? It's in the right margin jumps to paint
ret  nc                  ; No carry? Pass right

reprintPoint_1:
cp   POINTS_X1_R         ; Compare limit marker 1
jr   c, reprintPoint_1_print ; Carry? passes through marker 1
                         ; jumps to paint
jr   nz, reprintPoint_2  ; !=0? Passes right,jumps check step marker 2
reprintPoint_1_print:
ld   a, (p1points)       ; A = points player 1
call GetPointSprite      ; Sprite to be painted on marker
; 1st digit
ld   e, (hl)             ; E = lower part 1st digit address
inc  hl                  ; HL = high side
```

```
ld    d, (hl)              ; D = upper part
push  hl                   ; Preserves HL
ld    hl, POINTS_P1        ; HL = address where to paint points player 1
call  PrintPoint           ; Paint 1st digit marker player 1
pop   hl                   ; Retrieves HL
; 2nd digit
inc   hl                   ; HL = low part 2nd digit address
ld    e, (hl)              ; E = lower part
inc   hl                   ; HL = high part
ld    d, (hl)              ; D = upper part
ld    hl, POINTS_P1 + 1    ; HL = address where to paint 2nd digit
                           ; points player 1
jr    PrintPoint           ; Paint 2nd digit marker player 1

reprintPoint_2:
cp    POINTS_X2_L          ; Compare right boundary marker 2
ret   c                    ; Carry? Pass on the left
; Spirax
jr    printPoint_2_print   ; Paint marker player 2
```

We compile, load the emulator and check that everything still works.

Thanks a lot Spirax.

Ball strike bug at the bottom of the paddle

It's time to fix a bug we've had since we introduced the ability to change the speed and angle of the ball depending on the part of the paddle it hits. When the ball hits the last scanline of the paddle, it doesn't change its inclination, speed or vertical direction. Why is this?

The reason is the way we have implemented collision detection. Before evaluating in which part of the paddle it hits, we evaluate if it hits the paddle, and here is the error; when it hits the last scanline of the paddle, it exits the routine, indicating with the active Z flag that there is a collision, but without evaluating in which part of the paddle it hits.

We locate the CheckCrossY tag in the game.asm file, sixteen lines down we find this.

```
ret   nc                   ; Carry? No, ball passes underneath
                           ; or collide in the last scanline.
                           ; The latter case activates flag Z
```

If we read the comments, we get out of the routine if there is no carry. If there is no carry, the result is greater than or equal to zero. If the result is zero, we leave the routine with the Z flag activated (there is a collision) and without evaluating where the ball hit the paddle. If the result is greater than zero, we leave the routine with the Z flag deactivated (no collision).

To solve this, we will double check and add a new label to jump to.

The actual code for the part we want to touch is as follows.

```
ret   nc                   ; Carry? No, ball passes underneath
                           ; or collide in the last scanline.
```

```
                            ; The latter case activates flag Z

; Depending on collision location, inclination and speed
ld   a, c                   ; A = penultimate paddle scanline
```

Let's add a line before **RET NC** and a tag before **LD A, C**, so that the code looks like this:

```
jr   z, checkCrossY_eval  ; 0?, crash in last scanline
ret  nc                   ; No carry? Pass underneath

; Depending on collision location, inclination and speed
checkCrossY_eval:
ld   a, c                 ; A = penultimate paddle scanline
```

Even this **JR Z, checkCrossY_eval** could be changed to **JR Z, checkCrossY_5_5** as we know that the ball has hit the bottom of the paddle (try both ways).

We compile, load the emulator and see that we have fixed the bug.

Download the source code from here

https://tinyurl.com/22pxlpe3

Step 11: Sound and 16K

We have implemented sound effects when the ball hits the borders, the paddles and when a point is scored.

We create the folder Step11 and copy from the folder Step10: controls.asm, game.asm, main.asm, sprite.asm and video.asm. We create sound.asm to add the necessary counters and routines for our sound effects.

We will define three different sounds:

- When a point is marked.
- When the ball hits a paddle.
- When the ball hits the border.

For each sound, we need to define the note and the frequency. The frequency defines how long the note lasts; we identify it with the suffix FQ.

```
; Point
C_3:     EQU $0D07
C_3_FQ:  EQU $0082 / $10

; Paddle
C_4:     EQU $066E
C_4_FQ:  EQU $0105 / $10

; Border
C_5:     EQU $0326
C_5_FQ:  EQU $020B / $10
```

All the sounds we are going to use are C, but in different scales; the larger the scale, the higher the pitch.

The frequencies given are those that make the note last one second, so we'll divide them by 16. If we multiply them by 2, the note would last 2 seconds.

Each note in each scale has its own frequency. Appendix one contains tables of frequencies and notes, in decimal and hexadecimal.

The next constant is the memory address where the ROM BEEPER routine is located:

```
BEEPER: EQU $03B5
```

This routine receives the note in HL and the duration in DE, and changes the value of registers AF, BC, DE, HL and IX, as well as another aspect that we will see later.

Because the ROM BEEPER routine modifies so many registers, it is advisable not to call it directly; we implement a routine that does this.

This routine receives in A the type of sound to be emitted and does not change the value of any register:

- 1 = point
- 2 = paddle

- 3 = border

```
PlaySound:
push de
push hl
```

We preserve the value of the DE, **PUSH DE**, and HL, **PUSH HL**, registers.

```
cp    $01
jr    z, playSound_point
```

We check if the sound to be played is of type 1 (point), **CP $01**, and if so we skip, **JR Z, playSound_point**.

```
cp    $02
jr    z, playSound_paddle
```

If the sound is not type 1, we check if it is type 2 (paddle), **CP $02**, and if so we jump, JR Z, **playSound_paddle**.

If the sound is neither type 1 nor type 2, it is type 3 (border):

```
ld    hl, C_5
ld    de, C_5_FQ
jr    beep
```

We load the note in HL, **LD HL, C_5**, the duration in DE, **LD DE, C_5_FQ**, and play the sound, **JR beep**.

If the sound is of type 1 or 2, we do the same, with the values of each sound:

```
playSound_point:
ld    hl, C_3
ld    de, C_3_FQ
jr    beep

playSound_paddle:
ld    hl, C_4
ld    de, C_4_FQ
```

We are spared the last JR, as it is immediately followed by the routine that plays the sound:

```
beep:
push af
push bc
push ix
call BEEPER
pop  ix
pop  bc
pop  af

pop  hl
pop  de

ret
```

We keep AF, **PUSH AF**, BC, **PUSH BC**, and IX, **PUSH IX**. We then call the ROM routine, **CALL BEEPER**, and retrieve IX, **POP IX**, BC, **POP**

BC, AF, **POP AF**, HL, **POP HL**, and DE, **POP DE**. HL and DE are retained at the beginning of the PlaySound routine. We exit with, **RET**.

The final appearance of the sound.asm file is as follows:

```
; ------------------------------------------------------------------
; Sound.asm
; File with the sounds
; ------------------------------------------------------------------
; Point
C_3:    EQU $0D07
C_3_FQ: EQU $0082 / $10

; Paddle
C_4:    EQU $066E
C_4_FQ: EQU $0105 / $10

; Rebound
C_5:    EQU $0326
C_5_FQ: EQU $020B / $10

; ------------------------------------------------------------------
; ROM beeper routine.
;
; Input: HL -> Note.
;        DE -> Duration.
;
; Alters the value of the AF, BC, DE, HL and IX registers.
; ------------------------------------------------------------------
BEEPER: EQU $03B5

; ------------------------------------------------------------------
; Reproduces the sound of bouncing.
; Input: A -> Sound type: 1. Point
;                         2. Paddle
;                         3. Border
; ------------------------------------------------------------------
PlaySound:
; Preserves the value of records
push de
push hl

cp    $01                 ; Evaluates sound point
jr    z, playSound_point  ; Sound point? Jump

cp    $02                 ; Evaluates sound paddle
jr    z, playSound_paddle ; Sound paddle? Jump

; The border sound is emitted
ld    hl, C_5             ; HL = note
ld    de, C_5_FQ          ; DE = duration (frequency)
jr    beep                ; Jumps to beep

; The sound of point is emitted
playSound_point:
ld    hl, C_3             ; HL = note
ld    de, C_3_FQ          ; DE = duration (frequency)
jr    beep                ; Jumps to beep
```

```
; The paddle sound is emitted
playSound_paddle:
ld    hl, C_4              ; HL = note
ld    de, C_4_FQ           ; DE = duration (frequency)

; Sounds the note
beep:
; Preserves registers; ROM BEEPER routine alters them.
push af
push bc
push ix

call BEEPER               ; Call BEEPER from ROM

; Retrieves the value of the registers
pop   ix
pop   bc
pop   af

pop   hl
pop   de

ret
```

Now we need to call our new routine to play the sounds of the ball bouncing.

Open game.asm and locate checkBallCross_right. We will add two lines between **RET NZ** and **LD A, (ballSetting)**:

```
ld    a, $02
call PlaySound
```

We load the sound type in A, **LD A, $02**; we play it, **CALL PlaySound**.

We find the tag checkBallCross_left. Let's add the same two lines between **RET NZ** and **LD A, (ballSetting)**:

```
ld    a, $02
call PlaySound
```

We locate the moveBall_upChg tag. Below it, we add two lines, almost the same as above:

```
ld    a, $03
call PlaySound
```

Locate the moveBall_downChg tag and add the above two lines just below it:

```
ld    a, $03
call PlaySound
```

Locate the moveBall_rightChg tag below add:

```
ld    a, $01
call PlaySound
```

Five lines below that is CALL SetBallLeft; below that we add:

```
ld    a, $03
call PlaySound
```

Locate the moveBall_leftChg tag; below add:

```
ld    a, $01
call PlaySound
```

Five lines down is CALL SetBallRight, which we add just below:

```
ld    a, $03
call PlaySound
```

Finally, open main.asm, locate the Loop routine and add the following lines just above it:

```
ld    a, $03
call PlaySound
```

We go to the end of the file, in the "includes" part, we include the file sound.asm:

```
include "sound.asm"
```

If all goes well, we have reached the end. We compile, load into the emulator and...

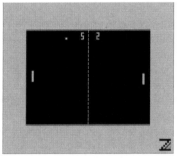

What about the border, why is it white? We have already seen that the ROM's BEEPER routine changes a lot of things, and one of them is the colour of the border, although it has a simple solution.

Fortunately, we have a system variable where we can store the border colour. The attributes of the bottom screen are also stored in this variable. The background of the bottom screen is the border colour.

We open video.asm and declare a constant at the top with the memory address of this system variable:

```
BORDCR: EQU $5c48
```

Locate the Cls routine, and add it just before the **INC HL** line:

```
ld    a, $07              ; Black background, white ink
```

We modify the line **LD (HL), $07** and leave it as follows:

```
ld    (hl), a
```

Finally, before RET, we add:

161

```
ld    (BORDCR), a
```

Compile, load into the emulator, and you're done - have we finished our ZX-Pong?

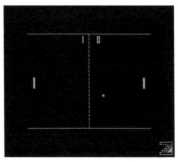

Is our programme compatible with the 16K model? Not yet, but since we're not using interrupts, it's very easy to make it compatible.

We open main.asm, find the two directives ORG and END, and replace $8000 with $5dad in ORG. In END, we replace the $8000 address with Main, the program entry label.

If we compile and load in the 16K model, our programme is compatible.

If we look closely, we can see that we have lost some speed. This loss is due to the fact that the second 16K of the ZX Spectrum, where we are now loading the program, is the so-called contained memory, which is shared with the ULA. When the ULA is working, everything stops.

We are going to change the speed at which the ball moves again.

Open sprite.asm, find ballSetting, comment out the line or $21 and write just below it:

```
; or    $21
or    $19
```

Now the ball starts at speed 3, which is the slowest speed.

Open game.asm, find SetBallLeft, go to line 7, comment it out and write just below it:

```
; or    $21
or    $19
```

If we now set the ball to come out of the left side of the screen, it will start at speed 3.

Find SetBallRight, comment out line 7 and type just below it:

```
; db    $61
db    $59
```

If we now set the ball to come out of the right side of the screen, it will start at speed 3.

Find the tag checkCrossY_1_5, comment out line 7 and write just below it:

```
; or   $21
or    $19
```

Now the ball speed is 3 instead of 4.

Find the tag checkCrossY_2_5, comment out line 7 and write just below it:

```
; or   $1a
or    $12
```

Now the ball speed is 2 instead of 3.

Find the tag checkCrossY_3_5, comment out line 7 and write just below it:

```
; or   $17
or    $0f
```

Now the ball speed is 1 instead of 2.

Find the tag checkCrossY_4_5, comment out line 7 and write just below it:

```
; or   $9a
or    $92
```

Now the ball speed is 2 instead of 3.

Find the tag checkCrossY_5_5, comment out line 3 and write just below it:

```
; or   $a1
or    $99
```

Now the ball speed is 3 instead of 4.

We compiled it, tested it in the emulator and we're almost done.

Download the source code from here

https://tinyurl.com/23hhmkzp

Step 12: Optimisation part 2

We have already mentioned that Spirax pointed out several optimisations. We have left for the end one that he showed for the sound routine and another that was implemented after the one he showed for the ReprintPoints routine.

Create a folder called Step12 and copy all the .asm files from the Step11 folder into it.

Optimising PlaySound

The first optimisation is in the sound routine, specifically in the way we evaluate the sound to be emitted.

Open sound.asm and locate the PlaySound tag, the first lines of which are:

```
PlaySound:
; Preserves the value of records
push de
push hl

cp    $01                  ; Sound of a point?
jr    z, playSound_point   ; Point sound, emits it

cp    $02                  ; Paddle sound?
jr    z, playSound_paddle  ; Paddle sound, emits it
```

In this routine we use **CP $01** and **CP $02** to check which sound should be output. Each CP instruction occupies 2 bytes and takes seven clock cycles. We replace these instructions with **DEC A**, which occupies 1 byte and takes 4 clock cycles, so we save 2 bytes and 6 clock cycles. DEC does change the value of the A register, but since we are concerned with the type of sound to be emitted, it does not affect us.

Let's see how the routine starts.

```
PlaySound:
; Preserves the value of records
push de
push hl

; Spirax
dec  a                     ; Decreasing A
jr   z, playSound_point    ; If 0, point sound
; Spirax
dec  a                     ; Decreasing A
jr   z, playSound_paddle   ; If 0, paddle sound
```

We preserve DE, **PUSH DE**, HL, **PUSH HL**, and decrement A, **DEC A**. If A was one, the result of the operation is zero and jumps to play the sound, **JR Z, playSound_point**.

If A was not one, the checks continue. We decrement A, **DEC A**, and if the result of the operation is zero, it jumps to play the sound, **JR Z,**

playSound_paddle. If it jumps, A was initially worth two, one with the first decrement and zero with this second.

If it does not jump, it remains as it was and emits the rim sound.

Compile, load into the emulator and check that it still works.

Optimisation of ReprintPoints

With this optimisation we save 20 bytes and one hundred and seven clock cycles. To achieve this, we are going to use the same method we used in step 10, following Spirax's comments; the way he pointed out.

As you may recall from step 10, we added a label so that the painting of player two's marker could be called independently; we will do the same for player one's marker. With this modification, the markers will take a little longer to paint (they are only painted at the start of the game and when marking a point), but we will simplify the ReprintPoints routine, saving bytes and clock cycles by eliminating redundant code.

Let's start by modifying the PrintPoints routine so that it can be called to print both players' markers independently.

Open video.asm and locate the PrintPoints tag. Underneath it we add another tag, the one we will call to paint the marker for player two:

```
printPoint_1_print:
```

Between the PrintPoints and printPoint_1_print tags we add the calls to paint the marker for each player:

```
call printPoint_1_print    ; Paints the marker of player 1
jr   printPoint_2_print    ; Paints the marker of player 2
```

We call to print player one's marker, **CALL printPoint_1_print**, and then jump to print player two's marker, **JR printPoint_1_print**.

There is only one more change we need to make in PrintPoints. We add **RET** just before the printPoint_2_print tag so that **CALL printPoint_1_print** is output correctly; remember that the rest of the jumps are output by the PrintPoint **RET**.

We add **RET** before printPoint_2_print:

```
ret
printPoint_2_print:
```

We have finished the necessary modifications to PrintPoints, but we have not saved anything, we have added code by adding bytes and clock cycles.

Let's start saving. We delete reprintPoint_1_print and the following lines until we reach the reprintPoint_2 tag; we do not delete it.

We locate the ReprintPoints tag and nine lines down we find the **JR Z, reprintPoint_1_print** statement. This tag no longer exists, so we need to change this line and leave it as follows:

```
jr   z, printPoint_1_print
```

We locate the reprintPoint_1 tag and make the final changes.

The code for this tag, after deleting the entire reprintPoint_1_print part, is as follows:

```
reprintPoint_1:
cp    POINTS_X1_R           ; Compare right boundary of marker 1
jr    c, reprintPoint_1_print ; Carry? Pass through marker 1, paint
jr    nz, reprintPoint_2     ; !=0? Passes right, jumps
```

We need to change the double check. As the reprintPoint_2 tag is now below the **JR NZ, reprintPoint_2** line, this jump is no longer necessary, but we do need to check if it is zero, in which case we need to paint the player a marker, **JR Z, printPoint_1_print**, and change the jump from **JR C, reprintPoint_1_print** to **JR C, printPoint_1_print**, so the code would look like this:

```
reprintPoint_1:
cp    POINTS_X1_R           ; Compare with right boundary marker 1
jr    z, printPoint_1_print
jr    c, printPoint_1_print ; 0 or carry? Pass marker 1, paint
```

The final appearance of PrintPoints and ReprintPoints is as follows:

```
; ------------------------------------------------------------------
; Paint the scoreboard.
; Each number is 1 byte wide by 16 bytes high.
; Alters the value of the AF, BC, DE and HL registers.
; ------------------------------------------------------------------
PrintPoints:
call printPoint_1_print    ; Paints marker player 1
jr   printPoint_2_print    ; Paints marker player 2

printPoint_1_print:
ld    a, (p1points)         ; A = points player 1
call GetPointSprite        ; Sprite to be painted on marker
; 1st digit of player 1
ld    e, (hl)              ; E = lower part 1st digit address
inc   hl                   ; HL = high side
ld    d, (hl)              ; D = upper part
push hl                    ; Preserves HL
ld    hl, POINTS_P1        ; HL = address where to paint digit
call PrintPoint            ; Paints 1st digit
pop  hl                    ; Retrieves HL

; 2nd digit of player 1
inc   hl                   ; HL = low part 2nd digit address
ld    e, (hl)              ; E = lower part
inc   hl                   ; HL = high part
ld    d, (hl)              ; D = upper part
; Spirax
ld    hl, POINTS_P1 + 1    ; HL = address where to paint digit
call PrintPoint            ; Paint2 2nd digit

ret

printPoint_2_print:
; 1st digit of player 2
ld    a, (p2points)        ; A = points player 2
```

```
call GetPointSprite      ; Sprite to be painted on marker
ld   e, (hl)             ; E = low part 1st digit address
inc  hl                  ; HL = high part
ld   d, (hl)             ; D = upper part
push hl                  ; Preserves HL
ld   hl, POINTS_P2       ; HL = address where digit
call PrintPoint          ; Paints 1st digit
pop  hl                  ; Retrieves HL

; 2nd digit of player 2
inc  hl                  ; HL = low part 2nd digit address
ld   e, (hl)             ; E = lower part
inc  hl                  ; HL = high part
ld   d, (hl)             ; D = upper part
; Spirax
ld   hl, POINTS_P2 + 1   ; HL address where to paint 2nd digit
; Paints the second digit of player 2's marker.

PrintPoint:
ld   b, $10              ; Each digit 1 byte by 16 (scanlines)

printPoint_printLoop:
ld   a, (de)             ; A = byte to be painted
ld   (hl), a             ; Paints the byte
inc  de                  ; DE = next byte
call NextScan            ; HL = next scanline
djnz printPoint_printLoop ; Until B = 0

ret

; ----------------------------------------------------------------
; Repaint the scoreboard.
; Each number is 1 byte wide by 16 bytes high.
; Alters the value of the AF, BC, DE and HL registers.
; ----------------------------------------------------------------
ReprintPoints:
ld   hl, (ballPos)       ; HL = ball position
call GetPtrY             ; Third, line and scanline ball position
cp   POINTS_Y_B          ; Compare lower limit marker
ret  nc                  ; No Carry? Pass underneath
ld   a, l                ; A = line and column ball position
and  $1f                 ; A = column
cp   POINTS_X1_L         ; Compare left boundary marker 1
ret  c                   ; Carry? Pass left
jr   z, printPoint_1_print ; 0? It's in left margin, paint

cp   POINTS_X2_R         ; Compare right boundary marker 2
jr   z, printPoint_2_print ; 0? It's in the right margin, paint
ret  nc                  ; No Carry? Pass on the right

reprintPoint_1:
cp   POINTS_X1_R         ; Compare right boundary marker 1
jr   z, printPoint_1_print
jr   c, printPoint_1_print ; Z or Carry? Pass marker 1, paint

reprintPoint_2:
cp   POINTS_X2_L         ; Compare right boundary marker 2
ret  c                   ; Carry? Pass on the left
; Spirax
```

```
jr    printPoint_2_print    ; Paint marker player 2
```

   If we compare the implementation of ReprintPoints with the one we did in step 10, we can see that the routine is much simpler, being practically reduced to the built-in checks, so that the marker is repainted only when necessary.

   All that's left is to compile, load in the emulator and check that everything still works.

   Or do you want to add a loading screen?

Download the source code from here

https://tinyurl.com/287qborj

Step 13: Loading screen

We left adding a loading screen for ZX-Pong until the end.

Create the folder Step13 and copy all .asm files from the folder Step12.

First download the loading screen I prepared or make your own. I'm not a graphic designer, so don't expect much, but it serves the purpose of this chapter.

https://tinyurl.com/26dfekly

We implement the loader

To create the loader we will not start from scratch, we will copy the loader that PASMO creates with the --tapbas option.

```
10 CLEAR 23981
20 POKE 23610,255
30 LOAD ""CODE
40 RANDOMIZE USR 23981
```

We are going to edit the first line, for which we will move the cursor up and once selected, press Shift + 1 to edit.

We are going to change the address where the program starts, because as we put more BASIC in, it is necessary to load the program in a higher memory location. We are going to change the **CLEAR 23980** to **CLEAR 24200**. Next we are going to change line 40 to put the memory address where the program is loaded, so that **RANDOMIZE USR 23981** we leave it as **RANDOMIZE USR 24200**.

Now we are going to extend line 20. We will edit it, go to the end and add a colon by pressing Ctrl + Z. After the colon we will add **POKE 23624, 0**, which we get with the O key. With this POKE we set the ink and black background in the ZX Spectrum command line part, we also set the border in black; address 23624 is where the system variable BORDCR is located.

We continue on line 20 and we put another **POKE** (don't forget the colon) to put a value in the system variable where the permanent attributes of the screen are set, **POKE 23693, 0**, to set the ink to black and the background to black on the whole screen.

Finally, we add another colon and **CLS**, pressing V.

```
10 CLEAR 24200
20 POKE 23610,255: POKE 23624,0: POKE 23693,0: CLS
30 LOAD ""CODE
40 RANDOMIZE USR 24200
```

Let's modify line 30, just before **LOAD ""CODE**, add **LOAD ""SCREEN$**: (LOAD by pressing J and SCREEN$ Control + K in extended mode).

After **SCREEN$**, we will add another **POKE** so that the rest of the blocks to be loaded are not displayed on the screen, and so that they do not erase part of the loading screen. I borrowed this **POKE** from one of AsteroideZX's videos, **POKE 23739, 111**.

It's time to record the changes to a tape, in this particular case we'll call it PongCargador.tap, as we'll be creating two other tapes: one for the loading screen and one for the programme.

To record we set **SAVE "Loader" LINE 10**. **SAVE** is obtained by pressing S and **LINE** is obtained by pressing Ctrl + 3 in extended mode. This will record the programme to tape and when we load it with **LOAD ""** it will run from line 10.

```
10 CLEAR 24200
20 POKE 23610,255: POKE 23624,0: POKE 23693,0: CLS
30 LOAD ""SCREEN$: POKE 23739,111: LOAD ""CODE
40 RANDOMIZE USR 24200
```

Restart the emulator and try the recorded file, you will see that it runs automatically and waits for the rest to load. Press Escape to stop the execution and press B, then 7 and Enter to make the border white. Then, in extended mode, press Control + C, then 7 and Enter, and we have the main screen background in white.

We add the loading screen

I designed the loading screen with ZX Paintbrush and exported it as PongScr.tap; it asked me to name the block and I called it PongScr.

It is very important to export as tap and not save as tap. If we record as tap, we will not be asked for the name of the header and it will not be loaded.

Now we are going to link the loader and the screen with Copy, in the command prompt (in my case it's Windows), don't forget to be in the working directory.

```
copy /b loader.tap+PongScr.tap ZX-Pong.tap
```

If you use Linux, it would be:

```
cat loader.tap PongScr.tap > ZX-Pong.tap
```

We concatenated loader.tap and PongScr.tap and wrote the result to ZX-Pong.tap.

The next step is to load the ZX-Pong.tap file into the emulator and see if it loads our screen.

Including ZX-Pong

Now we just have to compile our ZX-Pong with PASMO, without generating the BASIC loader.

First we open the file main.asm and change in the first line the **ORG $5dad** to **ORG $5e88** (24200), the address where our program should be loaded, as we specified in the loader.

It's time to compile with PASMO, but change the --tapbas we used so far to --tap.

```
pasmo --name ZX-Pong --tap main.asm pong.tap
```

Now we compile, but PASMO does not create a BASIC loader for us.

Finally we link the three files into one and check if our ZX-Pong still works.

```
copy /b loader.tap+PongScr.tap+pong.tap ZX-Pong.tap

cat loader.tap PongScr.tap pong.tap > ZX-Pong.tap
```

If all goes well, we load into the emulator and, after the loading screen, our programme loads, ready to play.

Download the source code from here

https://tinyurl.com/228sxg4w

If you have any doubts, you might be interested in watching the videos of the online workshop I did in collaboration with Retro Parla (Spanish).

https://tinyurl.com/2qh3qk9d

Space Battle

Introduction

Space Battle is a simple Mars killer developed for the ZX Spectrum in assembly language. The graphics are single character, UDG (User-Defined Graphic) is used and the movement is character based, so the differences to ZX-Pong are obvious.

In Space Battle I use interrupts, which I don't do in ZX-Pong. I also make more use of ROM routines, and when using UDG and RST $10 to paint, it is necessary to switch channels to paint at the top of the screen or on the command line.

The first steps will be to define the ship, move it around and continue with the enemies and shooting. Once this is done, we will implement the game mechanics, the collisions, the scores, the available lives, etc.

In the last steps we will implement the start menu, the choice of controls, the start and end of the game, markers, sound effects and generally decorate the final result a bit. Finally, the loading screen will be added.

Space Battle is compatible with the 16K, 48K and 128K models of the ZX Spectrum, can be controlled with keyboards and Sinclair and Kempston joysticks, and consists of thirty levels.

To say that it consists of thirty levels is perhaps a bit presumptuous, as the mechanics of the game do not change, although what does change are the enemies, with a total of thirty different enemies, one for each level.

The movement of the ship is horizontal, so I only need one graphic. The enemy movement is diagonal and I need four graphics:

- up/right
- top/left
- down/right
- down/left

The shooting of the ship is a single graphic, the explosion of the ship when it kills us is four graphics, and we will do a little animation when that happens.

We will define eight more graphics for the screen frame, and another empty graphic to erase the characters from the screen.

Much of what we will see has been explained before, so I will not give many instructions at times.

Don't forget to create the SpaceBattle folder.

Step 1: Definition of graphics

In this chapter we will define all the graphics used in Space Battle. We will learn how to do the hexadecimal/binary conversion on the fly by doing our first exercise.

You can use ZX Paintbrush, or you can use the templates I created for GIMP, which you can download from these addresses:

- https://sourcesolutions.itch.io/zx-paintbrush
- http://www.gimp.org.es/
- https://tinyurl.com/2on54ohh

The templates I have prepared are as follows:

- 8x8Template: for creating 8x8 pixel graphics.
- 256x192Template: the size of the ZX Spectrum's screen.

For Space Battle we will use 8x8 templates. I will show you the image of the graphics, the hexadecimal codes, and your job will be to convert the codes into pixels, head first, to draw the graphics on the templates.

Hexadecimal/binary conversion

Although at first it may seem complicated to convert a hexadecimal number to binary, and vice versa, it is very simple and practically straightforward. We need to know the value of each bit (pixel) in blocks of four, which gives us a value between 0 and F, a value that can be represented by each hexadecimal digit.

In a byte, each bit to one has the following values:

Bit	7	6	5	4	3	2	1	0
Value	128	64	32	16	8	4	2	1

When we convert from hexadecimal to binary, we divide the byte into two blocks of four bits (nibbles), resulting in a range of values between 0 and F (8 + 4 + 2 + 1 = 15 = F). To convert from binary to hexadecimal, we add the value of the bits to one of each nibble, which gives us the value in hexadecimal.

Suppose we have the following binary value:

0101 1001

If we add up the values of the nibbles, the result would be:

0 + 4 + 0 + 1 = 5   8 + 0 + 0 + 1 = 9

The result is that 01011001 is 59 in hexadecimal.

In hexadecimal a byte is represented by two digits. What if the value of some of the nibbles is greater than nine?

11011011 = 8 + 4 + 0 + 1 = 13 y 8 + 0 + 2 + 1 = 11

How do we represent thirteen and eleven with only one digit each? In hexadecimal, values from ten to fifteen are represented by letters.

Decimal	1	2	3	4	5	6	7	8	9	10	11	12	13	14	15
Hexadecimal	1	2	3	4	5	6	7	8	9	A	B	C	D	E	F

In the example above, the hexadecimal value of 11011011 is DB.

Practising hexadecimal/binary conversion

A good way to learn is by doing, and this is what I propose to do below. Let's look at the definition of all the UDGs we are going to use (the hexadecimal values) and draw them by doing the conversion from hexadecimal to binary.

If we work with nibbles (4 bits), the conversion table for a byte would be as follows:

Byte	7	6	5	4	3	2	1	0
Value	8	4	2	1	8	4	2	1

We will create a folder called Step01 and inside it a file called var.asm. Having this table at hand, we are going to draw the ship, whose definition in hexadecimal (which we are going to copy into the created file) is the following:

```
udgsCommon:
db $24, $42, $99, $bd, $ff, $18, $24, $5a ; $90 Ship
```

We convert to binary.

Byte	7	6	5	4	3	2	1	0
Value	8	4	2	1	8	4	2	1
$24			X			X		

	7	6	5	4	3	2	1	0
$42		X					X	
$99	X			X	X			X
$bd	X		X	X	X	X		X
$ff	X	X	X	X	X	X	X	X
$18				X	X			
$24			X			X		
$5a		X		X	X		X	

If you transfer this conversion to ZX Paintbrush, or to the templates, the result should look like this:

We are going to continue practising, doing the conversions for the shot and the animation of the explosion of the ship. It is important that you try to translate it from hexadecimal to binary and from there to the graphics.

```
db $00, $18, $24, $5a, $5a, $24, $18, $00 ; $91 Shot
```

Byte	7	6	5	4	3	2	1	0
Value	8	4	2	1	8	4	2	1
$00								
$18				X	X			
$24			X			X		
$5a		X		X	X		X	
$5a		X		X	X		X	
$24			X			X		
$18				X	X			

$00

```
db $00, $00, $00, $00, $24, $5a, $24, $18 ; $92 Blast 1
```

Byte	7	6	5	4	3	2	1	0
Value	8	4	2	1	8	4	2	1
$00								
$00								
$00								
$00								
$24			X			X		
$5a		X		X	X		X	
$24			X			X		
$18				X	X			

```
db $00, $00, $00, $14, $2a, $34, $24, $18 ; $93 Blast 2
```

Byte	7	6	5	4	3	2	1	0
Value	8	4	2	1	8	4	2	1
$00								
$00								
$00								
$14				X		X		
$2a		X		X		X		

Byte	7	6	5	4	3	2	1	0
Value	8	4	2	1	8	4	2	1
$34			X	X		X		
$24			X			X		
$18				X	X			

```
db $00, $00, $0c, $12, $2a, $56, $64, $18 ; $94 Blast 3
```

Byte	7	6	5	4	3	2	1	0
Value	8	4	2	1	8	4	2	1
$00								
$00								
$0c					X	X		
$12				X			X	
$2a			X		X		X	
$56		X		X		X	X	
$64		X	X			X		
$18				X	X			

```
db $20, $51, $92, $d5, $a9, $72, $2c, $18 ; $95 Blast 4
```

Byte	7	6	5	4	3	2	1	0
Value	8	4	2	1	8	4	2	1
$20			X					
$51		X		X				X
$92	X			X			X	
$d5	X	X		X		X		X

$a9	X		X		X			X	
$72			X	X	X			X	
$2c				X			X	X	
$18					X	X			

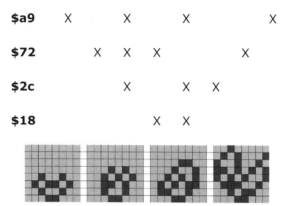

From here on, I will just give the hexadecimal definition and the image of the final appearance of each UDG.

If you are wondering what the number in the comments of each definition means, it is the code of the character we are redefining, i.e. the character code we are going to send to the printer to make the graphic. Don't worry if you don't understand it now, it will be much clearer later.

```
db $3f, $6a, $ff, $b8, $f3, $a7, $ef, $ae ; $96 Top/Left
db $ff, $aa, $ff, $00, $ff, $ff, $00, $00 ; $97 Top
db $fc, $ae, $fb, $1f, $cd, $e7, $f5, $77 ; $98 Top/Right
db $ec, $ac, $ec, $ac, $ec, $ac, $ec, $ac ; $99 Left
db $35, $37, $35, $37, $35, $37, $35, $37 ; $9a Right
db $ee, $af, $e7, $b3, $f8, $df, $75, $3f ; $9b Bottom/Left
db $00, $00, $ff, $ff, $00, $ff, $55, $ff ; $9c Bottom
db $75, $f7, $e5, $cf, $1d, $ff, $56, $fc ; $9d Bottom/Right
db $00, $00, $00, $00, $00, $00, $00, $00 ; $9e White
```

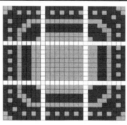

```
udgsEnemiesLevel1:
db $8c, $42, $2d, $1d, $b4, $be, $46, $30 ; $9f Left/Up
db $31, $42, $b4, $b8, $2d, $7d, $62, $0c ; $a0 Right/Up
db $30, $46, $be, $b4, $1d, $2d, $42, $8c ; $a1 Left/Down
db $0c, $62, $7d, $2d, $b8, $b4, $42, $31 ; $a2 Right/Down
```

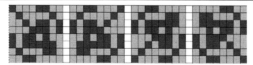

```
udgsEnemiesLevel2:
db $c0, $fb, $69, $5d, $7b, $14, $4a, $79 ; $9f Left/Up
db $03, $df, $96, $ba, $de, $28, $52, $9e ; $a0 Right/Up
```

```
db $79, $4a, $14, $7b, $5d, $69, $fb, $c0 ; $a1 Left/Down
db $9e, $52, $28, $de, $ba, $96, $df, $03 ; $a2 Right/Down
```

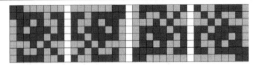

```
udgsEnemiesLevel3:
db $fc, $84, $b4, $af, $99, $f7, $14, $1c ; $9f Left/Up
db $3f, $21, $2d, $f5, $99, $ef, $28, $38 ; $a0 Right/Up
db $1c, $14, $f7, $99, $af, $b4, $84, $fc ; $a1 Left/Down
db $38, $28, $ef, $99, $f5, $2d, $21, $3f ; $a2 Right/Down
```

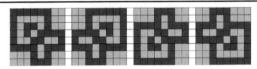

```
udgsEnemiesLevel4:
db $f2, $95, $98, $fe, $39, $55, $92, $4d ; $9f Left/Up
db $4f, $a9, $19, $7f, $9c, $aa, $49, $b2 ; $a0 Right/Up
db $4d, $92, $55, $39, $fe, $98, $95, $f2 ; $a1 Left/Down
db $b2, $49, $aa, $9c, $7f, $19, $a9, $4f ; $a2 Right/Down
```

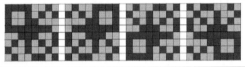

```
udgsEnemiesLevel5:
db $76, $99, $a4, $d4, $47, $bd, $8a, $4c ; $9f Left/Up
db $6e, $99, $25, $2b, $e2, $bd, $51, $32 ; $a0 Right/Up
db $4c, $8a, $bd, $47, $d4, $a4, $99, $76 ; $a1 Left/Down
db $32, $51, $bd, $e2, $2b, $25, $99, $6e ; $a2 Right/Down
```

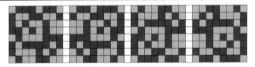

```
udgsEnemiesLevel6:
db $98, $66, $59, $aa, $b6, $49, $5a, $24 ; $9f Left/Up
db $19, $66, $9a, $55, $6d, $92, $5a, $24 ; $a0 Right/Up
db $24, $5a, $49, $b6, $aa, $59, $66, $98 ; $a1 Left/Down
db $24, $5a, $92, $6d, $55, $9a, $66, $19 ; $a2 Right/Down
```

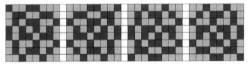

```
udgsEnemiesLevel7:
db $04, $72, $5d, $74, $2e, $be, $4c, $20 ; $9f Left/Up
db $20, $4e, $ba, $2e, $74, $7d, $32, $04 ; $a0 Right/Up
db $20, $4c, $be, $2e, $74, $5d, $72, $04 ; $a1 Left/Down
db $04, $32, $7d, $74, $2e, $ba, $4e, $20 ; $a2 Right/Down
```

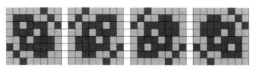

```
udgsEnemiesLevel8:
db $00, $7c, $5a, $68, $7c, $4f, $26, $04 ; $9f Left/Up
db $00, $3e, $5a, $16, $3e, $f2, $64, $20 ; $a0 Right/Up
db $04, $26, $4f, $7c, $68, $5a, $7c, $00 ; $a1 Left/Down
db $20, $64, $f2, $3e, $16, $5a, $3e, $00 ; $a2 Right/Down
```

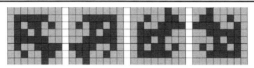

```
udgsEnemiesLevel9:
db $e0, $d8, $b6, $6e, $5b, $36, $3c, $08 ; $9f Left/Up
db $07, $1b, $6d, $76, $da, $6c, $3c, $10 ; $a0 Right/Up
db $08, $3c, $36, $5b, $6e, $b6, $d8, $e0 ; $a1 Left/Down
db $10, $3c, $6c, $da, $76, $6d, $1b, $07 ; $a2 Right/Down
```

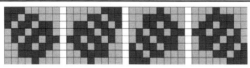

```
udgsEnemiesLevel10:
db $e0, $ce, $bf, $3c, $73, $75, $6a, $2c ; $9f Left/Up
db $07, $73, $fd, $3c, $ce, $ae, $56, $34 ; $a0 Right/Up
db $2c, $6a, $75, $73, $3c, $bf, $ce, $e0 ; $a1 Left/Down
db $34, $56, $ae, $ce, $3c, $fd, $73, $07 ; $a2 Right/Down
```

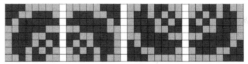

```
udgsEnemiesLevel11:
db $e0, $de, $bf, $7c, $7b, $75, $6a, $2c ; $9f Left/Up
db $07, $7b, $fd, $3e, $de, $ae, $56, $34 ; $a0 Right/Up
db $2c, $6a, $75, $7b, $7c, $bf, $de, $e0 ; $a1 Left/Down
db $34, $56, $ae, $de, $3e, $fd, $7b, $07 ; $a2 Right/Down
```

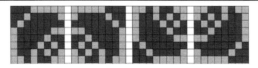

```
udgsEnemiesLevel12:
db $e0, $fe, $f7, $6c, $5f, $7e, $6c, $28 ; $9f Left/Up
db $07, $7f, $ef, $36, $fa, $7e, $36, $14 ; $a0 Right/Up
db $28, $6c, $7e, $5f, $6c, $f7, $fe, $e0 ; $a1 Left/Down
db $14, $36, $7e, $fa, $36, $ef, $7f, $07 ; $a2 Right/Down
```

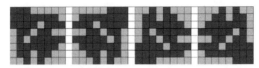

```
udgsEnemiesLevel13:
db $07, $6c, $7e, $34, $6f, $fb, $ae, $8c ; $9f Left/Up
db $e0, $36, $7e, $2c, $f6, $df, $75, $31 ; $a0 Right/Up
db $8c, $ae, $fb, $6f, $34, $7e, $6c, $07 ; $a1 Left/Down
db $31, $75, $df, $f6, $2c, $7e, $36, $e0 ; $a2 Right/Down
```

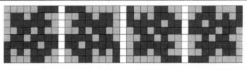

```
udgsEnemiesLevel14:
db $21, $1a, $96, $75, $4c, $3c, $62, $90 ; $9f Left/Up
db $84, $58, $69, $ae, $32, $3c, $46, $09 ; $a0 Right/Up
db $90, $62, $3c, $4c, $75, $96, $1a, $21 ; $a1 Left/Down
db $09, $46, $3c, $32, $ae, $69, $58, $84 ; $a2 Right/Down
```

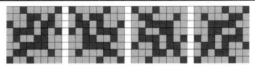

```
udgsEnemiesLevel15:
db $04, $02, $0d, $14, $28, $b0, $40, $20 ; $9f Left/Up
db $20, $40, $b0, $28, $14, $0d, $02, $04 ; $a0 Right/Up
db $20, $40, $b0, $28, $14, $0d, $02, $04 ; $a1 Left/Down
db $04, $02, $0d, $14, $28, $b0, $40, $20 ; $a2 Right/Down
```

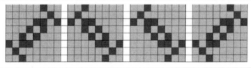

```
udgsEnemiesLevel16:
db $30, $48, $be, $b9, $7c, $2e, $27, $13 ; $9f Left/Up
db $0c, $12, $7d, $9d, $3e, $74, $e4, $c8 ; $a0 Right/Up
db $13, $27, $2e, $7c, $b9, $be, $48, $30 ; $a1 Left/Down
db $c8, $e4, $74, $3e, $9d, $7d, $12, $0c ; $a2 Right/Down
```

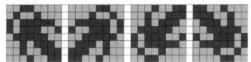

```
udgsEnemiesLevel17:
db $c0, $df, $36, $7c, $58, $77, $66, $44 ; $9f Left/Up
db $03, $fb, $6c, $3e, $1a, $ee, $66, $22 ; $a0 Right/Up
db $44, $66, $77, $58, $7c, $36, $df, $c0 ; $a1 Left/Down
db $22, $66, $ee, $1a, $3e, $6c, $fb, $03 ; $a2 Right/Down
```

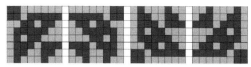

```
udgsEnemiesLevel18:
db $02, $71, $69, $57, $2f, $1e, $9e, $78 ; $9f Left/Up
db $40, $8e, $96, $ea, $f4, $78, $79, $1e ; $a0 Right/Up
db $78, $9e, $1e, $2f, $57, $69, $71, $02 ; $a1 Left/Down
db $1e, $79, $78, $f4, $ea, $96, $8e, $40 ; $a2 Right/Down
```

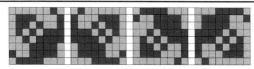

```
udgsEnemiesLevel19:
db $20, $7f, $e6, $4e, $5e, $79, $78, $44 ; $9f Left/Up
db $04, $fe, $67, $72, $7a, $9e, $1e, $22 ; $a0 Right/Up
db $44, $78, $79, $5e, $4e, $e6, $7f, $20 ; $a1 Left/Down
db $22, $1e, $9e, $7a, $72, $67, $fe, $02 ; $a2 Right/Down
```

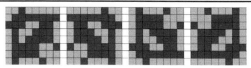

```
udgsEnemiesLevel20:
db $36, $2f, $db, $be, $7c, $db, $f6, $64 ; $9f Left/Up
db $6c, $f4, $db, $7d, $3e, $db, $6f, $26 ; $a0 Right/Up
db $64, $f6, $db, $7c, $be, $db, $2f, $36 ; $a1 Left/Down
db $26, $6f, $db, $3e, $7d, $db, $f4, $6c ; $a2 Right/Down
```

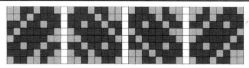

```
udgsEnemiesLevel21:
db $00, $70, $6e, $54, $2b, $34, $28, $08 ; $9f Left/Up
db $00, $0e, $76, $2a, $d4, $2c, $14, $10 ; $a0 Right/Up
db $08, $28, $34, $2b, $54, $6e, $70, $00 ; $a1 Left/Down
db $10, $14, $2c, $d4, $2a, $76, $0e, $00 ; $a2 Right/Down
```

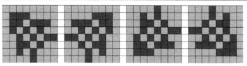

```
udgsEnemiesLevel22:
db $00, $78, $6e, $56, $6d, $3b, $34, $0c ; $9f Left/Up
db $00, $1e, $76, $6a, $b6, $dc, $2c, $30 ; $a0 Right/Up
db $0c, $34, $3b, $6d, $56, $6e, $78, $00 ; $a1 Left/Down
db $30, $2c, $dc, $b6, $6a, $76, $1e, $00 ; $a2 Right/Down
```

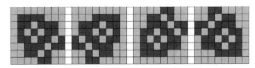

```
udgsEnemiesLevel23:
db $0c, $02, $3d, $35, $ac, $b8, $40, $30 ; $9f Left/Up
db $30, $40, $bc, $ac, $35, $1d, $02, $0c ; $a0 Right/Up
db $30, $40, $b8, $ac, $35, $3d, $02, $0c ; $a1 Left/Down
db $0c, $02, $1d, $35, $ac, $bc, $40, $30 ; $a2 Right/Down
```

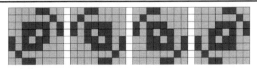

```
udgsEnemiesLevel24:
db $00, $77, $6e, $56, $2a, $74, $7b, $42 ; $9f Left/Up
db $00, $ee, $76, $6a, $54, $2e, $de, $42 ; $a0 Right/Up
db $42, $7b, $74, $2a, $56, $6e, $77, $00 ; $a1 Left/Down
db $42, $de, $2e, $54, $6a, $76, $ee, $00 ; $a2 Right/Down
```

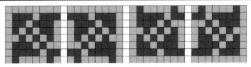

```
udgsEnemiesLevel25:
db $c0, $ff, $76, $6c, $5f, $7e, $6c, $48 ; $9f Left/Up
db $03, $ff, $6e, $36, $fa, $7e, $36, $12 ; $a0 Right/Up
db $48, $6c, $7e, $5f, $6c, $76, $ff, $c0 ; $a1 Left/Down
db $12, $36, $7e, $fa, $36, $6e, $ff, $03 ; $a2 Right/Down
```

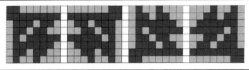

```
udgsEnemiesLevel26:
db $3c, $7e, $f7, $e8, $da, $e1, $68, $24 ; $9f Left/Up
db $3c, $7e, $ef, $17, $5b, $87, $16, $24 ; $a0 Right/Up
db $24, $68, $e1, $da, $e8, $f7, $7e, $3c ; $a1 Left/Down
db $24, $16, $87, $5b, $17, $ef, $7e, $3c ; $a2 Right/Down
```

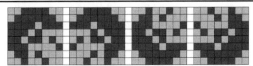

```
udgsEnemiesLevel27:
db $04, $02, $39, $2d, $3f, $9e, $4c, $38 ; $9f Left/Up
db $20, $40, $9c, $b4, $fc, $79, $32, $1c ; $a0 Right/Up
db $38, $4c, $9e, $3f, $2d, $39, $02, $04 ; $a1 Left/Down
db $1c, $32, $79, $fc, $b4, $9c, $40, $20 ; $a2 Right/Down
```

```
udgsEnemiesLevel28:
db $00, $37, $69, $5c, $34, $5f, $46, $64 ; $9f Left/Up
db $00, $ec, $96, $3a, $2c, $fa, $62, $26 ; $a0 Right/Up
db $64, $46, $5f, $34, $5c, $69, $37, $00 ; $a1 Left/Down
db $26, $62, $fa, $2c, $3a, $96, $ec, $00 ; $a2 Right/Down
```

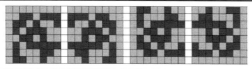

```
udgsEnemiesLevel29:
db $00, $37, $6d, $5e, $34, $7f, $56, $64 ; $9f Left/Up
db $00, $ec, $b6, $7a, $2c, $fe, $6a, $26 ; $a0 Right/Up
db $64, $56, $7f, $34, $5e, $6d, $37, $00 ; $a1 Left/Down
db $26, $6a, $fe, $2c, $7a, $b6, $ec, $00 ; $a2 Right/Down
```

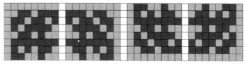

```
udgsEnemiesLevel30:
db $e0, $ff, $ed, $5b, $7e, $6e, $5f, $72 ; $9f Left/Up
db $07, $ff, $b7, $da, $7e, $76, $fa, $4e ; $a0 Right/Up
db $72, $5f, $6e, $7e, $5b, $ed, $ff, $e0 ; $a1 Left/Down
db $4e, $fa, $76, $7e, $da, $b7, $ff, $07 ; $a2 Right/Down
```

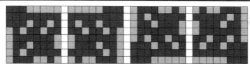

With this we have already defined the graphics we are going to use: the ship, the shot, the explosion, the frame of the screen and the enemies.

You may notice that all the enemies have the same character code, this is because there is a limited number of characters that can be used as UDGs. Don't worry, we'll see a way around this later on.

It's really very important to practice the hexadecimal to binary conversion, so don't leave it for another day, it's a very simple exercise.

Download the source code from here

https://tinyurl.com/22v23t2l

Step 2: Painting UDG

In this chapter we will start drawing with UDG. The ZX Spectrum character map consists of two hundred and fifty-six values, of which we can redefine twenty-one, namely those between $90 (144) and $A4 (164) inclusive.

Create a folder called Step02 and copy var.asm from Step01.

Where are the UDG?

The value of memory address $5C7B contains the memory address where the user-defined graphics are located, so all we need to do is load the address where our graphics are defined into that memory address. Once this is done, drawing any character between $90 and $A4 with RST $10 will draw the graphics we have defined.

We create the file called const.asm and add the following:

```
; Memory address where user-defined graphics are loaded.
UDG: EQU $5c7b
```

In this constant we will have the address where we store the address where our graphics are located.

We paint our UDGs

It's time for our first test, we're going to paint the UDGs. Create main.asm and add the following lines:

```
org   $5dad

Main:
ld    a, $90
ld    b, $15

Loop:
push af
rst   $10
pop   af
inc   a
djnz Loop

ret

end   Main
```

The first thing to do is to specify the address where we want to load the program, **ORG $5DAD**. We load the program at position $5DAD (23981) as it will be compatible with 16K models.

The next line is a label, **Main**, the entry point of the program.

Next we load one hundred and forty-four into A, **LD A, $90**, and twenty-one into B, **LD B, $15**, so we paint from character one hundred and forty-four to one hundred and sixty-four, for a total of twenty-one characters.

We make a loop of twenty-one iterations, starting with the loop label, **Loop**. We then keep the value of A, **PUSH AF**; the next instruction, **RST $10**, prints the character to which the code loaded into A belongs and modifies the register. We recover the value of A, **POP AF**.

We then increment A, **INC A**, so that it points to the next character, decrement B and jump to the loop if it has not reached zero, **DJNZ Loop**. Finally, we return to Basic, **RET**.

The last line tells PASMO to include the call to the address of the Main tag in the Basic loader.

Now it's time to compile and see the results in the emulator.

```
pasmo --name Martian --tapbas main.asm martian.tap martian.log
```

But have we painted our graphics?

We have painted the capital letters A to U because we have not indicated where our graphics are.

Next, we go to the main.asm file, and under the Main tag we add the following lines:

```
ld   hl, udgsCommon
ld   (UDG), hl
```

We load into HL the address where the graphics are, **LD HL, udgsCommon**, and load that value into the address where the location of our graphics is, **LD (UDG), HL**.

As both udgsCommon and UDG are not defined in the main.asm file, we need to add the includes for the const.asm and var.asm files after the **RET** statement.

```
include "const.asm"
include "var.asm"
```

Now we can recompile the program, load it into the emulator and see our graphics on the screen.

Much better, right? But we painted twenty-one graphics: the ship, the shot, the explosion, the frame, the blank character, the graphics of enemy one and part of the graphics of enemy two. How are we going to paint the other two graphics of enemy two and the rest?

We load the enemies' UDGs

Looking at the graphics definition, the first tag is called **udgsCommon**, and this should give us a clue as to how we're going to do this. We have defined fifteen common UDGs (ship, shot, explosion, frame and target), so we are going to define thirty-two bytes to be able to dump the enemy graphics into them; we do this because the enemies are one per level, and the dump is only done once, just at the level change.

In the var.asm file, above **udgsEnemiesLeve1**, let's add the following lines:

```
udgsExtension:
db $00, $00, $00, $00, $00, $00, $00, $00 ; $9f Left/Up
db $00, $00, $00, $00, $00, $00, $00, $00 ; $a0 Right/Up
db $00, $00, $00, $00, $00, $00, $00, $00 ; $a1 Left/Down
db $00, $00, $00, $00, $00, $00, $00, $00 ; $a2 Right/Down
```

In this block of memory we are going to dump the graphics of the enemies, depending on the level we are in.

Try compiling now and see how it looks. The enemy graphics are gone, aren't they? It's the udgsExtension painting.

We create the file graph.asm and implement in it the routine that loads into **udgsExtension** the graphics of the enemies of each of the levels, data that it receives in A.

To calculate the address where the graphics are, we multiply the level by thirty-two (bytes occupied by the graphics) and add the result to the address where the graphics of the first enemy are.

```
LoadUdgsEnemies:
dec   a
ld    h, $00
ld    l, a
```

Since the levels range from one to thirty, we decrement A, **DEC A**, so that it does not add one level too many (level one adds zero to udgsEnemies, level two adds one, etc.).

190

The next step is to load the level into HL, for which we load zero into H, **LD H, $00**, and the level into L, **LD L, A**.

```
add    hl, hl
add    hl, hl
add    hl, hl
add    hl, hl
add    hl, hl
```

We multiply the level by thirty-two by adding HL to itself five times, **ADD HL, HL**. The first addition is like multiplying by two, the second by four, by eight, by sixteen and by thirty-two.

```
ld     de, udgsEnemiesLevel1
add    hl, de
ld     de, udgsExtension
ld     bc, $20
ldir
ret
```

We load the address of the first enemy graphic into DE, **LD DE, udgsEnemiesLevel1**, and add it to HL, **ADD HL, DE**. We load the extension address DE, **LD DE, udgsExtension**, load the number of bytes we are going to load into udgsExtension, **LD BC, $20**, and load the thirty-two bytes of the level's enemy graphics into udgsExtension, **LDIR**. Finally we exit, **RET**.

The final aspect of the routine is as follows:

```
; -----------------------------------------------------------------
; Load user-defined graphics relating to enemies
;
; Entry: A -> Level from 1 to 30
;
; Alters the value of the A, BC, DE and HL registers.
; -----------------------------------------------------------------
LoadUdgsEnemies:
dec    a                   ; A = A - 1 which does not add one level more

ld     h, $00
ld     l, a                ; HL = level
add    hl, hl              ; HL = HL * 2
add    hl, hl              ; * 4
add    hl, hl              ; * 8
add    hl, hl              ; * 16
add    hl, hl              ; * 32
ld     de, udgsEnemiesLevel1 ; DE = address enemy graphics 1
add    hl, de              ; HL = HL + DE
ld     de, udgsExtension   ; DE = extension address
ld     bc, $20             ; BC = bytes to copy, 32
ldir                       ; Copies enemy bytes to extension

ret
```

Let's test the new routine by editing the main.asm file, starting by changing the **LD B, $15** instruction, above the Loop label, and leaving it as follows; it prints the first fifteen UDGs, the common ones:

```
ld     b, $0f
```

The rest is implemented between the **DJNZ Loop** instruction and the **RET** instruction.

```
ld    a, $01
ld    b, $1e
```

We load in A the first level, **LD A, $01**, in B the total number of levels (thirty), **LD B, $1E**, and implement a loop that draws the enemies of the thirty levels.

```
Loop2:
push af
push bc
call LoadUdgsEnemies
```

We keep AF, **PUSH AF**, and BC, **PUSH BC**, as we use A and B to control the enemies we paint and the loop iterations. Next, we call the routine that loads the level's enemy graphics into udgsExtension, **CALL LoadUdgsEnemies**.

```
ld    a, $9f
rst   $10
ld    a, $a0
rst   $10
ld    a, $a1
rst   $10
ld    a, $a2
rst   $10
```

The characters corresponding to the enemy graphics are $9F, $A0, $A1 and $A2; we load them into A, **LD A, $9F**, and paint, **RST $10**. We repeat the process with $A0, $A1 and $A2.

```
pop   bc
pop   af
inc   a
djnz Loop2
```

Recover BC, **POP BC**, AF, **POP AF**, increment A to go to the next level, **INC A**, and repeat until B is zero, **DJNZ Loop2**.

Finally, at the end of the file and before **END Main**, we insert the file graph.asm.

```
include "graph.asm"
```

The final main.asm code is as follows:

```
org  $5dad

Main:
ld   hl, udgsCommon
ld   (UDG), hl

ld   a, $90
ld   b, $0f
Loop:
push af
rst  $10
pop  af
```

```
inc   a
djnz Loop

ld    a, $01
ld    b, $1e
Loop2:
push af
push bc
call LoadUdgsEnemies
ld    a, $9f
rst   $10
ld    a, $a0
rst   $10
ld    a, $a1
rst   $10
ld    a, $a2
rst   $10
pop   bc
pop   af
inc   a
djnz Loop2

ret

include "const.asm"
include "graph.asm"
include "var.asm"

end   Main
```

We compile, load into the emulator and see that we have painted all our graphics.

At this point we have defined all the graphics and learned how to paint them.

Download the source code from here

https://tinyurl.com/2cg5mqho

Step 3: Play area

Create the folder Step03 and copy the files const.asm, graph.asm, main.asm and var.asm from the folder Step02.

Before starting to draw the game area, it is necessary to know that the ZX Spectrum screen is divided into two zones, the upper one with twenty-two lines (from zero to twenty-one) and the lower one (the line where the commands are entered).

If you load the program resulting from the previous chapter, when it is executed, pressing the ENTER key will display the basic list of the loader. Executing line 40 should paint the graphics, but this does not seem to be the case. They do draw, but they do so on the command line; look and you will see them draw and then disappear.

After running our program, the active part of the screen is the command line, so we need a mechanism to activate the part of the screen where we want to paint.

Changing the active display

The upper part of the screen is two, the lower part one. There is a routine in the ROM that activates one or the other channel depending on the value in register A.

Open the file const.asm and add the following lines:

```
; ------------------------------------------------------------------
; ROM routine that opens the display channel.
;
; Input: A -> 1 = command line
;             2 = top screen
; ------------------------------------------------------------------
OPENCHAN: EQU $1601
```

Next, we open the main.asm file and just below the Main tag we add the following lines:

```
ld    a, $02
call OPENCHAN
```

We load the channel we want to activate into A, **LD A, $02**, and then call the ROM routine to activate it, **CALL OPENCHAN**.

We compile, load into the emulator, press any key, execute line 40 and now our graphics are painted in the right place again.

We paint text strings

When working with UDG, we could say that we are painting characters, and as such we will be painting the game screen.

We implement a routine that paints strings, giving the address where the string is and the length of the string.

We create the file print.asm and implement PrintString, which takes the address of the string in HL and the length in B. This routine changes the value of the AF, B and HL registers.

```
PrintString:
ld    a, (hl)
rst   $10
inc   hl
djnz PrintString
ret
```

Loads the character to be drawn into A, **LD A, (HL)**, draws it, **RST $10**, points HL to the next character, **INC HL**, and repeats the operation until B is 0, **DJNZ PrintString**. Finally, it exits, **RET**.

The final aspect of the routine, once commented, is as follows:

```
; --------------------------------------------------------------------
; Paints chains.
;
; Input: HL = first memory location of the string.
;        B  = length of the chain.
; Alters the value of the AF, B and HL registers.
; --------------------------------------------------------------------
PrintString:
ld    a, (hl)             ; A = character to be painted
rst   $10                 ; Paint the character
inc   hl                  ; HL = next character
djnz PrintString          ; Until B has a value of 0
ret
```

The next step is testing, so let's edit the main.asm file. The first thing to do, so we don't forget, is to include the print.asm file before **END Main**:

```
include "print.asm"
```

Just before the includes, we are going to define a string with two tags, the string itself and a second tag to mark the end of the string.

```
String:
db 'Hello World'
String_End:
db $
```

Just before the **RET** that takes us out of Basic, we add the call to the new routine.

```
ld    hl, String
ld    b, String_End - String
call PrintString
```

We compile, load in the emulator and see the results.

As you can see, the string Hello World has been painted after the graphics.

We add codes before the string and leave it as it is:

```
db $16, $0a, $0a, 'Hello World'
```

We compile, load in the emulator and see the result.

As we can see, the Hello World string now appears more centred, which we have achieved by adding characters in front of the string, specifically $16, which is the control character of the Basic AT command, and the Y and X coordinates.

Below is a list of the control characters we can use when painting strings in this way, and the parameters to send.

Character	Code	Parameters	Values
DELETE	$0c		
ENTER	$0d		
INK	$10	Colour	From $00 to $07
PAPER	$11	Colour	From $00 to $07
FLASH	$12	No/Yes	From $00 to $01
BRIGHT	$13	No/Yes	From $00 to $01

INVERSE	$14	No/Yes	From $00 to $01
OVER	$15	No/Yes	From $00 to $01
AT	$16	Y and X coordinates	Y = from $00 to $15 X = from $00 to $1f
TAB	$17	Number of tabulations	

Control codes must be accompanied by their parameters to avoid unwanted results. If a string is printed after TAB, a space must be added as the first character of the string.

As an exercise, try different combinations of control codes, try colour, blinking, etc.

We paint the game screen

The game screen is surrounded by a frame, but before we paint anything, let's clean up main.asm, removing everything that's left over; we delete from the two lines before the **Loop** tag to the line before the **RET** statement, we also delete the definition of **String** and **String_End**.

main.asm should now look like this:

```
org   $5dad

Main:
ld    a, $02
call OPENCHAN
ld    hl, udgsCommon
ld    (UDG), hl
ret

include "const.asm"
include "graph.asm"
include "print.asm"
include "var.asm"

end Main
```

Now we define the strings to paint the frame in var.asm and include them before **udgsCommon**.

```
; ------------------------------------------------------------------
; Display frame
; ------------------------------------------------------------------
frameTopGraph:
db $16, $00, $00, $10, $01
db $96, $97, $97, $97, $97, $97, $97, $97, $97, $97, $97, $97, $97
db $97, $97, $97, $97, $97, $97, $97, $97, $97, $97, $97, $97, $97
db $97, $97, $97, $97, $97, $98
frameBottomGraph:
db $16, $15, $00
db $9b, $9c, $9c, $9c, $9c, $9c, $9c, $9c, $9c, $9c, $9c, $9c, $9c
db $9c, $9c, $9c, $9c, $9c, $9c, $9c, $9c, $9c, $9c, $9c, $9c, $9c
```

```
db $9c, $9c, $9c, $9c, $9c, $9d
frameEnd:
```

In the first **DB** line we define the position of the top, **$16, $00, $00** and the colour, **$10, $01**.

On the next line we define the top of the frame, first the top left corner, **$96**, then thirty top horizontal positions, **$97**, and finally the top right corner, **$98**; all these numbers are in the comments of the chart definition.

On the next line we define the position of the bottom, **$16, $15, $00**.

On the next line we define the bottom, first the lower left corner, **$9b**, then thirty lower horizontal positions, **$9c**, and finally the lower right corner, **$9d**.

Let's see how it all looks. We go back to main.asm and add the following lines just above the **RET**:

```
ld   hl, frameTopGraph
ld   b, frameEnd - frameTopGraph
call PrintString
```

We compile, load in the emulator and see the results.

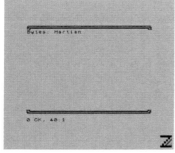

We have painted the top and bottom of the frame, although the frame is not complete as the sides are missing.

We will implement a routine that prints the frame and we will do this in print.asm.

```
PrintFrame:
ld   hl, frameTopGraph
ld   b, frameEnd - frameTopGraph
call PrintString
```

We load into HL the memory address of the top of the frame, **LD HL, frameTopGraph**, load into B the length by subtracting the start address of the top from the end address of the frame, **LD B, frameEnd - frameTopGraph**, and call the routine that prints the strings, **CALL PrintString**.

All that remains is to implement a loop to paint the sides.

```
ld   b, $01
printFrame_loop:
```

```
ld   a, $16
rst  $10
ld   a, b
rst  $10
ld   a, $00
rst  $10
ld   a, $99
rst  $10
```

We load into B the start line of the pages, **LD B, $01**, we load into A the AT control character, **LD A, $16**, and draw it, **RST $10**, we load the Y coordinate, **LD A, B**, and draw it, **RST $10**, we load the zero column, **LD A, $00**, and draw it, **RST $10**, and finally we load into A the left page character, **LD A, $99**, and draw it, **RST $10**.

We do the same with the right side, since the code is practically the same, we just mark the two lines that change.

```
ld   a, $16
rst  $10
ld   a, b
rst  $10
ld   a, $1f
rst  $10
ld   a, $9a
rst  $10
```

And so we come to the last part of the routine.

```
inc  b
ld   a, b
cp   $15
jr   nz, printFrame_loop

ret
```

We point B to the next line, **INC B**, load it into A, **LD A, B**, and check if B points to line twenty-one (the line where the bottom of the frame is), **CP $15**, and if not, repeat the loop until it reaches line twenty-one, **JR NZ, printFrame_loop**. As soon as B points to line twenty-one, we quit, **RET**.

The final aspect of the routine is as follows:

```
; ------------------------------------------------------------------
; Paint the frame of the screen.
;
; Alters the value of the HL, B and AF registers.
; ------------------------------------------------------------------
PrintFrame:
ld   hl, frameTopGraph      ; HL = top address
ld   b, frameEnd - frameTopGraph ; B = length
call PrintString            ; Paints the string

ld   b, $01                 ; B = line 1
printFrame_loop:
ld   a, $16                 ; A = control character AT
rst  $10                    ; Paints it
ld   a, b                   ; A = line
```

```
rst   $10                      ; Paints it
ld    a, $00                   ; A = column
rst   $10                      ; Paints it
ld    a, $99                   ; A = left lateral character
rst   $10                      ; Paints it

ld    a, $16                   ; A = control character AT
rst   $10                      ; Paints it
ld    a, b                     ; A = line
rst   $10                      ; Paints it
ld    a, $1f                   ; A = column
rst   $10                      ; Paints it
ld    a, $9a                   ; A = right-hand side character
rst   $10                      ; Paints it

inc   b                        ; B = next line
ld    a, b                     ; A = B
cp    $15                      ; B = 21?
jr    nz, printFrame_loop      ; B != 21, continue loop

ret
```

We will test if it paints the whole frame. Go back to main.asm and replace these lines:

```
ld    hl, frameTopGraph
ld    b, frameEnd - frameTopGraph
call PrintString
```

For this one:

```
call PrintFrame
```

We compile, load in the emulator and see the result.

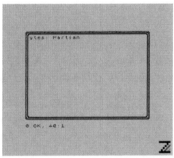

As you can see, we have already painted the frame of the screen, but there is still work to be done; we have not erased the screen and you can see things that should not be there.

We clean and colour the screen

Many of the Basic listings you see have a line similar to this:

```
BORDER 0: INK 7: PAPER 0: CLS
```

This line sets the screen border to black, the ink to white and the background to black. Finally, the screen is cleaned by applying the ink and background attributes.

We will use the ZX Spectrum ROM to set the ink and background, clean the screen and implement the border colour change.

We start with the part where we clean the screen by opening the const.asm file and adding the following lines:

```
; System variable where the permanent colour attributes are located.
ATTR_P: EQU $5c8d

; -----------------------------------------------------------------
; ROM routine that clears the screen using the value of ATTR_P
; -----------------------------------------------------------------
CLS: EQU $0daf
```

ATTR_P contains the permanent colour attributes in the format FBPPPIII, where F = FLASH (0/1), B = BRIGHT (0/1), PPP = PAPER (from 0 to 7) and III = INK (from 0 to 7). On the other hand, CLS clears the screen using the attributes in ATTR_P.

We go back to main.asm and add the following lines just before the PrintFrame call:

```
ld   hl, ATTR_P
ld   (hl), $07
call CLS
```

We load the memory address of the permanent attributes in HL, **LD HL, ATTR_P**; we set FLASH 0, BRIGHT 0, PAPER 0, INK 7, **LD (HL), $07**. Finally, we clear the screen, **CALL CLS**.

We compile, load into the emulator and see the results.

© OK, 40:1

Now we want to change the colour of the border. We have already seen in ZX-Pong that the BEEPER routine of the ROM changes the colour of the border, so it is necessary to store the attributes in a system variable; the attributes have the same format as seen for ATTR_P.

We go back to the const.asm file and add the constant for the system variable where the border attributes are stored.

```
; System variable where to store the border. Also used by BEEPER.
; The command line attributes are also stored here.
BORDCR: EQU $5c48
```

We go back to main.asm and set the border to black after **CALL CLS**.

```
xor   a
out   ($fe), a
ld    a, (BORDCR)
and   $c7
or    $07
ld    (BORDCR), a
```

We set A to zero, **XOR A**, and the border to black, **OUT ($FE), A**. We then load the value of BORDCR into A, **LD A, (BORDCR)**, discard the border colour and so set it to black, **AND $C7**. We set the colour to white, **OR $07**, and load the value into BORDCR, **LD (BORDCR), A**.

The **OR $07** command is only necessary while we are in Basic, remember that in BORDCR are the colour attributes of the command line, and if we don't change the ink to white, it will stay as it was originally, in black, the same colour we gave to the background (border).

We compile, load into the emulator and see the results.

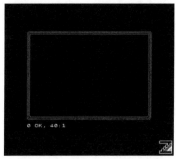

The only thing left to do is to paint the game information area, which we will do from the command line.

We paint the information of the game

The first thing to do is to define the title line of the game information area, at the beginning of var.asm.

```
; -----------------------------------------------------------------
; Title of the item information
; -----------------------------------------------------------------
infoGame:
db $10, $03, $16, $00, $00
db 'Lives   Points   Level    Enemies'
infoGame_end:
```

In the first line we set the colour to magenta and position the cursor at the coordinates 0,0. Next we define the titles of the information.

In print.asm we implement the routine that paints the titles of the information.

```
PrintInfoGame:
ld    a, $01
call OPENCHAN
```

When painting the titles of the information on the command line, the first thing to do is to activate channel one. We load one in A, **LD A, $01**, and call the channel change, **CALL OPENCHAN**.

```
ld   hl, infoGame
ld   b, infoGame_end - infoGame
call PrintString
```

We load in HL the address of the title of the information, **LD HL, infoGame**, in B the length, **LD B, infoGame_end - infoGame**, and then we call to print the string, **CALL PrintString**.

```
ld   a, $02
call OPENCHAN

ret
```

Finally, we reactivate channel two (the top screen) and exit.

The final aspect of the routine is as follows:

```
; ------------------------------------------------------------------
; Paint the game information headings.
; Alters the value of the A, C and HL registers.
; ------------------------------------------------------------------
PrintInfoGame:
ld   a, $01                  ; A = 1
call OPENCHAN                ; Activates channel 1
ld   hl, infoGame            ; HL = address string titles
ld   b, infoGame_end - infoGame ; B = length
call PrintString             ; Paints titles
ld   a, $02                  ; A = 2
call OPENCHAN                ; Activates channel 2

ret
```

We go back to main.asm and after **CALL PrintFrame** we add the call to paint the start information titles.

```
call PrintInfoGame
```

If we compile now, try it if you want, it seems that the last thing we implemented does not work, it does not paint the title information. Actually it does, but when we go back to Basic, the message **0 OK, 40:1** deletes it.

To avoid this, we'll stay in an infinite loop; we'll go to the **RET** statement that brings us back to Basic and change it to:

```
Main_loop:
jr   Main_loop
```

The final main.asm code is as follows:

```
org  $5dad

Main:
ld   a, $02
call OPENCHAN

ld   hl, udgsCommon
ld   (UDG), hl
```

```
ld    hl, ATTR_P
ld    (hl), $07
call CLS

xor   a
out   ($fe), a
ld    a, (BORDCR)
and   $c7
or    $07
ld    (BORDCR), a

call PrintFrame
call PrintInfoGame

Main_loop:
jr    Main_loop

include "const.asm"
include "graph.asm"
include "print.asm"
include "var.asm"

end   Main
```

We compile, load the emulator and see the result.

I don't know about you, but I don't like the fact that the titles are so close to the frame. Since we only have two lines in the command line without scrolling, and we need to draw the data below the title line, we have only one option left to remove a line from the play area.

In var.asm we find the **frameBottomGraph** tag, and one line down we see the **DB** that positions the cursor; we are going to change this line so that the Y coordinate is twenty instead of twenty-one.

```
db $16, $14, $00
```

In print.asm we now find the **printFrame_loop** tag. This loop runs until B is twenty-one; we need to change this condition so that it runs until it is twenty. Two lines above the **RET** of this routine we have **CP $15**, this is the line we need to modify, leaving it as follows:

```
cp    $14                    ; B = 20?
```

We compile, load into the emulator and see the results. Now we have our play area.

Download the source code from here

https://tinyurl.com/265k79ya

Step 4: Ship

Create the folder Step04 and copy the files const.asm, graph.asm, main.asm, print.asm and var.asm from Step03.

In this chapter we will implement the ship, its movement and therefore the controls.

On-screen positioning

So far we have been using the **AT** control character and coordinates to position ourselves on the screen, but this is slow.

We will open graph.asm and at the top of the file we will implement a routine that does the same thing, but is faster.

```
; -------------------------------------------------------------------
; Position the cursor at the specified coordinates.
;
; Input: B = Y-coordinate (24 to 3).
;        C = X-coordinate (32 to 1).
; Alters the value of the AF and BC registers.
; -------------------------------------------------------------------
At:
push de                       ; Preserves DE
push hl                       ; Preserves HL
call $0a23                    ; Call ROM routine
pop  hl                       ; Retrieve HL
pop  de                       ; Retrieve DE

ret
```

In this routine we use the ROM routine that positions the cursor. We store the value of DE, **PUSH DE**, and the value of HL, **PUSH HL**. Once this is done, we call the ROM routine, **CALL $0A23**, and retrieve the value of HL, **POP HL**, and also the value of DE, **POP DE**. Finally we exit, **RET**.

In the comments you can see that the routine also changes the value of AF and BC, but we don't keep them; we won't be affected by that, and so we save two **PUSH** and two **POP**.

Another thing to note, a hint is given in the comments, is that for the ROM routine the upper left corner is at coordinates Y=24 and X=32, so we will work with the coordinates inverted with respect to the **AT** instruction.

Open the file const.asm and add the coordinate constants.

```
; Screen coordinates for ROM routine positioning the cursor
; The play area (the frame).
COR_X: EQU $20 ; X-coordinate of the upper left corner
COR_Y: EQU $18 ; Y-coordinate of upper left corner
MIN_X: EQU $00 ; To be subtracted from COR_X for X upper left corner
MIN_Y: EQU $00 ; To be subtracted from COR_Y for Y upper left corner
MAX_X: EQU $1f ; To be subtracted from COR_X for X bottom right corner
MAX_Y: EQU $15 ; To be subtracted from COR_Y for Y lower right corner
```

The **EQU** directive does not compile, it does not expand the binary; it replaces the tag with its value wherever it is found.

We paint the ship

The first thing we're going to do is place the ship in our game area; it will move from left to right at the bottom of the game area.

Since the ship is a mobile element, we need to know its current and initial position, as we saw with the paddles in ZX-Pong.

We open the var.asm file and add the following lines after the game information title declarations:

```
; ------------------------------------------------------------------
; Statements of the graphics of the different characters
; and the coordinate configuration (Y, X)
; ------------------------------------------------------------------

; ------------------------------------------------------------------
; Nave
; ------------------------------------------------------------------
shipPos:
dw $0511
```

In the case of the ship, we only define the position, **DW $0511**, a two-byte value, first the Y-coordinate and then the X-coordinate, which we will load into BC during the game to position the ship. The position $0511 is the result of subtracting 19 ($13) and 15 ($0f) from the upper left corner used by the ROM routine ($1820).

We open const.asm and add constants for the ship character, the start position and the left and right tops.

```
; Character code of the ship, starting position and buffers
SHIP_GRAPH: EQU $90
SHIP_INI:   EQU $0511
SHIP_TOP_L: EQU $1e
SHIP_TOP_R: EQU $01
```

To paint the correct colours, and to avoid repeating the code, we implement a routine to change the ink colour in the graph.asm file. This routine receives the value of the colour in A.

Before implementing the routine, we add the constant memory location where the current colour attributes are stored. These attributes are those used by **RST $10** to assign the colour to the character it is drawing.

```
; System variable containing current colour attributes
ATTR_T: EQU $5c8f
```

We open the graph.asm file and implement the Ink routine.

```
; ------------------------------------------------------------------
; Change the ink
;
; Input: A -> Ink colour
; Alters the value of the A register.
; ------------------------------------------------------------------
Ink:
```

```
exx                          ; Preserves BC, DE and HL
ld    b, a                   ; B = ink
ld    a, (ATTR_T)            ; A = current attributes
and   $f8                    ; A = Ink 0
or    b                      ; A = Ink received
ld    (ATTR_T), a            ; Current attributes = A
exx                          ; Retrieves BC, DE and HL

ret
```

If we need to rely on the B register, the first thing we do is to preserve its value with the **EXX** instruction, which exchanges the value of the BC, DE and HL registers with the alternative registers 'BC, 'DE and 'HL, with only one byte and four clock cycles, which is faster and occupies less than if we used the stack.

We load the value of the colour into B, **LD B, A**, load the current attributes into A, **LD A, (ATTR_T)**, discard the colour, **AND $F8**, add the colour, **OR B**, and load it into the current attributes, **LD (ATTR_T), A**. Finally, we retrieve the value of the BC, DE and HL registers, **EXX**, and exit, **RET**.

We need a routine to paint the ship, which we implement in the file print.asm.

```
PrintShip:
ld    a, $07
call Ink
```

We load the white ink, **LD A, $07**, into A and call **CALL INK** to change it.

```
ld    bc, (shipPos)
call At
```

We load the position of the ship into BC, **LD BC, (shipPos)**, and position the cursor, **CALL At**.

```
ld    a, SHIP_GRAPH
rst   $10

ret
```

We load the ship character in A, **LD A, SHIP_GRAPH**, paint it, **RST $10**, and exit, **RET**.

We already have the routine that paints the ship, which looks like this:

```
; --------------------------------------------------------------
; Paints the ship at the current position.
; Alters the value of the A and BC registers.
; --------------------------------------------------------------
PrintShip:
ld    a, $07                 ; A = white ink
call Ink                     ; Change ink

ld    bc, (shipPos)          ; BC = ship position
call At                      ; Position cursor
```

```
ld   a, SHIP_GRAPH        ; A = ship character
rst  $10                  ; Pinta ship

ret
```

Before we leave the Print.asm file, we return to the routine that draws the frame, specifically the part where we create the loop that draws the sides.

```
printFrame_loop:
ld   a, $16               ; A = control character AT
rst  $10                  ; Paints it
ld   a, b                 ; A = line
rst  $10                  ; Paints it
ld   a, $00               ; A = column
rst  $10                  ; Paints it
ld   a, $99               ; A = left lateral character
rst  $10                  ; Paints it

ld   a, $16               ; A = control character AT
rst  $10                  ; Paints it
ld   a, b                 ; A = line
rst  $10                  ; Paints it
ld   a, $1f               ; A = column
rst  $10                  ; Paints it
ld   a, $9a               ; A = right-hand side character
rst  $10                  ; Paints it

inc  b                    ; B = next line
ld   a, b                 ; A = B
cp   $14                  ; A = 20?
jr   nz, printFrame_loop  ; A != 20, continue with loop
```

We see that the six lines following **printFrame_loop** position the cursor to paint on the left side, then six lines following printFrame_loop do the same for the right side.

I'm using Visual Studio Code with the Z80 Assembly meter extension, so I know that this routine, from **printFrame_loop** to **JR NZ, printFrame_loop**, consumes one hundred and sixty-five clock cycles and twenty-eight bytes.

Since we've already implemented a routine that positions the cursor, we've just implemented At, so let's replace these lines with calls to that routine.

Above printFrame_loop we modify the **LD B line, $01**, and leave it as follows:

```
ld   b, COR_Y - $01
```

Remember that the ROM routine works with inverted coordinates. We point B to line one, **LD B, COR_Y - $01**.

We delete the first six lines below **printFrame_loop** and replace them with the following:

```
ld   c, COR_X - MIN_X
call At
```

210

A few lines down, we delete from **LD A, $16** to **RST $10** just above **LD A, $9A**, and replace these lines with the following:

```
ld    c, COR_X - MAX_X
call At
```

Replacement from **INC B** to JR **NZ, printFrame_loop**.

```
dec   b
ld    a, COR_Y - MAX_Y + $01
sub   b
jr    nz, printFrame_loop
```

The final appearance of the modified part is as follows:

```
ld    b, COR_Y - $01        ; B = line 1
printFrame_loop:
ld    c, COR_X - MIN_X      ; C = column 0
call At                     ; Position cursor
ld    a, $99                ; A = left lateral character
rst   $10                   ; Paints it

ld    c, COR_X - MAX_X      ; C = column 31
call At                     ; Position cursor
ld    a, $9a                ; A = right-hand side character
rst   $10                   ; Paints it

dec   b                     ; B = B - 1
ld    a, COR_Y - MAX_Y + $01 ; A = line 20
sub   b                     ; Subtract next line
jr    nz, printFrame_loop   ; A - B != 0, continue loop
```

At first glance, the routine is shorter, consuming twenty-two bytes and one hundred and eleven clock cycles, but beware, all that glitters is not gold, to these clock cycles must be added the clock cycles of the At routine, which are sixty-nine (the bytes are not added because we are going to use the routine from more places).

When all the values are added up, the routine takes twenty-two bytes and each iteration of the loop consumes one hundred and eighty clock cycles, fifteen more than the previous implementation, although we have saved six bytes. In addition, the ROM routine takes less time than positioning using the **AT** control code.

What do we do now? How do we leave it?

Since the routine that paints the border is not critical, as we only paint it at the beginning of each level, and four clock cycles will not be noticed, we decided to keep the six-byte saving and stick with the new implementation.

We just need to paint the ship, we go to main.asm and just below **CALL PrintInfoGame** we add the call to paint the ship.

```
call PrintShip
```

We compile, load the emulator and see the results.

We move the ship

The ship must move in response to some action by the player, in our case by pressing three keys: Z to move the ship left, X to move the ship right and V to shoot.

We create the ctrl.asm file and implement the routine that reads the keyboard and returns the control keys pressed.

The routine we are going to implement returns the pressed keys in register D, similar to what was done in ZX-Pong; it sets bit zero to one if the Z key was pressed, bit one if the X key was pressed and bit two if the V key was pressed.

```
CheckCtrl:
ld    d, $00
ld    a, $fe
in    a, ($fe)
```

We set D to zero, **LD D, $00**, load the Cs-V half-stack into A, **LD A, $FE**, and read the keyboard, **IN A, ($FE)**.

```
checkCtrl_fire:
bit   $04, a
jr    nz, checkCtrl_left
set   $02, d
```

We check if the V key has been pressed, **BIT $04, A**. If it has not, we move on to check if the X key has been pressed, **JR NZ, checkCtrl_left**. If it was pressed, we set bit two of register D to one to indicate that the trigger was pressed, **SET $02, D**.

When we read from the keyboard, the status of the keys of the half stack read is in register A, with one for the keys that have not been pressed and zero for the keys that have been pressed (bit zero refers to the key furthest from the centre of the keyboard and four to the nearest).

The **BIT** instruction evaluates the status of the specified bit, $04, of the specified register, A, and, depending on whether it is set to zero or one, activates or deactivates the Z flag. The **SET** instruction sets the specified bit, $02, of the specified register, D, to one. The **RES** instruction is the opposite of **SET**, it sets the bit to zero. **RES** and **SET** do not affect the F register.

```
checkCtrl_left:
```

```
bit    $01, a
jr     nz, checkCtrl_right
set    $00, d
```

We check if the Z key has been pressed, **BIT $01, A**. If it has not, we move on to check if the X key has been pressed, **JR NZ, checkCtrl_right**. If it was pressed, we set the zero bit of the D register to one to indicate that the left key was pressed, **SET $00, D**.

```
checkCtrl_right:
bit    $02, a
ret    nz
set    $01, d
```

We check if the X key has been pressed, **BIT $02**, A. If it has not been pressed, we exit, **RET NZ**. If it was pressed, we set bit one of register D to one to indicate that it was pressed correctly, **SET $01, D**.

```
checkCtrl_testLR:
ld     a, d
and    $03
sub    $03
ret    nz
ld     a, d
and    $04
ld     d, a

checkCtrl_end:
ret
```

Finally, we check if left and right are pressed at the same time, in which case we disable both.

We load A with the value of D, **LD A, D**, we leave the value of the bits zero and one, **AND $03**, and we subtract three, **SUB $03**. If the result is not zero, we exit, **RET NZ**, because the two bits weren't set to one and we don't have to do anything.

If we have not exited, we load the value of D back into A, **LD A, D**, keeping only the value of bit two (trigger), **AND $04**, and load the value into D, **LD D, A**, thus disabling the simultaneous left and right keystrokes. Finally we exit, **RET**.

The last tag, **checkCtrl_end**, is not necessary, although we include it to make it clear where the routine ends.

The final aspect of the routine is as follows:

```
; --------------------------------------------------------------
; Evaluates whether any of the arrow keys have been pressed.
; The arrow keys are:
;               Z -> Left
;               X -> Right
;               V -> Shot
;
; Return: D -> Keys pressed.
;               Bit 0 -> Left
;               Bit 1 -> Right
;               Bit 2 -> Shot
;
```

```
;
; Alters the value of the registers A and D
; --------------------------------------------------------------
CheckCtrl:
ld   d, $00              ; D = 0
ld   a, $fe              ; A = half-stack Cs-V
in   a, ($fe)            ; Read keyboard

checkCtrl_fire:
bit  $04, a              ; V pressed?
jr   nz, checkCtrl_left  ; Not pressed, skip
set  $02, d              ; Set bit 2 of D

checkCtrl_left:
bit  $01, a              ; Z pressed?
jr   nz, checkCtrl_right ; Not pressed, skip
set  $00, d              ; Set bit 0 of D

checkCtrl_right:
bit  $02, a              ; X pressed?
ret  nz                  ; Not pressed, exits
set  $01, d              ; Set bit 1 of D

checkCtrl_testLR:
ld   a, d                ; A = D
and  $03                 ; Keeps bits 0 and 1
sub  $03                 ; Active both bits?
ret  nz                  ; Both not active (!=0), outputs
ld   a, d                ; A = D
and  $04                 ; Keeps bit 2
ld   d, a                ; D = A

checkCtrl_end:
ret
```

We open main.asm and in each iteration of the **Main_loop** we will call the routine we have just implemented. Just below the **Main_loop** tag, we add the following line:

```
call CheckCtrl
```

Below, in the part where we have the includes, we add the include for the ctrl.asm file.

```
include "ctrl.asm"
```

We compile and check that it compiles well; there are no errors.

When the ship is moved, we first erase it from the current position and repaint it at the new position.

In const.asm, we add the following constant to the constants we defined for the ship:

```
; Character code of the blank character
WHITE_GRAPH:    EQU $9e
```

We open print.asm and at the top we implement the routine that deletes the ship. As this routine will also be used to delete the enemies and the shot, it will be given the coordinates of the character we want to delete in BC.

```
DeleteChar:
call At
```

As DeleteChar receives the coordinates of the character to be deleted in BC, the first step is to position the cursor, **CALL At**.

```
ld   a, WHITE_GRAPH
rst  $10

ret
```

We load the character in bank A, **LD A, WHITE_GRAPH**, and paint it, **RST $10**, erasing the painted character at these coordinates.

The final aspect of the routine is as follows:

```
; --------------------------------------------------------------------
; Deletes a character from the display
;
; Input: BC -> Y/X coordinates of the character
; Alters the value of the AF registers
; --------------------------------------------------------------------
DeleteChar:
call At                       ; Position cursor

ld   a, WHITE_GRAPH           ; A = white character
rst  $10                      ; Paints it and erases the ship

ret
```

Open main.asm and add the following lines just below **CALL CheckCtrl** to see if it works:

```
ld   bc, (shipPos)
call DeleteChar
call PrintShip
```

With these lines we erase and paint the ship in each iteration of **Main_loop**. If we compile and load in the emulator, we will see that the ship is blinking constantly, a sign that the erasing is working.

Let's move the ship. We create a new file, game.asm, and implement the routine that changes the position of the ship and paints it. The routine gets the state of the controls in the D register (first we add the include from game.asm to main.asm).

```
MoveShip:
ld   bc, (shipPos)
bit  $01, d
jr   nz, moveShip_right
```

We load the ship's position into BC, **LD BC, (shipPos)**, check if the right-hand control is pressed, **BIT $01, D**, and if so we jump to the part that controls the right movement, **JR NZ, moveShip_right**.

```
bit  $00, d
ret  z
```

We check that the left-hand control has been pressed, **BIT $00, D**, and if it has not, we quit, **RET Z**.

```
moveShip_left:
ld    a, SHIP_TOP_L + $01
sub   c
ret   z
call DeleteChar
inc   c
ld    (shipPos), bc
jr    moveShip_print
```

If the left-hand control was pressed, we check if we can move the ship. We load into A the stop at which the ship can move to the left, **LD A, SHIP_TOP_L + $01**, and subtract the current column from the ship's position, **SUB C**. If the result is zero, the ship is already at the stop and cannot move to the right, so we exit, **RET Z**.

If we don't exit, we delete the ship, **CALL DeleteChar**, point C to the column just to the left, **INC C**, update the new position of the ship in memory, **LD (shipPos), BC**, and jump to the end of the routine, **JR moveShip_print**.

The routine that controls the movement of the ship to the right is almost the same as the one that controls the movement to the left, so we will only highlight and explain the changes.

```
moveShip_right:
ld    a, SHIP_TOP_R + $01
sub   c
ret   z
call DeleteChar
dec   c
ld    (shipPos), bc

moveShip_print:
call PrintShip

ret
```

In A we load the stop to which the ship can move to the right, **LD A, SHIP_TOP_R + 01**. In C we load the column to the right of the current position, **DEC C**. Finally, we paint the ship, **CALL PrintShip**.

The final aspect of the routine is as follows:

```
; ----------------------------------------------------------------
; Move the ship
;
; Input: D -> Controls status
; Alters the value of the AF and BC registers.
; ----------------------------------------------------------------
MoveShip:
ld    bc, (shipPos)        ; BC = ship position
bit   $01, d               ; Go right?
jr    nz, moveShip_right   ; If it goes right, jump

bit   $00, d               ; Go left?
ret   z                    ; Does not go left, exits
```

```
moveShip_left:
ld    a, SHIP_TOP_L + $01    ; A = stop for left-hand ship
sub   c                      ; A = A - C (column ship)
ret   z                      ; A = C? Yes, it comes out
call DeleteChar              ; Delete ship
inc   c                      ; C = left column of current
ld    (shipPos), bc          ; Update ship position
jr    moveShip_print         ; Jump to the end of the routine

moveShip_right:
ld    a, SHIP_TOP_R + $01    ; A = stop for right-hand ship
sub   c                      ; A = A - C (column ship)
ret   z                      ; A = C? Yes, it comes out
call DeleteChar              ; Delete ship
dec   c                      ; C = right column of current
ld    (shipPos), bc          ; Update ship position

moveShip_print:
call PrintShip               ; Paints ship

ret
```

Before continuing, remember that I commented earlier that At changed the value of the BC and AF registers, but did not affect us. Now that At is called from multiple locations, the change to BC does affect us. The solution is as simple as adding **PUSH BC** and **POP BC** to At to preserve and restore the value of BC.

However, we will do another implementation that saves bytes and clock cycles.

```
; -----------------------------------------------------------------
; Position the cursor at the specified coordinates.
;
; Input: B = Y-coordinate (24 to 3).
;        C = X-coordinate (32 to 1).
; Alters the value of the AF register
; -----------------------------------------------------------------
At:
push bc                      ; We preserve the value of BC
exx                          ; We preserve the value of BC, DE and HL
pop  bc                      ; Retrieve the value of BC
call $0a23                   ; Call the ROM routine
exx                          ; Retrieve the value of BC, DE and HL

ret
```

We keep the value of BC where the coordinates are, **PUSH BC**, keep the value of BC, DE and HL by swapping them with the alternative registers, **EXX**, retrieve BC (coordinates), **POP BC**, and call the ROM routine that positions the cursor, **CALL $0A23**.

At this point the values of BC, DE and HL have changed, we retrieve them from the alternate registers, **EXX**, and exit, **RET**.

The routine now occupies eight bytes and takes fifty-six clock cycles to execute, compared to ten bytes and ninety clock cycles if we use the stack for the three registers.

It's time to see if the ship is moving. We go back to main.asm and replace the lines we added earlier:

```
ld   bc, (shipPos)
call DeleteShip
call PrintShip
```

by:

```
call MoveShip
```

We compile, load the emulator and see the results.

The ship already moves left and right, but we have the same problem we had in ZX-Pong, it moves very fast, faster than the ZX-Pong paddles, because they moved pixel by pixel and the ship moves character by character.

We could solve it in the same way as we did then, by not moving the ship in each iteration of the loop, but since we are going to use the interrupts for other things, we are going to do it through them, and so we see something we didn't see in ZX-Pong.

Download the source code from here

https://tinyurl.com/274m83we

Step 5: Interruptions and shot

In this chapter we are going to implement interrupts; if you want to know more about them, read the chapter dedicated to them in the Compiler Software course, and how to implement them in 16K.

The ZX Spectrum generates a total of fifty interrupts per second on PAL systems, sixty on NTSC systems.

Create the folder Step05 and copy the files const.asm, ctrl.asm, game.asm, graph.asm, main.asm, print.asm and var.asm from the folder Step04.

Before we continue, let's look at the size of the program, which is about 1600 bytes.

Interruptions

The routine that is executed when an interrupt is generated is implemented in the int.asm file, so we create it.

Following the Compiler Software course, we will load $28 (40) into register I and our routine at address $7e5c (32348), giving us four hundred and nineteen bytes for the routine. Since the program loads at $5dad (23981), we have eight thousand three hundred and sixty-seven bytes for our game.

We open main.asm and before **Main_loop** we add the lines that prepare the interrupts.

```
di
ld    a, $28
ld    i, a
im    2
ei
```

We disable interrupts, **DI**, load $28 (40) into register A, **LD A, $28**, and load I, **LD I, A**. We change the interrupt mode to mode two, **IM 2**, and enable interrupts, **EI**.

We are going to implement the routine in the int.asm file, so open it and add the following lines:

```
org   $7e5c

Isr:
push hl
push de
push bc
push af
```

We load the **Isr** routine at address $7E5C (32348), **ORG $7E5C** and preserve HL, DE, BC and AF, **PUSH HL**, **PUSH DE**, **PUSH BC**, **PUSH AF**.

We do nothing more for the moment and leave.

```
Isr_end:
```

```
pop   af
pop   bc
pop   de
pop   hl
ei
reti
```

Get AF, BC, DE and HL, **POP AF**, **POP BC**, **POP DE**, **POP HL**, enable interrupts, **EI**, and exit, **RETI**.

Now we go to main.asm and just before **END Main** we include the file int.asm.

Compile, load into the emulator and test. Nothing seems to happen, but look at how much space our program now occupies. It takes up a whopping nine thousand bytes. Because we've loaded the routine at address $7E5C, PASMO fills all the space from where the program ended before to where it ends now with zeros, that's why it takes up so much space. Normally this doesn't matter when loading on an emulator, we can load it immediately, but on a ZX Spectrum we are adding unnecessary loading time.

We compile into multiple files

To prevent our program from growing like this, we will compile the int.asm file separately from the rest. We will also dispense with the loader generated by PASMO and make our own.

Creation of the loader

From the emulator we will generate a BASIC loader and save it as loader.tap. The code of the loader looks like this:

```
10 CLEAR 23980
20 LOAD ""CODE
30 LOAD ""CODE 32348
40 RANDOMIZE USR 23981
```

We save our loader with the following instruction:

```
SAVE "SPACEWAR" LINE 10
```

When the program is loaded, line ten is auto-executed.

Compilation in several files

We will compile the int.asm file separately, which will generate the int.tap file, and the rest of the program will generate martian.tap. Then we will concatenate the loader.tap, martian.tap and int.tap files into SpaceBattle.tap.

Since it is tedious to do this every time we want to compile and see the results, we will create a script. For those of you using Windows, create the file make.bat in the Paso05 folder, for those of you using Linux, run it from the command line:

```
touch make
```

Then grant permissions to run.

```
chmod +x make
```

Before we continue, open the main.asm file and delete the include of the int.asm file near the end.

We can now edit make or make.bat. On Windows and Linux, the first two lines are the same.

```
pasmo --name Martian --tap main.asm martian.tap martian.log
pasmo --name Int --tap int.asm int.tap int.log
```

First we compile the programme, then we compile the Int.asm file and generate the int.tap file. Note that instead of --tapbas we put --tap because we did the BASIC loader by hand.

Finally, we combine loader.tap, martian.tap and int.tap into SpaceBattle.tap.

For Linux users, add this line to the end of your make file:

```
cat loader.tap martian.tap int.tap > SpaceBattle.tap
```

For those of you using Windows, the line is as follows:

```
copy /b loader.tap+martian.tap+int.tap SpaceBattle.tap
```

From here, the way to compile will be to run make or make.bat, and in the emulator we will load the file SpaceBattle.tap.

We compile, load in the emulator and see that everything is the same, but the size of SpaceBattle.tap is less than two thousand bytes.

We slow down the ship

We saw in the previous chapter that the ship was moving too fast. To solve this, we will use the interrupts to move the ship a maximum of fifty times per second (on PAL systems, sixty on NTSC), i.e. we will move the ship when the interruption is triggered.

We open var.asm and add the following at the top:

```
; ----------------------------------------------------------------
; Indicators
;
; Bit 0 -> ship must be moved 0 = No, 1 = Yes
; ----------------------------------------------------------------
flags:
db $00
```

In int.asm, add the following lines after **PUSH AF:**

```
ld   hl, flags
set  00, (hl)
```

We load the flags memory address into HL, **LD HL, flags**, and set the zero bit to one, **SET $00, (HL)**.

Now go to the game.asm file and add the following lines just below the **MoveShip** tag:

```
ld   hl, flags        ; HL = address flags
bit  $00, (hl)        ; Check bit 0
ret  z                ; Bit 0 = 0? Yes, it comes out
res  $00, (hl)        ; Bit 0 = 0
```

We load the flags memory address into HL, **LD HL, flags**, we check if we need to move the ship, **BIT $00, (HL)**, and if not we exit, **RET Z**. If we do need to move the ship we set the bit to zero, **SET $00, (HL)**, this way we will not move the ship again until an interrupt occurs and we set the zero bit of flags back to one.

This will make our ship move fifty times per second (or sixty, depending on the system). We compile and...

Actually, we have a compilation error.

ERROR on line N of file Int.asm

ERROR: Symbol 'flags' is not defined

So far we have included all the .asm files we have in main.asm, but we have removed the **include** from int.asm to compile it separately, so the flags tag is not known in int.asm. The solution is simple, in int.asm we need to replace **LD HL, flags** with **LD HL, memoryaddress**.

Let's have a look at the line we used to compile.

```
pasmo --name Martian --tap main.asm martian.tap martian.log
```

The last parameter, **martian.log**, creates a file of that name in which we can see what memory address the tags are at. In this case, **flags** is at memory address $5EB5, so just go to int.asm and replace **LD HL, flags** with **LD HL, $5EB5**.

Now yes, we compile, load in the emulator and see that the ship moves slower, but we still have a problem; put a **NOP** at the beginning of main.asm, just before the **Main** tag.

Compile and you will see that it works fine. Load it into the emulator and it stopped working. If you go to martian.log, you will see that the flags tag is at address $5EB6, but in the int.asm file the value loaded in HL is $5EB5. Every time we change some code, it is very likely that the **flags** address will change, so we need to make sure that we change it in int.asm as well.

To prevent the **flags** address from changing, we open var.asm, cut the **flags** declaration and paste it at the top of main.asm, below **ORG $5DAD**. This ensures that **flags** is always located at $5DAD. Don't forget to replace $5EB5 with $5DAD in int.asm.

We compile, load it into the emulator and everything works, but this is because we initialised **flags** to zero, which is equivalent to **NOP**, which takes four clock cycles to execute, nothing more. If we had started it with a different value, say $C9, it would return to BASIC on execution because $C9 is **RET**. Try it and see.

This has an easy solution, before the **flags** tag we add **JR Main**, but as we only need the **flags** tag and it is zero, there is no problem, but be careful with this.

It is not necessary to add **JR Main**, but if you do, note that the **flags** address changes.

We implement the shot

As with the ship, we include the constants needed for the shot in const.asm.

```
; Shot character code and top
FIRE_GRAPH: EQU $91
FIRE_TOP_T: EQU COR_Y
```

Also in var.asm we add the tag to store the shot position.

```
; ------------------------------------------------------------------
; Shot
; ------------------------------------------------------------------
firePos:
dw $0000
```

In print.asm we will implement the routine that paints the shot.

```
PrintFire:
ld   a, $02
call Ink
```

We load red ink in A, **LD A, $02**, and call change, **CALL Ink**.

```
ld   bc, (firePos)
call At
```

We load into BC the position of the shot, **LD BC, (firePos)**, and call to position the cursor, **CALL At**.

```
ld   a, FIRE_GRAPH
rst  $10

ret
```

We load the shot character in A, **LD A, FIRE_GRAPH**, paints it, **RST $10**, and exit, **RET**.

The final aspect of the routine is as follows:

```
; -----------------------------------------------------------------
; Paints the shot at the current position.
; Alters the value of the AF and BC registers.
; -----------------------------------------------------------------
PrintFire:
ld   a, $02              ; A = red ink
call Ink                 ; Change ink

ld   bc, (firePos)       ; BC = shot position
call At                  ; Position cursor

ld   a, FIRE_GRAPH       ; A = shot character
rst  $10                 ; Paints it

ret
```

We implement the routine that moves the shot in game.asm.

```
MoveFire:
ld   hl, flags
bit  $01, (hl)
jr   nz, moveFire_try
bit  $02, d
ret  z
set  $01, (hl)
ld   bc, (shipPos)
inc  h
jr   moveFire_print
```

We load the flag address into HL, **LD HL, flags**, then check if bit one (shot) is set, **BIT $01, (HL)**, and if so we jump, **JR NZ, moveFire_try**. If bit one is not set, we check if the trigger control has been pressed, **BIT $02, D**, and if not we exit, **RET Z**. If it has, we set the trigger bit in flags, **SET $01, (HL)**, load the ship position in BC, **LD BC, (shipPos)**, point it to the top line, **INC B**, and jump to paints it, **JR moveFire_print**.

```
moveFire_try:
ld   bc, (firePos)
call DeleteChar
inc  b
ld   a, FIRE_TOP_T
sub  b
jr   nz, moveFire_print
res  $01, (hl)

ret
```

If the fire was active, we load its position in BC, **LD BC, (firePos)**, delete the fire, **CALL DeleteChar**, point B to the top line, **INC B**, load the top stop of the fire in A, **LD A, FIRE_TOP_T**, and subtract B, **SUB B**. If the result is not zero, the top stop has not been reached and we jump, **JR NZ, moveFire_print**. If we have reached the top, we deactivate the shot, **RES $01, (HL)**, and exit, **RET**.

```
moveFire_print:
ld   (firePos), bc
call PrintFire
```

```
ret
```

    If we have not reached the top or have just activated the shot, we update the position of the shot, **LD (firePos), BC**, paint it, **CALL PrintFire**, and exit, **RET**.

    The final aspect of the routine is as follows:

```
; --------------------------------------------------------------
; Move the shot
;
; Input: D -> Controls status
; Alters the value of the AF, BC and HL registers.
; --------------------------------------------------------------
MoveFire:
ld    hl, flags          ; HL = address flags
bit   $01, (hl)          ; Active fire?
jr    nz, moveFire_try   ; If active, jumps
bit   $02, d             ; Trigger control active?
ret   z                  ; If not active, exits
set   $01, (hl)          ; Enables trigger bit in flags
ld    bc, (shipPos)      ; BC = ship position
inc   b                  ; B = top line
jr    moveFire_print     ; Paint shot

moveFire_try:
ld    bc, (firePos)      ; BC = shot position
call  DeleteChar         ; Delete shot
inc   b                  ; B = top line
ld    a, FIRE_TOP_T      ; A = upper shot top
sub   b                  ; A = A - B (Y-coordinate shot)
jr    nz, moveFire_print ; A!= B, does not reach top, jumps
res   $01, (hl)          ; Deactivates shot

ret

moveFire_print:
ld    (firePos), bc      ; Update shot position
call  PrintFire          ; Paint shot

ret
```

    It's time to test the shot, so we open main.asm and at the beginning, in the **flags** declaration, we add the comment for bit one.

```
; Bit 1 -> shot is active 0 = No, 1 = Yes
```

    We locate **Main_loop**, and between the lines **CALL CheckCtrl** and **CALL MoveShip** we add the call to the shot movement.

```
call MoveFire
```

We compile, load the emulator and see the results.

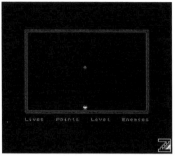

You can't see it in the picture, but in the emulator you can see that it looks like it's firing in bursts, and if you leave it pressed it looks like it doesn't stop firing. This is an optical effect caused by the camera moving faster than the ULA refreshes the screen. We leave it like that to make it look like we are shooting several times at once.

We started working with interrupts, timed the ship's movement and implemented triggering, as well as compiling the program into several files and customising the loader.

Download the source code from here

https://tinyurl.com/26amt7yf

Step 6: Enemies

In this chapter we will add the enemies. We create the folder Step06, copy from Step05 loader.tap, const.asm, ctrl.asm, game.asm, graph.asm, int.asm, main.asm, print.asm, var.asm and make or make.bat.

We define enemies

Enemies are moving objects, and as such we need to know their current and starting positions. In total we will have a maximum of twenty enemies on the screen, and we will use two bytes to specify the current position of the enemy and some other settings we need.

Open var.asm and add the enemy configuration after the frame definition.

```
; -----------------------------------------------------------------
; Enemy configuration
;
; 2 bytes per enemy.
; -----------------------------------------------------------------
; Byte 1                | Byte 2
; -----------------------------------------------------------------
; Bit 0-4: Y position   | Bit 0-4: Position X
; Bit 5:   Free         | Bit 5:   Free
; Bit 6:   Free         | Bit 6:   Direction X 0 = Left 1 = Right
; Bit 7:   Active 0/1   | Bit 7:   Direction Y 0 = Up   1 = Down
; -----------------------------------------------------------------
enemiesConfig:
db $96, $dd, $96, $d7, $96, $d1, $96, $cb, $96, $c5
db $93, $9d, $93, $97, $93, $91, $93, $8b, $93, $85
db $90, $dd, $90, $d7, $90, $d1, $90, $cb, $90, $c5
db $8d, $9d, $8d, $97, $8d, $91, $8d, $8b, $8d, $85
enemiesConfigIni:
db $96, $dd, $96, $d7, $96, $d1, $96, $cb, $96, $c5
db $93, $9d, $93, $97, $93, $91, $93, $8b, $93, $85
db $90, $dd, $90, $d7, $90, $d1, $90, $cb, $90, $c5
db $8d, $9d, $8d, $97, $8d, $91, $8d, $8b, $8d, $85
enemiesConfigEnd:
```

In the first byte we have the Y coordinate, bits zero to four, and whether the enemy is active or not, bit seven. In the second byte we have the X coordinate, bits zero to four, the horizontal direction, bit six, and the vertical direction, bit seven.

Bits six and seven of the second byte contain the direction of the enemy:

- 00b $00 Left / Top
- 01b $01 Left / Bottom
- 10b $02 Right / Top
- 11b $03 Right / Down

We add the definition of the enemy graphics before **enemiesConfig**.

```
; -----------------------------------------------------------------
```

```
; Enemy graphics
;
; 00 Up-Left
; 01 Up-Right
; 10 Down-Left
; 11 Down-Right
; ------------------------------------------------------------
enemiesGraph:
db $9f, $a0, $a1, $a2
```

If we look at the UDGs of the enemies, everything fits.

Going back to the enemy definition, we have twenty enemies in total, divided into four rows and five enemies per row.

The definition of the enemies from left to right and from top to bottom, remembering that we are working with inverted coordinates, is as follows:

Hexadecimal	Binary	Definition
$96, $dd	10010110, 11011101	Active Line 22 Down/Right Column 29
$96, $d7	10010110, 11010111	Active Line 22 Down/Right Column 23
$96, $d1	10010110, 11010001	Active Line 22 Line/Right Column 17
$96, $cb	10010110, 11001011	Active Line 22 Down/Right Column 11
$96, $c5	10010110, 11000101	Active Line 22 Down/Right Column 5

$93, $9d	10010011, 10011101	Active Line 19 Down/Left Column 29
$93, $97	10010011, 10010111	Active Line 19 Down/Left Column 23
$93, $91	10010011, 10010001	Active Line 19 Down/Left Column 17
$93, $8b	10010011, 10001011	Active Line 19 Down/Left Column 11
$93, $85	10010011, 10000101	Active Line 19 Down/Left Column 5
90, $dd	10010000, 11011101	Active Line 16 Down/Right Column 29
$90, $d7	10010000, 11010111	Active Line 16 Down/Right Column 23
$90, $d1	10010000, 11010001	Active Line 16 Down/Right Column 17

90, $cb	10010000, 11001011	Active Line 16 Down/Right Column 11
$90, $c5	10010000, 11000101	Active Line 16 Down/Right Column 5
$8d, $9d	10001101, 10011101	Active Line 13 Down/Left Column 29
$8d, $97	10001101, 10010111	Active Line 13 Down/Left Column 23
$8d, $91	10001101, 10010001	Active Line 13 Down/Left Column 17
$8d, $8b	10001101, 10001011	Active Line 13 Down/Left Column 11
$8d, $85	10001101, 10000101	Active Line 13 Down/Left Column 5

Once the graphics and their configuration have been defined, we go on to paint them.

We paint the enemies

The routine that paints the enemies is in print.asm.

```
PrintEnemies:
ld   a, $06
call Ink

ld   hl, enemiesConfig
ld   d, $14
```

We load the yellow ink in A, **LD A, $06**, change the ink, **CALL Ink**, load the address of the enemy configuration in HL, **LD HL, enemiesConfig**, and the number of enemies in D, **LD D, $14**.

```
printEnemies_loop:
bit  $07, (hl)
jr   z, printEnemies_endLoop
```

Check if the enemy is active, **BIT $07, (HL)**, if not jump, **JR Z, printEnemies_endLoop**.

```
push hl

ld   a, (hl)
and  $1f
ld   b, a
```

We keep the value of HL, **PUSH HL**, load the first byte of the enemy configuration into A, **LD A, (HL)**, keep the Y coordinate, **AND $1F**, and load it into B, **LD B, A**.

```
inc  hl
ld   a, (hl)
and  $1f
ld   c, a
call At
```

We point HL to the second byte of the enemy configuration, **INC HL**, load the value into A, **LD A, (HL)**, leave the X coordinate, **AND $1F**, load it into C, **LD C, A**, and position the cursor, **CALL At**.

```
ld   a, (hl)
and  $c0
rlca
rlca
ld   c, a
ld   b, $00
```

We load the second byte of the enemy configuration into A, **LD A, (HL)**, leave the address bits, **AND $c0**, pass the value to bits zero and one, **RLCA, RLCA**, load it into C, **LD C, A**, and set B to zero, **LD B, $00**.

```
ld   hl, enemiesGraph
add  hl, bc
ld   a, (hl)
rst  $10
```

We load in HL the direction in which we define the enemy figures, **LD HL, enemiesGraph**, we add the direction of the enemy (left, up, etc.), **ADD HL, BC**, we load in A the enemy figure to be painted, **LD A, (HL)**, and we paint it, **RST $10**.

```
pop   hl

printEnemies_endLoop:
inc   hl
inc   hl

dec   d
jr    nz, printEnemies_loop

ret
```

We take the value of HL, **POP HL**, point it to the first byte of the configuration of the next enemy, **INC HL**, **INC HL**, subtract one from D, **DEC D**, and continue until D is zero and we have traversed all the enemies. Finally we exit, **RET**.

The final aspect of the routine is as follows:

```
; ------------------------------------------------------------------
; Paint the enemies
;
; Alters the value of the AF, BC, D and HL registers.
; ------------------------------------------------------------------
PrintEnemies:
ld    a, $06              ; A = yellow ink
call Ink                  ; Change ink

ld    hl, enemiesConfig   ; HL = enemy configuration
ld    d, $14              ; D = 20 enemies

printEnemies_loop:
bit   $07, (hl)           ; Active enemy?
jr    z, printEnemies_endLoop ; If not active, skip

push hl                   ; Preserves HL
ld    a, (hl)             ; A = 1st byte value
and   $1f                 ; A = Y coordinate
ld    b, a                ; B = A

inc   hl                  ; HL = 2nd byte config
ld    a, (hl)             ; A = 2nd byte value
and   $1f                 ; A = X coordinate
ld    c, a                ; C = A
call At                   ; Position cursor

ld    a, (hl)             ; A = 2nd byte value
and   $c0                 ; A = direction (left...)
rlca                      ; Sets value in bits 0 and 1
rlca
ld    c, a                ; Load the value in C
ld    b, $00              ; Sets B to zero

ld    hl, enemiesGraph    ; HL = enemy graph
add   hl, bc              ; Add direction (left...)
ld    a, (hl)             ; A = enemy graph
rst   $10                 ; Paints it
pop   hl                  ; Retrieve HL

printEnemies_endLoop:
```

```
inc  hl                        ; HL = 1st byte configuration
inc  hl                        ; next enemy

dec  d                         ; D = D - 1
jr   nz, printEnemies_loop     ; Loop as long as D != 0

ret
```

To test if this works, we add the following lines to main.asm, just before Main_loop:

```
ld   a, $01
call LoadUdgsEnemies
call PrintEnemies
```

We load level one into A, **LD A, $01**, load the level's enemy graphics into udgsExtension, **CALL LoadUdgsEnemies**, and print them, **CALL PrintEnemies**.

We compile, load into the emulator and see the results.

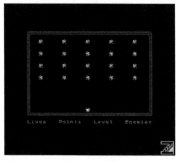

We move the enemies

The enemies are not moved every iteration of the loop, as we do with the trigger, but every N interrupts. So we add another comment in the flag tag, at the top of main.asm.

```
; Bit 2 -> enemies must be moved 0 = No, 1 = Yes
```

The next thing to do is to set the boundaries of the screen as far as the enemies can go. We set them in const.asm.

```
; Enemies' boundaries
ENEMY_TOP_T: EQU COR_Y - MIN_Y
ENEMY_TOP_B: EQU COR_Y - MAX_Y + $01
ENEMY_TOP_L: EQU COR_X - MIN_X
ENEMY_TOP_R: EQU COR_X - MAX_X
```

The boundaries we have set are top, bottom, left and right.

For the enemies to move every N interrupts, and as in **flags** we will use a bit to indicate whether they should move or not, in the int.asm file we will activate this bit. We add the following line under **SET $00, (HL)**:

```
set  02, (hl)
```

We are now ready to implement the routine that moves the enemies in game.asm.

```
MoveEnemies:
ld   hl, flags
bit  $02, (hl)
ret  z
res  2, (hl)
```

We load the address of the flags into HL, **LD HL, flags**. We must check if the enemy movement bit is set, **BIT $02, (HL)**, and if it is not, we exit, **RET Z**. If it is set, we disable it so that it does not happen in the next iteration of Main_loop, **RES $02, (HL)**.

```
ld   d, $14
ld   hl, enemiesConfig

moveEnemies_loop:
bit  $07, (hl)
jr   z, moveEnemies_ endLoop
```

We load the number of enemies in D, **LD D, $14**, the address of the configuration in HL, **LD HL, enemiesConfig**, see if the enemy is active, **BIT $07, (HL)**. If the enemy is not active, we jump to the next one, **JR Z, moveEnemies_loopEnd**.

```
push hl

ld   a, (hl)
and  $1f
ld   b, a

inc  hl
ld   a, (hl)
and  $1f
ld   c, a

call DeleteChar

pop  hl
```

We keep the value of HL, **PUSH HL**, load the first byte of the enemy configuration into A, **LD A, (HL)**, keep the Y-coordinate, **AND $1F**, and load it into B, **LD B, A**.

We point HL to the second byte of the enemy configuration, **INC HL**, load the value into A, **LD A, (HL)**, keep the X-coordinate, **AND $1F**, and load it into C, **LD C, A**.

Delete the enemy, **CALL DeleteChar**, restore HL, **POP HL**.

```
ld   b, (hl)
inc  hl
ld   c, (hl)
```

We load the first byte of the enemy configuration into B, **LD B, (HL)**, point HL to the second byte, **INC HL**, and load it into C, **LD C, (HL)**.

```
moveEnemies_X:
```

```
ld    a, c
and   $1f

bit   $06, c
jr    nz, moveEnemies_X_right
```

We load the value of the second byte of the configuration into A, **LD A, C**, and keep the X coordinate, **AND $1F**.

We check the horizontal direction bit of the enemy, **BIT $06, C**. If it is set to one, the enemy moves to the right and jumps, **JR Z, moveEnemies_X_right**. If not, the enemy moves to the left.

```
moveEnemies_X_left:
inc   a
sub   ENEMY_TOP_L
jr    z, moveEnemies_X_leftChg

inc   c
jr    moveEnemies_Y

moveEnemies_X_leftChg:
set   $06, c
jr    moveEnemies_Y
```

We increment A and so point to the column to the left of the current one, **INC A**, subtract the top left, **SUB ENEMY_TOP_L**, and if the result is zero, it has reached the top and jumps to change direction, **JR Z, moveEnemies_X_leftChg**.

If the direction is not to be changed, point C to the column to the left of the current column, **INC C**, and jump to the vertical move handle, **JR moveEnemies_Y**.

If the direction is to be changed, set bit six of C to set the horizontal direction to the right, **SET $06, C**, and jump to the vertical move handle, **JR moveEnemies_Y**.

If the enemy does not move to the left, it will move to the right.

```
moveEnemies_X_right:
dec   a
sub   ENEMY_TOP_R
jr    z, moveEnemies_X_rightChg

dec   c
jr    moveEnemies_Y

moveEnemies_X_rightChg:
res   $06, c
```

We decrement A to point to the column to the right of the current one, **DEC A**, subtract the right top, **SUB ENEMY_TOP_R**, and if the result is zero, it has reached the top and jumps to change direction, **JR Z, moveEnemies_X_rightChg**.

If the direction is not to be changed, point C to the right column, **DEC C**, and jump to vertical movement, **JR moveEnemies_Y**.

If you want to change the direction, turn off bit six of C to set the horizontal direction to the left, **RES $06**, C, and start the vertical movement.

```
moveEnemies_Y:
ld   a, b
and  $1f
bit  $07, c
jr   nz, moveEnemies_Y_down
```

We load the value of the first byte of the configuration into A, **LD A, B**, and leave the Y coordinate, **AND $1F**.

We check bit seven of C to get the vertical direction, **BIT $07, C**, and if it is one, the enemy moves down, **JR NZ, moveEnemies_Y_down**, and jumps.

If the bit is zero, the enemy moves up.

```
moveEnemies_Y_up:
inc  a
sub  ENEMY_TOP_T
jr   z, moveEnemies_Y_upChg

inc  b
jr   moveEnemies_endMove

moveEnemies_Y_upChg:
set  $07, c
jr   moveEnemies_endMove
```

We increment A to point to the line above the current line, **INC A**, subtract the top, **SUB ENEMY_TOP_T**, and if it is zero, we have reached the top and must jump, **JR Z, moveEnemies_Y_upChg**, to change direction.

If we have not reached the top, we increment B to point to the line above the current line, **INC B**, and jump to the end of the loop, **JR moveEnemies_endMove**.

If the direction is to be changed, we set bit seven of C to change the direction down, **SET $07, C**, and jump to the end of the loop, **JR moveEnemies_endMove**.

If the enemy does not move up, it moves down.

```
moveEnemies_Y_down:
dec  a
sub  ENEMY_TOP_B
jr   z, moveEnemies_Y_downChg

dec  b
jr   moveEnemies_endMove

moveEnemies_Y_downChg:
res  $07, c
```

We decrement A to point to the line below the current one, **DEC A**, subtract the top from the bottom, **SUB ENEMY_TOP_B**, and if it is zero, we have reached the top and jump because we have to change direction, **JR Z, moveEnemies_Y_downChg**.

If we have not reached the top, we decrement B to point to the line below the current line, **DEC B**, and jump to the end of the loop, **JR moveEnemies_endMove**.

If we want to change the direction, we disable bit seven of C and increment the direction, **RES $07, C**.

```
moveEnemies_endMove:
ld    (hl), c
dec   hl
ld    (hl), b

moveEnemies_endLoop:
inc   hl
inc   hl
dec   d
jr    nz, moveEnemies_loop
```

We update in memory the second byte of the configuration, **LD(HL), C**, point HL to the first byte, **DEC HL**, and update in memory, **LD(HL), B**.

We point HL to the first byte of the next enemy configuration, **INC HL, INC HL**, decrement D, **DEC D**, and continue in the loop until D is zero and we have traversed all twenty enemies, **JR Z, moveEnemies_loop**.

```
moveEnemies_end:
call PrintEnemies

ret
```

We print the enemies with the new positions, **CALL PrintEnemies**, and exit with **RET**.

We have implemented the routine that moves the enemies, whose final appearance is as follows:

```
; ----------------------------------------------------------------
; Moves enemies.
;
; Alters the value of the AF, BC, D and HL registers.
; ----------------------------------------------------------------
MoveEnemies:
ld    hl, flags           ; HL = address flags
bit   $02, (hl)           ; Bit 2 active?
ret   z                   ; Not active, exits
res   $02, (hl)           ; Disables bit 2

ld    d, $14              ; D = number of enemies (20)
ld    hl, enemiesConfig   ; HL = configuration address
moveEnemies_loop:
bit   $07, (hl)           ; Active enemy?
jr    z, moveEnemies_endLoop ; Not active, jumps

push  hl                  ; Preserves HL
ld    a, (hl)             ; A = value 1st byte config
```

```
and   $1f                  ; A = Y coordinate
ld    b, a                 ; B = A

inc   hl                   ; HL = 2nd byte config
ld    a, (hl)              ; A = value 2nd byte config
and   $1f                  ; A = X coordinate
ld    c, a                 ; C = A

call  DeleteChar           ; Deletes enemy
pop   hl                   ; Retrieve HL

ld    b, (hl)              ; B = value 1st byte config
inc   hl                   ; HL = 2nd byte config
ld    c, (hl)              ; C = 2nd byte config value

moveEnemies_X:
ld    a, c                 ; A = C
and   $1f                  ; A = X coordinate

bit   $06, c               ; Evaluates horizontal direction
jr    nz, moveEnemies_X_right ; != 0, right, jump

moveEnemies_X_left:
inc   a                    ; A = previous column
sub   ENEMY_TOP_L          ; A = A - left stop
jr    z, moveEnemies_X_leftChg ; = 0, stop has been reached, skip

inc   c                    ; C = previous column
jr    moveEnemies_Y        ; Jump to vertical movement

moveEnemies_X_leftChg:
set   $06, c               ; Horizontal dir = right
jr    moveEnemies_Y        ; Jump to vertical movement

moveEnemies_X_right:
dec   a                    ; A = back column
sub   ENEMY_TOP_R          ; A = A - right stop
jr    z, moveEnemies_X_rightChg ; = 0, has reached stop, skip

dec   c                    ; C = back column
jr    moveEnemies_Y        ; Jump to vertical movement

moveEnemies_X_rightChg:
res   $06, c               ; Horizontal dir = left

moveEnemies_Y:
ld    a, b                 ; A = first byte config
and   $1f                  ; A = Y coordinate
bit   $07, c               ; Evaluates vertical direction
jr    nz, moveEnemies_Y_down ; != 0, downwards, jump

moveEnemies_Y_up:
inc   a                    ; A = previous line
sub   ENEMY_TOP_T          ; A = A - top top
jr    z, moveEnemies_Y_upChg ; = 0, stop has been reached, skip

inc   b                    ; B = back line
jr    moveEnemies_endMove  ; Jump to end loop
```

```
moveEnemies_Y_upChg:
set  $07, c              ; Vertical dir = down
jr   moveEnemies_endMove ; Jump to end loop

moveEnemies_Y_down:
dec  a                   ; A = back line
sub  ENEMY_TOP_B         ; A = A - stop below
jr   z, moveEnemies_Y_downChg ; = 0, has arrived, jump

dec  b                   ; Aim B at the back line
jr   moveEnemies_endMove ; Jumps to the end of the loop

moveEnemies_Y_downChg:
res  $07, c              ; Vertical dir = top

moveEnemies_endMove:
ld   (hl), c             ; Update 2nd byte config
dec  hl                  ; HL = 1st byte config
ld   (hl), b             ; Update 1st byte config

moveEnemies_endLoop:
inc  hl
inc  hl                  ; HL 1st byte config
                         ; next enemy
dec  d                   ; D = D - 1
jr   nz, moveEnemies_loop ; Until D = 0 (20 enemies)

moveEnemies_end:
call PrintEnemies        ; Paint enemies

ret
```

Now it's time to see how the enemies move. Open main.asm and in the **Main_loop** tag, just below **CALL MoveShip**, add the following line:

```
call MoveEnemies
```

We compile, load in the emulator and see the results.

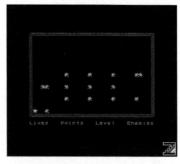

How's it going? Are the enemies moving? Yes, they're moving, but they're moving too fast and the firing has slowed down. We need to slow down the movement of the enemies, and we're going to do that from the interrupt routine, so let's go to the int.asm file.

239

We are going to do something similar to what we did in ZX-Pong, we are going to add a counter at the end of the file to control when we activate the movement of the enemies.

```
countEnemy: db $00
```

Between the lines **SET $00, (HL)** and **SET $02, (HL)** we now implement the use of this counter.

```
ld    a, (countEnemy)
inc   a
ld    (countEnemy), a
sub   $02
jr    nz, Isr_end
ld    (countEnemy), a
```

We load the value of the counter into A, **LD A, (countEnemy)**, increment A, **INC A**, and update the counter, **LD (countEnemy), A**, in memory. We subtract from A the value that the counter must reach to activate the movement, **SUB $03**, and if it has not reached it, we jump to the end of the routine, **JR NZ, Isr_end**.

If it has reached the value, we set it to zero, **LD (countEnemy), A**, and set the bit to move the enemies, **SET $02, (HL)**.

Compile and load into the emulator. We have regained the firing speed and the enemies are still moving fast.

We have all the elements of the game in motion.

Download the source code from here

https://tinyurl.com/2974uel5

Step 7: Collisions and level change

In this chapter we are going to include the collisions of the shot with the enemies, the enemies with the ship and the level changes.

We create the folder Step07 and copy from Step06: make, or make.bat if you are on Windows, loader.tap, const.asm, ctrl.asm, game.asm, graph.asm, int.asm, main.asm, print.asm and var.asm.

Enemy collisions with the shot

First we implement the collisions between the enemies and the shot. In the first byte of each enemy's configuration, bit seven, we are told whether it is active or not, so we can decide whether to paint it or not.

The routine we are going to implement checks if an enemy is in the same coordinates as the shot, and if so, deactivates it.

We implement this routine at the beginning of the file game.asm.

```
CheckCrashFire:
ld    a, (flags)
and   $02
ret   z
```

We load the value of the flags into A, **LD A, (flags)**, leave bit one to check if the shot is active, **AND $02**, and exit if it is not, **RET Z**.

```
ld    de, (firePos)
ld    hl, enemiesConfig
ld    b, enemiesConfigEnd - enemiesConfigIni
sra   b
```

We load in DE the coordinates of the shot, **LD DE, (firePos)**, in HL the configuration of the enemies, **LD HL, enemiesConfig**, in B the total number of bytes of configuration, **LD B, enemiesConfigEnd - enemiesConfigIni**, we divide it by two, **SRA B**, and in this way we obtain the number of enemies; the configuration of each one occupies two bytes.

SRA shifts all the bits to the right, sets bit zero in the carry and holds bit seven to preserve the sign. **SRA** does an integer division by two, and since the number of enemies we have is even, it works for us.

```
checkCrashFire_loop:
ld    a, (hl)
inc   hl
bit   $07, a
jr    z, checkCrashFire_endLoop
```

We load the first byte of the configuration into A, **LD A, (HL)**, point HL to the second byte, **INC HL**, check if the enemy is active, **BIT $07, A**, and jump, **JR Z, checkCrashFire_endLoop**, if not.

```
and   $1f
cp    d
jr    nz, checkCrashFire_endLoop
```

If the enemy is active, we keep the Y-coordinate, **AND $1F**, compare it with the shot, **CP D**, and jump if they are not the same, **JR NZ, checkCrashFire_endLoop**.

```
ld    a, (hl)
and   $1f
cp    e
jr    nz, checkCrashFire_endLoop
```

We load in A the second byte of the enemy configuration, **LD A, (HL)**, leave the X coordinate, **AND $1F**, compare it with the shot, **CP E**, and jump, **JR NZ, checkCrashFire_endLoop**, if they are not the same.

```
dec   hl
res   07, (hl)
ld    b, d
ld    c, e
call  DeleteChar

ret
```

If shot and enemy collide, we point HL to the first byte of the enemy configuration, **DEC HL**, disable the enemy, **RES $07, (HL)**, load the Y-coordinate of the shot into B, **LD B, D**, the X-coordinate into C, **LD C, E**, delete what is in the coordinates, **CALL DeleteChar**, and exit the routine, **RET**.

```
checkCrashFire_endLoop:
inc   hl
djnz  checkCrashFire_loop

ret
```

If fire and enemy do not collide, we point HL to the first byte of the next enemy configuration, **INC HL**, and repeat the loop until B is zero, **DJNZ checkCrashFire_loop**. At the end of the loop we exit the routine, **RET**.

The final aspect of the routine is as follows:

```
; -----------------------------------------------------------------
; Evaluates the collisions of the shot with enemies.
;
; Alters the value of the AF, BC, DE and HL registers.
; -----------------------------------------------------------------
CheckCrashFire:
ld    a, (flags)          ; A = flags
and   $02                 ; Active fire?
ret   z                   ; Not active, exits
ld    de, (firePos)       ; DE = firing position
ld    hl, enemiesConfig   ; HL = def 1st enemy
ld    b, enemiesConfigEnd-enemiesConfigIni ; B = number of config bytes
sra   b                   ; B = B / 2, number of enemies

checkCrashFire_loop:
ld    a, (hl)             ; A coord Y enemy
inc   hl                  ; HL = enemy coord X
bit   $07, a              ; Active enemy?
```

```
jr    z, checkCrashFire_endLoop ; Not active, skips
and   $1f                      ; A = coord Y enemy
cp    d                        ; Compare coord Y disp
jr    nz, checkCrashFire_endLoop ; Distinct, jumps
ld    a, (hl)                  ; A = enemy X coord
and   $1f                      ; A = coord X
cp    e                        ; Compare coord X disp
jr    nz, checkCrashFire_endLoop ; Distinct, jumps

dec   hl                       ; HL = coord Y enemy
res   $07, (hl)                ; Deactivates enemy
ld    b, d                     ; B = coord Y shot
ld    c, e                     ; C = coord X
call  DeleteChar               ; Delete trigger/enemy

ret                            ; Exits
checkCrashFire_endLoop:
inc   hl                       ; HL = coord Y next
djnz  checkCrashFire_loop      ; Loop as long as B > 0

ret
```

We test if the collisions work. We open main.asm, go to the **Main_loop** tag, and under **CALL MoveFire** we preserve the value of DE (it has the controls' keystrokes), **PUSH DE**. We include the call to the previous routine, **CALL CheckCrashFire**, and we restore the value of DE, **POP DE**, which looks like this:

```
Main_loop:
call CheckCtrl
call MoveFire
push de
call CheckCrashFire
pop  de
call MoveShip
call MoveEnemies
jr   Main_loop
```

We compile, load into the emulator and test. We see that we have two problems, one of which is inherited:

- If we don't move the ship, it will be erased and not painted again.
- Once there are no more ships, all we can do is reload the game.

The first problem will not be addressed. If the ship is destroyed after colliding with an enemy, we will include the explosion later.

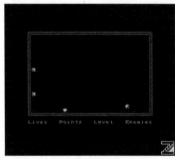

Level change

For the level change, the first thing we have to control is the number of active enemies, when we reach zero we have to change the level. The second thing is the number of levels there are, thirty in total. For now, when we reach level thirty-one, we go back to level one. Later the game will end.

We open var.asm and add a variable for the number of active enemies and another for the current level, at the beginning, after the game information title.

```
; --------------------------------------------------------------
; Information about the game
; --------------------------------------------------------------
enemiesCounter:
db $14
levelCounter:
db $01
```

Before implementing the level-changing routine, we made some changes to use levelCounter. We open the graph.asm file and locate the **LoadUdgsEnemies** routine. This routine receives the level in A, which is no longer necessary as it takes this value from **levelCounter**. We add the following line to the top of the routine:

```
ld    a, (levelCounter)
```

In A, we load the current level, LD A, (levelCounter).

In the comments of the routine, we delete the line referring to the entry in A of the level, leaving the following:

```
; --------------------------------------------------------------
; Load enemy-related graphics
;
; Alters the value of the AF, BC, DE and HL registers.
; --------------------------------------------------------------
LoadUdgsEnemies:
ld    a, (levelCounter)    ; A = level
dec   a                    ; A = A - 1, do not add one level of more
ld    h, $00               ; H = 0
ld    l, a                 ; L = A, HL = level - 1
add   hl, hl               ; Multiply by 2
add   hl, hl               ; by 4
add   hl, hl               ; by 8
add   hl, hl               ; by 16
add   hl, hl               ; by 32
ld    de, udgsEnemiesLevel1 ; DE = enemy address 1
add   hl, de               ; HL = HL + DE
ld    de, udgsExtension    ; DE = extension address
ld    bc, $20              ; BC = bytes to copy, 32
ldir                       ; Copies enemy bytes in extension

ret
```

In game.asm we look for the tag **checkCrahsFire_endLoop**, above it is a **RET** and above this **RET** we add the following lines:

```
ld    hl, enemiesCounter    ; HL = enemiesCounter
dec   (hl)                  ; Subtract one enemy
```

In main.asm, three lines above **Main_loop**, just before **CALL LoadUdgsEnemies**, we delete the line **LD A, $01**; we get the level from **levelCounter**.

Compile, load into the emulator and check that everything still works.

In game.asm we implement the level change: we load the graphics of the enemies of the next level, reset their configuration and update the counters added earlier.

```
ChangeLevel:
ld    a, (levelCounter)
inc   a
cp    $1f
jr    c, changeLevel_end
ld    a, $01
```

We load the current level into A, **LD A, (levelCounter)**, move to the next level by incrementing A, **INC A**, and check if we have reached level thirty-one, **CP $1F**. If we have not, we jump to the last part of the routine, **JR C, changeLevel_end**. If we have reached level thirty-one, remember we have thirty levels, we don't jump and set A to $01.

```
changeLevel_end:
ld    (levelCounter), a
call  LoadUdgsEnemies

ld    a, $14
ld    (enemiesCounter), a

ld    hl, enemiesConfigIni
ld    de, enemiesConfig
ld    bc, enemiesConfigEnd-enemiesConfigIni
ldir

ret
```

We load the next level into memory, **LD (levelCounter), A**, the enemy graphics, **CALL LoadUdgsEnemies**, the total number of enemies in A, **LD A, $14**, and update, **LD (enemiesCounter), A**.

We restart the configuration: we point HL to the initial configuration, **LD HL, enemiesConfigIni**, DE to the current configuration, **LD DE, enemiesConfig**, load the bytes occupied by the configuration into BC, **LD BC, enemiesConfigEnd - enemiesConfigIni**, pass the initial to the current, **LDIR**, and exit, **RET**.

The last aspect of the routine is as follows:

```
; --------------------------------------------------------------------
; Change level.
;
; Alters the value of the AF, BC, DE and HL registers.
; --------------------------------------------------------------------
```

```
ChangeLevel:
ld    a, (levelCounter)     ; A = current level
inc   a                     ; A = next level
cp    $1f                   ; Level 31?
jr    c, changeLevel_end    ; Is not 31, skip
ld    a, $01                ; If 31, level = 1

changeLevel_end:
ld    (levelCounter), a     ; Update level in memory
call  LoadUdgsEnemies       ; Load enemy graphics

ld    a, $14                ; A = total number of enemies
ld    (enemiesCounter), a   ; Loads it into memory

ld    hl, enemiesConfigIni  ; HL = initial configuration
ld    de, enemiesConfig     ; DE = current configuration
ld    bc, enemiesConfigEnd - enemiesConfigIni ; BC = long config
ldir                        ; Initial configuration = current

ret
```

Finally, we use the implementation. We go to main.asm, to the **MainLoop** routine, find the fifth line, **POP DE**, and add the following below it:

```
ld    a, (enemiesCounter)
or    a
jr    z, Main_restart
```

We load into A the number of enemies still active, **LD A, (enemiesCounter)**, check if we have reached zero, **OR A**, and jump if so, JR Z, Main_restart.

Go to the end of the file and add the following before the first include:

```
Main_restart:
call ChangeLevel
jr   Main_loop
```

We move to the next level, **CALL ChangeLevel**, and return to the start of the loop, **JR Main_loop**.

As main.asm grows, let's see how it should look now:

```
org   $5dad

; --------------------------------------------------------------------
; Indicators
;
; Bit 0 -> ship must be moved 0 = No, 1 = Yes
; Bit 1 -> Trigger is active 0 = No, 1 = Yes
; Bit 2 -> Enemies must be moved 0 = No, 1 = Yes
; --------------------------------------------------------------------
flags:
db $00

Main:
ld    a, $02
```

```
call OPENCHAN

ld   hl, udgsCommon
ld   (UDG), hl

ld   hl, ATTR_P
ld   (hl), $07
call CLS

xor  a
out  ($fe), a
ld   a, (BORDCR)
and  $c7
or   $07
ld   (BORDCR), a

call PrintFrame
call PrintInfoGame
call PrintShip

di
ld   a, $28
ld   i, a
im   2
ei

call LoadUdgsEnemies
call PrintEnemies

Main_loop:
call CheckCtrl
call MoveFire

push de
call CheckCrashFire
pop  de

ld   a, (enemiesCounter)
or   a
jr   z, Main_restart

call MoveShip
call MoveEnemies
jr   Main_loop

Main_restart:
call ChangeLevel
jr   Main_loop

include "const.asm"
include "var.asm"
include "graph.asm"
include "print.asm"
include "ctrl.asm"
include "game.asm"

end  Main
```

We compile, load into the emulator and, if all goes well, see how the enemies change when we have killed them all.

Collisions between enemies and the ship

In this first approach, we just paint an explosion when an enemy collides with the ship. Later we will subtract a life.

First we implement the routine that draws the explosion. Let's go to the print.asm file.

```
PrintExplosion:
ld   a, $02
call Ink

ld   bc, (shipPos)
ld   d, $04
ld   e, $92
```

In A we load two (two = red colour), **LD A, $02**, and change the colour of the ink, **CALL Ink**. We load into BC the position of the ship, **LD BC, (shipPos)**, into D the number of UDGs the explosion has, **LD D, $04**, and into E the first UDG of the explosion, **LD E, $92**.

```
printExplosion_loop:
call At
ld   a, e
rst  $10
halt
halt
halt
halt
inc  e
dec  d
jr   nz, printExplosion_loop

jp   PrintShip
```

We position the cursor on the ship's coordinates, **CALL At**, load the UDG in A, **LD A, E**, and paint it, **RST $10**. We wait four interrupts, **HALT**, **HALT**, **HALT**, **HALT**, point E to the next UDG, **INC E**, decrement D, **DEC D**, and continue in the loop, **JR NZ, printExplosion_loop**, until D reaches zero.

We paint the ship and walk away, **JP PrintShip**. We use PrintShip's **RET** to exit. We could call PrintShip and exit, but with JP we save one byte and seventeen clock cycles.

The final aspect of the routine is as follows:

```
; --------------------------------------------------------------
; Paints the explosion of the ship
;
; Alters the values of the AF, BC and DE registers.
; --------------------------------------------------------------
PrintExplosion:
ld    a, $02                ; A = 2 (red)
call  Ink                   ; Ink = red

ld    bc, (shipPos)         ; BC = ship position
ld    d, $04                ; D = UDG explosion number
ld    e, $92                ; E = 1st UDG explosion
printExplosion_loop:
call  At                    ; Position cursor
ld    a, e                  ; A = UDG
rst   $10                   ; Paints it
halt
halt
halt
halt                        ; Wait for 4 interruptions
inc   e                     ; E = next UDG
dec   d                     ; D = D-1
jr    nz, printExplosion_loop ; Loop until D = 0

jp    PrintShip             ; Paints ship and goes out that way
```

Now, in game.asm, we are going to implement the collisions between the enemies and the ship, which, as you will see, is very similar to the collision routine of the enemies with the shot.

```
CheckCrashShip:
ld    de, (shipPos)
ld    hl, enemiesConfig
ld    b, enemiesConfigEnd-enemiesConfigIni
sra   b
```

We load in HL the position of the ship, **LD DE, (shipPos)**, HL we point it to the configuration of the enemies, **LD HL, enemiesConfig**, we load in B the total number of bytes of the configuration, **LD B, enemiesConfigEnd - enemiesConfigIni**, and we divide it by two to get the number of enemies, **SRA B**.

```
checkCrashShip_loop:
ld    a, (hl)
inc   hl
bit   $07, a
jr    z, checkCrashShip_endLoop
```

We load the first byte of the enemy configuration into A, **LD A, (HL)**, point HL to the second byte, **INC HL**, check if the enemy is active, **BIT $07, A**, and skip if not, **JR Z, checkCrashShip_endLoop**.

```
and   $1f
```

```
cp    d
jr    nz, checkCrashShip_endLoop
```

We keep the Y-coordinate of the enemy at A, **AND $1F**, compare it with the Y-coordinate of the ship, **CP D**, and jump if they are not the same, **JR NZ, checkCrashShip_endLoop**.

```
ld    a, (hl)
and   $1f
cp    e
jr    nz, checkCrashShip_endLoop
```

We load the second byte of the enemy configuration in A, **LD A, (HL)**, keep the X coordinate, **AND $1F**, and see if it matches that of the ship, **CP E**. We skip, **JR NZ, checkCrashShip_endLoop**, if they are not the same.

```
dec   hl
res   07, (hl)

ld    hl, enemiesCounter
dec   (hl)

jp    PrintExplosion
```

If we go through here, there has been a collision. We point HL to the first byte of the enemy configuration, **DEC HL**, and disable the enemy, **RES $07,(HL)**. We point HL at the counter, **LD HL, enemiesCounter**, and subtract one, **DEC (HL)**. Finally, we jump to paint the explosion and exit, **JP PrintExplosion**, using the same technique we saw in **PrintExplosion**.

```
checkCrashShip_endLoop:
inc   hl
djnz  checkCrashShip_loop
ret
```

If there has been no collision, we point HL to the first byte of the next enemy's configuration, **INC HL**, and continue in the loop until B is zero and we have traversed all the enemies, **DJNZ checkCrashShip_loop**. Finally, we exit, **RET**.

The final aspect of the routine is as follows:

```
; ----------------------------------------------------------------
; Evaluates enemy collisions with the ship.
;
; Alters the value of the AF, BC, DE and HL registers.
; ----------------------------------------------------------------
CheckCrashShip:
ld    de, (shipPos)         ; DE = ship position
ld    hl, enemiesConfig     ; HL = enemiesConfig
ld    b, enemiesConfigEnd-enemiesConfigIni ; B = bytes config
sra   b                     ; B = B/2 = number of enemies

checkCrashShip_loop:
ld    a, (hl)               ; A = enemy Y-coordinate
inc   hl                    ; HL = coord X
bit   $07, a                ; Active enemy?
```

```
jr    z, checkCrashShip_endLoop ; Not active, skips

and   $1f                     ; A = coord Y enemy
cp    d                       ; Compare with ship
jr    nz, checkCrashShip_endLoop ; Distinct, skip

ld    a, (hl)                 ; A = enemy X coord
and   $1f                     ; A = coord X
cp    e                       ; Compare with ship
jr    nz, checkCrashShip_endLoop ; Distinct, skip

dec   hl                      ; HL = coord Y enemy
res   $07, (hl)               ; Deactivates enemy

ld    hl, enemiesCounter      ; HL = enemiesCounter
dec   (hl)                    ; Subtract one enemy

jp    PrintExplosion          ; Paint explosion and it comes out

checkCrashShip_endLoop:
inc   hl                      ; HL = coord Y next enemy
djnz  checkCrashShip_loop     ; Loop until B = 0

ret
```

It is time to test the collisions between the ship and the enemies. We open main.asm, locate **Main_loop** and see that the last line is **JR Main_loop**. Above this line we will add the call to test the collisions between the ship and the enemies:

```
call CheckCrashShip
```

We compile, load in the emulator and see the results.

We have implemented collisions between shot and enemy, and between enemy and ship. Also, the level changes when we destroy all the enemies.

251

Download the source code from here

https://tinyurl.com/289uvoyj

Step 8: Transition between levels and scoreboard

In this chapter we will implement the scoreboard and a transition between levels.

We create the folder Step08 and copy from the folder Step07 the files loader.tap, const.asm, ctrl.asm, game.asm, graph.asm, int.asm, main.asm, print.asm, var.asm and make or make.bat.

Level change transition

The first thing we implement is a routine that changes the colour attributes of the screen to those in the A register. We open graph.asm.

```
Cla:
ld    hl, $5800
ld    (hl), a
ld    de, $5801
ld    bc, $02ff
ldir

ret
```

We point HL to the attribute area, **LD HL, $5800**, load the new attributes at that address, **LD (HL), A**, point DE to the next address, **LD DE, $5801**, load into BC the attribute area positions but one (the first one is already changed), **LD BC, $02FF**, change the whole attribute area, **LDIR**, and exit, **RET**.

The appearance of the routine, once commented, is as follows:

```
; -----------------------------------------------------------------
; Changes the colour attributes of the display.
;
; Input: A = Colour attributes (FBPPPIII).
;
; Alters the value of the AF, BC, DE and HL registers.
; -----------------------------------------------------------------
Cla:
ld    hl, $5800          ; HL = 1st address attributes
ld    (hl), a            ; Load attributes
ld    de, $5801          ; DE = 2nd address attributes
ld    bc, $02ff          ; BC = positions to be exchanged
ldir                     ; Change display attributes

ret
```

We also implement in graph.asm the routine that we will use to transition from one level to another. This routine is a variation of the FadeScreen routine found in Compiler Software's Z80 Assembly course.

https://tinyurl.com/2l7qx68e

We will traverse the entire video area to make a maximum of eight moves on each byte to clean it up.

```
FadeScreen:
ld    b, $08

fadeScreen_loop1:
ld    hl, $4000
ld    de, $1800
```

We load into B the iterations of the outer loop, **LD B, $08**, HL we set it to the start of the video area, **LD HL, $4000**, and we load into DE the length of the area (the pixel part), **LD DE, $1800**.

```
fadeScreen_loop2:
ld    a, (hl)
or    a
jr    z, fadeScreen_cont

bit   $00, l
jr    z, fadeScreen_right

rla
jr    fadeScreen_cont

fadeScreen_right:
rra
```

We load in A the byte pointed to by HL, **LD A, (HL)**, check if it is clean (zeroed), **OR A**, and jump, **JR Z, fadeScreen_cont** if it is clean.

If we do not jump, we check if the address pointed to by HL is even or odd, **BIT $00, L**, and if it is even (bit 0 is zero) we jump, **JR Z, fadeScreen_right**. If odd, we do not jump, we turn A left, **RLA**, and jump, **JR fadeScreen_cont**. If the memory address is even, we rotate A to the right, **RRA**.

Before we continue, let's stop at three lines, **OR A** is the first. At this point we want to know if the byte in the video area pointed to by HL is clean (has all bits set to zero), and we can do this with **CP $00**, consuming two bytes and seven clock cycles. **OR A** only returns zero if A is zero, and uses one byte and four clock cycles; the flags are affected in much the same way, and in the carry flag the result is the same. Instead of **OR A** we can use **AND A**, the result is the same.

The next lines to look at are **RLA** and **RRA**. In both cases the A register is rotated: to the left in the case of **RLA** and to the right in the case of **RRA**.

- **RLA**: rotates the byte to the left, sets the value of bit 7 to the carry and passes the value of the carry to bit 0.
- **RRA**: rotates the byte to the right, places the value of bit 0 in the carry and passes the value of the carry to bit 7.

Carry = 1 Byte = 10000001

RLA	RRA
Carry = 1 Byte = 00000011	Carry = 1 Byte = 11000000
Carry = 0 Byte = 00000111	Carry = 0 Byte = 11100000
Carry = 0 Byte = 00001110	Carry = 0 Byte = 01110000

As we can see in this table, if at any point in the **FadeScreen** routine, before we do the rotation, the carry is set to one, we may have some pixels left without cleaning, but this will not happen because another of the things that **OR A** does is to set the carry to zero, the same as if we used **CP $00**.

This brings us to the final part of the routine.

```
fadeScreen_cont:
ld   (hl), a
inc  hl

dec  de
ld   a, d
or   e
jr   nz, fadeScreen_loop2

ld   a, b
dec  a
push bc
call Cla
pop  bc

djnz fadeScreen_loop1

ret
```

We update the video position that HL points to with the rotated value, **LD (HL), A**, and point HL to the next position in the video area, **INC HL**.

Decrement DE, **DEC DE**, load the value of D into A, **LD A, D**, mix it with E, **OR E**, and loop until DE is zero, **JR NZ, fadeScreen_loop2**.

We load the value of B into A, **LD A, B**, remove one from A so that the value is between seven and zero, **DEC A**, keep the value of BC, **PUSH BC**, change the screen colours, **CALL Cla**, get the value of BC, **POP BC**, and continue the loop until B is zero, **DJNZ fadeScreen_loop1**. Finally, we exit.

Let's pause again to explain one part of the code in more detail.

```
dec  de
ld   a, d
or   e
jr   nz, fadeScreen_loop2
```

So far we have implemented loops using 8-bit registers, as in this case the outer loop; we load eight into B, **LD B, $08**, and later, with **DJNZ**, we decrement B and if the result is not zero, we jump and continue in the loop, thanks to the fact that doing **INC** or **DEC** on an 8-bit register affects the Z flag.

In the case of 16-bit registers, **INC** and **DEC** do not affect the Z flag. If we just decrement the register and then check if the Z flag is set, we have an infinite loop. To make a loop using a 16-bit register, after decrementing the register, we have to load one of its parts into A and then **OR** the other part, and if both values are zero, as we have seen above, the result is zero, the Z flag is activated and we exit the loop.

The final result of the routine is as follows.

```
; -------------------------------------------------------
; Screen fade effect.
;
; Alters the value of the AF, BC, DE and HL registers.
; -------------------------------------------------------
FadeScreen:
ld   b, $08                ; External loop repeat 8 times, 1*bit

fadeScreen_loop1:
ld   hl, $4000             ; HL = home video area
ld   de, $1800             ; DE = length video area

fadeScreen_loop2:
ld   a, (hl)               ; A = byte pointed to by HL
or   a                     ; Any active pixels?
jr   z, fadeScreen_cont    ; None, skip

bit  $00, l                ; HL address even?
jr   z, fadeScreen_right   ; It's even, jump

rla                        ; Rotate A left
jr   fadeScreen_cont

fadeScreen_right:
rra                        ; Rotate A right

fadeScreen_cont:
ld   (hl), a               ; Update HL video position
inc  hl                    ; HL = next position

dec  de
ld   a, d
or   e
```

```
jr   nz, fadeScreen_loop2  ; Loop until BC = 0

ld   a, b                  ; B = A
dec  a                     ; A = A-1 (A between 0 and 7)
push bc                    ; Preserve BC
call Cla                   ; Change screen colours
pop  bc                    ; Retrieves BC

djnz fadeScreen_loop1      ; Loop until B = 0

ret
```

To test the implementation, open main.asm, locate the **Main_restart** routine and replace the **CALL ChangeLevel** line with the following:

```
call FadeScreen
call ChangeLevel
call PrintFrame
call PrintInfoGame
call PrintShip
```

We call the screen fade effect, **CALL FadeScreen**, paint the screen frame, **CALL PrintFrame**, the game information, **CALL PrintInfoGame**, and the ship, **CALL PrintShip**.

We compile, load the emulator, kill all the enemy ships and watch the screen fade effect.

Scoreboard

The scoreboard will show you how many lives you have, how many points you have scored, the level you are at and how many enemies you have left, so we need some more information and we are going to introduce a new concept, the BCD numbers.

BCD numbers

A byte can contain numbers in the range 0 to 255. When we work with numbers in BCD format, this range is reduced from 0 to 99. BCD numbers divide the byte into two nibbles (4 bits) and store values from 0 to 9 in each of them, so the hexadecimal value 0x10, which in decimal is 16, working with BCD would be 10, we would see the number in hexadecimal notation as if it were decimal, which is useful for example when painting or when working with numbers of more than 16 bits.

To be able to work with numbers in this way, we have the **DAA** (Decimal Adjust Accumulator) instruction, which works as follows:

- Checks bits 0, 1, 2 and 3 if they contain a non-BCD digit greater than nine or the H flag is set, adds or subtracts $06 (0000 0110b) to the byte depending on the operation performed.
- Checks bits 4, 5, 6 and 7 if they contain a non-BCD digit greater than nine or the C flag is set, adds or subtracts $60 (0110 0000b) from the byte depending on the operation performed.

After each arithmetic instruction, increment or decrement, **DAA** must be performed. Let's look at an example.

```
ld    a, $09        ; A = $09
inc   a             ; A = $0a
daa                 ; A = $10
dec   a             ; A = $0f
daa                 ; A = $09
add   a, $03        ; A = $0c
daa                 ; A = $12

sub   a, $03        ; A = $0f
daa                 ; A = $09
```

Number of enemies and level

Now let's open the var.asm file and locate the **enemiesCounter** tag, which defines twenty in hexadecimal ($14), and we'll change it to the value in BCD, $20. We locate **levelCounter** and see that it defines $01; in this case we won't change it, but we'll add a byte with the same value, using the first byte to load the enemies of each level and make the level change, and the second to paint the number of the level we're in.

```
; ------------------------------------------------------------------
; Information about the game
; ------------------------------------------------------------------
enemiesCounter:
db $20
levelCounter:
db $01, $01
```

We use these two labels in parts of our program, but we don't take into account that we are now working with BCD numbers, so we need to locate the places where they are used in order to modify their behaviour.

The first change is to the **ChangeLevel** routine in game.asm by adding seven lines. The first four lines are added at the beginning of the routine.

```
ld    a, (levelCounter + 1)
inc   a
daa
ld    b, a
```

We load the current level (which is already in BCD format) into A, **LD A, (levelCounter + 1)**, increment the level, **INC A**, do the decimal adjustment, **DAA**, and load the value into B, **LD B, A**.

Now add the following line above the **changeLevel_end** tag:

```
ld    b, a
```

If we go through here, the next level would be thirty-one and we only have thirty, so we load $01 into A and now we load this value into the register where we have the level in BCD format, **LD B, A**.

We continue with the reference to the **changeLevel_end** tag, after which we update the level in memory. Just below this line, **LD (levelCounter), A**, we add the lines that update the level in memory in BCD format.

```
ld    a, b
ld    (levelCounter + 1), a
```

We load the current level in BCD into A, **LD A, B**, and update it in memory, **LD (levelCounter + 1), A**.

Two lines later we change **LD A, $14** to **LD A, $20** to get the total number of enemies in BCD.

The final aspect of the routine is as follows:

```
; -----------------------------------------------------------------
; Change level.
;
; Alters the value of the AF, BC, DE and HL registers.
; -----------------------------------------------------------------
ChangeLevel:
ld    a, (levelCounter + 1) ; A = current level BCD
inc   a                     ; Increases level
daa                         ; Decimal adjust
ld    b, a                  ; B = A
ld    a, (levelCounter)     ; A = current level
inc   a                     ; A = next level
cp    $1f                   ; Level 31?
jr    c, changeLevel_end    ; Is not 31, skip
ld    a, $01                ; If 31, A = 1
ld    b, a                  ; B = A

changeLevel_end:
ld    (levelCounter), a     ; Update level in memory
ld    a, b                  ; A = BCD level
ld    (levelCounter + 1), a ; Update in memory
call  LoadUdgsEnemies       ; Load enemy graphics

ld    a, $20                ; A = total number of enemies
ld    (enemiesCounter), a   ; Load into memory

ld    hl, enemiesConfigIni  ; HL = initial configuration
ld    de, enemiesConfig     ; DE = configuration
ld    bc, enemiesConfigEnd-enemiesConfigIni ; BC = config length
ldir                        ; Load initial config in config
```

```
ret
```

If we were to compile now, we would see that killing all the enemies would not result in the level change. This is because the number of enemies is now $20 (32) and we have not yet adapted all the routines to work with BCD.

We continue in game.asm, we go to **checkCrashFire_endLoop**, above this label is a **RET**, and just above it are the instructions to subtract an enemy, **LD HL, enemiesCounter** and **DEC (HL)**. Let's replace these two lines with the following:

```
ld    a, (enemiesCounter)
dec   a
daa
ld    (enemiesCounter), a
```

We load the number of enemies remaining into A, **LD A, (enemiesCounter)**, subtract one, **DEC A**, make the adjustment, **DAA**, and update the value in memory, **LD (enemiesCounter), A**.

The final aspect of the routine is as follows:

```
; ---------------------------------------------------------------
; Evaluates the collisions of the shot with enemies.
;
; Alters the value of the AF, BC, DE and HL registers.
; ---------------------------------------------------------------
CheckCrashFire:
ld    a, (flags)           ; A = flags
and   $02                  ; Active fire?
ret   z                    ; Not active, exits

ld    de, (firePos)        ; DE = firing position
ld    hl, enemiesConfig    ; HL = 1st enemy definition
ld    b, enemiesConfigEnd-enemiesConfigIni ; B = bytes config
sra   b                    ; B = B/2, number of enemies

checkCrashFire_loop:
ld    a, (hl)              ; A = enemy Y-coordinate
inc   hl                   ; HL = enemy coord X
bit   $07, a               ; Enemy active?
jr    z, checkCrashFire_endLoop ; Not active, skips
and   $1f                  ; A = coord Y enemy
cp    d                    ; Compare with shot
jr    nz, checkCrashFire_endLoop ; Distinct, jumps
ld    a, (hl)              ; A = enemy X coord
and   $1f                  ; A = coord X
cp    e                    ; Compare with shot
jr    nz, checkCrashFire_endLoop ; Distinct, jumps

dec   hl                   ; HL = coord Y enemy
res   $07, (hl)            ; Deactivates enemy
ld    b, d                 ; B = coord Y shot
ld    c, e                 ; C = coord X shot
call  DeleteChar           ; Delete shot/enemy
ld    a, (enemiesCounter)  ; A = number of enemies
dec   a                    ; Subtract one
daa                        ; Decimal adjust
```

```
ld    (enemiesCounter), a    ; Update in memory

ret                          ; Exits

checkCrashFire_endLoop:
inc  hl                      ; HL = coord Y enemy next
djnz checkCrashFire_loop     ; Loop as long as B > 0

ret
```

There is another routine in which we subtract an enemy, which evaluates collisions between the ship and the enemy.

We find the tag **checkCrashShip_endLoop**, above it we find **JP PrintExplosion**, and above it two lines equal to the ones we have replaced, and we have to replace them as before.

The final aspect of the routine looks like this:

```
; -----------------------------------------------------------------
; Evaluates enemy collisions with the ship.
;
; Alters the value of the AF, BC, DE and HL registers.
; -----------------------------------------------------------------
CheckCrashShip:
ld    de, (shipPos)         ; DE = ship position
ld    hl, enemiesConfig     ; HL = enemiesConfig
ld    b, enemiesConfigEnd-enemiesConfigIni ; B = bytes config
sra   b                     ; B = B/2, number of enemies

checkCrashShip_loop:
ld    a, (hl)               ; A = enemy Y-coordinate
inc   hl                    ; HL = enemy coord X
bit   $07, a                ; Enemy active?
jr    z, checkCrashShip_endLoop ; Not active, skips

and   $1f                   ; A = coord Y enemy
cp    d                     ; Compare with ship
jr    nz, checkCrashShip_endLoop ; Distinct, skip

ld    a, (hl)               ; A = enemy X coord
and   $1f                   ; A = coord X
cp    e                     ; Compare with ship
jr    nz, checkCrashShip_endLoop ; Distinct, skip

dec   hl                    ; HL = coord Y enemy
res   $07, (hl)             ; Deactivates enemy

ld    a, (enemiesCounter)   ; A = number of enemies
dec   a                     ; Subtract one
daa                         ; Decimal adjust
ld    (enemiesCounter), a   ; Update in memory

jp    PrintExplosion        ; Paint explosion and it comes out

checkCrashShip_endLoop:
inc   hl                    ; HL = coord Y next enemy
djnz  checkCrashShip_loop   ; Loop until B = 0
```

```
ret
```

If we now compile and load in the emulator, everything works again.

Painting BCD numbers

We are going to implement a routine that draws the BCD numbers on the screen, and as you will see, it is relatively simple. To calculate the character code for each of the digits, just add the zero character.

We will open print.asm and implement the routine that draws the BCD numbers, receiving the address of the number to draw in HL.

```
PrintBCD:
ld   a, (hl)
and  $f0
rra
rra
rra
rra
add  a, '0'
rst  $10
```

We load the number to be painted in A, **LD A, (HL)**, we keep the tens, **AND $F0**, we set the value in bits zero to three, **RRA, RRA, RRA, RRA**, we add the code of character 0, **ADD A, '0'**, and we paint the tens, **RST $10**.

```
ld   a, (hl)
and  $0f
add  a, '0'
rst  $10

ret
```

We load the number to be painted in A, **LD A, (HL)**, we keep the units, **AND $0F**, we add the code of the character 0, **ADD A, '0'**, and we paint the units, **RST $10**. Finally, we exit, **RET**.

The final aspect of the routine is as follows:

```
; --------------------------------------------------------------------
; Paints numbers in BCD format
;
; Input: HL -> Pointer to number to be painted
;
; Alters the value of the AF registers.
; --------------------------------------------------------------------
PrintBCD:
ld   a, (hl)            ; A = number to be painted
and  $f0                ; A = tens
rra
rra
rra
rra                     ; Passes to bits 0 to 3
add  a, '0'             ; A = A + character 0
rst  $10                ; Paint digit
```

```
ld    a, (hl)        ; A = number to be painted
and   $0f            ; A = units
add   a, '0'         ; A = A + character 0
rst   $10            ; Paint digit

ret
```

Painting the scoreboard

We implement the routine that paints the scoreboard: lives, points, level and enemies.

The first thing to do is to define the location constants for each of the marker elements. We open const.asm and add:

```
COR_ENEMY: EQU $1705 ; Coord info enemies
COR_LEVEL: EQU $170d ; Coord info level
COR_LIVE:  EQU $171e ; Coord info lives
COR_POINT: EQU $1717 ; Coord info points
```

The values of the game information will be painted on the command line, we have two lines here. Remember that for the ROM routine that positions the cursor, the upper left corner is $1820, or Y = 24, X = 32, so the values will be painted in line 23 and in columns 5, 13, 23 and 30. If we subtract the row and column values from 24 and 32, the result is the coordinates if the top right corner were $0000.

In var.asm we will add definitions to keep track of lives and points.

```
livesCounter:
db $05
pointsCounter:
dw $0000
```

We open print.asm to implement the routine that will paint the marker values.

```
PrintInfoValue:
ld    a, $05
call Ink

ld    a, $01
call OPENCHAN
```

We load ink five into A, **LD A, $05**, and change it, **CALL Ink**. As the values are painted on the command line, we load into A channel one, **LD A, $01**, and open it, **CALL OPENCHAN**.

```
ld   bc, COR_LIVE
call At
ld   hl, livesCounter
call PrintBCD
```

We load into BC the position where we will draw the lives, **LD BC, COR_LIVE**, position the cursor, **CALL At**, point HL to the lives counter, **LD HL, livesCounter**, and draw the lives, **CALL PrintBCD**.

```
ld   bc, COR_POINT
call At
```

```
ld   hl, pointsCounter + 1
call PrintBCD
ld   hl, pointsCounter
call PrintBCD
```

We load into BC the position where we are going to draw the points, **LD BC, COR_POINT**, position the cursor, **CALL At**, point HL to the thousands and hundreds of points, **LD HL, pointsCounter + 1**, and draw it, **CALL PrintBCD**. We point HL to the tens and units of the points, **LD HL, pointsCounter**, and draw it, **CALL PrintBCD**.

```
ld   bc, COR_LEVEL
call At
ld   hl, levelCounter + 1
call PrintBCD
```

We load into BC the position where we want to draw the level, **LD BC, COR_LEVEL**, we position the cursor, **CALL At**, HL we point it to the level counter in BCD format, **LD HL, levelCounter + 1**, and we draw it, **CALL PrintBCD**.

```
ld   bc, COR_ENEMY
call At
ld   hl, enemiesCounter
call PrintBCD
```

We load into BC the position where we are going to print the enemy counter, **LD BC, COR_ENEMY**, position the cursor, **CALL At**, HL we point it at the enemy counter, **LD HL, enemiesCounter**, and paints it, **CALL PrintBCD**.

```
ld   a, $02
call OPENCHAN

ret
```

Before leaving, we activate the top screen. We load the channel in A, **LD A, $02**, change it, **CALL OPENCHAN**, and exit, **RET**.

The last aspect of the routine is as follows:

```
; -------------------------------------------------------------------
; Paints the values of the line item information.
;
; Alters the value of the AF, BC and HL registers.
; -------------------------------------------------------------------
PrintInfoValue:
ld   a, $05              ; A = ink 5
call Ink                 ; Change ink

ld   a, $01              ; A = channel 1
call OPENCHAN            ; Activate channel, command line

ld   bc, COR_LIVE        ; BC = position lives
call At                  ; Position cursor
ld   hl, livesCounter    ; HL = livesCounter
call PrintBCD            ; Paints it

ld   bc, COR_POINT       ; BC = position points
```

```
call  At                       ; Position cursor
ld    hl, pointsCounter+1      ; HL = units thousands and hundreds
call  PrintBCD                 ; Paints it
ld    hl, pointsCounter        ; HL = tens and units
call  PrintBCD                 ; Paints it

ld    bc, COR_LEVEL            ; BC = position levels
call  At                       ; Position cursor
ld    hl, levelCounter+1       ; HL = levelCounter in BCD
call  PrintBCD                 ; Paints it

ld    bc, COR_ENEMY            ; BC = enemy position
call  At                       ; Position cursor
ld    hl, enemiesCounter       ; HL = enemiesCounter
call  PrintBCD                 ; Paints it

ld    a, $02                   ; A = channel 2
call  OPENCHAN                 ; Activates channel, top screen

ret
```

Now it's time to see if what we've implemented works, open main.asm, locate **Main** and the **DI** statement, just above it we add the following line to paint the game information:

```
call PrintInfoValue
```

Find **Main_restart**, and just before the last line, **JR, Main_loop**, add the same line as before.

Compile, load into the emulator and see the results.

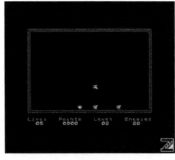

As you can see, only the level is updated, the rest of the game information is not. Also, it is not painted with the colour we have defined.

The colour part is the first thing we will fix. The system variable into which we load the screen attributes in the ink routine affects the top screen, so the command line is not affected. The command line attributes are in the same system variable as the border attributes (BORDCR), so we will make two changes.

We open print.asm, locate **PrintInfoValue** and delete the first two lines, **LD A, $05** and **CALL Ink**, because as we have seen, this does not change the command line attributes.

We go back to main.asm, locate **Main**, and modify the part where the border colour is assigned, which currently looks like this:

```
xor  a
out  ($fe), a
ld   a, (BORDCR)
and  $c7
or   $07
ld   (BORDCR), a
```

We will change lines four and five as follows:

```
xor  a
out  ($fe), a
ld   a, (BORDCR)
and  $c0
or   $05
ld   (BORDCR), a
```

We compile, load the emulator and see that the values are painted in the chosen colour.

Let's update the rest of the values. Every time the shot hits an enemy, we have to subtract one enemy and add five points. On the other hand, every time an enemy hits our ship, we have to subtract one life and one enemy.

We open game.asm, locate **checkCrahsFire_endLoop** and see that the lines above it already subtract one enemy from the counter.

```
ld   a, (enemiesCounter)    ; A = number of enemies
dec  a                      ; Subtract one
daa                         ; Decimal adjust
ld   (enemiesCounter), a    ; Update value in memory

ret
```

It remains to add five points for killing an enemy and painting the information. We add the following lines between **LD (enemiesCounter), A** and **RET**:

```
ld   a, (pointsCounter)
add  a, $05
daa
ld   (pointsCounter), a
ld   a, (pointsCounter + 1)
adc  a, $00
daa
ld   (pointsCounter + 1), a
call PrintInfoValue
```

We load the units and tens of points, **LD A, (pointsCounter)**, into A, add five, **ADD A, $05**, do the decimal adjustment, **DAA**, and load the value into memory, **LD (pointsCounter), A**.

The addition of five to the units and the decimal setting may cause a carry, for example if the value was ninety-five, which we need to add to the hundreds.

We load the hundreds and thousands, **LD A, (PointsCounter + 1)**, into A, add zero with carry to A, **ADC A, $00**, do the decimal adjustment, **DAA**, load the value into memory, **LD (PointsCounter + 1), A**, and print the line item information, **CALL PrintInfoValue**.

The final aspect of the routine is as follows:

```
; ------------------------------------------------------------------
; Evaluates the collisions of the shot with enemies.
;
; Alters the value of the AF, BC, DE and HL registers.
; ------------------------------------------------------------------
CheckCrashFire:
ld   a, (flags)            ; A = flags
and  $02                   ; Active fire?
ret  z                     ; Not active, exits

ld   de, (firePos)         ; DE = firing position
ld   hl, enemiesConfig     ; HL = 1st enemy definition
ld   b,enemiesConfigEnd-enemiesConfigIni ; B bytes config enemies
sra  b                     ; B = B/2, number of enemies

checkCrashFire_loop:
ld   a, (hl)               ; A = enemy Y-coordinate
inc  hl                    ; HL = enemy coord X
bit  $07, a                ; Enemy active?
jr   z, checkCrashFire_endLoop ; Not active, skips
and  $1f                   ; A = coord Y enemy
cp   d                     ; Compare with shot
jr   nz, checkCrashFire_endLoop ; Distinct, jumps
ld   a, (hl)               ; A = enemy X coord
and  $1f                   ; A = coord X
cp   e                     ; Compare with shot
jr   nz, checkCrashFire_endLoop ; Distinct, jumps

dec  hl                    ; HL = coord Y enemy
res  $07, (hl)             ; Deactivates enemy
ld   b, d                  ; B = coord Y shot
ld   c, e                  ; C = coord X shot
call DeleteChar            ; Delete trigger/enemy
ld   a, (enemiesCounter)   ; A = number of enemies
dec  a                     ; Subtract one
daa                        ; Decimal adjust
ld   (enemiesCounter), a   ; Update in memory
ld   a, (pointsCounter)    ; A = units and tens
add  a, $05                ; A = A + 5
daa                        ; Decimal adjust
ld   (pointsCounter), a    ; Update in memory
ld   a, (pointsCounter + 1) ; A = hundreds and ud thousand
adc  a, $00                ; A = A + 0 with carry over
daa                        ; Decimal adjust
ld   (pointsCounter + 1), a ; Update in memory
call PrintInfoValue        ; Paint InfoValue

ret                        ; Exits

checkCrashFire_endLoop:
inc  hl                    ; HL = coord Y next enemy
djnz checkCrashFire_loop   ; Loop to B = 0
```

```
ret
```

In this code we have used an instruction that we have not seen before, **ADC** (Add With Carry). This instruction adds the specified value to A, plus the value of the carry, so that if we add zero to A, and the carry is one, we would add one to A, which is commonly known as "I'll take one".

ADC possibilities are:

Mnemonic	Cycles	Bytes	S Z H P N C
ADC A, r	4	1	* * * V 0 *
ADC A, N	7	2	* * * V 0 *
ADC A, (HL)	7	1	* * * V 0 *
ADC A, (IX+N)	19	3	* * * V 0 *
ADC A, (IY+N)	19	3	* * * V 0 *
ADC HL, BC	15	2	* * ? V 0 *
ADC HL, DE	15	2	* * ? V 0 *
ADC HL, HL	15	2	* * ? V 0 *
ADC HL, SP	15	2	* * ? V 0 *

* Affects flag, V = overflow, 0 = sets flag to 0, ? = unknown value

We only need to subtract one life if the ship crashes into an enemy. We locate **checkCrashShip_endLoop**, just above it we find the line **JP PrintExplosion**, and just above it we add the following lines:

```
ld    a, (livesCounter)
dec   a
daa
ld    (livesCounter), a
call PrintInfoValue
```

We load the lives into A, **LD A, (livesCounter)**, remove one, **DEC A**, do the decimal adjustment, **DAA**, load the value into memory, **LD (livesCounter), A**, and paint the information, **CALL PrintInfoValue**. As we can see, since the lives counter is a single byte, the modification is less than the one we made for the score counter.

The final aspect of the routine is as follows:

```
; -----------------------------------------------------------------
; Evaluates enemy collisions with the ship.
;
; Alters the value of the AF, BC, DE and HL registers.
; -----------------------------------------------------------------
CheckCrashShip:
ld    de, (shipPos)      ; DE = ship position
ld    hl, enemiesConfig  ; HL = enemiesConfig
```

```
ld   b, enemiesConfigEnd-enemiesConfigIni ; B = bytes config
sra  b                     ; B = B/2, number of enemies

checkCrashShip_loop:
ld   a, (hl)               ; A = coord Y enemy
inc  hl                    ; HL = enemy coord X
bit  $07, a                ; Enemy active?
jr   z, checkCrashShip_endLoop ; Not active, skips

and  $1f                   ; A = coord Y enemy
cp   d                     ; Compare with ship
jr   nz, checkCrashShip_endLoop ; Distinct, skip

ld   a, (hl)               ; A = enemy X coord
and  $1f                   ; A = coord X
cp   e                     ; Compare with ship
jr   nz, checkCrashShip_endLoop ; Distinct, skip

dec  hl                    ; HL = coord Y enemy
res  $07, (hl)             ; Deactivates enemy

ld   a, (enemiesCounter)   ; A = number of enemies
dec  a                     ; Subtract one
daa                        ; Decimal adjust
ld   (enemiesCounter), a   ; Update in memory
ld   a, (livesCounter)     ; A = lives
dec  a                     ; Subtract a
daa                        ; Decimal adjuts
ld   (livesCounter), a     ; Update in memory
call PrintInfoValue        ; Paint information

jp   PrintExplosion        ; Paint explosion and it comes out

checkCrashShip_endLoop:
inc  hl                    ; HL = coord Y next enemy
djnz checkCrashShip_loop   ; Loop until B = 0

ret
```

We see if the implementation works. We compile it, load it into the emulator and see the results.

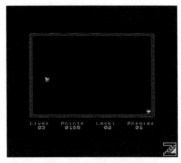

We are now ready to play our first games. We have implemented a transition between levels and the scoreboard.

Download the source code from here

https://tinyurl.com/24o6uohh

Step 9: Start the game

In this chapter we will implement the start and end of the game.

As in the previous chapters, we will create the folder Step09 and copy the files loader.tap, const.asm, ctrl.asm, game.asm, graph.asm, int.asm, main.asm, make or make.bat, print.asm and var.asm from the folder Step08.

Before we start with the aim of this chapter, we will review the PrintString routine to look at three variations.

PrintString routine

The PrintString variations we will see are implemented in a new file called testprint.asm, then we will decide which routine is the definitive one.

Open testprint.asm and add the following code.

```
org     $5dad

TestPrint:
ld    hl, string
ld    b, stringEOF - string
call PrintString

ld    hl, stringNull
call PrintStringNull

ld    hl, stringFF
call PrintStringFF

ret

; -----------------------------------------------------------------
; Paints chains.
;
; Input: HL = first position of the string
;        B  = length of the chain.
;
; Alters the value of the AF and HL registers.
; -----------------------------------------------------------------
PrintString:
ld    a, (hl)             ; A = character to be painted
rst   $10                 ; Paint the character
inc   hl                  ; HL = next character
djnz PrintString          ; Loop until B = 0

ret

; -----------------------------------------------------------------
; Paints chains.
;
; Input: HL = first position of the string
;
; Alters the value of the AF and HL registers.
; -----------------------------------------------------------------
```

```
PrintStringNull:
ld    a, (hl)               ; A = character to be painted
or    a                     ; Is it 0?
ret   z                     ; Is 0, exits
rst   $10                   ; Paint the character
inc   hl                    ; HL = next character
jr    PrintStringNull       ; Loop

; -----------------------------------------------------------------
; Paints chains.
;
; Input: HL = first position of the string
;
; Alters the value of the AF and HL registers.
; -----------------------------------------------------------------
PrintStringFF:
ld    a, (hl)               ; A = character to be painted
cp    $ff                   ; Is it $FF?
ret   z                     ; Is $FF, exits
rst   $10                   ; Paint the character
inc   hl                    ; HL = next character
jr    PrintStringFF         ; Loop

string:
db $10, $05, $11, $03, $16, $05, $0a, "Hello Assembly"
stringEOF:

stringNull:
db $10, $07, $11, $01, $16, $07, $0a, "Hello Assembly", $00

stringFF:
db $10, $02, $11, $07, $16, $09, $0a, "Hello Assembly", $ff

end   TestPrint
```

In this code we can see three PrintString routines:

- **PrintString**: the routine as we have it now.
- **PrintStringNull**: prints strings and uses the $00 character as the end.
- **PrintStringFF**: prints strings and uses the $FF character as the end.

The first of these routines we already know, so we will explain the PrintStringNull routine; PrintStringFF only differs in one line.

```
PrintStringNull:
ld      a, (hl)
or      a
ret     z
rst     $10
inc     hl
jr      PrintStringNull
```

PrintStringNull and **PrintStringFF**, get in HL the position of the string (same as **PrintString**), but do not need the length.

We load in A the character pointed to by HL, **LD A, (HL)**, see if it is zero, **OR A**, and if it is, **RET Z**.

The line that changes in **PrintStringFF** is **OR A**, which is **CP $FF**, since this is the character used as the end of the string in this case. Remember that the result of **OR A** is zero only if A is zero. With **CP** it is zero if A and the comparator are equal.

If the character loaded at A is not the end of the string, we print the character, **RST $10**, point HL to the next character, **INC HL**, and loop until the whole string is printed, **JR PrintStringNull**.

Using one or the other routine has its advantages and disadvantages. Let's do the first comparison on bytes and clock cycles.

	Bytes	Cycles
PrintString	6	47/42
PrintStringNull	7	51/45
PrintStringFF	8	54/48

Looking at this table, the most optimal routine is the first one, as it uses fewer bytes and is faster. In reality, it is faster, but it does not occupy fewer bytes, because each time we call it, we have to add two bytes of load in B to the length of the string. If we use it a lot, we quickly see that the byte saving does not happen.

The logical choice is the second routine, which is faster and uses fewer bytes than the third, but as we will see below, it has its disadvantages.

TestPrint is a single program, to compile it we call PASMO from the command line:

```
pasmo --name TestPrint --tapbas testprint.asm testprint.tap
```

We compile TestPrint, load it and see the results.

As you can see, everything went well. We have three strings and we have painted each one with a different routine.

Let's now look at the disadvantages of the second routine, for which we will modify the second string, which is now:

```
stringNull:
db $10, $07, $11, $01, $16, $07, $0a, "Hello Assembly", $00
```

And let's change the second byte, $07, to $00.

```
stringNull:
db $10, $00, $11, $01, $16, $16, $07, $0a, "Hello Assembly", $00
```

We compile, load and see the results.

Something is wrong. Let's review the definition of chains.

```
string:
db $10, $05, $11, $03, $16, $05, $0a, "Hello Assembly"
stringEOF:

stringNull:
db $10, $00, $11, $01, $16, $07, $0a, "Hello Assembly", $00

stringFF:
db $10, $02, $11, $07, $16, $09, $0a, "Hello Assembly", $ff
```

The second string, **stringNull**, is terminated with $00 because the routine paints until it reaches this value. The strings start with $10, which is the **INK** code, so the next byte must be a colour code, from $00 to $07.

When we pass **stringNull** to the **PrintStringNull** routine, it reads the first character, $10 (INK), reads the next character, $00, and exits.

Next we load the string **stringFF** into HL and call the **PrintStringFF** routine. This routine reads the first character, **$10 (INK)**, and prints it, but because the previous character was also an **INK**, it now expects a colour code, and what we give it is **$10 (16)**, an invalid colour, hence the message K Invalid Colour, 40:1.

We modify the second byte of the string **stringNull** again, setting it to $05, and also the second byte of the string **stringFF**, now worth $02, setting it to $00.

We compile, load into the emulator and see the results.

As we can see, it is working again and is printing the third string in black, $00, so we opt for **PrintStringFF**.

We copy the code from the routine, open print.asm, locate PrintString and replace the code from that routine with the code we just copied. The final appearance of the routine should be as follows:

```
; ------------------------------------------------------------------
; Paints strings ending in $FF.
;
; Input: HL = first position of the string
;
; Alters the value of the AF and HL registers.
; ------------------------------------------------------------------
PrintString:
ld   a, (hl)             ; A = character to be painted
cp   $ff                 ; Is it $FF?
ret  z                   ; Is $FF, exits
rst  $10                 ; Paint the character
inc  hl                  ; HL = next character
jr   PrintString         ; Loop
```

We need to change the definition of strings and **PrintString** calls.

We go to print.asm, find the **PrintFrame** tag, delete the second one and add two after **CALL PrintString**.

```
ld   hl, frameTopGraph       ; HL = top address
ld   b, frameEnd-framTopGraph ; Loads the length in B
call PrintString             ; Paints the string

ld   hl, frameBottomGraph    ; HL = bottom direction
call PrintString             ; Paints the string
```

Find **PrintInfoGame** and delete the fourth line.

```
ld   a, $01              ; A = channel 1
call OPENCHAN            ; Activate channel, command line
ld   hl, infoGame        ; HL = address string titles
ld   b, infoGame_end-infoGame ; Load length into B
```

Open the var.asm file, find the **infoGame** tag and add **$FF** after the enemies. Delete the **infoGame_end** tag as it is no longer useful.

```
infoGame:
db $10, $03, $16, $00, $00
db 'Lives   Points   Level   Enemies', $ff
```

~~infoGame_end:~~

We locate the **frameTopGraph** tag and add the byte **$FF** to the end of the definition. In the **frameBottomGraph** tag we do the same and delete the **frameEnd** tag, which is no longer useful.

```
frameTopGraph:
db $16, $00, $00, $10, $01
db $96, $97, $97, $97, $97, $97, $97, $97, $97, $97, $97, $97, $97
db $97, $97, $97, $97, $97, $97, $97, $97, $97, $97, $97, $97
db $97, $97, $97, $97, $97, $98, $ff
frameBottomGraph:
db $16, $14, $00
db $9b, $9c, $9c, $9c, $9c, $9c, $9c, $9c, $9c, $9c, $9c, $9c, $9c
db $9c, $9c, $9c, $9c, $9c, $9c, $9c, $9c, $9c, $9c, $9c, $9c
db $9c, $9c, $9c, $9c, $9c, $9d, $ff
```

We compile (we do this again by running make or make.bat), load it into the emulator and see that it works. We can also see that the program now takes up three bytes less; for each line we removed where we loaded the length of the string into B, we saved two bytes (six in total), but by putting $ff at the end of the strings we have added three bytes again.

Start and end of the game

We will implement a start screen as a menu and two endings, one for when we are killed without finishing the game, the other for when we manage to finish it.

Start of the game

On the start screen we show an introductory text, the control buttons and the selection of the different control types.

We open var.asm and add the definition of the splash screen at the top.

```
title:
db $10, $02, $16, $00, $0a, "SPACE BATTLE", $0d, $0d, $0d, $ff

firstScreen:
db $10, $06, "  Alien ships attack the Earth,", $0d
db "the future depends on you.", $0d, $0d
db "  Destroy all enemies that you", $0d
db "can, and protect the planet.", $0d, $0d, $0d
db $10, $03, "Z - Left", $16, $0a, $17, "X - Right"
db $16, $0c, $0c, "V - Shot", $0d, $0d
db $10, $04, "1 - Keyboard     3 - Sinclair 1", $0d, $0d
db "2 - Kempston     4 - Sinclair 2", $0d, $0d, $0d
db $10, $05, "  Aim, shoot and dodge the enemy", $0d
db "ships, defeat and release to the", $0d
db "planet of the threat."
db $ff
```

We set the colour to red, **$10, $02**, position the cursor on line 0, column 8, **$16, $00, $08**, paint the name of the game, **SPACE BATTLE**, and add three line breaks, **$0d, $0d, $0d**. We continue defining the rest of the lines until we reach the string delimiter, **$FF**, the value the **PrintString** routine expects to know the end of the string.

We will now open the print.asm file and at the end of it we will implement the routine that draws the splash screen and will soon save the choice of controls.

```
PrintFirstScreen:
call CLS
ld   hl, title
call PrintString
ld   hl, firstScreen
call PrintString
```

We clear the screen, **CALL CLS**, load into HL the memory address where the title definition starts, **LD HL, title**, paint it, **CALL PrintString**, load into HL the start address of the screen definition, **LD HL, firstScreen**, and call the routine that paints the strings, **CALL PrintString**.

As we are going to allow a choice of different control types later on, we are preparing them.

```
printFirstScreen_op:
ld   a, $f7
in   a, ($fe)
bit  $00, a
jr   nz, printFirstScreen_op
call FadeScreen

ret
```

We load the half stack 1-5 in A, **LD A, $F7**, read the keyboard, **IN A, ($FE)**, check if the one (Keyboard) is pressed, **BIT $00, A**, and if not, continue until it is pressed, **JR NZ, printFirstScreen_op**. We perform the fade effect, **CALL FadeScreen**, and exit, **RET**.

The final aspect of the routine is as follows:

```
; -------------------------------------------------------------------
; Display screen and selection of controls.
;
; Alters the value of the AF and HL registers.
; -------------------------------------------------------------------
PrintFirstScreen:
call CLS                     ; Clear screen
ld   hl, title               ; HL = title definition
call PrintString             ; Print title
ld   hl, firstScreen         ; HL = screen definition
call PrintString             ; Paint screen

printFirstScreen_op:
ld   a, $f7                  ; A = half-row 1-5
in   a, ($fe)                ; Read keyboard
bit  $00, a                  ; 1 pressed?
jr   nz, printFirstScreen_op ; Not pressed, loop
call FadeScreen              ; Fade screen

ret
```

It's time to see if the implementation works. We open the main.asm file, locate the **Main** tag and within it the call to print the frame, **CALL PrintFrame**. Just above this call, we will include the call to the routine that paints the splash screen.

```
call    PrintFirstScreen
```

We compile, load the emulator and see the results.

As you can see, we're now in the start screen, and we won't leave it until we press one. There is still more to do, but for now we will leave it at that and move on to the end of the game.

End of the game

The end of the game can happen in two different ways: we run out of five lives and lose, or we pass level thirty and win.

Based on the previous paragraph, we will define two different end screens. We go back to var.asm and after the definition of **firstScreen** we add the definition of the two end screens.

```
gameOverScreen:
db $10, $06, "  You have lost all your ships,"
db "you have not been able to save the Earth.", $0d, $0d
db "  The planet has been invaded by aliens.", $0d, $0d
db "  You can try again, it's up to you to save the Earth.", $ff

winScreen:
db $10, $06, "Congratulations, you have destroyed the aliens, you saved
the Earth.", $0d, $0d
db "The inhabitants of the planet will be eternally grateful to you.",
$ff

pressEnter:
db $10, $04, $16, $10, $03, "Press enter to continue", $ff
```

As with the start screen, we will implement the routines that print the end screens and wait for the Enter key to continue. Let's go to print.asm and place ourselves at the end of it.

The routine we are going to implement will have A set to zero if it is the end of the game because we have lost, and non-zero if it is the end of the game because we have won.

```
PrintEndScreen:
push af
call FadeScreen
ld   hl, title
call PrintString
pop  af
or   a
jr   nz, printEndScreen_Win
```

We preserve the value of A, **PUSH AF**, fade the screen, **CALL FadeScreen**, point HL to the start of the title, **LD HL, title**, and paint it, **CALL PrintString**. Get the value of AF, **POP AF**, evaluate if A is zero, **OR A**, and skip if not, **JR NZ, printEndScreen_Win**.

```
printEndScreen_GameOver:
ld   hl, gameOverScreen
call PrintString
jr   printEndScreen_WaitKey
```

If the value of A is zero, we point HL to the beginning of the end-of-game screen definition, because we have lost the end-of-game screen, **LD HL, gameOverScreen**, draw it, **CALL PrintString**, and jump to wait for the Enter key to be pressed, **JR printEndScreen_WaitKey**.

```
printEndScreen_Win:
ld   hl, winScreen
call PrintString
```

If the value of A is not zero, we point HL to the beginning of the end-of-game screen definition, because we won, **LD HL, winScreen**, and print it, **CALL PrintString**.

We prepare the rest to wait for the player to press Enter.

```
printEndScreen_WaitKey:
ld   hl, pressEnter
call PrintString
call PrintInfoGame
call PrintInfoValue
```

We point HL to the beginning of the string that asks for the Enter key to be pressed, **LD HL, pressEnter**, paint it, **CALL PrintString**, then the titles of the game information, **CALL PrintInfoGame**, and finally we print the game information to show the player the level he has reached and the points he has scored, **CALL PrintInfoValue**.

```
printEndScreen_WaitKeyLoop:
ld   a, $bf
in   a, ($fe)
rra
jr   c, printEndScreen_WaitKeyLoop
call FadeScreen

ret
```

We load the Enter-H half stack into A, **LD A, $BF**, read it, **IN A, ($FE)**, rotate A to the right, **RRA**, and loop until carry is disabled, **JR C,**

printEndScreen_WaitKeyLoop. If Enter is pressed (carry is disabled), we fade the screen, **CALL FadeScreen**, and exit, **RET**.

To evaluate whether Enter was pressed, we read the Enter-H half stack; the zero bit indicates whether Enter was pressed or not, with a value of one if it was not pressed and zero if it was. Turning A clockwise sets the value of the zero bit in the carry, so that if it is on, Enter has not been pressed, and if it is off, it has.

The final aspect of the routine is as follows:

```
; -------------------------------------------------------------
; End of game screen.
;
; Input: A -> End type, 0 = Game Over, !0 = Win.
;
; Alters the value of the AF and HL registers.
; -------------------------------------------------------------
PrintEndScreen:
push af                    ; Preserve AF
call FadeScreen            ; Fade screen
ld   hl, title             ; HL = title
call PrintString           ; Print title
pop  af                    ; Retrieves AF
or   a                     ; ¿A = 0?
jr   nz, printEndScreen_Win ; 0 != 0, skip

printEndScreen_GameOver:
ld   hl, gameOverScreen    ; HL = Game Over screen
call PrintString           ; Paint it
jr   printEndScreen_WaitKey ; Skip waiting for Enter keystroke

printEndScreen_Win:
ld   hl, winScreen         ; HL = WinScreen
call PrintString           ; Paint it

printEndScreen_WaitKey:
ld   hl, pressEnter        ; HL = string 'Press Enter
call PrintString           ; Paint it
call PrintInfoGame         ; Paint game info. titles
call PrintInfoValue        ; Paint game data

printEndScreen_WaitKeyLoop:
ld   a, $bf                ; A = half-stack Enter-H
in   a, ($fe)             ; Reads the keyboard
rra                        ; Rota A right, status Enter
jr   c, printEndScreen_WaitKeyLoop ; Carry, not clicked, loop
call FadeScreen            ; Fade screen

ret
```

Now we need to test that our end of game screens are displayed correctly, so we go to main.asm, find the **CALL PrintFirstScreen** line that we added earlier, and just above it we add the following lines:

```
xor  a
call PrintEndScreen
ld   a, $01
call PrintEndScreen
```

Set A to zero, **XOR A**, print the end of game screen, **CALL PrintEndScreen**, set A to one, **LD A, $01**, and paint the end of game.

We compile, load into the emulator and see the result.

The first call we make to the routine that draws the end, we make it with A at zero, and so it draws the screen that corresponds to when we lost all our lives. When we press Enter, we set A to one and call the routine again.

This time it will paint the screen corresponding to the fact that we have passed all thirty levels.

Press Enter and you should see the start screen.

Now we need to put everything together so that everything is in its place. First we'll remove the last four lines we used to test the **PrintEndScreen** routine and replace them with the following lines to initialise the game data:

```
Main_start:
xor  a
ld   hl, enemiesCounter
ld   (hl), $20
inc  hl
ld   (hl), a ; $1d
inc  hl
ld   (hl), a ; $29
inc  hl
ld   (hl), $05
inc  hl
ld   (hl), a
inc  hl
```

```
ld   (hl), a
call ChangeLevel
```

Set A to zero, **XOR A**. We point HL to the enemy counter, **LD HL, enemiesCounter**, and set it to twenty in BCD, **LD (HL), $20**. We point HL to the level counter, **INC HL**, and set it to zero, **LD (HL), A**. We point HL to the BCD level counter, **INC HL**, and set it to zero, **LD (HL), A**. We point HL to the life counter, **INC HL**, and set it to five, **LD (HL), $05**. We point HL to the first byte of the BCD point marker, **INC HL**, and set it to zero, **LD (HL), A**. We point HL to the second byte, **INC HL**, and set it to zero, **LD (HL), A**. Finally, we call level change to reset the enemies and load level one.

In the lines where we load the level, we have commented the values **$1D** and **$29**. Later, we will use these values to test the end of the game by playing only the last level.

We look for the load lines of the interrupt vector, from **DI** to **EI**, cut them and paste them on top of **Main_start**.

We find the **Main_loop** tag and right at the end, above **JR Main_loop**, we add the check if we have lives.

```
ld   a, (livesCounter)
or   a
jr   z, GameOver
```

We load A in lives, **LD A, (livesCounter)**, evaluate if it is zero, **OR A**, and jump if it is, **JR Z, GameOver**.

Look for **Main_restart**, and under it add the check if we have passed the last level.

```
ld   a, (levelCounter)
cp   $1e
jr   z, Win
```

We load the level in A, **LD A, (levelCounter)**, check if it is the last one, **CP $1E**, and jump if it is, **JR Z, Win**.

Find the line **CALL ChangeLevel**, which is almost at the end of **Main_restart**, cut and paste it under **CALL FadeScreen**, so it is the fifth line of **Main_restart**.

Let's go to the end of **Main_restart**, and below that we will implement the end of game.

```
GameOver:
xor  a
call PrintEndScreen
jp   Main_start
```

We set A to zero, **XOR A**, paint the end screen, **CALL PrintEndScreen**, and return to the start, **JP MainStart**.

```
Win:
ld   a, $01
call PrintEndScreen
```

```
jp   Main_start
```

We set A to one, **LD A, $01**, print the end screen, **CALL PrintEndScreen**, and return to the start, JP MainStart.

As you can see we have used **JP** instead of **JR** because if we put **JR Main_start** in **Win** we get an out of range jump error.

We are going to make a new change, we are going to make the ship paint at the start position when we change levels. Go into the game.asm file, find the **changeLevel_end** tag and add the following before the **RET**:

```
ld   hl, shipPos        ; HL = position of the ship
ld   (hl), SHIP_INI     ; Updates it with the initial
```

We point HL to the ship's position, **LD HL, shipPos**, and update it with the initial position, **LD (HL), SHIP_INI**. Since the Z80 is little-endian, HL points to the ship's X-coordinate; loading **SHIP_INI** into (HL) loads the second byte defined in **SHIP_INI** at the ship's X-coordinate, **LD (HL), $11**.

And then we come to the moment of truth, we compile, load the game into the emulator and if all goes well, when we lose the five lives, the game ends, Game Over.

Back to Main.asm and the lines:

```
ld   (hl), a            ; $1d
inc  hl
ld   (hl), a            ; $29
```

We leave them as they are:

```
ld   (hl), $1d
inc  hl
ld   (hl), $29
```

We compile, load and start the game at level thirty. We beat it and game over, win.

Since we have changed a few things in main.asm, we can see how it should look now:

```
org  $5dad

; --------------------------------------------------------------
; Indicators
;
; Bit 0 -> ship must be moved 0 = No, 1 = Yes
; Bit 1 -> Trigger is active 0 = No, 1 = Yes
; Bit 2 -> Enemies must be moved 0 = No, 1 = Yes
; --------------------------------------------------------------
flags:
db $00

Main:
ld   a, $02
call OPENCHAN

ld   hl, udgsCommon
```

```
ld   (UDG), hl

ld   hl, ATTR_P
ld   (hl), $07
call CLS

xor  a
out  ($fe), a
ld   a, (BORDCR)
and  $c0
or   $05
ld   (BORDCR), a

di
ld   a, $28
ld   i, a
im   2
ei

Main_start:
xor  a
ld   hl, enemiesCounter
ld   (hl), $20
inc  hl
ld   (hl), a ; $1d
inc  hl
ld   (hl), a ; $29
inc  hl
ld   (hl), $05
inc  hl
ld   (hl), a
inc  hl
ld   (hl), a

call ChangeLevel
call PrintFirstScreen
call PrintFrame
call PrintInfoGame
call PrintShip
call PrintInfoValue

call LoadUdgsEnemies
call PrintEnemies

Main_loop:
call CheckCtrl
call MoveFire

push de
call CheckCrashFire
pop  de

ld   a, (enemiesCounter)
cp   $00
jr   z, Main_restart

call MoveShip
call MoveEnemies
call CheckCrashShip
```

```
ld    a, (livesCounter)
or    a
jr    z, GameOver

jr    Main_loop

Main_restart:
ld    a, (levelCounter)
cp    $1e
jr    z, Win

call FadeScreen
call ChangeLevel
call PrintFrame
call PrintInfoGame
call PrintShip
call PrintInfoValue
jr    Main_loop

GameOver:
Xor   a
call PrintEndScreen
jp    Main_start

Win:
ld    a, $01
call PrintEndScreen
jp    Main_start

include "ctrl.asm"
include "const.asm"
include "game.asm"
include "graph.asm"
include "print.asm"
include "var.asm"

end   Main
```

At this point we can play, but there is still work to be done.

Download the source code from here

https://tinyurl.com/2y49z8yh

Step 10: Joystick and extra life

In this chapter we are going to implement joystick control and get an extra life every five hundred points.

We create the folder Step10 and copy the files loader.tap, const.asm, ctrl.asm, game.asm, graph.asm, int.asm, main.asm, make or make.bat, print.asm and var.asm from the folder Step09.

First we implemented a delay between levels to give us time to prepare.

Delay

We will open game.asm and at the end of it we will implement the routine that will produce about half a second of delay. The ULA produces fifty interrupts per second on PAL systems, sixty on NTSC. We will implement a loop that waits for twenty-five interrupts.

```
; ------------------------------------------------------------------
; Wait for twenty-five interruptions.
; ------------------------------------------------------------------
Sleep:
ld    b, $19              ; B = 25
sleep_Loop:
halt                     ; Wait for interruption
djnz sleep_Loop          ; Loop until B = 0

ret
```

We won't explain the code, you already have enough knowledge to understand it.

To see how this routine works, open main.asm, locate the **Main_start** tag, and at the end, just after **CALL PrintEnemies**, add the call to the delay routine.

```
call Sleep
```

Locate **Main_restart** and at the end, before **JR Main_loop**, add the following lines:

```
call PrintEnemies
call Sleep
```

Now we compile, load into the emulator and see that there is a delay between the time the enemies beep and the time they move.

Joystick

Since we are going to use the joystick to control the game, we have three other control options in addition to the buttons, and we need to store somewhere the type of control the player has chosen. We open var.asm, locate **enemiesCounter** and add a new label just above it:

```
controls:
```

```
db $00
```

This is where we will store the player's choice of controls.

Open print.asm and locate **printFirstScreen_op**. We will delete the lines **BIT $00, A** and **JR NZ, printFirstScreen_op**. We will replace them with the new implementation. We will leave the rest of the lines as they are and add them just above **CALL FadeScreen**:

```
printFirstScreen_end:
ld    a, b
ld    (controls), a
```

We have added a new tag, **printFirstScreen_end**, and as you can see we have selected the controls in B, we load them into A, **LD A, B**, and from there we load them into memory, **LD (controls), A**.

We implement the rest of the routine in the place where the deleted lines were, just below the keyboard display, **IN A, ($FE)**.

```
ld    b, $01
rra
jr    nc, printFirstScreen_end
inc   b
rra
jr    nc, printFirstScreen_end
inc   b
rra
jr    nc, printFirstScreen_end
inc   b
rra
jr    c, printFirstScreen_op
```

It should be remembered that when reading the keyboard, the status of the keys is given in bits zero to four, where bit zero corresponds to the key furthest from the centre of the keyboard and bit four corresponds to the key closest to the centre of the keyboard. Similarly, the bit is set to zero if the key has been pressed and to one if it has not.

We set B to one, the key option, **LD B, $01**, rotate A to the right, set the value of the zero bit (key 1) in the carry flag, **RRA**, and if the carry flag is disabled, the bit has been set to zero, the key has been pressed and we jump, **JR NC, printFirstScreen_end**, because they have selected keyboard.

If carry is enabled, we increment B to two (Kempston), rotate by setting the value of the zero bit (key 2 after the previous rotation) in the carry flag, **RRA**, and jump as before, **JR NC, printFirstScreen_end**, if carry is disabled.

If 2 has not been pressed, we rotate and check keys 3 and 4, paying attention to the last **JR**, in this case **JR C, printFirstScreen_op**. If 4 has not been pressed either, the carry is active and we read the keyboard and continue the loop until any key from 1 to 4 is pressed.

The final aspect of the routine is as follows:

```
; --------------------------------------------------------------------
```

```
; Display screen and selection of controls.
;
; Alters the value of the AF and HL registers.
; --------------------------------------------------------------
PrintFirstScreen:
call CLS                    ; Clear screen
ld   hl, title             ; HL = title definition
call PrintString           ; Paint title
ld   hl, firstScreen       ; HL = screen definition
call PrintString           ; Paint screen

printFirstScreen_op:
ld   a, $f7                ; A = half-row 1-5
in   a, ($fe)             ; Read keyboard
ld   b, $01                ; B = 1, option keys
rra                        ; Rotate A right
jr   nc, printFirstScreen_end ; Carry? No, pressed
inc  b                     ; B = B+1, option Kempston
rra                        ; Rotate A right
jr   nc, printFirstScreen_end ; Carry? No, pressed
inc  b                     ; B = B+1, option Sinclair 1
rra                        ; Rotate A right
jr   nc, printFirstScreen_end ; Carry? No, pressed
inc  b                     ; B = B+1, option Sinclair 2
rra                        ; Rotate A right
jr   c, printFirstScreen_op ; Carry? Yes, not pressed

printFirstScreen_end:
ld   a, b                 ; A = selected option
ld   (controls), a        ; Load into memory
call FadeScreen           ; Fade screen

ret
```

Now you need to use the controls you have chosen, and the first thing you need to know is how to read the joysticks.

In the case of the Sinclair joysticks, each joystick is mapped to a half row of the keyboard, which is not the case with the Kempston. Another difference is that the Sinclair joysticks set the pressed directions to zero, whereas the Kempston joysticks set them to one.

Below is a table detailing how to read the joystick keystrokes and in which bit we have each address.

Joystick	Half-row	Port	Up	Below	Left	Right.	Fire
Sinclair 1	$EF(0-6)	$FE	1	2	4	3	0
Sinclair 2	$F7(1-5)	$FE	3	2	0	1	4
Kempston		$1F	3	2	1	0	4

We open ctrl.asm and modify **CheckCtrl** to take into account the four types of controls available.

The first line of this routine is **LD D, $00**, and just below this we will implement the management of the controls. We delete from just below **LD D, $00** to just above **RET** as follows:

```
CheckCtrl:
ld   d, $00              ; D = 0

ret
```

At the end of the routine it checked if both left and right were pressed at the same time, **checkCtrl_testLR**, and if so both were skipped. We will remove this check because if both are pressed the ship will move to the right (see **MoveShip** in game.asm) and by removing this part we save ten bytes and thirty-eight or forty-four clock cycles.

And now we start the implementation right after **LD D, $00**.

```
ld   a, (controls)
dec  a
jr   z, checkCtrl_Keys
dec  a
jr   z, checkCtrl_Kempston
dec  a
jr   z, checkCtrl_Sinclair1
```

We load into A the selected controls, a value between one and four, **LD A, (controls)**, and decrement A, **DEC A**. If the value of A was one, after decrementing it is zero and we jump, **JR Z, checkCtrl_Keys**. If the keyboard was not selected, we decrement A and check if Kempston was selected, and if not we do the same to see if Sinclair 1 was selected. If neither has been selected, then Sinclair 2 has been selected.

Previously we checked if a key was pressed with the instruction **BIT n, r**, which takes two bytes and eight clock cycles. Since a single read of the port gives us the status of all addresses, this time we will use rotations of register A, which occupy one byte and take four clock cycles. We use a maximum of five rotations, occupying five bytes and taking twenty clock cycles. The alternative is to use three **BIT** instructions, occupying six bytes and taking twenty-eight clock cycles; with rotations we save bytes and clock cycles.

```
checkCtrl_Sinclair2:
ld   a, $f7
in   a, ($fe)
checkCtrl_Sinclair2_left:
rra
jr   c, checkCtrl_Sinclair2_right
set  $00, d
checkCtrl_Sinclair2_right:
rra
jr   c, checkCtrl_Sinclair2_fire
set  $01, d
checkCtrl_Sinclair2_fire:
and  $04
ret  nz
set  $02, d
ret
```

We load the half stack 1-5 into A, **LD A, $F7**, and read the keyboard, **IN A, ($FE)**. We rotate A to the right to see if the left direction, **RRA**, has been pressed, and if not, the carry flag is set and jumps, **JR C, chechCtrl_Sinclair2_right**. If pressed, we set the zero bit of D, **SET $00, D**.

We rotate A to the right to check if the right direction, **RRA**, has been pressed, and if not, the carry is activated and jumps, **JR C, chechCtrl_Sinclair2_fire**. If it has been pressed, we set bit one of D, **SET $01, D.**

Now the shot is in bit two, check if it is set, **AND $04**, and exit if it is not, **RET NZ**. If it is, we activate bit two of D, **SET $02, D**, and exit, **RET**.

We will now manage the Kempston selection.

```
checkCtrl_Kempston:
in    a, ($1f)
checkCtrl_Kempston_right:
rra
jr   nc, checkCtrl_Kempston_left
set  $01, d
checkCtrl_Kempston_left:
rra
jr   nc, checkCtrl_Kempston_fire
set  $00, d
checkCtrl_Kempston_fire:
and  $04
ret  z
set  $02, d
ret
```

We read port thirty-one, **IN A, ($1F)**. We rotate A to the right to check if the right direction, **RRA**, has been pressed and turn off the carry and jump, **JR NC, chechCtrl_Kempston_left**, if it has not been pressed. If it was pressed, we set bit one of D, **SET $01, D**.

We rotate A to the right to check if the left direction, **RRA**, has been pressed and if not, the carry flag is disabled and jumps, **JR NC, chechCtrl_Kempston_fire**. If it was pressed, we set bit one of D, **SET $00, D**.

Now the shot is in bit two, we check if it is pressed, **AND $04**, and if not, **RET Z**. If it is pressed, we activate bit two of D, **SET $02, D**, and exit, RET.

The management of Sinclair 1 and the keyboard is the same as for Sinclair 2, only the order of the tests is different, so let's look at the last aspect of the routine.

```
; ------------------------------------------------------------------
; Evaluates whether an direction has been clicked.
; Kempston, Sinclair 1 and Sinclair 2
; The keys are:
;          Z -> Left
;          X -> Right
;          V -> Trigger
```

```
;
; Return: D -> Keys pressed:
;              Bit 0 -> Left
;              Bit 1 -> Right
;              Bit 2 -> Trigger
;
; Alters the value of the registers A and D
; ----------------------------------------------------------------
CheckCtrl:
ld   d, $00              ; Sets D to 0
ld   a, (controls)       ; A = selection controls
dec  a                   ; A = A-1
jr   z, checkCtrl_Keys   ; Zero, skip
dec  a                   ; A = A-1
jr   z, checkCtrl_Kempston ; Zero, skip
dec  a                   ; A = A-1
jr   z, checkCtrl_Sinclair1 ; Zero, skip

; Sinclair 2 control
checkCtrl_Sinclair2:
ld   a, $f7              ; A = half-row 1-5
in   a, ($fe)            ; Read keyboard
checkCtrl_Sinclair2_left:
rra                      ; Rotate A, check left
jr   c, checkCtrl_Sinclair2_right ; Carry, not pressed, skip
set  $00, d              ; No carry, set bit left
checkCtrl_Sinclair2_right:
rra                      ; Rotate A, check der
jr   c, checkCtrl_Sinclair2_fire ; Carry, not pressed, skip
set  $01, d              ; No carry, set right bit
checkCtrl_Sinclair2_fire:
and  $04                 ; Check shot
ret  nz                  ; Non-zero, not pressed, exits
set  $02, d              ; If zero, set shot bit
ret                      ; Exits

; Kempston control
checkCtrl_Kempston:
in   a, ($1f)            ; Read port 31
checkCtrl_Kempston_right:
rra                      ; Rotate A, check right
jr   nc, checkCtrl_Kempston_left ; No carry, not pressed, skip
set  $01, d              ; Carry, set right bit
checkCtrl_Kempston_left:
rra                      ; Rotate A, check left
jr   nc, checkCtrl_Kempston_fire ; No carry, not pressed, skip
set  $00, d              ; Carry, set left bit
checkCtrl_Kempston_fire:
and  $04                 ; Check shot
ret  z                   ; Zero, not pressed, exits
set  $02, d              ; Non-zero, set shot bit
ret                      ; Exits

; Sinclair 1 control
checkCtrl_Sinclair1:
ld   a, $ef              ; A = half-row 0-6
in   a, ($fe)            ; Read keyboard
checkCtrl_Sinclair1_fire:
rra                      ; Rota A, check shot
```

```
jr   c, checkCtrl_Sinclair1_right ; Carry, not pressed, skip
set  $02, d                ; No carry, set bit shot
checkCtrl_Sinclair1_right:
rra
rra
rra                        ; Rotate A, check right
jr   c, checkCtrl_Sinclair1_left ; Carry, not pressed, skip
set  $01, d                ; No carry, set right bit
checkCtrl_Sinclair1_left:
rra                        ; Rotate A, check left
ret  c                     ; Carry, not pressed, exit
set  $00, d                ; No carry, set left bit
ret                        ; Exits

; Keyboard control
checkCtrl_Keys:
ld   a, $fe                ; A = half-stack Cs-V
in   a, ($fe)              ; Read keyboard
checkCtrl_Key_left:
rra
rra                        ; Rotate A, check left
jr   c, checkCtrl_right    ; Carry, not pressed, skip
set  $00, d                ; No carry, set bit left
checkCtrl_right:
rra                        ; Rotate A, check right
jr   c, checkCtrl_fire     ; Carry, not pressed, skip
set  $01, d                ; No carry, set right bit
checkCtrl_fire:
and  $02                   ; Check shot
ret  nz                    ; Non-zero, not pressed, exits
set  $02, d                ; Zero, set shot bit
ret                        ; Exits
```

We compile, load in the emulator and test the different controls.

Extra life

We're going to implement that every five hundred fucks you get, you get an extra life.

We open var.asm, locate **pointsCounter**, and just below it we add a new label:

```
extraCounter:
dw $0000
```

In **extraCounter** we control the accumulation of points until it reaches five hundred to give an extra life.

We initialise **extraCounter** at the start of each game. We go to the main.asm file, locate the **Main_start** tag, and look at the first few lines:

```
xor  a
ld   hl, enemiesCounter
ld   (hl), $20
inc  hl
ld   (hl), a ; $1d
inc  hl
ld   (hl), a ; $29
```

292

```
inc   hl
ld    (hl), $05
inc   hl
ld    (hl), a
inc   hl
ld    (hl), a
```

In this part we initialise the values of the game, which occupies seventeen bytes and takes ninety-two clock cycles. The pair **INC HL** and **LD (HL), A**, occupies two bytes and takes thirteen clock cycles. Since we would have to add two more pairs to initialise the two new bytes we added with the **extraCounter** tag, we would add four bytes and twenty-six clock cycles, for a total of twenty-one bytes and one hundred and eighteen clock cycles, plus the code grows repetitively.

Instead of initialising the values as we do now, we will use the **LDIR** instruction. We delete the code we used to initialise the values and replace it with the following:

```
ld    hl, enemiesCounter
ld    de, enemiesCounter + 1
ld    (hl), $00
ld    bc, $08
ldir
ld    a, $05
ld    (livesCounter), a
```

We point HL to the location of the enemies counter, **LD HL, enemiesCounter**, and point DE to the next location.

We set the memory location to which HL points to zero, **LD(HL), $00**, load the number of locations to be set to zero in addition to the first into BC, **LD BC, $08**, and set the remaining memory locations to zero, **LDIR**.

Not all values start at zero, lives are done at five, so we load five into A, **LD A, $05**, and load them into memory, **LD (livesCounter), A**.

The way we have implemented the initialisation, the code occupies eighteen bytes and takes eighty-one clock cycles, so we have gained bytes and processing time. The code is more readable, and if we need to add more bytes to initialise, all we have to do is change the value of BC.

The final appearance of **Main_start** is as follows:

```
Main_start:
ld    hl, enemiesCounter
ld    de, enemiesCounter + 1
ld    (hl), $00
ld    bc, $08
ldir
ld    a, $05
ld    (livesCounter), a

call ChangeLevel
```

All that's left is the last part, which accumulates points in **extraCounter**, gives an extra life and resets the counter to zero when you reach five hundred.

Open game.asm, find the **CheckCrashFire** tag and scroll to the end of it; it looks like this:

```
ld   (pointsCounter + 1), a ; Update in memory
call PrintInfoValue         ; Print InfoValue

ret                         ; Exits

checkCrashFire_endLoop:
inc  hl                     ; HL = coord Y next enemy
djnz checkCrashFire_loop    ; Loop as long as B > 0

ret
```

The part where we accumulate the points to get the extra life is between **LD (pointsCounter + 1), A** and **CALL PrintInfoValue**, so we continue:

```
ld   hl, (extraCounter)
ld   bc, $0005
add  hl, bc
ld   (extraCounter), hl
ld   bc, $01f4
sbc  hl, bc
jr   nz, checkCrashFire_cont
ld   (extraCounter), hl
ld   a, (livesCounter)
inc  a
daa
ld   (livesCounter), a
checkCrashFire_cont:
```

If you have reached this part of the routine, it is because you have hit an enemy and scored five points.

We load the extra life counter into HL, **LD HL, (extraCounter)**, load the five points to be added into BC, **LD BC, $0005**, add it to HL, **ADD HL, BC**, and update it in memory, **LD (extraCounter), HL**.

We load five hundred into BC, **LD BC, $01F4**, subtract it from HL, **SBC HL, BC**, and if the result is not zero, we jump because we have not reached five hundred points, **JR NZ, checkCrashFire_cont**. If the result of the subtraction was zero, we would have reached five hundred points.

SBC is subtraction with carry, the only one available to the Z80 when working with 16-bit registers. It is very important that the carry is disabled, which we know it is because before the subtraction we added five to HL and in our case the value of HL will never exceed five hundred.

If we had not jumped, the value of HL would have reached five hundred and would now be zero. We update the counter in memory by setting it to zero, **LD (extraCounter), HL**, load the number of lives we have left in A, **LD A, (livesCounter)**, increment A to have one more life,

INC A, do the decimal adjustment, **DAA**, and update the value in memory, **LD (livesCounter), A**.

Finally, before **CALL PrintInfoValue**, we set the label to jump to if five hundred is not reached, **checkCrashFire_cont**.

The final aspect of the routine is as follows:

```
; -----------------------------------------------------------------
; Evaluates the collisions of the shot with enemies.
;
; Alters the value of the AF, BC, DE and HL registers.
; -----------------------------------------------------------------
CheckCrashFire:
ld    a, (flags)                ; A = flags
and   $02                       ; Active shot?
ret   z                         ; Not active, exits

ld    de, (firePos)             ; DE = shot position
ld    hl, enemiesConfig         ; HL = 1st enemy definition
ld    b, enemiesConfigEnd-enemiesConfigIni ; B = bytes config enemies
sra   b                         ; B = B/2 number of enemies

checkCrashFire_loop:
ld    a, (hl)                   ; A = enemy Y-coordinate
inc   hl                        ; HL = coord X
bit   $07, a                    ; Active enemy?
jr    z, checkCrashFire_endLoop ; Not active, skips
and   $1f                       ; A = coord Y enemy
cp    d                         ; Compare coord Y shot
jr    nz, checkCrashFire_endLoop ; Not the same, skip
ld    a, (hl)                   ; A = coord X enemy
and   $1f                       ; A = coord X
cp    e                         ; Compare coord X shot
jr    nz, checkCrashFire_endLoop ; Not the same, skip

dec   hl                        ; HL = coord Y enemy
res   $07, (hl)                 ; Deactivates enemy
ld    b, d                      ; B = coord Y shot
ld    c, e                      ; C = coord X shot
call  DeleteChar                ; Delete shot/enemy
ld    a, (enemiesCounter)       ; A = number of enemies
dec   a                         ; Subtract one
daa                             ; Decimal adjust
ld    (enemiesCounter), a       ; Refresh memory
ld    a, (pointsCounter)        ; A = units and tens
add   a, $05                    ; A = A+5
daa                             ; Decimal adjust
ld    (pointsCounter), a        ; Refresh memory
ld    a, (pointsCounter + 1)    ; A hundreds and ud thousands
adc   a, $00                    ; A = A+1 with carry
daa                             ; Decimal adjust
ld    (pointsCounter + 1), a    ; Refresh memory
ld    hl, (extraCounter)        ; HL = extra life counter
ld    bc, $0005                 ; BC = 5
add   hl, bc                    ; HL = HL+BC
ld    (extraCounter), hl        ; Update memory
ld    bc, $01f4                 ; BC = 500
sbc   hl, bc                    ; HL = HL-BC
```

```
jr   nz, checkCrashFire_cont  ; !0, skip
ld   (extraCounter), hl       ; 0, extra life counter = 0
ld   a, (livesCounter)        ; A = lives
inc  a                        ; Add a life
daa                           ; Decimal adjust
ld   (livesCounter), a        ; Refresh memory
checkCrashFire_cont:
call PrintInfoValue           ; Print InfoValue

ret                           ; Exits

checkCrashFire_endLoop:
inc  hl                       ; HL = coord Y next enemy
djnz checkCrashFire_loop      ; Loop as long as B > 0

ret
```

We compile, load into the emulator and see the results. Every five hundred points we get an extra life.

To see if it works, we can start the game with **extraCounter** at $1EF (495) and when we hit an enemy we get a life.

You can also do something that you may have already noticed, if you start the level with the trigger pressed, move to the right and stay there, you will get through almost all the levels without getting killed. This is something we need to change, otherwise you can get through all thirty levels using this technique.

Change of shot

The first thing we will do is change the shot to see if that solves anything. Continue in game.asm, locate **MoveFire**, and after the first line, **LD HL, flags**, add the following:

```
bit  00, (hl)
ret  z
```

We check if the zero bit is active, **BIT $00, (HL)**, and if not we quit.

The zero bit of the flags indicates whether we should move the ship, so now the trigger moves at the same speed as the ship.

We compile, load into the emulator and see the results.

As you can see, the technique of moving to the right no longer works, but I like it better than the shot, which gives a sense of continuity, and also the movement should be polished more, as it does some strange things when there are few enemies left.

We are going to comment on the two lines we added, as we are going to solve them by changing the behaviour of the enemies.

In this chapter we added a delay for switching between levels, joystick control and extra lives. We also saw a trick to get through all the levels without the slightest effort, and we tried to change the shooting behaviour to avoid it, but we weren't convinced.

Download the source code from here

https://tinyurl.com/2a5blh2o

Step 11: Enemy behaviour

In this chapter we will focus on the behaviour of the enemies.

We create Step11 and copy from Step10 loader.tap, const.asm, ctrl.asm, game.asm, graph.asm, int.asm, main.asm, make or make.bat, print.asm and var.asm.

Changes of direction

To make enemy movement a little less predictable, the direction of the enemies will change every four seconds.

The first thing to do is to open main.asm, locate the **flags** tag and add a comment for bit three.

```
; --------------------------------------------------------------
; Indicators
;
; Bit 0 -> ship must be moved 0 = No, 1 = Yes
; Bit 1 -> shot is active 0 = No, 1 = Yes
; Bit 2 -> enemies must be moved 0 = No, 1 = Yes
; Bit 3 -> change address enemies 0 = No, 1 = Yes
; --------------------------------------------------------------
flags:
db $00
```

Every four seconds we will activate bit three and the enemies will change direction.

So that the enemies do not always change direction, we will use an extra tag. Open var.asm, go to the **extraCounter** tag and add the following lines:

```
; --------------------------------------------------------------
; Auxiliary values
; --------------------------------------------------------------
swEnemies:
db $00
enemiesColor:
db $06
```

The tag we are going to use is **swEnemies**. As you can see, I've added another tag that we're going to use to add a little colour effect to the enemies.

Now we are going to implement the routine that will change the direction of the enemies. We will open game.asm and implement the routine that changes the direction of the enemies at the beginning.

```
ChangeEnemies:
ld   hl, flags
bit  $03, (hl)
ret  z
res  03, (hl)
ld   b, $14
ld   hl, enemiesConfig
```

```
ld   a, (swEnemies)
ld   c, a
```

We load into HL the address of the flags memory, **LD HL, flags**, check if bit three is set (address change), **BIT $03, (HL)**, and exit if it is not, **RET Z**.

Deactivate the bit if it is set, **RES $03, (HL)**, load into B the total number of enemies, **LD B, $14**, load into HL the address of the enemy configuration, **LD HL, enemiesConfig**, load into A the value of the auxiliary tag indicating the change of enemy address, **LD A, (swEnemies)**, and preserve the value by loading it into C, **LD C, A**.

```
changeEnemies_loop:
bit  $07, (hl)
jr   z, changeEnemies_endLoop

inc  hl
ld   a, (hl)
and  $3f
or   c
ld   (hl), a

dec  hl
ld   a, c
add  a, $40
ld   c, a
```

We check if the enemy is active, **BIT $07, (HL)**, and if not, we jump.

The address of the enemy is in bits six and seven of the second byte of the configuration, so we point HL to this second byte, **INC HL**, load it into A, **LD A, (HL)**, discard the current address, **AND $3F**, add the new one, **OR C**, and update in memory, **LD (HL), A**.

Point HL back to the first byte of the configuration, **DEC HL**, load the new address into A, **LD A, C**, add one ($40 = **01**00 0000), **ADD A, $40**, and load the value into C, **LD C, A**.

```
changeEnemies_endLoop:
inc  hl
inc  hl
djnz changeEnemies_loop
```

We point HL to the first byte of the next enemy, **INC HL, INC HL**, and repeat until B is zero and we have gone through all the enemies, **DJNZ changeEnemies_loop**.

```
changeEnemies_end:
ld   a, c
ld   (swEnemies), a
ret
```

We load the new address into A, **LD A, C**, load the value into memory for the next time the address needs to be changed, **LD (swEnemies), A**, and exit, **RET**.

The last aspect of the routine is as follows:

```
; ------------------------------------------------------------------
; Changes the direction of enemies.
;
; Alters the value of the AF, BC and HL registers.
; ------------------------------------------------------------------
ChangeEnemies:
ld    hl, flags            ; HL = address flags
bit   $03, (hl)            ; Bit 3 active?
ret   z                    ; Not active, exits
res   $03, (hl)            ; Disables bit 3
ld    b, $14               ; B = number of enemies (20)
ld    hl, enemiesConfig    ; HL = enemiesConfig
ld    a, (swEnemies)       ; A = aux change direction
ld    c, a                 ; C = A (new address)
changeEnemies_loop:
bit   $07, (hl)            ; Active enemy?
jr    z, changeEnemies_endLoop ; Not active, skips

inc   hl                   ; HL = 2nd byte config
ld    a, (hl)              ; A = 2nd byte
and   $3f                  ; Discard the address
or    c                    ; A = new address
ld    (hl), a              ; Update in memory

dec   hl                   ; HL = 1st byte config
ld    a, c                 ; A = C (new address)
add   a, $40               ; Add one dir ($40=01000000)
ld    c, a                 ; C = A (new address)

changeEnemies_endLoop:
inc   hl                   ; HL 1st byte next config
inc   hl                   ; enemy
djnz  changeEnemies_loop   ; Until B = 0 (20 enemies)

changeEnemies_end:
ld    a, c                 ; A = C (new address)
ld    (swEnemies), a       ; Update in-memory

ret
```

This new routine needs to be called from the main loop of the program. Go back to main.asm, find **Main_loop**, find the **CALL MoveShip** line, and add the following just below it:

```
call ChangeEnemies
```

Try to compile, load in the emulator and you will see that everything remains the same, we have not broken anything and the address change does not occur because we do not activate bit three of the flags.

We open int.asm to implement the activation of this bit every four seconds (on PAL systems), thus using interrupts.

The first thing we will do is add a constant to the top of the file, just below **ORG $7E5C**:

```
T1: EQU $c8
```

We assign $C8 (two hundred) to T1, which is the result of multiplying fifty interrupts per second by four seconds.

At the end of the file we add a tag to keep track of the interrupts until they reach two hundred and four seconds.

```
countT1:    db $00
```

Now we modify the interrupt routine. We locate the **Isr_end** tag, and just above it we implement the part that controls the four seconds we talked about.

```
Isr_T1:
ld   a, (countT1)
inc  a
ld   (countT1), a
sub  T1
jr   nz, Isr_end
ld   (countT1), a
set  03, (hl)
```

We load the counter in A, **LD A, (countT1)**, add one, **INC A**, and update the value of the counter, **LD (countT1), A**.

We subtract the interrupts that must be reached to activate the change of direction flag, **SUB T1**, and skip them if they are not reached, **JR NZ, Isr_end**.

When four seconds have been reached, the result of the above subtraction is zero and we update the counter, **LD (countT1), A**. Finally, we set the address change bit, **SET $03, (HL)**.

Three lines above **Isr_T1** we find the **JR NZ line, Isr_end**, which we change to this:

```
jr   nz, Isr_T1
```

Now we compile, load the emulator and check that the enemies change direction every four seconds. In the same way, we can see that going to the right and shooting doesn't work so well, maybe in the first level, but not in the following ones.

We are forcing the player to move, but the enemy's speed does not allow us to see where he is going, so we should slow down the enemy's speed. We go back to int.asm and find the part where the bit for moving enemies is activated:

```
ld   a, (countEnemy)
inc  a
ld   (countEnemy), a
sub  $02
jr   nz, Isr_T1
ld   (countEnemy), a
set  02, (hl)
```

Change **SUB $02** to **SUB $03**.

Compile, load in the emulator and see if it runs better. Adjust the speed to your liking; we still need to work on the behaviour of the enemies.

Colour change

As I mentioned earlier in this chapter, we are going to add a colour effect to the movement of the enemies, for which we have added the **enemiesColor** tag to var.asm.

The effect is to change the colour of the enemies from one (blue) to seven (white) every time they move.

Let's go to print.asm and locate **PrintEnemies**, and just below that we'll add the implementation of the colour effect.

The first thing we need to do is change the first line of the rutia, LD A, $06.

```
ld    a, (enemiesColor)        ; A = ink
```

The colour in which the enemies are painted is taken from this new label.

The first time we paint the enemies in each level, we paint them yellow. Open game.asm, locate **ChangeLevel** and add these two lines at the top:

```
ld    a, $06               ; A = yellow
ld    (enemiesColor), a    ; Update colour in memory
```

When we compile and load in the emulator, we see that the enemies are still painted in yellow.

We follow game.asm and find the **MoveEnemies** tag, which looks like this:

```
MoveEnemies:
ld    hl, flags            ; HL = flags memory address
bit   $02, (hl)            ; Bit 2 active?
ret   z                    ; Not active, exits
res   $02, (hl)            ; Disables bit 2 of flags

ld    d, $14               ; D = total number of enemies (20)
ld    hl, enemiesConfig    ; HL = enemies config address
moveEnemies_loop:
```

The colour change is implemented immediately after the **RES $02, (HL)** line.

```
ld    a, (enemiesColor)
inc   a
cp    $08
jr    c, moveEnemies_cont
ld    a, $01

moveEnemies_cont:
ld    (enemiesColor), a
```

We load the colour in A, **LD A, (enemiesColor)**, add one, **INC A**, check if it has reached eight, **CP $08**, and jump if it hasn't, **JR C, moveEnemies_cont**. If we didn't jump, we reached eight and set the colour to blue, **LD A, $01**. Finally, we update the colour in memory, **LD (enemiesColor), A**.

The start of the routine looks like this:

```
MoveEnemies:
ld   hl, flags              ; HL = flags memory address
bit  $02, (hl)              ; Bit 2 active?
ret  z                      ; Not active, exits
res  $02, (hl)              ; Disables bit 2 of flags

ld   a, (enemiesColor)      ; A = enemiesColor
inc  a                      ; It increases it
cp   $08                    ; ¿A = 8?
jr   c, moveEnemies_cont    ; Distinct, jumps
ld   a, $01                 ; A = colour blue

moveEnemies_cont:
ld   (enemiesColor), a      ; Update colour in memory
ld   d, $14                 ; D = total number of enemies (20)
ld   hl, enemiesConfig      ; HL = dir config enemies
moveEnemies_loop:
```

Compile and load into the emulator. Now we can see how the enemies change colour.

Enemy shots

We've changed the behaviour of the enemies, firstly so that we don't just get through the thirty levels by staying in one part of the screen, and secondly to make the game more eye-catching.

The time has come for the most important change, we are going to equip our enemies with shooting.

Shooting enemies will be activated when they are above us, and there will be a maximum of five active shots at any one time.

The first step is to declare the constants we need. Open const.asm and look for WHITE_GRAPH, which is an EQU directive with a value of $9E, code that corresponds to the graphic defined for the blank, which is unnecessary since the blank character is defined in the ZX Spectrum, it is the character $20 (32). We leave the line as follows:

```
WHITE_GRAPH: EQU $20
```

Now locate **ENEMY_TOP_R** and just below it we will add constants for the total number of enemies, the character code for enemy shot and the number of shots that can be active at the same time.

```
ENEMIES:     EQU $14
ENEMY_GRA_F: EQU $9e
FIRES:       EQU $05
```

We see that the character code $9E becomes the enemy shot.

Open var.asm, find **udgsCommon** and go to the last line:

```
db $00, $00, $00, $00, $00, $00, $00, $00 ; $9e White
```

We change this line and leave it as follows:

```
db $00, $3c, $2c, $2c, $2c, $2c, $18, $00 ; $9e Enemy shot
```

If you have done the exercises in **Step 1: Definition of graphics**, you should be able to draw the representation of the enemy shot on paper or on the provided templates, you just need to do the conversion from hexadecimal to binary.

Just above **udgsCommon** we will add tags to configure the shots and to keep track of the number of active shots.

```
; ------------------------------------------------------------------
; Enemy shots configuration
;
; 2 bytes per shot.
; ------------------------------------------------------------------
; Byte 1              | Byte 2
; ------------------------------------------------------------------
; Bit 0-4: Position Y | Bit 0-4: X position
; Bit 5:    Free      | Bit 5:    Free
; Bit 6:    Free      | Bit 6:    Free
; Bit 7:    Active 1/0 | Bit 7:    Free
; ------------------------------------------------------------------
enemiesFire:
ds FIRES * $02
enemiesFireCount:
db $00
```

With **DEFS**, we reserve as many bytes as the result of multiplying **FIRES** (maximum number of enemy shots simultaneously) by two (bytes per shot). As you can see, the configuration of the enemy shots has some similarity to the configuration of the enemies.

Open up game.asm and let's start with the implementation necessary for enemies to shoot and make things difficult.

We will implement a routine to disable all enemy shots, which we will call every time we start a new level. We will place this routine just before the **Sleep** routine.

```
ResetEnemiesFire:
ld   hl, enemiesFire
ld   de, enemiesFire + $01
ld   bc, FIRES * $02
ld   (hl), $00
ldir

ret
```

We point HL to the first byte of the enemiesFire configuration, **LD HL, enemiesFire**, DE we point it to the next byte, **LD DE, enemiesFire + $01**, we load into BC the number of bytes to clear, **LD BC, FIRES * $02**, we clear the first one, **LD (HL), $02**, we clear the rest, **LDIR**, and exit, **RET**.

Actually, we are also clearing (resetting) the active firing counter, which is not a problem. However, if you want to avoid this, you can set **LD BC, FIRES * $02 - $01**.

The appearance of the routine, once annotated, is as follows:

```
; -------------------------------------------------------------
; Initialises the enemy firing configuration
;
; Alters the value of the BC, DE and HL registers.
; -------------------------------------------------------------
ResetEnemiesFire:
ld    hl, enemiesFire        ; HL = shot configuration
ld    de, enemiesFire + $01  ; DE = next byte
ld    bc, FIRES * $02        ; BC = bytes to be cleared
ld    (hl), $00              ; Clean 1st byte
ldir                         ; Clean remainder

ret
```

The enemy firing configuration is a kind of list. We need a routine that updates this list, sees which shots are active, puts them at the beginning and updates the number of active shots in memory. We'll implement this just before **ResetEnemiesFire**.

We are unlikely to have more than five enemy shots active at any one time, maybe even less. Based on that, we are going to do a routine that is not the most optimal, but it works.

The routine will go through the whole list for each item, so we will use two nested loops. Finally, we implement a third loop that updates the number of active shots.

```
RefreshEnemiesFire:
ld   b, FIRES
xor  a
refreshEnemiesFire_loopExt:
push bc
ld   ix, enemiesFire
ld   b, FIRES
```

We load the maximum number of shots into B as the outer loop counter, **LD B, FIRES**, and set A to zero, **XOR A**. We keep BC, **PUSH BC**, point IX to the part of the enemy firing configuration, **LD IX, enemiesFire**, and reload the maximum number of shots into B as the inner loop counter, **LD B, FIRES**.

```
refreshEnemiesFire_loopInt:
bit  $07, (ix+$00)
jr   nz, refreshEnemiesFire_loopIntCont
ld   c, (ix+$02)
ld   (ix+$00), c
ld   c, (ix+$03)
ld   (ix+$01), c
ld   (ix+$02), a
```

We evaluate if the fire is active, **BIT $07, (IX+$00)**, and if it is, we skip, **JR NZ, refreshEnemiesFire_loopIntCont**.

If it is not active, we load the first byte of the next shot into C, **LD C, (IX+$02)**, and load it into the first byte of the shot pointed to by IX, **LD (IX+$00), C**. We load the second byte of the next shot into C, **LD C, (IX+$03)**, and load it into the second byte of the shot pointed to by IX, **LD (IX+$01), C**.

Finally, we set the first byte of the second shot to zero, **LD(IX+$02), A**.

```
refreshEnemiesFire_loopIntCont:
inc  ix
inc  ix
djnz refreshEnemiesFire_loopInt

pop  bc
djnz refreshEnemiesFire_loopExt
```

We point IX to the first byte of the next shot, **INC IX**, **INC IX**, and repeat the operations in a loop, **DJNZ refreshEnemiesFire_loopInt**, until B is zero.

We get BC (this is the outer loop counter), **PUSH BC**, and repeat the loop operations, **DJNZ refreshEnemiesFire_loopExt**, until the value of B reaches zero.

At this point we have the active shots at the top of the list, and all that remains is to count how many shots are active. We will count the active shots in A, remembering that we already set it to zero at the beginning of the routine, **XOR A**.

```
ld   b, FIRES
ld   hl, enemiesFire
refreshEnemiesFire_loopCount:
bit  $07, (hl)
jr   z, refreshEnemiesFire_end
inc  a
refreshEnemiesFire_loopCountCont:
inc  hl
inc  hl
djnz refreshEnemiesFire_loopCount
refreshEnemiesFire_end:
ld   (enemiesFireCount), a

ret
```

We load the maximum number of shots in B, **LD B, FIRES**, and aim HL at its setting, **LD HL, enemiesFire**.

Evaluate if the fire is active, **BIT $07, (HL)**, and jump if not, **JR Z, refreshEnemiesFire_end**.

If active, we increment A to add an active fire, **INC A**, point HL to the first byte of the next fire, **INC HL**, **INC HL**, and continue the loop until the value of B becomes zero, **DJNZ refreshEnemiesFire_loopCount**.

Finally, we update in memory the number of shots still active, **LD (enemiesFireCount), A**, and exit, **RET**.

The final aspect of the routine is as follows:

```
; ------------------------------------------------------------------
; Updates enemy shots settings
;
; Alters the value of the AD, BC, HL and IX registers.
; ------------------------------------------------------------------
RefreshEnemiesFire:
ld   b, FIRES                ; B = maximum number of shots
xor  a                       ; A = 0
refreshEnemiesFire_loopExt:
push bc                      ; Preserve BC
ld   ix, enemiesFire         ; IX = config shots
ld   b, FIRES                ; B = maximum number of shots
refreshEnemiesFire_loopInt:
bit  $07, (ix+$00)           ; Active shot?
jr   nz, refreshEnemiesFire_loopIntCont ; Active, jumps
ld   c, (ix+$02)             ; C = byte 1 next shot
ld   (ix+$00), c             ; Byte 1 of the current = C
ld   c, (ix+$03)             ; C = byte 2 next shot
ld   (ix+$01), c             ; Byte 2 of the current = C
ld   (ix+$02), a             ; Byte 1 next shot = 0
refreshEnemiesFire_loopIntCont:
inc  ix
inc  ix                      ; IX = byte 1 next shot
djnz refreshEnemiesFire_loopInt ; Loop until B = 0

pop  bc                      ; Retrieves BC (outer loop)
djnz refreshEnemiesFire_loopExt ; Loop until B = 0

; Updates the number of active shots
ld   b, FIRES                ; B = maximum number of shots
ld   hl, enemiesFire         ; HL = fire configuration
refreshEnemiesFire_loopCount:
bit  $07, (hl)               ; Active shot?
jr   z, refreshEnemiesFire_end ; Not active, skips
inc  a                       ; A=A+1 (shot counter)
refreshEnemiesFire_loopCountCont:
inc  hl
inc  hl                      ; HL = byte 1 next shot
djnz refreshEnemiesFire_loopCount ; Loop until B = 0

refreshEnemiesFire_end:
ld   (enemiesFireCount), a ; Update shot counter

ret
```

Next, we implement the routine that triggers the shots. The shots will be fired when the enemy is in the same horizontal coordinate as the ship and when they are not all active.

We continue in game.asm, locate the **MoveEnemies** tag and implement the trigger activation routine on top of it.

```
EnableEnemiesFire:
ld   de, (shipPos)
ld   hl, enemiesConfig
ld   b, ENEMIES
```

We load in DE the position of the ship, **LD DE, (shipPos)**, point HL to the address of the enemies configuration, **LD HL, enemiesConfig**, and we load in B the maximum number of enemies, **LD B, ENEMIES**.

```
enableEnemiesFire_loop:
ld    a, (enemiesFireCount)
cp    FIRES
ret   nc

push  bc
ld    a, (hl)
ld    b, a
inc   hl
and   $80
jr    z, enableEnemiesFire_loopCont

ld    a, (hl)
and   $1f
cp    e
jr    nz, enableEnemiesFire_loopCont
```

We load into register A the number of active shots, **LD A, (enemiesFireCount)**, compare it with the maximum number of shots, **CP FIRES**, and quit when we have reached it, **RET NC**.

We keep the value of BC, **PUSH BC**, load the first byte of the enemy configuration in A, **LD A, (HL)**, load it in B, **LD B, A**, point HL to the second byte, **INC HL**, see if the enemy is active, **AND $80**, and if not jump, **JR Z, enableEnemiesFire_loopCont**.

If the enemy is active, we load the second byte of the configuration into A, **LD A, (HL)**, keep the X-coordinate, **AND $1F**, compare with the X-coordinate of the ship, **CP E**, and skip if they are not the same, **JR NZ, enableEnemiesFire_loopCont**.

If we have not jumped, we need to enable the shot.

```
ld    c, a
push hl
push bc
ld    hl, enemiesFire
ld    a, (enemiesFireCount)
add   a, a
ld    b, $00
ld    c, a
add   hl, bc
pop   bc
ld    (hl), b
inc   hl
ld    (hl), c
ld    hl, enemiesFireCount
inc   (hl)
pop   hl
```

We load the enemy's x-coordinate into C, **LD C, A**, and we have the firing configuration. Preserve HL, **PUSH HL**, preserve BC, **PUSH BC**, point HL to the enemy shots configuration, **LD HL, enemiesFire**, load into A the number of active shots, **LD A, (enemiesFireCount)**, multiply by two, **ADD**

A, A, set B to zero, **LD B, $00**, load into C the number of bytes to move, **LD C, A**, and add it to HL so that it points to the position in the list where we are going to set the shot configuration, **ADD HL, BC**.

We retrieve the shot configuration, **POP BC**, load the first byte into memory, **LD (HL), B**, point HL to the second byte in the list, **INC HL**, load the second byte into memory, **LD (HL), C**, point HL to the shots counter, **LD HL, enemiesFireCount**, increment it, **INC (HL)**, and retrieve HL to point to the second byte of the enemy configuration, **POP HL**.

```
enableEnemiesFire_loopCont:
pop  bc
inc  hl
djnz enableEnemiesFire_loop

ret
```

We get the value of BC, get the loop counter, **POP BC**, point HL to the first byte of the next enemy configuration, **INC HL**, and keep looping, **DJNZ enebleEnemiesFire_loop,** until we have looped through all the enemies. Finally we exit, **RET**.

The final aspect of the routine is as follows:

```
; -----------------------------------------------------------------
; Enables enemy fire.
;
; Alters the value of the AF, BC, DE and HL registers.
; -----------------------------------------------------------------
EnableEnemiesFire:
ld   de, (shipPos)         ; DE = ship position
ld   hl, enemiesConfig     ; HL = enemiesConfig
ld   b, ENEMIES            ; B = total number of enemies

enableEnemiesFire_loop:
ld   a, (enemiesFireCount) ; A = number of active shots
cp   FIRES                 ; Compares with max. shots
ret  nc                    ; Reached, exits (NC)

push bc                    ; Preserve BC
ld   a, (hl)               ; A = 1st byte enemy config
ld   b, a                  ; B = A
inc  hl                    ; HL = 2nd byte config
and  $80                   ; Active enemy?
jr   z, enableEnemiesFire_loopCont ; Not active, skip

ld   a, (hl)               ; A = 2nd byte enemy config
and  $1f                   ; A = coord X
cp   e                     ; Compare with ship
jr   nz, enableEnemiesFire_loopCont ; Not equal, skip

; Activate the shot
; The shot configuration is that of the enemy
ld   c, a                  ; C = enemy coord X
push hl                    ; Preserves HL
push bc                    ; Preserves BC, config shot
ld   hl, enemiesFire       ; HL = enemy fire
ld   a, (enemiesFireCount) ; A = shots counter
```

```
add   a, a                  ; A = A*2, two bytes shot
ld    b, $00
ld    c, a                  ; BC = offset
add   hl, bc                ; HL = HL+BC, shot to activate
pop   bc                    ; BC, config trigger
ld    (hl), b               ; Load into memory 1st byte config
inc   hl                    ; HL = 2nd byte config
ld    (hl), c               ; Load in memory
ld    hl, enemiesFireCount  ; HL = shots counter
inc   (hl)                  ; Increments in memory
pop   hl                    ; HL = 2nd byte config

enableEnemiesFire_loopCont:
pop   bc                    ; B = total number of enemies
inc   hl                    ; HL = 1st byte enemy config next
djnz enableEnemiesFire_loop ; Until it runs through all the enemies
                            ; B = 0

ret
```

Shots is enabled when the enemies are in the same horizontal coordinate as the ship, so it's called from within the **MoveEnemies** routine.

In **MoveEnemies** we will change two things: first we go to the **moveEnemies_cont** tag, and the second line, which now looks like this:

```
ld    d, $14                ; D = total number of enemies (20)
```

We leave it at that:

```
ld    d, ENEMIES            ; D = total number of enemies
```

Earlier we declared the constant **ENEMIES**, and now we need to reference it in all the places where the number of enemies is loaded.

Look for **moveEnemies_end** and after the first line:

```
call PrintEnemies           ; Print Enemies
```

We add the **EnableEnemiesFire** call:

```
call EnableEnemiesFire       ; Enables enemy fire
```

We implement a routine for moving enemy shots, just as we have one for moving enemies.

We continue in game.asm, locate **MoveFire** and implement the routine that moves the enemy shots just before it.

```
MoveEnemiesFire:
ld    a, $03
call Ink
ld    hl, flags
bit  $04, (hl)
ret  z
res  04, (hl)
```

We load in A the magenta ink, **LD A, $03**, and change it, **CALL Ink**. We load the flags in HL, **LD HL, flags**, and check if bit four is active, **BIT $04, (HL)**. If the bit is not set, we exit, **RET Z**, otherwise we disable it, **RES $04, (HL)**.

As you may have noticed, we are going to use another bit of flags.

```
ld    d, FIRES
ld    hl, enemiesFire
moveEnemiesFire_loop:
ld    b, (hl)
inc   hl
ld    c, (hl)
dec   hl
```

We load the maximum number of shots into D, **LD D, FIRES**, point HL to the shot configuration, **LD HL, enemiesFire**, load the first byte into B, **LD B, (HL)**, point HL to the second byte, **INC HL**, load it into C, **LD C, (HL)**, and point HL back to the first byte, **DEC HL**.

```
bit   $07, b
jr    z, moveEnemiesFire_loopCont
res   $07, b
call DeleteChar
ld    a, ENEMY_TOP_B + $01
cp    b
jr    z, moveEnemiesFire_loopCont
dec   b
call At
ld    a, ENEMY_GRA_F
rst   $10
set   $07, b
```

We evaluate if the shot is active, **BIT $07, B**, and jump if it is not, **JR Z, moveEnemiesFire_loopCont**. If it's inactive, we could exit the routine, but we don't, so that the routine always takes the same time to execute, or at least as close as possible between each execution.

If it is active, we keep the Y-coordinate, **RES $07, B**, delete the fire from its current position, **CALL DeleteChar**, load the vertical stop of the fire from below in A, **LD A, ENEMY_TOP_B+$01**, compare with the Y-coordinate, **CP B**, and jump, **JR Z, moveEnemiesFire_loopCont**, if we have reached it.

If we have not reached the top, we set the Y-coordinate to the next line, **DEC B**, position the cursor, **CALL At**, load the graph of the enemy shot in A, **LD A, ENEMY_GRA_F**, draw it, **RST $10**, and leave the shot activated, **SET $07, B**.

```
moveEnemiesFire_loopCont:
ld    (hl), b
inc   hl
inc   hl

dec   d
jr    nz, moveEnemiesFire_loop

jp    RefreshEnemiesFire
```

At this point we have enabled or disabled the shot and updated the Y coordinate accordingly. We update the first byte of the in-memory configuration, **LD (HL), D**, point HL to the first byte of the next shot, **INC HL, INC HL**, decrement D where we have the number of iterations of the loop, **DEC D**, and continue, **JR NZ, moveEnemiesFire_loop**, until D is zero.

Finally, we jump to refresh the shot list and exit, **JP RefreshEnemiesFire**.

The final aspect of the routine is as follows:

```
; -----------------------------------------------------------------
; Moves the enemy's shot.
;
; Alters the value of the AF, BC, DE and HL registers.
; -----------------------------------------------------------------
MoveEnemiesFire:
ld    a, $03              ; A = ink 3
call  Ink                 ; Change ink
ld    hl, flags           ; HL = flags
bit   $04, (hl)           ; Active move enemy shot?
ret   z                   ; Not active, exits
res   $04, (hl)           ; Deactivates flag move shot

ld    d, FIRES            ; D = maximum number of shots
ld    hl, enemiesFire     ; HL = enemy shot
moveEnemiesFire_loop:
ld    b, (hl)             ; B = coord Y shot
inc   hl                  ; HL = coord X
ld    c, (hl)             ; C = coord X
dec   hl                  ; HL = coord Y

bit   $07, b              ; Active shot?
jr    z, moveEnemiesFire_loopCont ; Not active, skip
res   $07, b              ; B = coord Y
call  DeleteChar          ; Delete shot
ld    a, ENEMY_TOP_B + $01 ; A = limit at the bottom
cp    b                   ; Compare with coord Y
jr    z, moveEnemiesFire_loopCont ; Equals, jump
dec   b                   ; B = next line
call  At                  ; Position cursor
ld    a, ENEMY_GRA_F      ; A = shot graph
rst   $10                 ; Paints it
set   $07, b              ; Activates shot

moveEnemiesFire_loopCont:
ld    (hl), b             ; Update coord Y shot
inc   hl
inc   hl                  ; HL = 1st byte enemy config next

dec   d                   ; D = D - 1
jr    nz, moveEnemiesFire_loop ; Loop until D = 0

jp    RefreshEnemiesFire  ; Refreshes shots and exits
```

We are almost ready to see enemy fire on the screen.

At the start of the **MoveEnemies** routine, we get the value of the **flags** tag and evaluate whether bit four is set.

We go to Main.asm and add the following to the **flags** comments:

```
; Bit 4 -> move enemy shot 0 = No, 1 = Yes
```

We continue in Main.asm and take the opportunity to include the calls to some of the routines we have implemented.

We locate the **Main_start** tag and, before **CALL ChangeLevel**, we include the call to initialise the shots:

```
call ResetEnemiesFire
```

We locate the **Main_loop** routine and, between **CALL MoveEnemies** and **CALL CheckCrashShip**, we add the call to the routine that moves the enemy shots:

```
call MoveEnemiesFire
```

We'll take this opportunity to comment out the **CALL CheckCrashShip** line so that we don't get killed by enemies and we can see what the shots look like.

Finally, we find the **Main_restart** routine and almost at the end, just before **CALL Sleep**, we add another call to initialise enemy shots:

```
call ResetEnemiesFire
```

We're done in main.asm, but we still need to set bit four of the **flags** to make everything work.

Let's go to int.asm, and the first thing we need to do is decide what speed the enemy shot will move at. There is no need to implement anything new to have two speeds available:

- The speed at which the ship is moving.
- The speed at which enemies move.

I chose the second one. Find the line **SET $02, (HL)**, and add just below it:

```
set   $04, (hl)
```

If you want it to move at the speed of the ship, this line should be placed just below **SET $00, (HL)**.

We have implemented a good number of lines. It's time to test and see the results; we'll compile, load and see what happens.

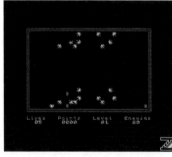

If all goes well, you can already see the enemy shots.

I commented that five shots at once might be too much. To get a better idea, we located **MoveEnemies** on game.asm and commented on the **CALL PrintEnemies** line towards the end to see it better.

We compile, load into the emulator and see the results.

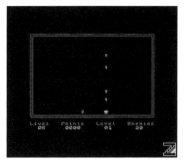

If we add the enemies, it might be too much. We uncomment the **CALL PrintEnemies** line, and in main.asm, in the MainLoop routine, we find the **CALL CheckCrashShip** line and remove the comment.

We compile, load and see that the enemies kill us again. The only thing left to do is to make the enemy shoot at us.

Before implementing the collisions between the ship and enemy shots, remember that we declared a constant with the total number of enemies, **ENEMIES**, but we still have parts of the code where we do not use it.

We go to print.asm, locate **PrintEnemies** and modify the line **LD D, $14** as follows:

```
ld    d, ENEMIES
```

The rest of the changes are made in game.asm.

We locate the **ChangeEnemies** routine, locate the **LD B, $14** line and modify it accordingly:

```
ld    b, ENEMIES
```

Find the **CheckCrashFire** routine and delete the lines:

```
ld    b, enemiesConfigEnd - enemiesConfigIni
sra   b
```

And we replace them with:

```
ld    b, ENEMIES
```

We make the same change to the **CheckCrashShip** routine.

And now we implement the collisions between the ship and the enemy shots. We continue in the **CheckCrashShip** routine, go to the end and just before **RET** we add the new collisions.

```
checkCrashShipFire:
ld    de, (shipPos)
ld    a, (enemiesFireCount)
```

```
ld    b, a
ld    hl, enemiesFire
```

We load into DE the position of the ship, **LD DE, (shipPos)**, into A the number of shots fired, **LD A, (enemiesFireCount)**, then into B, **LD B, A**, and point HL to the shots configuration, **LD HL, enemiesFire**.

```
checkCrashShipFire_loop:
ld    a, (hl)
inc   hl
res   $07, a
cp    d
jr    nz, checkCrashShipFire_loopCont
ld    a, (hl)
cp    e
jr    nz, checkCrashShipFire_loopCont
```

We load the first byte of the configuration into A, **LD A, (HL)**, point HL to the second byte, **INC HL**, leave the Y-coordinate, **RES $07, A**, compare it with the ship's coordinate, **CP D**, and skip if they are not the same, **JR NZ, checkCrashShipFire_loopCont**.

If the coordinates are the same, we load into A the X coordinate of the shot, **LD A, (HL)**, compare it with that of the ship, **CP E**, and jump if they are not the same, **JR NZ, checkCrashShipFire_loopCont**.

```
dec   hl
res   07, (hl)
ld    a, (livesCounter)
dec   a
daa
ld    (livesCounter), a
call  PrintInfoValue
call  PrintExplosion
jp    RefreshEnemiesFire
```

If there is a collision of the shot with the ship, we point HL to the first byte of the shots configuration, **DEC HL**, disable the shot, **RES $07, (HL)**, load the lives into A, **LD A, (livesCounter)**, remove one, **DEC A**, do the decimal adjustment, **DAA**, and update in memory, **LD (livesCounter), A**.

We print the game information, **CALL PrintInfoValue**, paint the explosion, **CALL PrintExploxion**, and refresh the enemy shot list and exit that way, **JP RefreshEnemiesFire**.

```
checkCrashShipFire_loopCont:
inc   hl
djnz  checkCrashShipFire_loop
```

If there was no collision, point HL to the first byte of the next shot configuration, **INC HL**, and loop until all shots have been traversed, **DJNZ checkCrashShipFire_loop**.

The final aspect of collision detection between the ship and enemies (enemy ships and shots) is as follows:

```
; --------------------------------------------------------------------
```

```
; Evaluates enemy collisions and shots with the ship.
;
; Alters the value of the AF, BC, DE and HL registers.
; ----------------------------------------------------------------
CheckCrashShip:
ld   de, (shipPos)        ; DE = ship position
ld   hl, enemiesConfig    ; HL = enemiesConfig
ld   b, ENEMIES          ; B = number of enemies
checkCrashShip_loop:
ld   a, (hl)             ; A = enemy Y-coordinate
inc  hl                  ; HL = enemy coord X
bit  $07, a              ; Enemy active?
jr   z, checkCrashShip_endLoop ; Not active, skips

and  $1f                 ; A = coord Y enemy
cp   d                   ; Compare with ship
jr   nz, checkCrashShip_endLoop ; Not the same, skip

ld   a, (hl)             ; A = enemy X coord
and  $1f                 ; A = coord X
cp   e                   ; Compare ship
jr   nz, checkCrashShip_endLoop ; Not the same, skip

dec  hl                  ; HL = coord Y enemy
res  $07, (hl)           ; Deactivates enemy

ld   a, (enemiesCounter) ; A = number of enemies
dec  a                   ; Subtract one
daa                      ; Decimal adjust
ld   (enemiesCounter), a ; Updates in memory
ld   a, (livesCounter)   ; A = lives
dec  a                   ; Remove one
daa                      ; Decimal adjust
ld   (livesCounter), a   ; Update in memory
call PrintInfoValue      ; Paint info. value
jp   PrintExplosion      ; Paint explosion and it comes out

checkCrashShip_endLoop:
inc  hl                  ; HL = coord Y next enemy
djnz checkCrashShip_loop ; Loop until B = 0

checkCrashShipFire:
; Checks for collisions between enemy shot and ship
ld   de, (shipPos)       ; DE = ship position
ld   a, (enemiesFireCount)
ld   b, a                ; B = number of active shots
ld   hl, enemiesFire     ; HL = shots configuration
checkCrashShipFire_loop:
ld   a, (hl)             ; A = coord Y shot
inc  hl                  ; HL = coord X
res  $07, a              ; A = coord Y
cp   d                   ; Compare with ship
jr   nz, checkCrashShipFire_loopCont ; Distinct, skip
ld   a, (hl)             ; A = coord X shot
cp   e                   ; Compare with ship
jr   nz, checkCrashShipFire_loopCont ; Distinct, skip

; If it gets here, the ship has collided with the shot.
dec  hl                  ; HL = 1st byte of config
```

316

```
res   $07, (hl)             ; Deactivate shot
ld    a, (livesCounter)     ; A = lives
dec   a                     ; Removes one
daa                         ; Decimal adjust
ld    (livesCounter), a     ; Update in memory
call  PrintInfoValue        ; Paint info. value
call  PrintExplosion        ; Paint Explosion
jp    RefreshEnemiesFire    ; Refreshes shots and exits

checkCrashShipFire_loopCont:
inc   hl                    ; HL = next shot
djnz  checkCrashShipFire_loop ; Loop until B = 0

ret
```

Now we have the enemy shot. Compile, load into the emulator and see the results.

Difficulty setting

Maybe the difficulty is too high now, maybe not. Either way, let's look at some small changes we can make to adjust the difficulty.

The changes I am suggesting are for you to test, but do not leave them permanently, as we will later add an option in the menu for the player to choose between different levels of difficulty.

The first way to reduce the difficulty is to reduce the speed at which enemies move and shoot. Locate the line **SUB $03** in int.asm and replace $03 with $04, $05, $06, etc. Remember that the higher this number is, the slower the enemies will move. Try it and you will see how it reduces.

We can reduce the difficulty by reducing the number of simultaneous shots. Go into the const.asm file, find the FIRES tag and change its value to $01, $02, etc. We compile and see how the difficulty is reduced as there are fewer simultaneous shots.

We can also reduce the difficulty if the enemies and the ship do not collide. We locate the **moveEnemies_Y_down** tag and two lines down we have **SUB ENEMY_TOP_B**, we modify this line and leave it as follows:

```
sub   ENEMY_TOP_B + $01
```

As you can see, the enemies and the ship no longer collide, which reduces the difficulty. If this reduces the difficulty too much, increase the number of simultaneous shots.

By not colliding with the ship, we could save a lot of the **CheckCrashShip** routine, but as we are going to change this based on player selection, we will leave it as it is.

Another way to reduce the difficulty is a la **Galactic Plague**, the first game I loaded on my Amstrad CPC 464, where you have three lives to complete each level.

To start each level with five lives, go to main.asm, locate Main_restart, and add the following lines before **CALL FadeScreen**:

```
ld    hl, livesCounter
ld    (hl), $05
```

With these lines, we will have five lives at the start of each level.

We've changed the behaviour of the enemies, we've given them a shot and we've also looked at different ways of adjusting the difficulty.

Download the source code from here

https://tinyurl.com/25fh9gk8

Step 12: Sound

In this chapter we will prepare the in-game music and sound effects.

Create the folder Step12 and copy the files loader.tap, const.asm, ctrl.asm, game.asm, graph.asm, int.asm, main.asm, make or make.bat, print.asm and var.asm from the folder Step11.

Testing, testing

Before we implement the sound, we are going to do a series of tests to see how we do it.

Inside the Step12 folder we will create the Sound folder, and inside it we will add the code files of the tests we are going to carry out.

Inside the Sound folder, we will create the const.asm file to add the constants we will need, such as the memory address of the **BEEPER** routine of the ROM that will play the notes we send.

```
;   ----------------------------------------------------------------
;   ROM beeper routine.
;
;   Input: HL -> Note.
;          DE -> Duration.
;
;   Alters the value of the AF, BC, DE, HL and IX registers.
;   ----------------------------------------------------------------
BEEP:    EQU $03b5
```

We can see from the comments that this routine receives the note in the HL register and the duration (frequency) in the DE register.

Next, we will add the notes and frequencies to the file.

```
;   ----------------------------------------------------------------
;   Notes to be uploaded to HL
;   ----------------------------------------------------------------
C_0:     EQU $6868
Cs_0:    EQU $628d
D_0:     EQU $5d03
Ds_0:    EQU $57bf
E_0:     EQU $52d7
F_0:     EQU $4e2b
Fs_0:    EQU $49cc
G_0:     EQU $45a3
Gs_0:    EQU $41b6
A_0:     EQU $3e06
As_0:    EQU $3a87
B_0:     EQU $373e
C_1:     EQU $3425
Cs_1:    EQU $3134
D_1:     EQU $2e6f
Ds_1:    EQU $2bd3
E_1:     EQU $295c
F_1:     EQU $2708
Fs_1:    EQU $24d5
```

```
G_1:      EQU $22c2
Gs_1:     EQU $20cd
A_1:      EQU $1ef4
As_1:     EQU $1d36
B_1:      EQU $1b90
C_2:      EQU $1a02
Cs_2:     EQU $188b
D_2:      EQU $1728
Ds_2:     EQU $15da
E_2:      EQU $149e
F_2:      EQU $1374
Fs_2:     EQU $125b
G_2:      EQU $1152
Gs_2:     EQU $1058
A_2:      EQU $0f6b
As_2:     EQU $0e9d
B_2:      EQU $0db8
C_3:      EQU $0cf2
Cs_3:     EQU $0c36
D_3:      EQU $0b86
Ds_3:     EQU $0add
E_3:      EQU $0a40
F_3:      EQU $09ab
Fs_3:     EQU $091e
G_3:      EQU $089a
Gs_3:     EQU $081c
A_3:      EQU $07a6
As_3:     EQU $0736
B_3:      EQU $06cd
C_4:      EQU $066a
Cs_4:     EQU $060c
D_4:      EQU $05b3
Ds_4:     EQU $0560
E_4:      EQU $0511
F_4:      EQU $04c6
Fs_4:     EQU $0480
G_4:      EQU $043d
Gs_4:     EQU $03ff
A_4:      EQU $03c4
As_4:     EQU $038c
B_4:      EQU $0357
C_5:      EQU $0325
Cs_5:     EQU $02f7
D_5:      EQU $02ca
Ds_5:     EQU $02a0
E_5:      EQU $0279
F_5:      EQU $0254
Fs_5:     EQU $0231
G_5:      EQU $020f
Gs_5:     EQU $01f0
A_5:      EQU $01d3
As_5:     EQU $01b7
B_5:      EQU $019c
C_6:      EQU $0183
Cs_6:     EQU $016c
D_6:      EQU $0156
Ds_6:     EQU $0141
E_6:      EQU $012d
F_6:      EQU $011b
```

```
Fs_6:    EQU $0109
G_6:     EQU $00f8
Gs_6:    EQU $00e9
A_6:     EQU $00da
As_6:    EQU $00cc
B_6:     EQU $00bf
C_7:     EQU $00b2
Cs_7:    EQU $00a7
D_7:     EQU $009c
Ds_7:    EQU $0091
E_7:     EQU $0087
F_7:     EQU $007e
Fs_7:    EQU $0075
G_7:     EQU $006d
Gs_7:    EQU $0065
A_7:     EQU $005e
As_7:    EQU $0057
B_7:     EQU $0050
C_8:     EQU $004a
Cs_8:    EQU $0044
D_8:     EQU $003e
Ds_8:    EQU $0039
E_8:     EQU $0034
F_8:     EQU $0030
Fs_8:    EQU $002b
G_8:     EQU $0027
Gs_8:    EQU $0023
A_8:     EQU $0020
As_8:    EQU $001c
B_8:     EQU $0019
```

The lower case "S" after some notes indicates that it is a sustained note, the number is the scale. If the number is smaller, the note is lower, if it is larger, the note is higher.

We also add the frequencies, using the same notation, but adding **_f** to distinguish them from the notes. These frequencies make the notes sound for one second, but if we divide them by two, they would sound for half a second. Be careful, while a sound is being emitted our programme stops, so we divide the frequencies by thirty-two.

```
; -------------------------------------------------------------
; Frequencies to be loaded in DE, 1 second ( / 2 = 0.5 ....)
; -------------------------------------------------------------
C_0_f:  EQU $0010 / $20
Cs_0_f: EQU $0011 / $20
D_0_f:  EQU $0012 / $20
Ds_0_f: EQU $0013 / $20
E_0_f:  EQU $0014 / $20
F_0_f:  EQU $0015 / $20
Fs_0_f: EQU $0017 / $20
G_0_f:  EQU $0018 / $20
Gs_0_f: EQU $0019 / $20
A_0_f:  EQU $001b / $20
As_0_f: EQU $001d / $20
B_0_f:  EQU $001e / $20
C_1_f:  EQU $0020 / $20
Cs_1_f: EQU $0022 / $20
```

```
D_1_f:   EQU $0024 / $20
Ds_1_f:  EQU $0026 / $20
E_1_f:   EQU $0029 / $20
F_1_f:   EQU $002b / $20
Fs_1_f:  EQU $002e / $20
G_1_f:   EQU $0031 / $20
Gs_1_f:  EQU $0033 / $20
A_1_f:   EQU $0037 / $20
As_1_f:  EQU $003a / $20
B_1_f:   EQU $003d / $20
C_2_f:   EQU $0041 / $20
Cs_2_f:  EQU $0045 / $20
D_2_f:   EQU $0049 / $20
Ds_2_f:  EQU $004d / $20
E_2_f:   EQU $0052 / $20
F_2_f:   EQU $0057 / $20
Fs_2_f:  EQU $005c / $20
G_2_f:   EQU $0062 / $20
Gs_2_f:  EQU $0067 / $20
A_2_f:   EQU $006e / $20
As_2_f:  EQU $0074 / $20
B_2_f:   EQU $007b / $20
C_3_f:   EQU $0082 / $20
Cs_3_f:  EQU $008a / $20
D_3_f:   EQU $0092 / $20
Ds_3_f:  EQU $009b / $20
E_3_f:   EQU $00a4 / $20
F_3_f:   EQU $00ae / $20
Fs_3_f:  EQU $00b9 / $20
G_3_f:   EQU $00c4 / $20
Gs_3_f:  EQU $00cf / $20
A_3_f:   EQU $00dc / $20
As_3_f:  EQU $00e9 / $20
B_3_f:   EQU $00f6 / $20
C_4_f:   EQU $0105 / $20
Cs_4_f:  EQU $0115 / $20
D_4_f:   EQU $0125 / $20
Ds_4_f:  EQU $0137 / $20
E_4_f:   EQU $0149 / $20
F_4_f:   EQU $015d / $20
Fs_4_f:  EQU $0172 / $20
G_4_f:   EQU $0188 / $20
Gs_4_f:  EQU $019f / $20
A_4_f:   EQU $01b8 / $20
As_4_f:  EQU $01d2 / $20
B_4_f:   EQU $01ed / $20
C_5_f:   EQU $020b / $20
Cs_5_f:  EQU $022a / $20
D_5_f:   EQU $024b / $20
Ds_5_f:  EQU $026e / $20
E_5_f:   EQU $0293 / $20
F_5_f:   EQU $02ba / $20
Fs_5_f:  EQU $02e4 / $20
G_5_f:   EQU $0310 / $20
Gs_5_f:  EQU $033e / $20
A_5_f:   EQU $0370 / $20
As_5_f:  EQU $03a4 / $20
B_5_f:   EQU $03db / $20
C_6_f:   EQU $0417 / $20
```

```
Cs_6_f:  EQU $0455 / $20
D_6_f:   EQU $0497 / $20
Ds_6_f:  EQU $04dd / $20
E_6_f:   EQU $0527 / $20
F_6_f:   EQU $0575 / $20
Fs_6_f:  EQU $05c8 / $20
G_6_f:   EQU $0620 / $20
Gs_6_f:  EQU $067d / $20
A_6_f:   EQU $06e0 / $20
As_6_f:  EQU $0749 / $20
B_6_f:   EQU $07b8 / $20
C_7_f:   EQU $082d / $20
Cs_7_f:  EQU $08a9 / $20
D_7_f:   EQU $092d / $20
Ds_7_f:  EQU $09b9 / $20
E_7_f:   EQU $0a4d / $20
F_7_f:   EQU $0aea / $20
Fs_7_f:  EQU $0b90 / $20
G_7_f:   EQU $0c40 / $20
Gs_7_f:  EQU $0cfa / $20
A_7_f:   EQU $0dc0 / $20
As_7_f:  EQU $0e91 / $20
B_7_f:   EQU $0f6f / $20
C_8_f:   EQU $105a / $20
Cs_8_f:  EQU $1153 / $20
D_8_f:   EQU $125b / $20
Ds_8_f:  EQU $1372 / $20
E_8_f:   EQU $149a / $20
F_8_f:   EQU $15d4 / $20
Fs_8_f:  EQU $1720 / $20
G_8_f:   EQU $1880 / $20
Gs_8_f:  EQU $19f5 / $20
A_8_f:   EQU $1b80 / $20
As_8_f:  EQU $1d23 / $20
B_8_f:   EQU $1ede / $20
```

We've added a lot of constants, but remember that **EQU** is not compiled, so it doesn't take up any space. When compiled, the **EQU** tag will be replaced with the value it represents wherever it appears.

Now that we have defined the notes and their frequencies, we will define the songs, which in our case will be two. You won't see them now, but you will see them later.

To define the songs we will use the tags added to const.asm. We create the var.asm file (in the Sound folder) and add the first song.

```
Song_1:
dw G_2_f,G_2,    G_2_f, G_2,   G_2_f,G_2,    Ds_2_f,Ds_2, As_2_f,As_2
dw G_2_f,G_2,    Ds_2_f,Ds_2, As_2_f,As_2,   G_2_f,G_2,   G_2_f,G_2
dw G_2_f,G_2,    G_2_f, G_2,   Ds_2_f,Ds_2,   As_2_f,As_2, G_2_f,G_2
dw Ds_2_f,Ds_2, As_2_f,As_2,  G_2_f,G_2,     D_3_f,D_3,   D_3_f,D_3
dw D_3_f,D_3,    Ds_3_f,Ds_3, As_2_f,As_2,   Fs_2_f,Fs_2, Ds_2_f,Ds_2
dw As_2_f,As_2,  G_2_f,G_2

dw G_3_f,G_3,    G_2_f,G_2,    G_2_f, G_2,    G_3_f,G_3,   Fs_3_f,Fs_3
dw F_3_f,F_3,    E_3_f,E_3,    Ds_3_f,Ds_3,   E_3_f,E_3,   Gs_2_f,Gs_2
dw Cs_3_f,Cs_3, C_3_f,C_3,    B_2_f,B_2,     As_2_f,As_2, A_2_f,A_2
dw As_2_f,As_2, Ds_2_f,Ds_2, Fs_2_f,Fs_2,   Ds_2_f,Ds_2, Fs_2_f,Fs_2
```

```
dw As_2_f,As_2,  G_2_f,G_2,    As_2_f,As_2,   D_3_f,D_3

dw G_3_f,G_3,    G_2_f,G_2,    G_2_f,G_2,    G_3_f,G_3,    Fs_3_f,Fs_3
dw F_3_f,F_3,    E_3_f,E_3,    Ds_3_f,Ds_3,   E_3_f,E_3,    Gs_2_f,Gs_2
dw Cs_3_f,Cs_3,  C_3_f,C_3,    B_2_f,B_2,    As_2_f,As_2,  A_2_f,A_2
dw As_2_f,As_2,  Ds_2_f,Ds_2,  Fs_2_f,Fs_2,   Ds_2_f,Ds_2,  As_2_f,As_2
dw G_2_f,G_2,    A_2_f,A_2,    G_2_f,G_2

dw G_2_f,G_2,    G_2_f, G_2,   G_2_f,G_2,    Ds_2_f,Ds_2,  As_2_f,As_2
dw G_2_f,G_2,    Ds_2_f,Ds_2,  As_2_f,As_2,   G_2_f,G_2,    G_2_f,G_2
dw G_2_f,G_2,    G_2_f,G_2,    Ds_2_f,Ds_2,   As_2_f,As_2,  G_2_f,G_2
dw Ds_2_f,Ds_2,  As_2_f,As_2,  G_2_f,G_2
```

As you can see, the definition consists of 16-bit value pairs (using the labels defined in const.asm), frequency and note.

Now let us add the second of the songs.

```
Song_2:
dw D_4_f,D_4,  D_4_f,D_4,  D_4_f,D_4,  G_4_f,G_4,  D_5_f,D_5
dw C_5_f,C_5,  B_4_f,B_4,  A_4_f,A_4,  G_5_f,G_5,  D_5_f,D_5
dw C_5_f,C_5,  B_4_f,B_4,  A_4_f,A_4,  G_5_f,G_5,  D_5_f,D_5
dw C_5_f,C_5,  B_4_f,B_4,  C_5_f,C_5,  A_4_f,A_4

dw D_4_f,D_4,  D_4_f,D_4,  D_4_f,D_4,  G_4_f,G_4,  D_5_f,D_5
dw C_5_f,C_5,  B_4_f,B_4,  A_4_f,A_4,  G_5_f,G_5,  D_5_f,D_5
dw C_5_f,C_5,  B_4_f,B_4,  A_4_f,A_4,  G_5_f,G_5,  D_5_f,D_5
dw C_5_f,C_5,  B_4_f,B_4,  C_5_f,C_5,  A_4_f,A_4

dw D_4_f,D_4,  D_4_f,D_4,  E_4_f,E_4,  E_4_f,E_4,  C_5_f,C_5
dw B_4_f,B_4,  A_4_f,A_4,  G_4_f,G_4,  G_4_f,G_4,  A_4_f,A_4
dw B_4_f,B_4,  A_4_f,A_4,  E_4_f,E_4,  Fs_4_f,Fs_4,  D_4_f,D_4
dw D_4_f,D_4,  E_4_f,E_4,  E_4_f,E_4,  C_5_f,C_5,  C_5_f,C_5
dw B_4_f,B_4,  A_4_f,A_4,  G_4_f,G_4,  D_5_f,D_5,  D_5_f,D_5
dw A_4_f,A_4,  D_4_f,D_4,  D_4_f,D_4,  E_4_f,E_4,  E_4_f,E_4
dw C_5_f,C_5,  B_4_f,B_4,  A_4_f,A_4,  G_4_f,G_4,  G_4_f,G_4
dw A_4_f,A_4,  B_4_f,B_4,  A_4_f,A_4,  E_4_f,E_4,  Fs_4_f,Fs_4

dw D_5_f,D_5,  D_5_f,D_5,  G_5_f,G_5,  F_5_f,F_5,  Ds_5_f, Ds_5
dw D_5_f,D_5,  C_5_f,C_5,  B_4_f,B_4,  A_4_f,A_4,  G_4_f, G_4
dw D_5_f,D_5

dw D_4_f,D_4,  D_4_f,D_4,  D_4_f,D_4,  G_4_f,G_4,  D_5_f,D_5
dw C_5_f,C_5,  B_4_f,B_4,  A_4_f,A_4,  G_5_f,G_5,  D_5_f,D_5
dw C_5_f,C_5,  B_4_f,B_4,  A_4_f,A_4,  G_5_f,G_5,  D_5_f,D_5
dw C_5_f,C_5,  B_4_f,B_4,  C_5_f,C_5,  A_4_f,A_4
dw $0000
```

The last line is **DW $0000**. We use this value to indicate that the songs are finished, and from here we go back to the beginning of the songs.

Finally, we add the variable to store the next note.

```
ptrSound:
dw Song_2
```

Now it's time to implement the routine we'll use to play the songs. We will create sound.asm and implement Play.

```
Play:
ld    hl, (ptrSound)
ld    e, (hl)
inc   hl
ld    d, (hl)
ld    a, d
or    e
jr    nz, play_cont
```

We load the direction of the sound into HL, **LD HL, (ptrSound)**, the lower byte of the frequency into E, **LD E, (HL)**, we set HL to the top, **INC HL**, and load it into D, **LD D, (HL)**. We load the value of D into A, **LD A, D**, check if the frequency value is $0000 to know if we are at the end of the song, **OR E**, and if not we jump, **JR NZ, play_cont**.

```
play_reset:
ld    hl, Song_1
ld    (ptrSound), hl
ret
```

When we have reached the end of the songs, we load the address of song one in HL, **LD HL, Song_1**, update in memory, **LD (ptrSound), HL**, and exit, **RET**.

```
play_cont:
inc   hl
ld    c, (hl)
inc   hl
ld    b, (hl)
inc   hl
ld    (ptrSound), hl
ld    h, b
ld    l, c

call BEEP

ret
```

If we haven't reached the end of the song, we point HL to the lower byte of the note, **INC HL**, load it into C, **LD C, (HL)**, point HL to the upper byte of the note, **INC HL**, load it into B, **LD B, (HL)**, point HL to the lower byte of the frequency of the next note, **INC HL**, and update it in memory, **LD (ptrSound), HL**. We load the high byte of the note into H, **LD H, B**, load the low byte into L, **LD L, C**, sound the note, **CALL BEEP**, and exit, **RET**.

Let's see if it works. We create the file test1.asm and add the following lines:

```
org   $5dad

Loop:
call Play

jr    Loop

include "const.asm"
include "sound.asm"
```

```
include "var.asm"

end   Loop
```

We set the memory address where the program will be loaded to be compatible with 16K models, **ORG $5DAD**, we call the routine responsible for playing the songs, **CALL Play**, and we stay in an infinite loop, **JR Loop**.

In the last part of the archive we include the necessary files.

To see if it works, we compile, load and listen. To compile we use the command line.

```
pasmo --tapbas test1.asm test1.tap
```

If all goes well, you will be able to distinguish two different songs, and those with better hearing will even be able to tell which songs they are, although it is very difficult.

Rhythm and beat

In fact, the music does not sound good. It is necessary to control the rhythm in which the notes sound, and we will use the interruptions to do this. We create the file test2.asm and start the implementation.

```
org   $5dad

; --------------------------------------------------------------
; Indicators for music.
;
; Bit 7 -> Play sound 1 = Yes / 0 = No
; --------------------------------------------------------------
music:
db $00
```

We start with the address where we load the program, **ORG $5DAD**, and declare a label that will be used to interact with the interrupts, **music**.

```
Main:
ld    hl, Song_2
ld    (ptrSound), hl

di
ld    a, $28
ld    i, a
im    2
ei
```

We point HL to the second song, **LD HL, Song_2**, load the value into memory, **LD (ptrSound), HL**, disable interrupts, **DI**, load forty into A, **LD A, $28**, then into I, **LD I, A**, go to interrupt mode two, **IM 2**, and enable them, **EI**. They don't actually become active until the next instruction.

```
Loop:
ld    a, (music)
bit   $07, a
```

```
jr    z, Loop
and   $7f
ld    (music), a

call Play

jr    Loop
```

We load the value of music into A, **LD A, (music)**, check if bit seven is set to one, **BIT $07, A**, and jump, **JR Z, Loop**, if not.

If the bit is one, we set it to zero, **AND $7F**, load to memory, **LD (music), A**, play sound, **CALL Play**, and continue looping, **JR Loop**.

```
include "const.asm"
include "sound.asm"
include "var.asm"

end   Main
```

Finally, we include the files and tell PASMO to include the program call in the loader.

The only thing left to do is to use the interrupts and control the rhythm. We create the file int2.asm and start.

```
org   $7e5c

MUSIC: EQU $5dad

counter:
db $00
```

We indicate where to load the interrupt routine, **ORG $7E5C**, declare a constant with the address where the labels of the indicators for the music are, and a counter for the number of interrupts to pass before we emit a sound.

The rest of the implementation is done between **MUSIC** and **counter**.

```
Isr:
push af
push bc
push de
push hl

ld    a, (counter)
inc   a
ld    (counter), a
cp    $06
jr    nz, isr_end

xor   a
ld    (counter), a

ld    hl, MUSIC
set   07, (hl)
```

```
isr_end:
pop  hl
pop  de
pop  bc
pop  af

ei
reti
```

We keep the value of the **PUSH** registers. We load the value of the counter into A, **LD A, (counter)**, increment it by one, **INC A**, load it into memory, **LD (counter), A**, evaluate if it has reached six, **CP $06**, and jump if not, **JR NZ, isr_end**.

If the counter has reached six, we set it to zero, **XOR A**, load into memory, **LD (counter), A**, point HL to the music indicator, **LD HL, MUSIC**, and set bit seven, **SET $07, (HL)**.

We retrieve the registers, **POP**, activate the interrupts, **EI**, and exit, **RETI**.

We go back to test2.asm and just above END **Main** we insert int2.asm.

```
include "int2.asm"
```

The order in which the files are included is very important in this case. Let's compile and see how it sounds.

```
pasmo --tapbas test2.asm test2.tap
```

Now we can tell the songs apart, even though they have the same rhythm and should not.

This is the waveform we see in the emulator (Menu \ Audio \ Waveform).

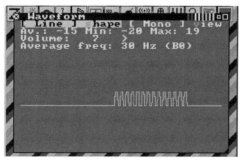

As for the order of the **include**, try putting int2.asm before var.asm. Compile, load with the 16K model and see what happens... It doesn't work!

Check the size of test2.tap, it should be about 9324 bytes. Leave the **include** as they were, compile and check the size, it should be about 8520 bytes. What is the reason for this difference?

Unlike the game, we do not compile the files separately, we only compile one file thanks to the **include**.

The memory of the 16K models goes from position $0000 to $7FFF. We load the interrupt routine at $7E5C, and we have 419 bytes to go to $7FFF, but be careful, we have to count with the stack.

If we put the int2.asm **include** at the end, we load thirty-two bytes from $7E5C, which takes up the interrupt routine and is well short of the four hundred and nineteen bytes we have available.

If we put the var.asm **include** after the int.asm **include**, after the thirty-two bytes of the interrupt routine, the bytes of the song definition are loaded, eight hundred and four bytes, for a total of eight hundred and thirty-six bytes ($0344). If we add these bytes to the address where we load the interrupts, $7E5C+$0344, we get $81A0, beyond the capacity of the 16K models.

Different rhythms

To make the songs, or even part of them, go to different beats, we are going to add a new 16-bit value: in the upper byte we are going to put $FF, which tells our programme that it is a beat change, while in the lower byte we are going to put the beat, a value from $00 to $0F.

We will create var3.asm and copy all the code from Var.asm into it. We will add two rhythm changes. Locate the **Song_1** tag and add below it:

```
dw $ff0c
```

When the program encounters this, it interprets it as a beat change ($FF) and expects twelve pauses between each note ($0C).

Locate **Song_2** and add to it:

```
dw $ff06
```

In this case there will be six pauses ($06) between each note, so we can deduce that the second song will play twice as fast as the first.

Create int3.asm and copy all the code from int2.asm into it. Create test3.asm and copy all the code from test2.asm into it.

We start by modifying test3.asm. In the **include** we replace var.asm and int.asm with var3.asm and int3.asm and add a comment line to the **music** tag.

```
; Bit 0 to 3 -> Rhythm
```

The rest of the changes are made just before **DI** by adding the following lines.

```
ld   a, (hl)
and  $0f
ld   (music), a
```

Previously we pointed HL to **Song_2**, now we load the value pointed to by HL into A, **LD A, (HL)**, keep the rhythm bits, **AND $0F**, and load the value into the flags for the music, **LD (music), A**.

Let's go to the int3.asm file and add a new tag at the end, just below the **counter**, to store the rhythm of the song.

```
times: db $00
```

Now we locate the label Isr and five lines below it **LD A, (counter)**. Just above this line we add the following line:

```
isr_cont:
```

Four lines down we find **CP $06**. We change this line to read as follows:

```
cp    (hl)
```

Another four lines down we find **LD HL, MUSIC**. Just above this line we add the next one:

```
isr_set:
```

Now we go back to the Isr tag and after the four **PUSH** we implement the part where we control the rhythm changes.

```
ld    a, (MUSIC)
and   $0f
ld    hl, times
cp    (hl)
jr    z, isr_cont
ld    (hl), a
xor   a
ld    (counter), a
jr    isr_set
```

We load in A the value of the indicators, **LD A, (MUSIC)**, we keep the rhythm, **AND $0F**, we point to HL where we store the rhythm that the song has, **LD HL, times**, we compare with the rhythm of the indicators, **CP (HL)**, and if they are the same we jump, **JR Z, isr_cont**, there is no change in the rhythm.

If the rhythm has changed, we store the new rhythm, **LD (HL), A**, set A to zero, **XOR A**, and counter, **LD (counter), A**. Finally we jump, **JR isr_set**.

This is what int3.asm should look like:

```
org   $7e5c

MUSIC: EQU $5dad

Isr:
push af
push bc
push de
push hl

ld    a, (MUSIC)
```

```
and  $0f
ld   hl, times
cp   (hl)
jr   z, isr_cont
ld   (hl), a
xor  a
ld   (counter), a
jr   isr_set

isr_cont:
ld   a, (counter)
inc  a
ld   (counter), a
cp   (hl)
jr   nz, isr_end

xor  a
ld   (counter), a

isr_set:
ld   hl, MUSIC
set  07, (hl)

isr_end:
pop  hl
pop  de
pop  bc
pop  af

ei
reti

counter: db $00
times:   db $00
```

All that remains is to modify the **Play** routine so that it takes the rhythm changes into account. We go to the sound.asm file and after the sixth line, **OR E**, we add the following lines:

```
jr   z, play_reset
cp   $ff
```

With **OR E** we check if we have reached the end of the songs, in which case we skip, **JR Z, play_reset**. If we have not reached the end of the songs, we check if it is a change of tempo, **CP $FF**.

The next line we already had, **JR NZ, play_cont**, and now what it does is to skip if there is no change of tempo.

We keep adding lines under **JR NZ, play_cont**.

```
ld   a, e
ld   (music), a
inc  hl
ld   (ptrSound), hl
ret
```

If we have not skipped, the rhythm will change. We load the new beat into A, **LD A, E**, load it into the pointers for music, **LD (music), A**, point HL to the next note (at the frequency), **INC HL**, update the pointer value to the next note, **LD (ptrSound), HL**, and exit, **RET**. The rest of the routine stays the same.

Now it's time to see how it sounds. We compile, load into the emulator and listen to the results.

```
pasmo --tapbas test3.asm test3.tap
```

If all goes well, the two songs will play at different speeds, which you can see by listening or watching the waveform.

We have done the necessary tests and already know how to implement the music.

Download the source code from here

https://tinyurl.com/2bofykqp

Step 13: Music

It is time to integrate everything we saw in the previous chapter into our game, there will be some small variations, but it is practically the same. Also, it is time to comment all the code, there are parts that are not commented yet and if we leave it like this, it is possible that in time it will be difficult to know what we are doing there and, more importantly, why?

Create the folder Step13 and copy from the folder Step12 the files loader.tap, const.asm, ctrl.asm, game.asm, graph.asm, int.asm, main.asm, make or make.bat, print.asm, var.asm and the folder sound.

Constants

We start by declaring the necessary constants in the const.asm file, starting with the ROM routine we are going to use. Locate the UDG tag and add the following just below it:

```
; ------------------------------------------------------------
; ROM beeper routine.
;
; Input: HL -> Note.
;        DE -> Duration.
;
; Alters the value of the AF, BC, DE, HL and IX registers.
; ------------------------------------------------------------
BEEP: EQU $03b5
```

It is very important to read the comments, as we can see that this ROM routine changes the value of almost all the registers. We did not take this into account in the previous chapter, but we will in this chapter.

At the end of the const.asm file we will add the note constants and frequencies we saw in the previous chapter.

Variables

The next step is to add the necessary variables: the pointer to the next note and the songs. Open var.asm and add the following lines at the end:

```
; ------------------------------------------------------------
; Necessary data for music.
; ------------------------------------------------------------

; ------------------------------------------------------------
; Next note
; ------------------------------------------------------------
ptrSound:
dw $0000

; ------------------------------------------------------------
; Songs
; ------------------------------------------------------------
Song_1:
dw $ff0c
```

```
dw G_2_f,G_2,    G_2_f,G_2,    G_2_f,G_2,    Ds_2_f,Ds_2,  As_2_f,As_2
dw G_2_f,G_2,    Ds_2_f,Ds_2,  As_2_f,As_2,  G_2_f, G_2,   G_2_f,G_2
dw G_2_f,G_2,    G_2_f,G_2,    Ds_2_f,Ds_2,  As_2_f,As_2,  G_2_f,G_2
dw Ds_2_f,Ds_2,  As_2_f,As_2,  G_2_f,G_2,    D_3_f,D_3,    D_3_f,D_3
dw D_3_f,D_3,    Ds_3_f,Ds_3,  As_2_f,As_2,  Fs_2_f,Fs_2,  Ds_2_f,Ds_2
dw As_2_f,As_2,  G_2_f,G_2

dw G_3_f,G_3,    G_2_f,G_2,    G_2_f,G_2,    G_3_f,G_3,    Fs_3_f,Fs_3
dw F_3_f,F_3,    E_3_f,E_3,    Ds_3_f,Ds_3,  E_3_f,E_3,    Gs_2_f,Gs_2
dw Cs_3_f,Cs_3,  C_3_f,C_3,    B_2_f,B_2,    As_2_f,As_2,  A_2_f,A_2
dw As_2_f,As_2,  Ds_2_f,Ds_2,  Fs_2_f,Fs_2,  Ds_2_f,Ds_2,  Fs_2_f,Fs_2
dw As_2_f,As_2,  G_2_f,G_2,    As_2_f,As_2,  D_3_f,D_3

dw G_3_f,G_3,    G_2_f,G_2,    G_2_f,G_2,    G_3_f,G_3,    Fs_3_f,Fs_3
dw F_3_f,F_3,    E_3_f,E_3,    Ds_3_f,Ds_3,  E_3_f,E_3,    Gs_2_f,Gs_2
dw Cs_3_f,Cs_3,  C_3_f,C_3,    B_2_f,B_2,    As_2_f,As_2,  A_2_f,A_2
dw As_2_f,As_2,  Ds_2_f,Ds_2,  Fs_2_f,Fs_2,  Ds_2_f,Ds_2,  As_2_f,As_2
dw G_2_f,G_2,    A_2_f,A_2,    G_2_f,G_2

dw G_2_f,G_2,    G_2_f,G_2,    G_2_f,G_2,    Ds_2_f,Ds_2,  As_2_f,As_2
dw G_2_f,G_2,    Ds_2_f,Ds_2,  As_2_f,As_2,  G_2_f,G_2,    G_2_f,G_2
dw G_2_f,G_2,    G_2_f,G_2,    Ds_2_f,Ds_2,  As_2_f,As_2,  G_2_f,G_2
dw Ds_2_f,Ds_2,  As_2_f,As_2,  G_2_f,G_2

Song_2:
dw $ff05
dw D_4_f,D_4,    D_4_f,D_4,    D_4_f,D_4,    G_4_f,G_4,    D_5_f,D_5
dw C_5_f,C_5,    B_4_f,B_4,    A_4_f,A_4,    G_5_f,G_5,    D_5_f,D_5
dw C_5_f,C_5,    B_4_f,B_4,    A_4_f,A_4,    G_5_f,G_5,    D_5_f,D_5
dw C_5_f,C_5,    B_4_f,B_4,    C_5_f,C_5,    A_4_f,A_4

dw D_4_f,D_4,    D_4_f,D_4,    D_4_f,D_4,    G_4_f,G_4,    D_5_f,D_5
dw C_5_f,C_5,    B_4_f,B_4,    A_4_f,A_4,    G_5_f,G_5,    D_5_f,D_5
dw C_5_f,C_5,    B_4_f,B_4,    A_4_f,A_4,    G_5_f,G_5,    D_5_f,D_5
dw C_5_f,C_5,    B_4_f,B_4,    C_5_f,C_5,    A_4_f,A_4

dw D_4_f,D_4,    D_4_f,D_4,    E_4_f,E_4,    E_4_f,E_4,    C_5_f,C_5
dw B_4_f,B_4,    A_4_f,A_4,    G_4_f,G_4,    G_4_f,G_4,    A_4_f,A_4
dw B_4_f,B_4,    A_4_f,A_4,    E_4_f,E_4,    Fs_4_f,Fs_4,  D_4_f,D_4
dw D_4_f,D_4,    E_4_f,E_4,    E_4_f,E_4,    C_5_f,C_5,    C_5_f,C_5
dw B_4_f,B_4,    A_4_f,A_4,    G_4_f,G_4,    D_5_f,D_5,    D_5_f,D_5
dw A_4_f,A_4,    D_4_f,D_4,    D_4_f,D_4,    E_4_f,E_4,    E_4_f,E_4
dw C_5_f,C_5,    B_4_f,B_4,    A_4_f,A_4,    G_4_f,G_4,    G_4_f,G_4
dw A_4_f,A_4,    B_4_f,B_4,    A_4_f,A_4,    E_4_f,E_4,    Fs_4_f,Fs_4
dw D_5_f,D_5,    D_5_f,D_5,    G_5_f,G_5,    F_5_f,F_5,    Ds_5_f,Ds_5
dw D_5_f,D_5,    C_5_f,C_5,    B_4_f,B_4,    A_4_f,A_4,    G_4_f,G_4
dw D_5_f,D_5

dw D_4_f,D_4,    D_4_f,D_4,    D_4_f,D_4,    G_4_f,G_4,    D_5_f,D_5
dw C_5_f,C_5,    B_4_f,B_4,    A_4_f,A_4,    G_5_f,G_5,    D_5_f,D_5
dw C_5_f,C_5,    B_4_f,B_4,    A_4_f,A_4,    G_5_f,G_5,    D_5_f,D_5
dw C_5_f,C_5,    B_4_f,B_4,    C_5_f,C_5,    A_4_f,A_4
dw $0000
```

As we saw in the previous chapter, we need a flags variable for the music. Let's go to main.asm and the game **flags**. Just below that we add the flags for the music.

```
; -----------------------------------------------------------------
```

```
; Music indicators
;
; Bit 0 to 3 -> Rhythm
; Bit 7      -> sounds 0 = No, 1 = Yes
; --------------------------------------------------------------
music:
db $00
```

Remember that these labels must be set to zero at the start, otherwise everything may stop working.

Reproduction

We continue with the routine that will be responsible for playing the sound; we go to game.asm.

It is necessary to specify the song to be played and the rhythm. Since we have two songs, we start with the first song on even levels and the second song on odd levels.

We locate ChangeLevel and see that it is the eighth and ninth lines:

```
inc  a
cp   $1f
```

Right between these two lines we will implement the change of song depending on the level:

```
ld   hl, Song_1
bit  $00, a
jr   z, changeLevel_cont
ld   hl, Song_2
changeLevel_cont:
ld   (ptrSound), hl

ex   af, af'
ld   a, (hl)
ld   (music), a
ex   af, af'
```

We point HL to the first song, **LD HL, Song_1**, look at the zero bit of A to see if the next level is odd or even, **BIT $00, A**, and skip if it is even. If it is odd, we point HL to the next song, **LD HL, Song_2**.

We update the pointer to the note (to the beat), **LD (ptrSound), HL**, keep the value of AF since A contains the next level, **EX AF, AF'**, load the beat in A, **LD A, (HL)**, update the indicators, **LD (music)**, A, and restore the value of AF, **EX AF, AF'**.

The final aspect of the routine is as follows:

```
; --------------------------------------------------------------
; Change level.
;
; Alters the value of the AF, BC, DE and HL registers.
; --------------------------------------------------------------
ChangeLevel:
ld   a, $06              ; A = yellow colour
ld   (enemiesColor), a   ; Update in memory
```

```
ld    a, (levelCounter + 1) ; A = current level in BCD
inc   a                     ; Increases level
daa                         ; Decimal adjust
ld    b, a                  ; B = A
ld    a, (levelCounter)     ; A = current level
inc   a                     ; A = next level

ld    hl, Song_1            ; HL = song 1
bit   $00, a                ; Even level?
jr    z, changeLevel_cont   ; Yes, jump
ld    hl, Song_2            ; No, HL = song 2

changeLevel_cont:
ld    (ptrSound), hl        ; Update next note
ex    af, af'               ; Preserves AF (A = next level)
ld    a, (hl)               ; A = lower byte note (beat)
ld    (music), a            ; Updates indicators
ex    af, af'               ; Retrieves AF
cp    $1f                   ; Level 31?
jr    c, changeLevel_end    ; No, skip
ld    a, $01                ; Yes, set it to 1
ld    b, a                  ; B = A

changeLevel_end:
ld    (levelCounter), a     ; Update level in memory
ld    a, b                  ; A = B (BCD level)
ld    (levelCounter + 1), a ; Update in memory
call  LoadUdgsEnemies       ; Load enemy graphics

ld    a, $20                ; A = total number of enemies, 20 BCD
ld    (enemiesCounter), a   ; Updates in memory

ld    hl, enemiesConfigIni  ; HL = enemies initial config
ld    de, enemiesConfig     ; HL = enemies config
ld    bc, enemiesConfigEnd-enemiesConfigIni ; BC = config length
ldir                        ; Load initial config in config

ld    hl, shipPos           ; HL = ship position
ld    (hl), SHIP_INI        ; Update in memory

ret
```

Now let's implement the routine that plays the songs; we'll do this before the **RefreshEnemiesFire** routine.

```
Play:
ld    hl, (ptrSound)
ld    e, (hl)
inc   hl
ld    d, (hl)
ld    a, d
or    e
jr    z, play_reset
```

We load the note address into HL, **LD HL, (ptrSound)**, the lower byte of the frequency into E, **LD E, (HL)**, point HL to the upper byte, **INC HL**, load it into D, **LD D, (HL)**, load it into A, **LD A, D**, and check whether the end of the song has been reached, **OR E**, in which case we jump, **JR Z, play_reset**.

```
cp    $ff
jr    nz, play_cont
ld    a, e
ld    (music), a
inc   hl
ld    (ptrSound), hl
ret
```

If we have not skipped, we check if the note is actually a beat change, **CP $FF**, and skip if it is not, **JR NZ, play_cont**.

If it is a beat change, we load it into A, **LD A, E**, update the music pointer, **LD (music), A**, point HL to the next note (frequency), **INC HL**, update the pointer, **LD (ptrSound), HL**, and exit, **RET**.

```
play_reset:
ld    hl, Song_1
ld    (ptrSound), hl
ret
```

If it is the end of the songs, we point HL to the first song, **LD HL, Song_1**, update pointer, **LD (ptrSound), HL**, and exit, **RET**.

```
play_cont:
inc   hl
ld    c, (hl)
inc   hl
ld    b, (hl)
inc   hl
ld    (ptrSound), hl
ld    h, b
ld    l, c
```

If we have not reached the end of the songs and there has been no tempo change, we point HL to the lower byte of the note, **INC HL**, load it into C, **LD C, (HL)**, point HL to the upper byte, **INC HL**, load it into B, **LD B, (HL)**, point HL to the next note, **INC HL**, update pointer, **LD (ptrSound), HL**, load the upper byte of the note into H, **LD H, B**, and the lower byte into L, **LD L, C**.

At the beginning of the chapter we declared the **BEEP** tag with the value of the memory address where the ROM BEEPER routine is located, which receives the note in HL and the frequency in DE. We can now call it.

This is the main difference from the implementation we did in the previous chapter. We are going to add some sort of special effect, so we are going to implement the ROM call in our own routine.

```
Play_beep:
push  af
push  bc
push  de
push  hl
call  BEEP
pop   hl
pop   de
```

```
pop   bc
pop   af

ret
```

We hold the register values, **PUSH**, call the ROM routine to play the note, **CALL BEEP**, retrieve the register value, **POP**, and exit, **RET**.

We can now call **Play** to play music during the game, and **Play_beep** to play single notes, such as sound effects.

It is not possible to change the order in which the routines are implemented, please note that **Play** comes from **Play_beep**, if we change the order the result may not be what we want.

The final aspect of the routine is as follows:

```
; ----------------------------------------------------------------
; He plays the songs.
;
; Alters the value of the AF, BC, DE and HL registers.
; ----------------------------------------------------------------
Play:
ld    hl, (ptrSound)        ; HL = current note address
ld    e, (hl)              ; E = lower byte frequency
inc   hl                   ; HL = upper byte
ld    d, (hl)              ; D = upper byte
ld    a, d                 ; A = D
or    e                    ; End songs?
jr    z, play_reset        ; Yes, jump
cp    $ff                  ; Does it change tempo?
jr    nz, play_cont        ; No, jump
ld    a, e                 ; A = new rhythm
ld    (music), a           ; Update in memory
inc   hl                   ; HL = next note
ld    (ptrSound), hl       ; Update pointer
ret

play_reset:
ld    hl, Song_1           ; HL = first song
ld    (ptrSound), hl       ; Update pointer
ret

play_cont:
inc   hl                   ; HL = lower byte note
ld    c, (hl)              ; C = lower byte note
inc   hl                   ; HL = upper byte
ld    b, (hl)              ; B = upper byte
inc   hl                   ; HL = frequency next note
ld    (ptrSound), hl       ; Update pointer
ld    h, b
ld    l, c                 ; HL = note

; ----------------------------------------------------------------
; He sounds a note.
;
; Input: HL -> Note
;        DE -> Frequency
; ----------------------------------------------------------------
```

```
Play_beep:
push af
push bc
push de
push hl                      ; Preserves records
call BEEP                    ; Call ROM routine
pop  hl
pop  de
pop  bc
pop  af                      ; Retrieves records

ret
```

We need to put the call to Play inside the main loop. We go back to main.asm, find **Main_loop** and within it the line **CALL CheckCrashShip**. Below this line we add:

```
ld   hl, music
bit  $07, (hl)
jr   z, main_loopCont
res  07, (hl)
call Play

main_loopCont:
```

We point HL to the music flags, **LD HL, music**, check if bit seven is set, **BIT $07, (HL)**, and skip if not, **JR Z, main_loopCont**.

We deactivate it if it is active, **RES $07, (HL)**, and make the next note sound, **CALL Play**.

Finally, we add the tag to jump to if bit seven is not active, **main_loopCont**.

The appearance of main.asm after commenting is as follows:

```
org  $5dad

;  ---------------------------------------------------------------
;  Indicators
;
;  Bit 0 -> ship must be moved 0 = No, 1 = Yes
;  Bit 1 -> shot is active 0 = No, 1 = Yes
;  Bit 2 -> enemies must be moved 0 = No, 1 = Yes
;  Bit 3 -> change address enemies 0 = No, 1 = Yes
;  Bit 4 -> move enemy shot 0 = No, 1 = Yes
;  ---------------------------------------------------------------
flags:
db $00


;  ---------------------------------------------------------------
;  Music indicators
;
;  Bit 0 to 3 -> Rhythm
;  Bit 7      -> sounds 0 = No, 1 = Yes
;  ---------------------------------------------------------------
music:
db $00

Main:
```

```
ld   a, $02
call OPENCHAN              ; Opens channel 2, top screen

ld   hl, udgsCommon        ; HL = UDG address
ld   (UDG), hl             ; Update UDG address

ld   hl, ATTR_P            ; HL = address permanent attributes
ld   (hl), $07             ; White ink and black background
call CLS                   ; Clear screen

xor  a                     ; A = 0
out  ($fe), a              ; Border = black
ld   a, (BORDCR)           ; A = BORDCR
and  $c0                   ; A = brightness and flash
or   $05                   ; A += ink 5 and background 0
ld   (BORDCR), a           ; Update BORDCR

di                         ; Disables interrupts
ld   a, $28                ; A = 40
ld   i, a                  ; I = A
im   2                     ; Mode 2 interruptions
ei                         ; Activates interruptions

ld   a, (flags)            ; A = flags
Main_start:
ld   hl, enemiesCounter    ; HL = enemiesCounter
ld   de, enemiesCounter+$01 ; DE = level counter
ld   (hl), $00             ; Enemies counter = 0
ld   bc, $08               ; BC number of bytes to clear
ldir                       ; Clean bytes
ld   a, $05
ld   (livesCounter), a     ; Lives = 5

call ResetEnemiesFire      ; Initialises enemy shot
call ChangeLevel           ; Change level
call PrintFirstScreen      ; Paint menu screen and wait
call PrintFrame            ; Paint frame
call PrintInfoGame         ; Paint game info titles
call PrintShip             ; Paint ship
call PrintInfoValue        ; Paint info. value

call LoadUdgsEnemies       ; Load enemies
call PrintEnemies          ; Paints them
; Delay
call Sleep                 ; Delay before starting the level

; Main loop
Main_loop:
call CheckCtrl             ; Check controls
call MoveFire              ; Move fire

push de                    ; Preserves DE
call CheckCrashFire        ; Evaluates enemy collision/shootback
pop  de                    ; Retrieve DE

ld   a, (enemiesCounter)   ; A = number of active enemies
or   a                     ; Is it 0?
jr   z, Main_restart       ; Yes, jump
```

```
call MoveShip            ; Move ship
call ChangeEnemies       ; Change enemies address if applicable
call MoveEnemies         ; Move enemies
call MoveEnemiesFire     ; Move enemy fire
call CheckCrashShip      ; Evaluates ship/enemies/shot collision

ld   hl, music           ; HL = music indicators
bit  $07, (hl)           ; Sound note?
jr   z, main_loopCont    ; No, jump
res  $07, (hl)           ; Disables bit seven of music
call Play                ; Play note

main_loopCont:
ld   a, (livesCounter)   ; A = lives
or   a                   ; Is it 0?
jr   z, GameOver         ; Yes, GAME OVER!

jr   Main_loop           ; Main loop

Main_restart:
ld   a, (levelCounter)   ; A = level
cp   $1e                 ; Is it 31 (we have 30)
jr   z, Win              ; Yes, VICTORY!

call FadeScreen          ; Fade screen
call ChangeLevel         ; Change level
call PrintFrame          ; Paint frame
call PrintInfoGame       ; Paint game info titles
call PrintShip           ; Paint ship
call PrintInfoValue      ; Print info. value
call PrintEnemies        ; Paint Enemies
call ResetEnemiesFire    ; Resets enemy shots
; Delay
call Sleep               ; Delay
jr   Main_loop           ; Main loop

; GAME OVER!
GameOver:
xor  a                   ; A = 0
call PrintEndScreen      ; Print end screen and wait
jp   Main_start          ; Main menu

; VICTORY!
Win:
ld   a, $01              ; A = 1
call PrintEndScreen      ; Paint end screen and wait
jp   Main_start          ; Main menu

include "const.asm"
include "ctrl.asm"
include "game.asm"
include "graph.asm"
include "print.asm"
include "var.asm"

end  Main
```

Music control by interruptions

The interrupt routine is where we indicate when a new note needs to be played. We go to int.asm and the first thing we do is add two constants before **T1: EQU $C8**:

```
FLAGS: EQU $5dad
MUSIC: EQU $5dae
```

These tags refer to the memory locations where we have defined the flags in main.asm.

After the four **PUSH** of the **Isr** label, we find the line **LD HL, $5DAD**, which we will modify as follows:

```
ld    hl, FLAGS
```

At the end of the file we will add the variables to store the rhythm of the song, and the counter to know if the bit to play a note should be activated.

```
countTempo: db $00
tempo:      db $00
```

Locate **Isr_T1**, modify the fifth line, **JR NZ, Isr_end** and leave it as follows:

```
jr    nz, Isr_sound
```

We locate **Isr_end** and implement the music control above it.

```
Isr_sound:
ld    a, (MUSIC)
and   $0f
ld    hl, tempo
cp    (hl)
jr    z, Isr_soundCont
ld    (hl), a
jr    Isr_soundEnd
```

We load into A the music flags, **LD A, (MUSIC)**, keep the beat, **AND $0F**, point HL to the current tempo, **LD HL**, and compare it with the beat in the music flags, **CP (HL)**. If the two values are the same, there is no tempo change and we jump, **JR Z, Isr_soundCount**. If they are different, we update, **LD (HL), A**, and jump, **JR Isr_soundEnd**.

```
Isr_soundCont:
ld    a, (countTempo)
inc   a
ld    (countTempo), a
cp    (hl)
jr    nz, Isr_end
```

We load the beat counter into A, **LD A, (countTempo)**, increment it, **INC A**, update in memory, **LD (countTempo), A**, compare them, **CP (HL)**, if they are different we don't have to play the note and jump, **JR NZ, Isr_end**.

```
Isr_soundEnd:
xor   a
ld    (countTempo), a
ld    hl, MUSIC
set   07, (hl)
```

If we have not jumped, we must sound the note. Set A to zero, **XOR A**, update the beat counter, **LD (countTempo)**, A, point HL to the indicators, **LD HL, MUSIC**, and set bit seven to indicate that a note should be played, **SET $07, (HL)**.

The final appearance of int.asm, once commented, is as follows:

```
org  $7e5c

FLAGS: EQU $5dad          ; General indicators
MUSIC: EQU $5dae          ; Indicators music
T1:    EQU $c8            ; Interruptions to activate change
                         ; of enemy leadership

Isr:
push hl
push de
push bc
push af                   ; Preserves records

ld    hl, FLAGS           ; HL = indicators
set   $00, (hl)           ; Activate bit 0, move ship

ld    a, (countEnemy)     ; A = counter move enemies
inc   a                   ; A = A+1
ld    (countEnemy), a     ; Update in memory
sub   $03                 ; A = A+3
jr    nz, Isr_T1          ; Non-zero, jumps
ld    (countEnemy), a     ; Counter = zero
set   $02, (hl)           ; Activate bit 2, move enemies
set   $04, (hl)           ; Activate bit 4, move enemy shot

; Change of direction of enemies
Isr_T1:
ld    a, (countT1)        ; A = counter change address
inc   a                   ; A = A+1
ld    (countT1), a        ; Update in memory
sub   T1                  ; A = A-T1 (interruptions to be passed)
jr    nz, Isr_sound       ; Non-zero, skip
ld    (countT1), a        ; Counter = zero
set   $03, (hl)           ; Activates bit 3 flags
                         ; change address enemies

; Sound
Isr_sound:
ld    a, (MUSIC)          ; A = music indicators
and   $0f                 ; A = tempo
ld    hl, tempo           ; HL = current tempo
cp    (hl)                ; Compares tempo
jr    z, Isr_soundCont    ; Equals, jumps
ld    (hl), a             ; Different, current tempo
jr    Isr_soundEnd        ; Jump to sound note
```

```
Isr_soundCont:
ld    a, (countTempo)       ; A = countTempo
inc   a                     ; A = A+1
ld    (countTempo), a       ; Update in memory
cp    (hl)                  ; Compare with current rate
jr    nz, Isr_end           ; Distinct, jumps

Isr_soundEnd:
xor   a                     ; A = 0
ld    (countTempo), a       ; Tempo counter = 0
ld    hl, MUSIC             ; HL = music indicators
set   $07, (hl)             ; Activate bit 7, sound

Isr_end:
pop   af
pop   bc
pop   de
pop   hl                    ; Retrieves records
ei                          ; Activates interruptions
reti                        ; Exits

countT1:    db $00          ; Counter change direction enemies
countEnemy: db $00          ; Enemy movement counter
countTempo: db $00          ; Counter to sound notes
tempo:      db $00          ; Current tempo
```

When we compile and load it into the emulator, there should be music playing during the game, and on every level, whether odd or even, one song or another should start playing.

If the difficulty is too high, comment out the line **CALL CheckCrashShip** in the main loop to avoid being killed.

Sound effects

Apart from the music, we will implement three different types of sound effects:

- Enemy movement.
- Explosion of the ship.
- Shot.

We implement these sound effects in separate routines within game.asm. Since we've already seen how to make each note sound, let's look at the final code of the routines without going into detail.

Locate the **RefreshEnemiesFire** routine and add the following lines before it:

```
; ------------------------------------------------------------------
; Emits the sound of enemy movement.
;
; Alters the value of the HL and DE registers.
; ------------------------------------------------------------------
PlayEnemiesMove:
ld    hl, $0a               ; HL = note
ld    de, $00               ; DE = frequency
call Play_beep              ; Play the sound
```

```
ld   hl, $14          ; HL = note
ld   de, $20          ; DE = frequency
call Play_beep        ; Play the sound

ld   hl, $0a          ; HL = note
ld   de, $10          ; DE = frequency
call Play_beep        ; Play the sound

ld   hl, $30          ; HL = note
ld   de, $1e          ; DE = frequency
jr   Play_beep        ; Play the sound and exit

; -----------------------------------------------------------------
; Emits the sound of the ship's explosion.
;
; Alters the value of the HL and DE registers.
; -----------------------------------------------------------------
PlayExplosion:
ld   hl, $27a0        ; HL = note
ld   de, $2b/$20      ; DE = frequency
call Play_beep        ; Play the sound

ld   hl, $13f4        ; HL = note
ld   de, $37/$20      ; DE = frequency
call Play_beep        ; Play the sound

ld   hl, $14b9        ; HL = note
ld   de, $52/$20      ; DE = frequency
call Play_beep        ; Play the sound

ld   hl, $1a2c        ; HL = note
ld   de, $41/$20      ; DE = frequency
jr   Play_beep        ; Play the sound and exit

; -----------------------------------------------------------------
; Emits the sound of the ship's gunfire
;
; Alters the value of the HL and DE registers.
; -----------------------------------------------------------------
PlayFire:
ld   hl, $64          ; HL = note
ld   de, $01          ; DE = frequency
jr   Play_beep        ; Play sound and exit
```

As we can see, in the three routines we load notes in HL, frequencies in DE, and we emit sounds, **CALL Play_beep**, except in the last note of each effect, in which case we use **JR** to exit with the **RET** of Play_beep.

All that remains now is to call the implemented routines. We locate **MoveEnemiesFire** and its last line, which is **JP RefreshEnemiesFire**. Just above this line we add the call to the sound we want to make when the enemies move, more specifically when they shots.

```
call PlayEnemiesMove       ; Play EnemiesMove
```

The next call we add is to the sound that is made when the gun is fired. We locate **MoveFire** and after the sixth line, **SET $01, (HL)**, we add the following lines:

```
push hl              ; Preserves HL
call PlayFire        ; Play shot sound
pop  hl              ; Retrieves HL
```

In the case of the explosion sound, we will not call it from game.asm, even though it seems inconsistent.

If we locate the **checkCrashShip_endLoop** tag, which is inside the **CheckCrashShip** routine, and we look at the previous line **JP PrintExplosion**, we can deduce that when the ship is hit we paint the explosion, and if we go to **PrintExplosion** we see that it paints the explosion and jumps to paint the ship, **JP PrintShip** and goes out that way.

So, in order not to change the current behaviour, and even though it is not coherent, the call to the sound emission will be made from **PrintExplosion**. We go to the print.asm file, find the **PrintExplosion** routine and the last line, which is **JP PrintShip**. On top of this line we add the following line:

```
call PlayExplosion       ; Emits explosion sound
```

We now have the music and all the sound effects for our game. Compile, load into the emulator and see the results.

Download the source code from here

https://tinyurl.com/26a25wfk

Step 14: Difficulty, mute and loading screen

In this chapter we will allow you to choose between five difficulty levels, mute the music during the game and include the loading screen.

Create the folder Step14 and copy the files loader.tap, const.asm, ctrl.asm, game.asm, graph.asm, int.asm, main.asm, make or make.bat, print.asm and var.asm from the folder Step13.

Difficulty

Depending on the difficulty level selected, we will change the behaviour of the enemies and the number of lives as follows:

- **Level one**: Enemies do not reach our ship's position. The number of simultaneous shots fired by the enemies is one.
- **Level two**: Enemies do not reach our ship's position. The number of simultaneous enemy shots is five.
- **Level three**: The number of simultaneous shots is one.
- **Level four**: The number of simultaneous shots is five. Each time you complete a level, you start with five lives, Galactic Plague style.
- **Level five**: the number of simultaneous shots is five.

As we are giving the option of choosing between five difficulty levels, we need to modify the start screen.

We go to var.asm and modify **title** and **firstScreen**, leaving them as follows:

```
title:
db $10, $02, $16, $00, $0a, "SPACE BATTLE", $0d, $0d, $ff

firstScreen:
db $10, $06, "  Alien ships attack the Earth,", $0d
db "the future depends on you.", $0d, $0d
db "  Destroy all enemies that you", $0d
db "can, and protect the planet.", $0d, $0d
db $10, $03, $16, $08, $02, "Z - Left"
db $16, $08, $14, "X - Right"
db $0d, $0d, $16, $0a, $02, "V - Shot"
db $16, $0a, $14, "M - Sound", $0d, $0d
db $10, $04, "1 - Keyboard      3 - Sinclair 1", $0d, $0d
db "2 - Kempston      4 - Sinclair 2", $0d, $0d
db $10, $07, $16, $10, $08, "5 - Difficulty", $0d, $0d
db $10, $05, "  Aim, shoot and dodge the enemy", $0d
db "ships, defeat and release to the", $0d
db "planet of the threat."
db $ff
```

As we add new options, we remove a line break in the title and several in the rest of the screen to make everything fit.

We continue in var.asm, locate the **enemiesColor** tag and under the value (DB $06) add the tag we will use to store the selected difficulty.

```
hardness:
db $03
```

Now that we have the modified splash screen, we need to display the chosen difficulty level. We go to print.asm and after the **PrintFrame** routine we implement the routine that paints the difficulty:

```
; -----------------------------------------------------------------
; Paints the selected difficulty in the menu
;
; Alters the value of the AF and BC registers.
; -----------------------------------------------------------------
PrintHardness:
ld    a, $02            ; A = red ink
call Ink                ; Change ink
ld    b, $08            ; B = coord Y (inverted)
ld    c, $09            ; C = coord X (inverted)
call At                 ; Position cursor
ld    a, (hardness)     ; A = hardness
add   a, '0'            ; A = A + character 0
rst   $10               ; Paints the difficulty

ret
```

At this stage we have a certain level of knowledge, so we will only explain the routine in detail.

We set the ink to red (2), position the cursor, load the difficulty, add the character '0' to get the difficulty character and paint it.

We continue in print.asm, find the **PrintFirstScreen** routine and after the fifth line, **CALL PrintString**, we add the call to paint the selected difficulty.

```
call PrintHardness
```

We compile, load the emulator and see the results.

We removed the line breaks, added a new control button to turn the music on and off, and added the option to select the difficulty level.

Now we add the implementation of the difficulty selection. Continuing with print.asm, locate the **printFirstScreen_end** tag, and just above it we have the **JR C line, printFirstScreen_op**. Just above this we add the following lines:

```
jr    nc, printFirstScreen_end
rra
```

If key 4 has been pressed, we go to the end of the routine, **JR NC, printFirstScreen_end**. If not, we turn A to the right to see if key 5 has been pressed.

The next line was already there, **JR C, printFirstScreen_op**, and we leave it as it is, if the 5 has not been pressed it jumps and continues in the loop.

Below this line we add the following lines, which will be executed if the 5 is pressed:

```
ld    a, (hardness)
inc   a
cp    $06
jr    nz, printFirstScreen_opCont
ld    a, $01
```

We load the difficulty level selected in A, **LD A, (hardness)**, increment it, **INC A**, check if it has reached six, **CP $06**, skip if not, **JR NZ, printFirstScreen_opCont**, and if it has, set it to one, **LD A, $01**.

```
printFirstScreen_opCont:
ld    (hardness), a
call PrintHardness
jr    printFirstScreen_op
```

We update the difficulty in memory, **LD (hardness), A**, paint it, **CALL PrintHardess**, and continue in the loop waiting for a key to be pressed from 1 to 4.

The look and feel of the routine is as follows:

```
; -----------------------------------------------------------------
; Display screen and selection of controls.
;
; Alters the value of the AF, BC and HL registers.
; -----------------------------------------------------------------
PrintFirstScreen:
call CLS                    ; Clear screen
ld   hl, title             ; HL = title definition
call PrintString           ; Print title
ld   hl, firstScreen       ; HL = screen definition
call PrintString           ; Paint screen
call PrintHardness         ; Paint difficulty

printFirstScreen_op:
ld   b, $01                ; B = 1, option keys
ld   a, $f7                ; A = half-row 1-5
in   a, ($fe)              ; Read keyboard
rra                        ; Rotate A right, 1 pressed?
jr   nc, printFirstScreen_end ; No carry, click and skip
inc  b                     ; B = B+1, option Kempston
rra                        ; Rotate A right, 2 pressed?
jr   nc, printFirstScreen_end ; No carry, click and skip
inc  b                     ; B = B+1, option Sinclair 1
rra                        ; Rotate A right, 3 pressed?
jr   nc, printFirstScreen_end ; No carry, click and skip
inc  b                     ; Increments B, Sinclair 2
rra                        ; Rotate A right, 4 pressed?
```

```
jr   nc, printFirstScreen_end ; No carry, click and skip
rra                          ; Rotate A right, 5 pressed?
jr   c, printFirstScreen_op ; Carry, NOT pressed, loop
ld   a, (hardness)           ; A = hardness
inc  a                       ; A = A+1
cp   $06                     ; A = 6?
jr   nz, printFirstScreen_opCont ; A < 6, skip
ld   a, $01                  ; A = 1

printFirstScreen_opCont:
ld   (hardness), a           ; Upgrades difficulty
call PrintHardness           ; Paint it
jr   printFirstScreen_op     ; Loop to press 1 to 4

printFirstScreen_end:
ld   a, b                    ; A = selected option
ld   (controls), a           ; Load into memory
call FadeScreen              ; Fade screen

ret
```

We compile, load the emulator and test the difficulty setting.

It doesn't work, at least not the way we want it to. It is very fast and extremely difficult to select the desired difficulty.

We are going to change the part of the routine that evaluates which keys are pressed, relying on the ROM routines that control that there is a pause between each key detection to avoid repetition.

Let's switch to interrupt mode 1 so that all system variables are automatically updated.

We go to const.am and add two counters pointing to two system variables that we need to know which key was last pressed using the ROM routines.

```
; ----------------------------------------------------------------
; Address where the keypad status flags are located when
; the interrupts are active in mode 1.
;
; Bit 3 = 1 input in L mode, 0 input in K mode.
; Bit 5 = 1 a key has been pressed, 0 has not been pressed.
; Bit 6 = 1 numeric character, 0 alphanumeric.
; ----------------------------------------------------------------
FLAGS_KEY: equ $5c3b

; ----------------------------------------------------------------
; Memory address where the last pressed key is located,
; when mode 1 interrupts are active.
; ----------------------------------------------------------------
LAST_KEY: equ $5c08
```

If we read the comments we will know what is what.

We go back to print.asm, find **printFirstScreen_op** and delete the lines just below **LD B, $01** to line **JR C, printFirstScreen_op**, including this last line. Just above **printFirstScreen_op** we add the following lines:

```
di
```

```
im    1
ei

ld    hl, FLAGS_KEY
set   03, (hl)
```

Disable interrupts, **DI**, switch mode to one, **IM 1**, re-enable interrupts, **EI**, load the address of the keyboard flags in HL, **LD HL, FLAGS_KEY**, and set the input mode to L, **SET $03, (HL)**.

Just below **printFirstScreen_op** we implement the keyboard reading using ROM:

```
bit   $05, (hl)
jr    z, printFirstScreen_op
res   05, (hl)
```

We check if a key has been pressed, **BIT $05, (HL)**, if it has not we return to the loop, **JR Z, printFirstScreen_op**, and if it has we set bit 5 to zero for future checks, **RES $05, (HL)**.

The next line is **LD B, $01**. We continue to implement below it.

```
ld    c, '0' + $01
ld    a, (LAST_KEY)
cp    c
jr    z, printFirstScreen_end
```

We load in C the ASCII code of the one, **LD C, '0' + $01**, in A the last key pressed, **LD A, (LAST_KEY)**, we check if it is the one, **CP C**, and if so we jump, **JR Z, printFirstScreen_end**.

```
inc   b
inc   c
cp    c
jr    z, printFirstScreen_end
```

Increment B (Kempston option), **INC B**, increment C (key two), **INC C**, check if pressed, **CP C**, and jump, **JR Z, printFirstScreen_end**, if so.

We do the same to check if three or four (Sinclair 1 and 2) has been pressed:

```
inc   b
inc   c
cp    c
jr    z, printFirstScreen_end
inc   b
inc   c
cp    c
jr    z, printFirstScreen_end
```

All that remains is to check that five (difficulty) has been pressed:

```
inc   c
cp    c
jr    nz, printFirstScreen_op
```

Increment C (key 5), **INC C**, see if it is pressed, **CP C**, and skip if not, **JR NZ, printFirstScreen_op**.

All that remains is to find **printFirstScreen_end** and add the following lines before **RET**:

```
di
im   2
ei
```

We deactivate the interrupts, **DI**, switch to mode two, **IM 2**, and activate them, **EI**.

The final aspect of the routine is as follows:

```
; -----------------------------------------------------------------
; Presentation screen, selection of controls and difficulty.
;
; Alters the value of the AF, BC and HL registers.
; -----------------------------------------------------------------
PrintFirstScreen:
call CLS                    ; Clear screen
ld   hl, title              ; HL = title definition
call PrintString            ; Paint title
ld   hl, firstScreen        ; HL = screen definition
call PrintString            ; Paint screen
call PrintHardness          ; Paint difficulty

di                          ; Disables interrupts
im   1                      ; Switches to mode 1
ei                          ; Activates interrupts

ld   hl, FLAGS_KEY          ; HL = keyboard flags address
set  $03, (hl)              ; L-mode input
printFirstScreen_op:
bit  $05, (hl)              ; Any key pressed?
jr   z, printFirstScreen_op ; No, returns to loop
res  $05, (hl)              ; Bit 5 = 5, required for future inspections
ld   b, $01                 ; B = 1, option keys
ld   c, '0' + $01           ; C = ASCII code 1
ld   a, (LAST_KEY)          ; A = last key pressed
cp   c                      ; 1 pressed?
jr   z, printFirstScreen_end ; Yes, jump
inc  b                      ; B = B+1, option Kempston
inc  c                      ; C = C+1, key 2
cp   c                      ; 2 pressed?
jr   z, printFirstScreen_end ; Yes, jump
inc  b                      ; B = B+1, option Sinclair 1
inc  c                      ; C = C+1, key 3
cp   c                      ; 3 pressed?
jr   z, printFirstScreen_end ; Yes, jump
inc  b                      ; B = B+1, option Sinclair 2
inc  c                      ; C = C+1, key 4
cp   c                      ; 4 pressed?
jr   z, printFirstScreen_end ; Yes, jump
inc  c                      ; C = C+1, key 5
cp   c                      ; 5 pressed?
jr   nz, printFirstScreen_op ; No, loop
ld   a, (hardness)          ; A = hardness
inc  a                      ; A = A+1
```

```
cp    $06                    ; ¿A = 6?
jr    nz, printFirstScreen_opCont ; No, skip
ld    a, $01                 ; A = 1
printFirstScreen_opCont:
ld    (hardness), a          ; Upgrades difficulty
call  PrintHardness          ; Paint it
jr    printFirstScreen_op    ; Loop until key is pressed 1 to 4

printFirstScreen_end:
ld    a, b                   ; A = selected option
ld    (controls), a          ; Load into memory
call  FadeScreen             ; Fade screen

di                           ; Disables interruptions
im    2                      ; Switches to mode 2
ei                           ; Activates interruptions

ret
```

We compile, load the game into the emulator and see that we can select the difficulty we want.

Now that we have selected the difficulty, we need to change the behaviour of the game depending on the selected difficulty: the enemies may or may not reach the line where our ship is, and there are one to five enemy fires at the same time. We control this with the constants **ENEMY_TOP_B** and **FIRES**, so these values must be variable.

Open var.asm, locate the **hardness** tag, and add these lines just above it:

```
enemiesTopB:
db ENEMY_TOP_B
firesTop:
db FIRES
```

We have our variables, now we need to use them. Go to game.asm, find the tag **moveEnemies_Y_down** and the line **SUB ENEMY_TOP_B**. We replace this line with the following, reading the comments we know what it does:

```
push hl                      ; Preserves HL
ld   hl, enemiesTopB         ; HL = top at the bottom
sub  (hl)                    ; Subtract it
pop  hl                      ; Retrieve HL
```

Continuing with game.asm, locate **enableEnemiesFire_loop** and the line **CP FIRES**. We will replace this line with the following lines:

```
push hl                      ; Preserves HL
ld   hl, firesTop            ; HL = maximum number of shots
ld   c, (hl)                 ; C = maximum number of shots
pop  hl                      ; Retrieve HL
cp   c                       ; Compares maximum shots with active
```

This controls how far the enemy ships can reach from below, and how many shots can be fired at once.

We need a routine that changes the **enemiesTop** and **firesTop** values depending on the selected difficulty.

We continue in game.asm, locate Sleep and implement it just above it:

```
SetHardness:
ld   hl, enemiesTopB
ld   (hl), ENEMY_TOP_B
ld   a, (hardness)
cp   $03
jr   nc, setHardness_Fire
inc  (hl)
```

Aim HL at the enemy position stop below, **LD HL, enemyTopB**, update to default top, **LD (HL), ENEMY_TOP_B**, load difficulty in A, **LD A, (hardness)**, see if it is three, **CP $03**, if no carry is greater than or equal and jump, **JR NC, setHardness_Fire**. If there is carry, the hardness is less than three, we increase the top of the enemy position below by one line, **INC (HL)**. Remember that we are working with inverted coordinates.

```
setHardness_Fire:
ld   hl, firesTop
ld   (hl), $01
cp   $01
ret  z
cp   $03
ret  z
ld   (hl), FIRES

ret
```

We aim HL at the maximum number of simultaneous shots, **LD HL firesTop**, set it to one, **LD (HL), $01**, check if we are on difficulty one, **CP $01**, quit if so, **RET Z**, check if it is three, **CP $03**, quit if so. If not, we load the default maximum number of shots, **LD (HL), FIRES**, and exit, **RET**.

The final aspect of the routine is as follows:

```
; ------------------------------------------------------------------
; Assign difficulty
;
; Alters the value of the AF and HL registers.
; ------------------------------------------------------------------
SetHardness:
ld   hl, enemiesTopB         ; HL = top bottom enemies
ld   (hl), ENEMY_TOP_B       ; Update with default buffer
ld   a, (hardness)           ; A = hardness
cp   $03                     ; Compares it with 3
jr   nc, setHardness_Fire    ; No carry A => 3, skip
inc  (hl)                    ; Up one stop line below enemies
setHardness_Fire:
ld   hl, firesTop            ; HL = maximum fires
ld   (hl), $01               ; Sets it to 1
cp   $01                     ; Difficulty 1?
ret  z                       ; Yes, exits
cp   $03                     ; Difficulty 3?
```

```
ret  z                      ; Yes, exits
ld   (hl), FIRES            ; Load default maximum shots

ret
```

Now it's time to test if the level selection behaves as we want it to. We go to main.asm, find **Main_start** and the line **CALL PrintFirstScreen**. Immediately after this line we add the call to the difficulty setting:

```
call SetHardness            ; Assigns the difficulty
```

Now there is only one of the aspects we pointed out at the beginning; if the selected difficulty level is four, we start each level with five lives.

We continue in main.asm, look for the **Main_restart** tag and the line **JR Z, Win**. Just below this line we will implement the last aspect of difficulty:

```
ld   a, (hardness)
cp   $04
jr   nz, main_restartCont
ld   a, $05
ld   (livesCounter), a
main_restartCont:
```

We load the difficulty into A, **LD A, (hardness)**, check if it is four, **CP $04**, and skip if not, **JR NZ, main_restartCont**.

If we don't jump, we load five into A, **LD A, $05**, and update the number of lives in memory, **LD (livesCounter), A**, to start each level with five.

The last aspect of the routine is as follows:

```
Main_restart:
ld   a, (levelCounter)      ; A = level
cp   $1e                    ; A = 31? (we have 30)
jr   z, Win                 ; Yes, jump, VICTORY!

ld   a, (hardness)          ; A = hardness
cp   $04                    ; Is it 4?
jr   nz, main_restartCont   ; No, skip
ld   a, $05                 ; A = 5
ld   (livesCounter), a      ; Lives = 5

main_restartCont:
call FadeScreen             ; Fade screen
call ChangeLevel            ; Change level
call PrintFrame             ; Paint frame
call PrintInfoGame          ; Paint info titles
call PrintShip              ; Paint ship
call PrintInfoValue         ; Paint info values
call PrintEnemies           ; Paint enemies
call ResetEnemiesFire       ; Resets enemy shots
; Delay
call Sleep                  ; Produces delay
jr   Main_loop              ; Main loop
```

We compile, load the emulator and check that the different difficulty levels behave as we have defined.

Muting

The implementation of turning the music on and off is simple. We go to main.asm and add a new comment to the flags tag:

```
; Bit 5 -> mute 0 = No, 1 = Yes
```

In bit five of the flags we will indicate whether the mute is active or not.

Now we need to implement the enabling or disabling of this bit. Locate **Main_loop** and add the new implementation just below it:

```
rst   $38
ld    hl, FLAGS_KEY
set   03, (hl)
bit   $05, (hl)
jr    z, main_loopCheck
```

We update the system variables, **RST $38**, point HL to the keyboard flags, **LD HL, FLAGS_KEY**, put the input in L mode, **SET $03, (HL)**, check if a key has been pressed, **BIT $05, (HL)**, and if not, we jump.

```
res   05, (hl)
ld    a, (LAST_KEY)
cp    'M'
jr    z, main_loopMute
cp    'm'
jr    nz, main_loopCheck
```

We set bit five to zero for future inspection, **RES $05, (HL)**, load the key pressed in A, **LD A, (LAST_KEY)**, see if M was pressed, **CP 'M'**, skip if so, **JR Z, main_loopMute**, see if m was pressed, **CP 'm'**, and skip if not, **JR NZ, main_loopCheck**.

```
main_loopMute:
ld    a, (flags)
xor   $20
ld    (flags), a

main_loopCheck:
```

If m has been pressed, either uppercase or lowercase, we load the flags in A, **LD A, (flags)**, invert bit five, **XOR $20**, and update the value in memory, **LD (flags), A**. Finally, we include the tag we jumped to that did not exist, **main_loopCheck**.

This is a good time to remember how **XOR** works at bit level:

```
0 XOR 0 = 0
0 XOR 1 = 1
1 XOR 0 = 1
1 XOR 1 = 0
```

If the two bits are the same, the result is 0, if they are different, the result is 1. With **XOR $20**, if bit 5 is set to 1, the result is 0, if it is set to 1, the result is 1. The rest of the bits are unaffected.

The final appearance of the beginning of the **Main_loop** routine is as follows:

```
; Main loop
Main_loop:
rst  $38                  ; Update system variables
ld   hl, FLAGS_KEY        ; HL = keypad flags address
set  $03, (hl)            ; L-mode input
bit  $05, (hl)            ; Key pressed?
jr   z, main_loopCheck    ; No, skip
res  $05, (hl)            ; Bit 5 = 0, for future inspections
ld   a, (LAST_KEY)        ; A = last key pressed
cp   'M'                  ; M pressed?
jr   z, main_loopMute     ; Yes, skip
cp   'm'                  ; m pressed?
jr   nz, main_loopCheck   ; No, skip
main_loopMute:
ld   a, (flags)           ; A = flags
xor  $20                  ; Reverse bit 5 (mute)
ld   (flags), a           ; Update in memory

main_loopCheck:
call CheckCtrl            ; Check keystroke controls
call MoveFire             ; Move fire
```

Finally, we locate **GameOver**, we see that the top line is this:

```
jr   Main_loop            ; Main loop
```

We replace **JR** with **JP** because after adding several lines, **JR** would give us an out-of-range jump error.

Now that we've enabled or disabled the mute bit by pressing the M key, let's take it into account when we play or don't play the music. We go to Int.asm, find the **Isr_sound** tag and add the following lines just below it:

```
bit  $05, (hl)            ; Bit 5 active (mute)?
jr   nz, Isr_end          ; Yes, jump
```

When we reach **Isr_soung** HL points to **flags** of main.asm. We evaluate if bit five (mute) is set, **BIT $05, (HL)**, and jump if it is, **JR NZ, Isr_end**.

It's time to check that we have implemented the mute correctly. We compile, load the emulator, start the game and check that when we press M (without pressing any other key at the same time) the music is muted, when we press it again it starts playing again. The sound effects still play.

Loading screen

We come to the last point in the development of Space Battle, the loading screen.

Since the beginning of the tutorial we have been dragging an aspect that will cause an error when including the loading screen, we saw it in ZX-Pong, we fixed it, but again I have fallen into it; we have to change the start address of our game.

We go to main.asm and change the start address, which is now **ORG $5DAD**, to **ORG $5DFD**.

We go to int.asm and change **FLAGS: EQU $5DAD** and leave it as **FLAGS: EQU $5DFD**. We also change **MUSIC: EQU $5DAE** and leave it as **MUSIC: EQU $5DFE**.

If we now compile and load, we may get an error, because we have not changed the addresses in the loader. In addition to the addresses, we will add a **POKE**, which we already used in ZX-Pong, and the loading of the loading screen.

The final appearance of the loader should look like this:

```
10 CLEAR 24059
20 POKE 23739,111: LOAD ""SCREEN$
30 LOAD ""CODE: LOAD ""CODE 32348
40 RANDOMIZE USR 24060
```

The loading screen, which you should download and leave in the Step14 folder, should look like this:

Download the loading screen from here

https://tinyurl.com/2efp7vca

We now have the modified loader and the loading screen in the directory. All that remains is to include the loading screen in SpaceBattle.tap.

If we are working on Linux, we edit make and leave it as it is:

```
pasmo --name Martian --tap main.asm martian.tap martian.log
```

```
pasmo --name Int --tap int.asm int.tap int.log
cat loader.tap MarcianoScr.tap martian.tap int.tap > SpaceBattle.tap
```

If we are working on Windows, we edit make.bat and leave it as it is:

```
pasmo --name Martian --tap main.asm martian.tap martian.log
pasmo --name Int --tap int.asm int.tap int.log
copy /b loader.tap+MarcianoScr.tap+martian.tap+int.tap SpaceBattle.tap
```

We have added the loading screen to SpaceBattle.tap.

Run make or make.bat, load the emulator and we have our game, unless you want to change something...

Download the source code from here

https://tinyurl.com/28ol2tx6

Let´s make a game?

Tic-tac-toe

Introduction

Tic-tac-toe was born from reading the book "ZX Spectrum Game Programming Club" by Gary Plowman. When we finish typing the Basic list in the book, he suggests adding the single player mode as an exercise.

Having concluded that Basic was not my thing, I decided to develop the game from scratch in Assembly, with the following options:

- One and two player modes.
- Possibility to specify the names of the players.
- Points to be earned to finish the game.
- Maximum time per move.

In Space Battle we saw the use of the ROM routine for keyboard handling, but it is in Tic Tac Toe where it is used most intensively.

We will also use interrupts to control the maximum time per move and give the user a countdown of the seconds left to move; he will lose his turn if he uses them up without having made the move.

At this point in the book you should already have a certain level, so we will not explain the instructions one by one; we will explain what the routine does as a whole, which together with the comments should be sufficient for your understanding.

Step 1: Game board

The first thing we are going to do is to design and paint the game board, which consists of a grid of nine cells.

We create the folder TicTacToe and the files:

- Main.asm
- Rom.asm
- Screen.asm
- Sprite.asm
- Var.asm

This time I won't create folders for each step, but if you prefer you can continue this way.

Sprites

We define the graphics in sprite.asm: the X for player one, the O for player two, the board crosshairs and the vertical and horizontal lines. As in Space Battle, we will use the UDGs.

The appearance of the graphics in sprite.asm is as follows:

```
; ------------------------------------------------------------------
; File: sprite.asm
;
; Definition of graphs.
; ------------------------------------------------------------------
; Sprite player 1
Sprite_P1:
db $c0, $e0, $70, $38, $1c, $0e, $07, $03 ; $90
db $03, $07, $0e, $1c, $38, $70, $e0, $c0 ; $91

; Sprite player 2
Sprite_P2:
db $03, $0f, $1c, $30, $60, $60, $c0, $c0 ; $92 Top/Left
db $c0, $f0, $38, $0c, $06, $06, $03, $03 ; $93 Up/right
db $c0, $c0, $60, $60, $30, $1c, $0f, $03 ; $94 Down/Left
db $03, $03, $06, $06, $0c, $38, $f0, $c0 ; $95 Down/Right

; Sprite crosshead
Sprite_CROSS:
db $18, $18, $18, $ff, $ff, $18, $18, $18 ; $96

; Sprite vertical line
Sprite_SLASH:
db $18, $18, $18, $18, $18, $18, $18, $18 ; $97

; Sprite horizontal line
Sprite_MINUS:
db $00, $00, $00, $ff, $ff, $00, $00, $00 ; $98
```

With the practice you got in Space Battle, you should be able to draw the sprites on paper to see how they look.

The next step is to draw the board. Constants are needed to reference the ROM, define positions, data to be painted and routines to paint it.

ROM routines and variables

The ROM constants are defined in rom.asm.

```
; -------------------------------------------------------------------
; File: rom.asm
;
; ROM routines and system variables.
; -------------------------------------------------------------------

; Permanent attributes of screen 2, main screen.
ATTR_S: equ $5c8d

; Current display attributes 2.
ATTR_T: equ $5c8f

; Edge attribute and screen 1. Used by BEEPER.
BORDCR: equ $5c48

; Address of starting coordinates X and Y (PLOT)
COORDX: equ $5c7d
COORDY: equ $5c7e

;----------------------------------------------------------------
; Address where the keypad status flags are located when
; the interruptions are not active.
;
; Bit 3 = 1 input in L mode, 0 input in K mode.
; Bit 5 = 1 a key has been pressed, 0 has not been pressed.
; Bit 6 = 1 numeric character, 0 alphanumeric.
;----------------------------------------------------------------
FLAGS_KEY: equ $5c3b

;----------------------------------------------------------------
; Address where the last key was pressed
; when interrupts are not active.
;----------------------------------------------------------------
LAST_KEY: equ $5c08

; Direction of user-defined graphics.
UDG: equ $5c7b

; Start address of the graphics area of the VideoRAM.
VIDEORAM: equ $4000

; Length of the graphics area of the VideoRAM.
VIDEORAM_L: equ $1800

; Start address of the VideoRAM attributes area.
VIDEOATT: equ $5800

; Length of the VideoRAM attribute area.
VIDEOATT_L: equ $0300
```

```
; ------------------------------------------------------------------
; ROM beeper routine.
;
; Input: HL -> Note.
;        DE -> Duration.
;
; Alters the value of the AF, BC, DE, HL and IX registers.
; ------------------------------------------------------------------
BEEPER: equ $03b5


; ------------------------------------------------------------------
; Draw a line from the COORDS coordinates.
;
; Input: B -> Vertical displacement of the line.
;        C -> Horizontal displacement of the line.
;        D -> Vertical orientation of the line:
;               $01 = Up, $FF = Down.
;        E -> Horizontal orientation of the line:
;               $01 = Left, $FF = Right.
;
; Alters the value of the AF, BC and HL registers.
; ------------------------------------------------------------------
DRAW: equ $24ba


; ------------------------------------------------------------------
; ROM AT routine. Position the cursor.
;
; Input: B -> Y-coordinate.
;        C -> X-coordinate.
;
; The top left corner of the screen is 24, 33.
; (0-21) (0-31)
; ------------------------------------------------------------------
LOCATE: equ $0dd9


; ------------------------------------------------------------------
; ROM routine that opens the output channel.
;
; Input: A -> Channel (1 = lower display, 2 = upper display).
; ------------------------------------------------------------------
OPENCHAN: equ $1601
```

As you will see, we have added variables and routines that we have not seen before. Don't worry, we'll see them as we go along.

Variables

In var.asm we add the necessary data to paint the board.

```
; ------------------------------------------------------------------
; File: var.asm
;
; Variable and constant declarations.
; ------------------------------------------------------------------

; Board ink
INKBOARD: equ $04
```

```
; Position Y = 0 for LOCATE.
INI_TOP:  equ $18
; Position X = 0 for LOCATE.
INI_LEFT: equ $21
; Positions for painting OXO elements.
POS1_TOP: equ INI_TOP   - $07
POS2_TOP: equ POS1_TOP - $05
POS3_TOP: equ POS2_TOP - $05

POS1_LEFT: equ INI_LEFT   - $0a
POS2_LEFT: equ POS1_LEFT - $05
POS3_LEFT: equ POS2_LEFT - $05
; -----------------------------------------------------------
; Graphics.
; -----------------------------------------------------------
; Vertical lines of the board.
Board_1:
db $20, $20, $20, $20, $97, $20, $20, $20, $20, $97, $20, $20, $20
db $20, $ff

; Horizontal lines of the board.
Board_2:
db $98, $98, $98, $98, $96, $98, $98, $98, $98, $96, $98, $98, $98
db $98, $ff

; -----------------------------------------------------------
; Parts of the screen.
; -----------------------------------------------------------
; Guide numbers so that the player knows which key to press
; to place the tokens (O X O)
Board_Helper:
; Magenta ink
db $10, $03
; AT,Y,X,number
db $16, $08, $0a, "1", $16, $08, $10, "2", $16, $08, $15, "3"
db $16, $0d, $0a, "4", $16, $0d, $10, "5", $16, $0d, $15, "6"
db $16, $12, $0a, "7", $16, $12, $10, "8", $16, $12, $15, "9"
db $ff
```

Screen

In screen.asm we will implement the necessary routines to draw the elements on the screen.

```
; -----------------------------------------------------------
; Position the cursor. The upper corner is at 24.33.
;
; Input: B -> Y.
;        C -> X.
; -----------------------------------------------------------
AT:
push af
push bc
push de
push hl                      ; Preserve records

call LOCATE                  ; Position cursor
```

```
pop   hl
pop   de
pop   bc
pop   af                    ; Retrieves records
ret
```

The AT routine receives the Y and X coordinates simultaneously in the B and C registers (they are inverted coordinates). It calls the ROM routine that positions the cursor.

We will manage the different colour attributes in a differentiated way, with one routine for each attribute.

```
; ----------------------------------------------------------------
; Change the border colour.
;
; Input: A -> Colour for the border.
;
; Alters the value of the AF registers.
; ----------------------------------------------------------------
BORDER:
push bc                    ; Preserves BC
and  $07                   ; A = colour
out  ($fe), a              ; Change border colour

rlca
rlca
rlca                       ; Rotate three bits to the left to set
                           ; colour in paper/border bits
ld   b, a                  ; B = A
ld   a, (BORDCR)           ; A = system variable BORDCR
and  $c7                   ; Remove the paper/border bits
or   b                     ; Adds the paper/border colour

ld   (BORDCR), a           ; BORDCR = A, so that BEEPER does not change
pop  bc                    ; Retrieves BC

ret
```

The BORDER routine receives in A the colour to be assigned to the border. To make sure it is the right colour, we keep bits 0, 1 and 2. We change the border colour and then set the value in the system variable BORDCR so that BEEPER does not change it.

```
; ----------------------------------------------------------------
; Assigns the colour of the ink.
;
; Input: A -> Ink colour.
;             FBPPPIII
;
; Alters the value of the AF registers.
; ----------------------------------------------------------------
INK:
push bc                    ; Preserves BC
and  $07                   ; A = INK
ld   b, a                  ; B = A

ld   a, (ATTR_T)           ; A = current attribute
and  $f8                   ; A = FLASH, BRIGHT and PAPER
```

```
or    b                        ; Add INK

ld    (ATTR_T), a              ; Update current attribute
ld    (ATTR_S), a              ; Update permanent attribute
pop   bc                       ; Retrieves BC

ret
```

The INK routine gets the ink colour in A. We make sure to keep only the ink colour, get the current attributes, leave the flicker, brightness and background and add the ink. We update the system variables queried by RST $10 and by changing the channel to apply the colour attributes.

```
; ----------------------------------------------------------------
; Assigns the background colour.
;
; Input: A -> Background colour.
;
; Alters the value of the AF registers.
; ----------------------------------------------------------------
PAPER:
push  bc                       ; Preserves BC
and   $07                      ; A = colour
rlca
rlca
rlca                           ; Rotate three bits to the left to set
                               ; colour in paper/border bits
ld    b, a                     ; B = A
ld    a, (ATTR_T)              ; A = current attribute
and   $c7                      ; Remove background

or    b                        ; Add background
ld    (ATTR_T), a              ; Update current attribute
ld    (ATTR_S), a              ; Update permanent attribute
pop   bc                       ; Retrieves BC

ret
```

The PAPER routine gets the colour in A. We keep the colour, rotate it three bits to the left to put it in the background bits, and store it in B. We get the current attributes, remove the background, and add the one that came in A.

```
; ----------------------------------------------------------------
; Paints strings ending in $FF.
;
; Input: HL -> Address of the string.
;
; Alters the value of the AF and HL registers.
; ----------------------------------------------------------------
PrintString:
ld    a, (hl)                  ; A = character to paint
cp    $ff                      ; Is it $FF?
ret   z                        ; Yes, exit
rst   $10                      ; Paints character
inc   hl                       ; HL = next character
jr    PrintString              ; Loop to end of string
```

The PrintString routine has already been seen in Space Battle, so it needs no explanation.

We will implement routines to clean up the whole screen, a line and the attributes.

```
; ------------------------------------------------------------------
; Changes the attributes of the VideoRAM with the specified attribute.
;
; Input: A -> Specified attribute (FBPPPIII)
;            Bits 0-2 Ink colour (0-7).
;            Bits 3-5 Paper colour (0-7).
;            Bit  6   Brightness (0/1).
;            Bit  7   Blink (0/1).
;
; Alters the value of the BC, DE and HL registers.
; ------------------------------------------------------------------
CLA:
ld   hl, VIDEOATT        ; HL = start attributes
ld   (hl), a             ; Change attribute
ld   de, VIDEOATT+1      ; DE = 2nd address attributes VideoRAM
ld   bc, VIDEOATT_L-1    ; BC = length attributes - 1
ldir                     ; Changes the attributes

ld   (ATTR_T), a         ; Updates system variable
ld   (ATTR_S), a         ; current attribute, permanent
ld   (BORDCR), a         ; and border
ret
```

The CLA routine receives in A the attributes to be assigned to the screen, in the format already seen above. It modifies them and updates the current, permanent and border attribute system variables.

```
; ------------------------------------------------------------------
; Deletes the specified screen line.
;
; Input: B -> Screen line to be deleted.
;            Inverted coordinates.
;
; Alters the value of the AF registers.
; ------------------------------------------------------------------
CLL:
ld   a, (ATTR_T)         ; A = current attributes
and  $3f                 ; A = PAPER + INK
ld   (ATTR_T), a         ; Update in memory

push bc                  ; Preserves BC

ld   c, INI_LEFT         ; C = 1st column
call AT                  ; Position cursor
ld   b, $20              ; B = 32 columns*line
CLL_loop:
ld   a, $20              ; A = space
rst  $10                 ; Prints it out
djnz CLL_loop            ; Loop while B > 0

pop  bc                  ; Recover BC

ret
```

The CLL routine receives the line to be deleted in A (with inverted coordinates) and deletes it. Before it does this, it removes the brightness and blinking of the current attributes.

```
; -----------------------------------------------------------------
; Deletes the graphics from the VideoRAM.
;
; Alters the value of the BC, DE and HL registers.
; -----------------------------------------------------------------
CLS:
ld    hl, VIDEORAM          ; HL = VideoRAM address
ld    de, VIDEORAM+1        ; DE = 2nd address VideoRAM
ld    bc, VIDEORAM_L-1      ; BC = length VideoRAM - 1
ld    (hl), $00            ; Clean 1st position
ldir                       ; Clean up the rest

ret
```

The CLS routine erases the graphic area of the screen, the pixels.

As in Space Battle, we will draw some numerical data in BDC format, but this time, because the range of numbers will be between zero and ten, we will check if the ten is zero to draw a space instead.

```
; -----------------------------------------------------------------
; Paints the value of BCD numbers.
;
; It only paints numbers from 0 to 99.
;
; Input: HL -> Pointer to the number to be painted.
;
; Alters the value of the AF register.
; -----------------------------------------------------------------
PrintBCD:
ld    a, (hl)              ; A = number to paint
and   $f0                  ; A = tens
rrca
rrca
rrca
rrca                       ; Tens to bits from 0 to 3
or    a                    ; Tens = 0?
jr    nz, PrintBCD_ascii   ; No, skip
ld    a, ' '               ; Tens = 0
jr    PrintBCD_continue    ; Paint space

PrintBCD_ascii:
add   a, '0'               ; A = A + Ascii code of 0

PrintBCD_continue:
rst   $10                  ; Paint 1st digit
ld    a, (hl)              ; A = number to paint
and   $0f                  ; Keeps the units
add   a, '0'               ; A = A + Ascii code of 0
rst   $10                  ; Print 2nd digit
ret
```

PrintBCD gets the HL pointer to the number to paint, loads it into A, takes the tens and if they are zero, paints a space. The rest of the routine is the same as in Space Battle.

We have almost everything ready to paint the board, we just need the routine to do it.

```
; ------------------------------------------------------------------
; Paint the board.
;
; Alters the value of the AF, BC, D and HL registers.
; ------------------------------------------------------------------
PrintBoard:
ld    a, INKBOARD           ; A = ink
call INK                    ; Change ink

; Initial coordinates of the board
ld    b, INI_TOP-$06        ; B = coord Y
ld    c, INI_LEFT-$09       ; C = coord X
ld    d, $0e                ; D = number of rows board

printBoard_1:
call AT                     ; Position cursor
ld   hl, Board_1            ; HL = vertical line
call PrintString            ; Paints vertical line characters
dec  b                      ; B-=1, next line
dec  d                      ; D-=1
jr   nz, printBoard_1       ; Loop while D > 0

printBoard_2:
; Coordinates of the first horizontal line
ld    b, INI_TOP-$0a        ; B = coord Y
ld    c, INI_LEFT-$09       ; C = coord X
call AT                     ; Position cursor
ld   hl, Board_2            ; HL = horizontal line
call PrintString            ; Paint horizontal line

; Coordinates of the second horizontal line,
; X-coordinate does not change.
ld    b, INI_TOP-$0f        ; B = coord Y
call AT                     ; Position cursor
ld   hl, Board_2
call PrintString            ; Paint horizontal line

printBoard_3:
; Paints the guide numbers so that the user knows which key to press
; to place the tokens (O X O)
ld   hl, Board_Helper       ; HL = helper
jp    PrintString           ; Paints helper and exits
```

PrintBoard paints the board, changes the ink and prepares everything for painting the vertical line, which is painted on printBoard_1. The horizontal line is painted on printBoard_2 and the guide for the player to know which keys to press is painted on printBoard_3.

When the vertical and horizontal lines are drawn, the vertical line is erased where it crosses. Look closely at the definition of board2 and you will see that the same character is not painted over the whole board.

Main

To see if everything works, we implement the first version of the main.asm file.

```
org   $5e88

Main:
ld    hl, Sprite_P1
ld    (UDG), hl
ld    a, $02
call OPENCHAN

xor   a
call BORDER
call CLA
call CLS

Init:
call PrintBoard

Loop:
jr    Loop

include "rom.asm".
include "screen.asm"
include "sprite.asm"
include "var.asm"

end   Main
```

We set the start address, bearing in mind that we will be making a custom loader. We show where the UDGs are, open channel two, change the border, attributes, clear the screen and paint the board. We stay in an infinite loop, which will be the main loop.

We compile, load into the emulator and see the results.

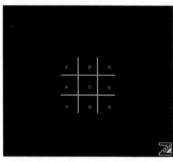

We already have the board on which the game will be played.

Download the source code from here

https://tinyurl.com/22oz5y2m

Step 2: scoreboards and a two player game

The next step will be to implement the scoreboards and the two-player game, which will form a large part of the programme.

Information

First we add the name of the programme, the players, the markers and the moving piece.

In var.asm we add the necessary data.

```
LENNAME: equ $0c              ; Length name players

; Information
Info:               db $10, $07, $16, $00, $03, "Three in a row at "
info_points:        db "5 point"
info_gt1:           db "s"

player1_title:      db $10, $05, $16, $02, $00
player1_name:       defs LENNAME, " "
player1_figure:     db $16, $04, $00, $90, $91, $0d, $91, $90

player_tie:         db $10, $02, $16, $02, $0d, "Tables"

player2_title:      db $10, $06, $16, $02, $14
player2_name:       defs LENNAME, " "
player2_figure:     db $16, $04, $1b, $92, $93, $16, $05, $1b
                    db $94, $95, $ff

; Titles
TitleTurn:          db $16, $15, $05, $13, $01
                    db "Shift for "
TitleTurn_name:     defs LENNAME, " "
                    db $ff
TitleError:         db $10, $02, $16, $15, $0a, $12, $01, $13, $01
                    defm "Box occupied", $ff
TitleEspamatica:    defm "Espamatica 2019", $ff
TitleGameOver:      db $10, $07, $16, $15, $03, $12, $01, $13, $01
                    defm "Game terminated. Other?", $ff
TitleLostMovement:  db $10, $02, $12, $01, $13, $01, $16, $15, $05
                    defm "Lose turn "
TitleLostMov_name:  defs LENNAME, " "
                    db $ff
TitleOptionStart:   defm "0. Start", $ff
TitleOptionPlayer:  defm "1. Players", $ff
TitleOptionPoint:   defm "2. Points", $ff
TitleOptionTime:    defm "3. Time", $ff
TitlePlayerName:    defm "Player "
TitlePlayerNumber:  db " : ", $ff
TitlePointFor:      db $10, $07, $16, $15, $05, $12, $01, $13, $01
                    defm "Point for "
TitlePointName:     defs LENNAME, " "
                    db $ff
TitleTie:           db $10, $07, $16, $15, $0d, $12, $01, $13, $01
                    defm "Tables", $ff
```

```
; ----------------------------------------------------------------
; Development of the game.
; ----------------------------------------------------------------
; Board squares. One byte per square, from 1 to 9.
; Bit 0, square occupied by player 1.
; Bit 4, square occupied by player 2.
Grid:           db $00, $00, $00, $00, $00, $00, $00, $00, $00
; Positions of the pieces on the board, 2 bytes per piece X, Y
GridPos:        db POS1_LEFT, POS1_TOP ; 1
                db POS2_LEFT, POS1_TOP ; 2
                db POS3_LEFT, POS1_TOP ; 3
                db POS1_LEFT, POS2_TOP ; 4
                db POS2_LEFT, POS2_TOP ; 5
                db POS3_LEFT, POS2_TOP ; 6
                db POS1_LEFT, POS3_TOP ; 7
                db POS2_LEFT, POS3_TOP ; 8
                db POS3_LEFT, POS3_TOP ; 9

Points_p1:      db $00              ; Points player 1
Points_p2:      db $00              ; Points player 2
Points_tie:     db $00              ; Points tables
PlayerMoves:    db $00              ; Player who moves

MaxPlayers:     db $01              ; Maximum players
MaxPoints:      db $05              ; Maximum Points
MaxSeconds:     db $10              ; Maximum seconds

Name_p1:        db "Amstrad CPC " ; Player name 1
Name_p2:        db "ZX Spectrum " ; Player name 2
Name_p2Default:db "ZX Spectrum " ; Default name
```

In the Info tag, we define the literals that will be displayed at the top of the screen. Although it may seem strange, the division into several labels is due to the fact that there are values that change depending on the choices made by the players:

- Points needed to win the game.
- If it is more than one point, it is written in the plural.
- The names of the players.

We also define the labels we will use to keep track of each player's score and name.

We go to screen.asm and implement one routine to draw the information and another to draw the score.

```
; ----------------------------------------------------------------
; Paint the information of the game.
;
; Alters the value of HL.
; ----------------------------------------------------------------
PrintInfo:
ld   hl, Info              ; HL = information
jp   PrintString           ; Paints it
```

PrintInfo paints the information to be displayed at the top of the screen. It does not assign ink colours or positions, as this is all defined in the Info tag.

```
; ------------------------------------------------------------------
; Paint the score.
;
; Alters the value of AF, BC, DE and HL.
; ------------------------------------------------------------------
PrintPoints:
ld    a, $05                ; A = cyan ink
call  INK                   ; Change ink
ld    b, INI_TOP-$04        ; B = coord Y
ld    c, INI_LEFT-$03       ; C = coord X
call  AT                    ; Position cursor
ld    hl, Points_p1         ; HL = points player 1
call  PrintBCD              ; Paints them

ld    a, $02                ; A = red ink
call  INK                   ; Change ink
ld    b, INI_TOP-$04        ; B = coord Y
ld    c, INI_LEFT-$0f       ; C = coord X
call  AT                    ; Position cursor
ld    hl, Points_tie        ; HL = points tables
call  PrintBCD              ; Paints them

ld    a, $06                ; A = yellow ink
call  INK                   ; Change ink
ld    b, INI_TOP-$04        ; B = coord Y
ld    c, INI_LEFT-$1e       ; C = coord X
call  AT                    ; Position cursor
ld    hl, Points_p2         ; HL = points player 2
jp    PrintBCD              ; Paints them in and out
```

PrintPoints paints the players' scores and tables. For each score, it changes the ink, positions the cursor and paints the score.

Now we have everything ready. We go to main.asm and after the call to PrintBoard we add the code that paints the information and the score.

```
ld    hl, Name_p1
ld    de, player1_name
ld    bc, LENNAME
ldir
ld    hl, Name_p2
ld    de, player2_name
ld    bc, LENNAME
ldir
call  PrintInfo

xor   a
ld    hl, Points_p1
ld    de, Points_p1+$01
ld    bc, $03
ld    (hl), a
ldir
call  PrintPoints
```

The names of the players are in the Name_p1 and Name_p2 tags, so we need to pass them to the appropriate place in the information. We initialise the score and draw it.

We compile, load into the emulator and see the results.

Two-player game

We will implement the two-player game: controls, tile moves, checks for correctness, and tic-tac-toe performance.

In var.asm we include a series of constants with ink colours, lines on which the three dashes occur, and key codes, which we will use together with the ROM routine to check the controls.

```
INKWARNING: equ $C2        ; Ink Warnings
INKPLAYER1: equ $05        ; Player ink 1
INKPLAYER2: equ $06        ; Player 2 ink
INKTIE:     equ $07        ; Ink tables

KEYDEL:     equ $0c        ; Delete key
KEYENT:     equ $0d        ; Enter Key
KEYSPC:     equ $20        ; Space Key
KEY0:       equ $30        ; Key 0
KEY1:       equ $31        ; Key 1
KEY2:       equ $32        ; Key 2
KEY3:       equ $33        ; Key 3
KEY4:       equ $34        ; Key 4
KEY5:       equ $35        ; Key 5
KEY6:       equ $36        ; Key 6
KEY7:       equ $37        ; Key 7
KEY8:       equ $38        ; Key 8
KEY9:       equ $39        ; Key 9

WINNERLINE123: equ $01     ; Winning line 123
WINNERLINE456: equ $02     ; Winning line 456
WINNERLINE789: equ $03     ; Winning line 789
WINNERLINE147: equ $04     ; Winning line 147
WINNERLINE258: equ $05     ; Winning line 258
WINNERLINE369: equ $06     ; Winning line 369
WINNERLINE159: equ $07     ; Winning line 159
WINNERLINE357: equ $08     ; Winning line 357
```

We implement the logic in the file game.asm. We build it and add the include to main.asm.

```
; --------------------------------------------------------------------
; Wait for a key to be pressed on the board.
; During the game the interruptions are activated in order
; to perform the countdown.
```

```
; With interrupts enabled, it does not update FLAGS_KEY/LAST_KEY.
;
; Output: C -> Key pressed.
;
; Alters the value of the AF and BC registers.
; -------------------------------------------------------------------
WaitKeyBoard:
ld    a, $f7           ; A = half-row 1-5
in    a, ($fe)         ; Read half-row
cpl                    ; Invert bits, keys pressed to 1
and   $1F              ; A = bits 1 to 4
jr    z, waitKey_cont  ; No key pressed, skips

; Evaluates the key pressed from 1 to 5.
ld    c, KEY1          ; C = key 1
ld    b, $05           ; B = keys to check
waitKey_1_5:
rra                    ; Pulsed key?
ret   c                ; Pressed, exit
inc   c                ; C = code next key
djnz  waitKey_1_5      ; Loop for 5 keys

waitKey_cont:
ld    a, $ef           ; A = half-row 0-6
in    a, ($fe)         ; Read half-row
cpl                    ; Invert bits, keys pressed to 1
and   $1F              ; A = bits 1 to 4
jr    z, waitKey_end   ; No key pressed, skip

; Evaluates the key pressed 9 to 6
rra                    ; Skip zero key
ld    c, KEY9          ; C = key 9
ld    b, $04           ; B = keys to check
waitKey_9_6:
rra                    ; Pulsed key?
ret   c                ; Pressed, exit
dec   c                ; C = next key code
djnz  waitKey_9_6      ; Loop for 4 keys

; No key has been pressed
waitKey_end:
ld    c, KEY0
ret
```

With WaitKeyBoard we will check if any of the keys on the board, from one to nine, have been pressed. In this case we will not use the ROM routine, because later we will have the mode two interrupts active, and neither FLAGS_KEY nor LAST_KEY will be updated, and the ROM will not be able to tell us the last key pressed.

The key check is very similar to the one we did in Space Battle, with the following variations:

- CPL: we invert the bits and evaluate if any keys were pressed with AND $1F; we skip if none were pressed.
- What we return, in this case in C, is the ASCII code of the key pressed; of the zero key if none was pressed.

We can also see that, before checking the keys 9 to 6, we make a rotation to ignore the 0 key.

We now continue with the logic of the token movement.

```
; ------------------------------------------------------------------
; Check and carry out the movement if it is correct.
;
; Input:  C  -> Key pressed
; Output: Z  -> Correct movement
;         NZ -> Incorrect movement
;
; Alters the value of the AF and HL registers.
; ------------------------------------------------------------------
ToMove:
push bc                    ; Preserves BC
ld   hl, Grid              ; HL = grid address
ld   a, c                  ; A = C (key code)
sub  $30                   ; A = numeric value key
dec  a                     ; A-=1, so that it does not add up
                           ; to one more
ld   b, $00                ; B = 0
ld   c, a                  ; C = A, BC = offset
add  hl, bc                ; HL = key box address
pop  bc                    ; Retrieves BC

ld   a, (hl)               ; A = box value
or   a                     ; Are you free?
ret  nz                    ; Busy, exits

ld   a, (PlayerMoves)      ; A = player moving
or   a                     ; Player 1?
jr   nz, toMove_p2         ; Player 2, jump
set  $00, (hl)             ; Activate box player 1
jr   toMove_end            ; Skip

toMove_p2:
set  $04, (hl)             ; Activate player 2 box

toMove_end:
xor  a                     ; Puts flag Z
ret                        ; Exits
```

ToMove receives the code of the key pressed in C. We calculate the value by subtracting the ASCII code from zero, subtracting one so as not to add too much to the offset, and point to the cell corresponding to the key pressed. We check that the cell is not occupied, if it is not, we activate bits one or four of the cell according to the player who is moving. If the cell is occupied, it goes out with NZ, if not, it goes out with Z (XOR A).

We need a routine that paints the tile in the right place; we implement this in screen.asm.

```
; ------------------------------------------------------------------
; Paint the card.
;
; Input: C -> Key pressed.
;
; Alters the value of the AF, BC and HL registers.
```

```
; -------------------------------------------------------------------
PrintOXO:
; Calculation of the card position
ld    a, c                  ; A = key
sub   $30                   ; A = key value
dec   a                     ; A-=1, so as not to over-add in offset
add   a, a                  ; A+=A, offset, two bytes per position
ld    b, $00                ; B = 0
ld    c, a                  ; C = A
ld    hl, GridPos           ; HL = address grid positions
add   hl, bc                ; HL+=BC, address coord X cell
ld    c, (hl)               ; C = coord X cell
inc   hl                    ; HL = address coord Y
ld    b, (hl)               ; B = coord Y cell
call  AT                    ; Position cursor

; Calculation sheet
ld    a, (PlayerMoves)      ; A = player who moves
or    a                     ; Check player
jr    nz, printOXO_Y        ; Non-zero, skip

printOXO_X:
ld    a, INKPLAYER1         ; A = ink player 1
call  INK                   ; Change ink
ld    a, $90                ; A = 1st sprite
rst   $10                   ; Paints it
ld    a, $91                ; A = 2nd sprite
rst   $10                   ; Paints it
dec   b                     ; B = bottom line
call  AT                    ; Position cursor
ld    a, $91                ; A = 2nd sprite
rst   $10                   ; Paints it
ld    a, $90                ; A = 1st sprite
rst   $10                   ; Paints it
ret                         ; Exists

printOXO_Y:
ld    a, INKPLAYER2         ; A = ink player 2
call  INK                   ; Change ink
ld    a, $92                ; A = 1st sprite
rst   $10                   ; Paints it
ld    a, $93                ; A = 2nd sprite
rst   $10                   ; Paints it
dec   b                     ; B = bottom line
call  AT                    ; Position cursor
ld    a, $94                ; A = 3rd sprite
rst   $10                   ; Paints it
ld    a, $95                ; A = 4th sprite
rst   $10                   ; Paints it
ret                         ; Exits
```

In the first part of PrintOXO, the offset is calculated to obtain the coordinates where to paint the piece, the cursor is obtained and positioned. Then you get the moving player.

The way to paint one tile or the other is almost identical: change the colour, paint the top part, position the cursor on the bottom line and paint the bottom part before leaving.

Now we can start testing how everything we have implemented looks in the program. We go to main.asm and under the Loop tag, before JR Loop, we add the calls to the implemented routines.

```
call WaitKeyBoard
ld   a, c
cp   KEY0
jr   z, loop_cont
call ToMove
jr   nz, loop_cont
call PrintOXO
ld   a, (PlayerMoves)
xor  $01
ld   (PlayerMoves), a
loop_cont:
```

We wait for the player to press a key, and when he does, we check that the move is correct, and if it is, we paint the piece and change players.

We compile, load the emulator and see the results.

We see how the tiles are painted and once the whole board is occupied we can only restart and reload, so we have to implement the following:

- When the board is full, reset it.
- Display information messages.
- Check if there is a tic-tac-toe or a board.
- Refresh the scoreboard.

Resetting the board

In var.asm, before PlayersMoves, we add a tag to keep track of the number of moves. The board is full when the value reaches nine.

We put it first because PlayersMoves is only restarted at the start of a game. If we reset it with every point, player one would always move first.

```
MoveCounter: db $00        ; Move counter
```

Also in var.asm, we add a constant at the beginning where we specify the length of data to initialise in each line item.

```
LENDATA: equ $04           ; Length of data to be initialised
```

As we need to add more data to initialise, we change the value of this constant.

In main.asm we locate the Loop tag and four lines before the line LD BC, $03. Replace this line with the following:

```
ld   bc, LENDATA
```

Compile, load into the emulator and check that everything still works.

As we have mentioned, we will not always initialise all the data, so it is a good idea to implement a routine that can be passed the length of the data to be initialised, so that it can be called from different places with different values.

The values we want to initialise are:

- Points_p1
- Points_p2
- Points_tie
- MoveCounter
- PlayerMoves (only at the start of the game)

There are more values to initialise, but they are higher up, so either we initialise them in two parts, or we change the label. The label is Grid (each player's moves) and we need to set all the values to zero at the start of each point. Let's change the position of the label, just above Points_p1, like this:

```
; -------------------------------------------------------------------
; Development of the game.
; -------------------------------------------------------------------
; Positions of the pieces on the board, 2 bytes per piece Y, X
GridPos:      db POS1_LEFT, POS1_TOP ; 1
              db POS2_LEFT, POS1_TOP ; 2
              db POS3_LEFT, POS1_TOP ; 3
              db POS1_LEFT, POS2_TOP ; 4
              db POS2_LEFT, POS2_TOP ; 5
              db POS3_LEFT, POS2_TOP ; 6
              db POS1_LEFT, POS3_TOP ; 7
              db POS2_LEFT, POS3_TOP ; 8
              db POS3_LEFT, POS3_TOP ; 9

; Board squares. One byte per square, from 1 to 9.
; Bit 0 to 1, square occupied by player 1.
; Bit 4 to 1, square occupied by player 2.
Grid:        db $00, $00, $00, $00, $00, $00, $00, $00, $00
Points_p1:   db $00          ; Points player 1
Points_p2:   db $00          ; Points player 2
Points_tie:  db $00          ; Points tables
MoveCounter: db $00          ; Move counter
PlayerMoves: db $00          ; Player moving
```

The value of LENDATA has to be changed to $0D.

We implement the initialisation routine in game.asm.

```
; -------------------------------------------------------------------
```

```
; Initialises the values of the item/item.
;
; Input: BC -> Length of the values to be initialised.
;
; Alters the value of the BC, DE and HL registers.
; -----------------------------------------------------------------
ResetValues:
ld    hl, Grid              ; HL = Grid address
ld    de, Grid+$01          ; DE = address of Grid+1
ld    (hl), $00             ; Resets first position to zero
ldir                        ; Resets the remainder (BC) to zero

ret
```

ResetValues gets the number of bytes to clear in BC (must be one less than the total length, that's why LENDATA is $0D instead of $0E), points HL and DE to the first and second grid positions, clears the first and then the rest.

If you look closely, this routine should look very familiar, take a look at the CLS routine in screen.asm. They are almost identical!

We could implement a routine with the lines LD (HL), $00, LDIR and RET, bearing in mind that before calling it we would have to load the necessary values in HL and BC, and remove CLS and ResetValues. I'll leave it up to you, I'm going to leave it as it is now.

We go back to main.asm, find Loop and a few lines above XOR A. From XOR A to CALL PrintPoint, we keep only the lines LD BC, LENDATA and CALL PrintPoints, the rest we delete.

Between LD BC, LENDATA and CALL PrintPoints, we add the call to initialise the values, as follows:

```
call PrintInfo

ld    bc, LENDATA
call ResetValues
call PrintPoints

Loop:
```

After loading the length of data to be cleaned into BC, we call the initialisation of the values and draw the points.

We compile, load into the emulator and see that everything still works.

To know if the board is full, we need to update MoveCounter with every move and check if it has reached nine.

Locate loop_cont and add the following lines just above it, after LD (PlayerMoves), A:

```
ld    hl, MoveCounter
inc   (hl)
ld    a, $09
cp    (hl)
jr    nz, loop_cont
```

```
ld    bc, LENDATA-$01
call  ResetValues
call  PrintBoard
```

We increment the move counter, check if it has reached nine, in which case we load into BC the length of the data to be erased minus one (so as not to erase the moving player), initialise the data and draw the board empty.

Compile and load into the emulator. If we press the keys from one to nine until the board is full, the player whose turn it is to move has not been cleared and will move the player whose turn it was in the next turn.

Information messages

During the course of the game there are several messages that need to be displayed to the players: if the move is wrong, which player is moving, who gets the point, if there is a draw and when the game is over.

The messages have been defined at the beginning of the chapter, and in each of them the ink, brightness, flicker and location, so all we need to do is call PrintString with the address of the message in HL.

There are two reasons why this cannot be done:

- The messages Turn to, Missed turn and Point to are not complete, they are completed with the name of the player who has the turn.
- Before writing a message, the line must be cleared.

We will implement two routines, one in game.asm and the other in screen.asm; these routines will act as a bridge when we call PrintString.

We will start with the routine we have implemented in screen.asm.

```
; ------------------------------------------------------------------
; Paint the messages
;
; Input: HL-> message address
; ------------------------------------------------------------------
PrintMsg:
ld    b, INI_TOP-$15      ; B = coord Y line to be deleted (inverted)
call  CLL                 ; Deletes the line
jp    PrintString         ; Paint the message
```

PrintMsg receives the address of the message in HL, clears the message line and jumps to paint the message, where it exits. Clearing the line before painting a new message is the only use of this routine.

We implement the game.asm routine, which completes the three messages that paint the player's name.

```
; ------------------------------------------------------------------
; Completes the messages in which the player's name is displayed.
;
; Input: HL -> message address
;        DE -> address where the name should go
;
; Alters the value of the AF, BC and DE registers.
; ------------------------------------------------------------------
```

```
DoMsg:
push hl                         ; Preserves HL
ld    hl, player1_name          ; HL = name player 1
ld    a, (PlayerMoves)          ; A = player
or    a                         ; Player 1?
ld    a, INKPLAYER1             ; A = ink player 1
jr    z, doMsg_cont             ; Player 1, skip
ld    hl, player2_name          ; HL = name player 2
ld    a, INKPLAYER2             ; A = ink player 2
doMsg_cont:
call INK                        ; Change ink
ld    bc, LENNAME               ; BC = length name
ldir                            ; Pass player name to message
pop  hl                         ; Retrieve HL
jp    PrintMsg                  ; Paint message
```

DoMsg receives the address of the message to be painted in HL and the address where the player's name is to be placed in DE. He checks which player's turn it is, places one or the other name and the player's ink. He paints the message and leaves.

We go to main.asm and paint all the messages we can, starting with who has the turn.

Locate Loop and add the following lines just below it:

```
ld    b, $19
loop_wait:
halt
djnz loop_wait
ld    hl, TitleTurn
ld    de, TitleTurn_name
call DoMsg
loop_key:
```

Each time we go through the loop, we paint the player whose turn it is to move. Before we do this, we pause for about half a second to allow time to read the messages.

Now find the line CP KEY0 and just below it in the line JR Z, loop_cont, change loop_cont to loop_key.

Compile, load it into the emulator and you will see that we can see which player has the turn to move.

Let's also draw the busy box error message. Find the CALL ToMove line, delete the following line, JR NZ, loop_cont, and add the following lines:

```
jr    z, loop_print
ld    hl, TitleError
call PrintMsg
jr    Loop
loop_print:
```

If it returns from the ToMove routine with the Z flag active, this means that the movement is correct and we jump to loop_print, the label we added before CALL PrintOXO. If not, the move is incorrect and we print the error message and go back to the start of the loop.

Compile, load into the emulator and try to move to an occupied square. The error message should be painted, even if it's only visible for a short time; don't worry, we'll remove the pause at the beginning of the loop later and use the sound effects for timing.

Table check

The draw check is simple; if there are nine moves and no three in a row, there is a draw.

Find the loop_cont tag and four lines above it, between JR NZ, loop_cont and LD BC, LENDATA-$01, add the following:

```
ld    hl, Points_tie
inc   (hl)
ld    hl, TitleTie
call PrintMsg
```

With these lines, if nine moves are reached without three in a row, one move is added to the draw score.

Go to the loop_key tag and add the following line above it:

```
call PrintPoints
```

Now, in each iteration of the loop, we draw the notes. The CALL PrintPoints just above the Loop tag can be removed.

Compile, load in the emulator and you will see that not everything works as it should, the table marker is not updated.

Actually everything works as it should, the problem is that ResetValues is resetting the scores, which is easy to fix, but we will fix it later.

We also notice that when repainting the board the flashing is active because the message Tables leaves it that way.

To solve this we could implement a routine to remove the flickering, but we decided to solve it in the board definition. We go to var.asm and just below the Board_1 tag we add the following line to disable the flickering and glowing when the board is painted.

```
db $12, $00, $13, $00
```

Compile, load into the emulator, move until the board is full and check that there is no flickering when repainting.

Tic-tac-toe check

The three in a row check should not be made until at least three moves have been made. In principle, there should be at least five moves before there are three in a row, but since we are going to implement the possibility of the player losing the turn if it takes longer than the set time, it is possible that there will be three in a row with three moves. However, we are going to perform the operation each time a piece is moved, so it will always take the same (approximate) time for each iteration of the loop.

In game.asm we add the routine that checks for tic-tac-toe.

```
; ------------------------------------------------------------------
; Check if there are three in a row.
;
; Return: A -> tic-tac-toe line
;         Z if there are three in a row, NZ otherwise.
;
; Alters the value of the AF, B and IX registers.
; ------------------------------------------------------------------
CheckWinner:
ld    ix, Grid-$01         ; IX = grid address - 1
ld    b, $03               ; B = sum cells player 1
ld    a, (PlayerMoves)     ; A = player
or    a                    ; Player 1?
jr    z, CheckWinner_check ; Player 1, skip
ld    b, $30               ; B = sum cells player 2

CheckWinner_check:
ld    a, (ix+1)            ; A = cell 1
add   a, (ix+2)            ; A+= cell 2
add   a, (ix+3)            ; A+= cell 3
cp    b                    ; Three in a row?
ld    a, WINNERLINE123     ; A = flag line 123
ret   z                    ; Tic-tac-toe, exits

ld    a, (ix+4)            ; A = cell 4
add   a, (ix+5)            ; A+= cell 5
add   a, (ix+6)            ; A+= cell 6
cp    b                    ; Three in a row?
ld    a, WINNERLINE456     ; A = indicator line 456
ret   z                    ; Tic-tac-toe, exits

ld    a, (ix+7)            ; A = cell 7
add   a, (ix+8)            ; A+= cell 8
add   a, (ix+9)            ; A+= cell 9
cp    b                    ; Three in a row?
ld    a, WINNERLINE789     ; A = line indicator line 789
ret   z                    ; Tic-tac-toe, exits

ld    a, (ix+1)            ; A = cell 1
add   a, (ix+4)            ; A+= cell 4
add   a, (ix+7)            ; A+= cell 7
cp    b                    ; Three in a row?
ld    a, WINNERLINE147     ; A = indicator line 147
```

```
ret   z                       ; Tic-tac-toe, exits

ld    a, (ix+2)               ; A = cell 2
add   a, (ix+5)               ; A+= cell 5
add   a, (ix+8)               ; A+= cell 8
cp    b                       ; Three in a row?
ld    a, WINNERLINE258        ; A = indicator line 258
ret   z                       ; Tic-tac-toe, exits

ld    a, (ix+3)               ; A = cell 3
add   a, (ix+6)               ; A+= cell 6
add   a, (ix+9)               ; A+= cell 9
cp    b                       ; Three in a row?
ld    a, WINNERLINE369        ; A = indicator line 369
ret   z                       ; Tic-tac-toe, exits

ld    a, (ix+1)               ; A = cell 1
add   a, (ix+5)               ; A+= cell 5
add   a, (ix+9)               ; A+= cell 9
cp    b                       ; Three in a row?
ld    a, WINNERLINE159        ; A = indicator line 159
ret   z                       ; Tic-tac-toe, exits

ld    a, (ix+3)               ; A = cell 3
add   a, (ix+5)               ; A+= cell 5
add   a, (ix+7)               ; A+= cell 7
cp    b                       ; Three in a row?
ld    a, WINNERLINE357        ; A = line indicator 357
ret                           ; Last condition, always comes out
```

In CheckWinner we point IX to the address above the grid, in B we load the value that the cells should add if one or the other player wins: three for player one and thirty for player two.

Then we check the possible combinations of three in a row that exist and leave if there were any, with the winning combination in A and the Z flag activated. To check if there were three in a row, we add up the values of the cells in A and check with B.

In the final check, if there are no three in a row, the Z flag is deactivated (NZ).

In main.asm we will add the lines to do the three in a row check and to act on whether it is successful or not. We add the following lines just below CALL PrintOXO.

```
loop_checkWinner:
call CheckWinner
jr    nz, loop_tie
ld    hl, TitlePointFor
ld    de, TitlePointName
call DoMsg
ld    hl, Points_p1
ld    a, (PlayerMoves)
or    a
jr    z, loop_win
inc   hl
loop_win:
```

```
inc  (hl)
jr   loop_reset
loop_tie:
```

We call the tic-tac-toe check and skip if there are no tic-tac-toes. If there are three in a row, we draw the point-to message, find out which player made it and increase their score.

Just below loop_tie are these lines:

```
ld   a, (PlayerMoves)
xor  $01
ld   (PlayerMoves), a
```

We remove it and put it under the loop_cont tag, otherwise the next point will be started by the same player who won the previous one.

Finally, we add the loop_reset tag before LD BC, LENDATA-$01.

We compile, load into the emulator and everything seems to work, except for the bookmarks, which still don't update.

We will visually mark where the three in a row have occurred by drawing a diagonal across the three tiles. We implement this routine in screen.asm.

```
; -------------------------------------------------------------------
; Print the winning line.
;
; Entry: A -> Winning line
;
; Alters the value of the AF, BC, DE and HL registers.
; -------------------------------------------------------------------
PrintWinnerLine:
ld   hl, COORDX            ; HL = coord X
ld   bc, $6c6c             ; BC = displacement
ld   de, $01ff             ; DE = orientation
cp   WINNERLINE159         ; Does line 159 win?
jr   z, printWinnerLine_159; Yes, skip
ld   e, $01                ; DE = orientation
cp   WINNERLINE357         ; Does line 357 win?
jr   z, printWinnerLine_357; Yes, skip

ld   c, $00                ; Displacement
cp   WINNERLINE147         ; Do you win line 147?
jr   z, printWinnerLine_147; Yes, skip
cp   WINNERLINE258         ; Does line 258 win?
jr   z, printWinnerLine_258; Yes, skip
cp   WINNERLINE369         ; Does line 369 win?
jr   z, printWinnerLine_369; Yes, skip

ld   bc, $006c             ; Displacement
ld   (hl), $48             ; Coord X
inc  hl                    ; Aim HL at coord Y
cp   WINNERLINE123         ; Do you win line 123?
jr   z, printWinnerLine_123; Yes, skip
cp   WINNERLINE456         ; Do you win line 456?
jr   z, printWinnerLine_456; Yes, skip
cp   WINNERLINE789         ; Does line 789 win?
jr   z, printWinnerLine_789; If so, jump to painting it
```

```
printWinnerLine_159:
ld   (hl), $b7            ; Coord X
jr   printWinnerLine_Y

printWinnerLine_357:
ld   (hl), $48            ; Coord X
jr   printWinnerLine_Y

printWinnerLine_147:
ld   (hl), $58            ; Coord X
jr   printWinnerLine_Y

printWinnerLine_258:
ld   (hl), $80            ; Coord X
jr   printWinnerLine_Y

printWinnerLine_369:
ld   (hl), $a8            ; Coord X

printWinnerLine_Y:
inc  hl                   ; Aim HL at coord Y
ld   (hl), $10            ; Coord Y
jr   printWinnerLine_end  ; Paint the line

printWinnerLine_123:
ld   (hl), $70            ; Coord Y
jr   printWinnerLine_end  ; Paint the line

printWinnerLine_456:
ld   (hl), $47            ; Coord Y
jr   printWinnerLine_end  ; Paint the line

printWinnerLine_789:
ld   (hl), $20            ; Coord Y

printWinnerLine_end:
jp   DRAW                 ; Paint the line
```

PrintWinnerLine gets the winning line in A. First we evaluate which is the line to jump to one part of the routine or another. As the different lines to be drawn share common data, we only change the data that differs and call DRAW to draw the line and exit (see the DRAW comments in ROM.asm for more information).

In main.asm, locate the loop_checkWinner tag and add the following line under JR NZ, loop_tie:

```
call PrintWinnerLine
```

We compile, load in the emulator and see the results.

As we can see, a line is drawn by marking the three in a row, although it is so fast that we can hardly see it. In the next chapter we will use sound for timing.

However, if you want to check that the line is drawn, you can put these two lines below CALL PrintWinnerLine:

```
tmp:
jr    tmp
```

Don't forget to remove them afterwards.

Scoreboard update

We are going to fix the long-standing bug that causes the scoreboard not to be updated.

In var.asm we locate the Grid tag and see that below it are the Points_p1, Points_p2 and Point_tie tags. We move these three tags to just below MoveCounter.

```
; -------------------------------------------------------------------
; Development of the game.
; -------------------------------------------------------------------
; Positions of the pieces on the board, 2 bytes per piece Y, X
GridPos:      db POS1_LEFT, POS1_TOP ; 1
              db POS2_LEFT, POS1_TOP ; 2
              db POS3_LEFT, POS1_TOP ; 3
              db POS1_LEFT, POS2_TOP ; 4
              db POS2_LEFT, POS2_TOP ; 5
              db POS3_LEFT, POS2_TOP ; 6
              db POS1_LEFT, POS3_TOP ; 7
              db POS2_LEFT, POS3_TOP ; 8
              db POS3_LEFT, POS3_TOP ; 9

; Board squares. One byte per square, from 1 to 9.
; Bit 0 to 1, square occupied by player 1.
; Bit 4 to 1, square occupied by player 2.
Grid:         db $00, $00, $00, $00, $00, $00, $00, $00, $00
MoveCounter:  db $00           ; Move counter
Points_p1:    db $00           ; Points player 1
Points_p2:    db $00           ; Points player 2
Points_tie:   db $00           ; Points tables
PlayerMoves:  db $00           ; Player moving
```

In main.asm, find the loop_reset tag, and on the bottom line, LD BC, LENDATA-$01, replace $01 with $04.

Compile, load into the emulator, and now the bookmarks are updated.

Download the source code from here

https://tinyurl.com/2brbm95l

Step 3: Sound

We will implement different sounds and use them for timing by pausing between events.

We will create the file sound.asm and add the include to main.asm.

In sound.asm we will add the definition of the different sounds and melodies.

```
; ------------------------------------------------------------------
; Sounds.
;
; Sounds end in $00, the byte indicating the end.
; ------------------------------------------------------------------
; Countdown
SoundCountDown:
db $03, $8c, $3a, $00

; Error
SoundError:
db $0d, $c6, $1e, $16, $13, $13, $00

; Loss of movement
SoundLostMovement:
db $0d, $07, $10, $0b, $96, $12, $0a, $4d, $14
db $0b, $96, $12, $1a, $2c, $08, $00

; Next player
SoundNextPlayer:
db $01, $9d, $7b, $00

; Spectrum Movement
SoundSpectrum:
db $06, $6e, $20, $06, $6e, $20, $05, $b7, $24
db $06, $6e, $20, $05, $13, $29, $05, $b7, $24
db $06, $6e, $20, $00

; Tables
SoundTie:
db $0d, $07, $10, $0b, $96, $12, $06, $d4, $1e
db $0b, $96, $12, $07, $a6, $1b, $0b, $96, $12
db $08, $a5, $18, $0b, $96, $12, $09, $b4, $15
db $0b, $96, $12, $0a, $4d, $14, $0b, $96, $12
db $0d, $07, $10, $00

; Point
SoundWinGame:
db $06, $6e, $20, $05, $13, $29, $04, $40, $30
db $06, $6e, $20, $05, $13, $29, $04, $40, $30
db $06, $6e, $20, $05, $13, $29, $04, $c7, $2b
db $05, $13, $29, $05, $b7, $24, $05, $13, $29
db $06, $6e, $20, $05, $13, $29, $04, $40, $30
db $06, $6e, $20, $05, $13, $29, $04, $40, $30
db $06, $6e, $20, $05, $13, $29, $04, $c7, $2b
db $05, $13, $29, $05, $b7, $24, $06, $6e, $20
db $00
```

All sounds have a zero byte as their last byte, which we will use in the routine that plays them to know when they are finished.

In these definitions, each note is made up of three bytes instead of four, the first two being the note and the third being the low byte of the duration, all of which are sixteenths and/or half notes.

We implement the routine that plays the tones.

```
; ------------------------------------------------------------------
; Plays a melody or sound.
;
; Input: BC = Start address of the melody.
;
; To save is done byte by byte, with the duration always being fuzzy
; or half-fuse; only one byte is needed for the duration.
; This routine is adapted for this operation.
; ------------------------------------------------------------------
PlayMusic:
push af
push bc
push de
push hl
push ix                   ; Preserves records

playMusic_loop:
ld   a, (bc)              ; A = high byte note
ld   h, a                 ; H = A
or   a                    ; A = 0?
jr   z, playMusic_end     ; A = 0, end

inc  bc                   ; BC = next value
ld   a, (bc)              ; A = byte under note
ld   l, a                 ; L = A

inc  bc                   ; BC = next value
ld   a, (bc)              ; A = duration note
ld   e, a                 ; E = A
ld   d, $00               ; D = 0 (fuse or half-fuse)
inc  bc                   ; BC = next value

push bc                   ; Preserves BC
call BEEPER               ; Play note
pop  bc                   ; Recover BC

jr   playMusic_loop       ; Loop until it reaches 0 end melody

playMusic_end:
pop  ix
pop  hl
pop  de
pop  bc
pop  af                   ; Retrieves records
ret
```

PlayMusic receives the address of the sound to be played in BC, loads the note in HL, the duration in DE, plays it and loops until it reaches the zero byte which marks the end of the sound. D is always zero, only one byte is used for the duration.

In main.asm we will add the necessary calls to play the sounds.

We locate the Loop tag and delete from LD B, $19 to DJNZ loop_wait as we will be timing with the sound. Below this, after CALL PrintPoints, we add the next player sound:

```
ld   bc, SoundNextPlayer
call PlayMusic
```

Locate the loop_print tag and just above it the JR Loop line. Above this line we add the error sound:

```
ld   bc, SoundError
call PlayMusic
```

Locate the loop_win tag and just below it the INC (HL) line. Below this line we add the dot winner sound:

```
ld   bc, SoundWinGame
call PlayMusic
```

Locate the loop_reset tag and just above it add the table sound:

```
ld   bc, SoundTie
call PlayMusic
```

We compile, load into the emulator and listen to every single sound.

The main.asm file has grown considerably since we started, so it's time to see what it looks like after commenting.

```
org  $5e88              ; Loading address

Main:
ld   hl, Sprite_P1      ; HL = address Sprite_P1
ld   (UDG), hl          ; UDG = address Sprite_p1
ld   a, $02             ; A = 2
call OPENCHAN           ; Open channel 2

xor  a                  ; A = 0, Z = 0, C = 0
call BORDER             ; Change border
call CLA                ; Changes display attributes
call CLS                ; Clear screen

Init:
call PrintBoard         ; Paint board

ld   hl, Name_p1        ; HL = name player 1
ld   de, player1_name   ; DE = player1_name
ld   bc, LENNAME        ; BC = length name
ldir                    ; Pass data
ld   hl, Name_p2        ; HL = name player 2
ld   de, player2_name   ; DE = player 2 name
ld   bc, LENNAME        ; BC = length name
ldir                    ; Pass data
call PrintInfo          ; Paint info

ld   bc, LENDATA        ; BC = length of starting data
call ResetValues        ; Clear data

Loop:
```

```
ld    hl, TitleTurn            ; HL = shift address
ld    de, TitleTurn_name       ; DE = address name in turn name in turn
call  DoMsg                    ; Compose and paint shift
call  PrintPoints              ; PaintPoints
ld    bc, SoundNextPlayer      ; BC = sound direction
call  PlayMusic                ; Play sound
loop_key:
call  WaitKeyBoard             ; Wait for key press
ld    a, c                     ; A = C
cp    KEY0                     ; Key pressed?
jr    z, loop_key              ; No, loop
call  ToMove                   ; Check movement
jr    z, loop_print            ; Correct, skip
ld    hl, TitleError           ; HL = address error
call  PrintMsg                 ; Paint Error
ld    bc, SoundError           ; BC = sound address
call  PlayMusic                ; Play sound
jr    Loop                     ; Main loop
loop_print:
call  PrintOXO                 ; Paint token
loop_checkWinner:
call  CheckWinner              ; Any winners?
jr    nz, loop_tie             ; No, check tables
call  PrintWinnerLine          ; Paints winning line
ld    hl, TitlePointFor        ; HL = winning address
ld    de, TitlePointName       ; HL = address winning name
call  DoMsg                    ; Compose and paint winner
ld    hl, Points_p1            ; HL = address points player 1
ld    a, (PlayerMoves)         ; A = player that moved
or    a                        ; Player 1?
jr    z, loop_win              ; Yes, skip
inc   hl                       ; HL = address points player 2
loop_win:
inc   (hl)                     ; Increases score
ld    bc, SoundWinGame         ; BC = sound address
call  PlayMusic                ; Play sound
jr    loop_reset               ; Jump
loop_tie:
ld    hl, MoveCounter          ; HL = move counter address
inc   (hl)                     ; Increments counter
ld    a, $09                   ; A = 9
cp    (hl)                     ; Counter = 9?
jr    nz, loop_cont            ; No, skip
ld    hl, Points_tie           ; HL = address points tables
inc   (hl)                     ; Increases score
ld    hl, TitleTie             ; HL = address tables
call  PrintMsg                 ; Paint tables
ld    bc, SoundTie             ; BC = sound direction
call  PlayMusic                ; Play sound
loop_reset:
ld    bc, LENDATA-$04          ; BC = data length clean data
call  ResetValues              ; Clear data
call  PrintBoard               ; Paint board
loop_cont:
ld    a, (PlayerMoves)         ; A = player who moved
xor   $01                      ; A = next player
ld    (PlayerMoves), a         ; Refresh in memory
jr    Loop                     ; Main loop
```

```
include "game.asm"
include "rom.asm"
include "screen.asm"
include "sprite.asm"
include "sound.asm"
include "var.asm"

end  Main
```

We have a large part of the game developed and working. We can play our first games with friends and/or family and we have sound.

In the next chapter we will implement the different options of the game and the end of the game.

Download the source code from here

https://tinyurl.com/283e38v7

Step 4: Options and end of game

In this chapter we will implement the different options of the game and the end of the game; as we left off in the previous chapter, the game continues indefinitely. The options will be selected from a start menu.

In var.asm we will add the following constants for the colours to avoid having to use numbers and to make it easier to change the colours during the game.

```
INK0: equ $00
INK1: equ $01
INK2: equ $02
INK3: equ $03
INK4: equ $04
INK5: equ $05
INK6: equ $06
INK7: equ $07
```

As an exercise, go through the title and text declarations and where you see $10, change the number that follows it to the corresponding INK tag.

In the same way, look for INK calls in the rest of the files, and instead of loading the ink number in A, load the corresponding INK tag.

Menu

Some of the start menu texts are already defined in ar.asm: the TitleEspamatica tag and from TitleOptionStart to TitleOptionTime.

We will delete all these lines as we are going to reimplement it, adding colours and positions, and it will look like this:

```
Title3InStripe:     db $10, INK2, $13, $01, $16, $02, $09
                    defm "Three in a row"
TitleOptionStart:   db $10, INK1, $13, $01, $16, $08, $08, "0. "
                    db $10, INK5
                    defm "Start"
TitleOptionPlayer:  db $10, INK7, $13, $01, $16, $0a, $08, "1. "
                    db $10, INK6
                    defm "Players"
TitleOptionPoint:   db $10, INK7, $16, $0c, $08, "2. ", $10, INK6
                    defm "Points"
TitleOptionTime:    db $10, INK7, $16, $0e, $08, "3. ", $10, INK6
                    defm "Time"
TitleEspamatica:    db $16, $14, $08
                    db $10, INK2, "E", $10, INK6, "s"
                    db $10, INK4, "p", $10, INK5, "a"
                    db $10, INK2, "m", $10, INK6, "a"
                    db $10, INK4, "t", $10, INK5, "i"
                    db $10, INK2, "c", $10, INK6, "a"
                    db $10, INK7, " 2019", $ff
```

Now we have the definition of the start menu almost ready to paint, we just need a routine to paint the values of the options. We implement this in screen.asm.

```
; -----------------------------------------------------------------
; Paint the values of the options.
;
; Alters the value of the AF, BC and HL registers.
; -----------------------------------------------------------------
PrintOptions:
ld    a, INK4               ; A = green ink
call  INK                   ; Change ink
ld    b, INI_TOP-$0a        ; B = coord Y
ld    c, INI_LEFT-$15       ; C = coord X
call  AT                    ; Positions cursor
ld    hl, MaxPlayers        ; HL = value players
call  PrintBCD              ; Paints it
ld    b, INI_TOP-$0c        ; B = coord Y
call  AT                    ; Positions cursor
ld    hl, MaxPoints         ; HL = points value
call  PrintBCD              ; Paints it
ld    b, INI_TOP-$0e        ; B = coord Y
call  AT                    ; Positions cursor
ld    hl, MaxSeconds        ; HL = time value
jp    PrintBCD              ; Paints it and exits
```

PrintOptions paints the values of the options in green. It positions the cursor and paints each of the values.

Let's see what the start menu looks like. We locate Main in main.asm, and under CALL OPENCHAN we add these lines:

```
Menu:
di                          ; Deactivate interruptions
im    $01                   ; Interruptions = mode 1
ei                          ; Activates interruptions
```

We have added a label for the menu part, disabled the interrupts to switch to mode one and enabled them again. We will then use the interrupts in mode two, so these lines are needed here.

At the bottom we find CALL CLS and then add the following lines:

```
ld    hl, Title3InStripe    ; HL = address three-inline
call  PrintString           ; Paints the menu
menu_op:
call  PrintOptions          ; Paint the options
jr    menu_op               ; Menu loop
```

We draw the start screen and the values of the options. We remain in an infinite loop as this is where we will implement the menu logic.

With the menu definition and a few lines we have painted it, but we still need to make it work.

Compile it, load it into the emulator and see how it looks.

Before implementing the menu logic, we will implement a routine in game.asm that uses the ROM to read the keyboard and return the ASCII code of the last key pressed. This routine will be used for the menu options and for the player name query.

```
; ----------------------------------------------------------------------
; Wait for a key to be pressed and return its Ascii code.
;
; Output: A -> Ascii code of the key.
;
; Alters the value of the AF and HL registers.
; ----------------------------------------------------------------------
WaitKeyAlpha:
ld    hl, FLAGS_KEY          ; HL = address flag keyboard
set   $03, (hl)              ; Input mode L

; Loop until a key is obtained.
WaitKeyAlpha_loop:
bit   $05, (hl)              ; Key pressed?
jr    z, WaitKeyAlpha_loop   ; Not pressed, loop
res   $05, (hl)              ; Bit set to 0 for future inspections

; Gets the Ascii of the key pressed.
; Valid Ascii 12 ($0C), 13 ($0D) and from 32 ($20) to 127 ($7F)
; If the key pressed is Space, load ' ' in A
WaitKeyAlpha_loadKey:
ld    hl, LAST_KEY           ; HL = last key pressed address
ld    a, (hl)                ; A = last key pressed
cp    $80                    ; Ascii > 127?
jr    nc, WaitKeyAlpha       ; Yes, invalid key, loop
cp    KEYDEL                 ; Pushed Delete?
ret   z                      ; Yes, exit
cp    KEYENT                 ; Press Enter?
ret   z                      ; Yes, exit
cp    KEYSPC                 ; Powered Space?
jr    c, WaitKeyAlpha        ; Ascii < space, invalid, loop
ret                          ; Exits
```

WaitKeyAlpha waits until a key is pressed that is valid for us, that is: delete, enter or an ASCII code between thirty-two and one hundred and twenty-seven. When a valid key is pressed, it returns the ASCII code for that key in A.

We implement the menu routine in main.asm, just after CALL PrintOptions, and the final aspect is this:

```
menu_op:
call PrintOptions          ; Paint the options
call WaitKeyAlpha          ; Wait for keypress
cp   KEY0                   ; Pushed 0?
jr   z, Init               ; Yes, start game
menu_Players:
cp   KEY1                   ; Pushed 1?
jr   nz, menu_Points       ; No, skip
ld   a, (MaxPlayers)       ; A = players
xor  $03                    ; Alternates between 1 and 2
ld   (MaxPlayers), a       ; Update in memory
jr   menu_op               ; Loop
menu_Points:
cp   KEY2                   ; Pushed 2?
jr   nz, menu_Time         ; No, skip
ld   a, (MaxPoints)        ; A = points
inc  a                      ; A += 1
cp   $06                    ; A = 6?
jr   nz, menu_PointsDo     ; No, skip
ld   a, $01                 ; A = 1
menu_PointsDo:
ld   (MaxPoints), a        ; Update in memory
add  a, '0'                 ; A = value ascii
ld   (info_points), a      ; Update in memory
cp   '1'                    ; Points 1?
jr   z, menu_Points1       ; Yes, skip
ld   a, 's'                 ; Plural
jr   menu_PointsEnd        ; Jump
menu_Points1:
ld   a, ' '                 ; Singular
menu_PointsEnd:
ld   (info_gt1), a         ; Update in memory
jr   menu_op               ; Loop
menu_Time:
cp   KEY3                   ; Pushed 3?
jr   nz, menu_op           ; No, loop
ld   a, (MaxSeconds)       ; A = seconds
add  a, $05                 ; A += 5
daa                         ; Decimal setting
cp   $35                    ; A = 35 BCD?
jr   nz, menu_TimeDo       ; No, skip
ld   a, $05                 ; A = 5
menu_TimeDo:
ld   (MaxSeconds), a       ; Refreshes in memory
jr   menu_op               ; Loop
```

After calling the routine that checks if a valid key has been pressed, it evaluates if it is any key between zero and three, and depending on which it is, it acts in one way or another. Note that it only does the decimal adjustment when incrementing seconds; it is the only option whose value is greater than nine.

We compile, load the emulator and see the results. Everything seems to go well until we press zero, start the game and the menu remains.

To fix this, we add the following line below the Init tag:

```
call CLS                    ; Clear screen
```

400

Start of game

When the game starts, the first thing we will do is ask for the names of the players. First, we add another constant to rom.asm; this address contains the coordinates of the cursor.

```
; Cursor position on screen 2.
; If loaded at BC -> B = Y, C = X.
CURSOR: equ $5c88
```

We implement the routine responsible for retrieving the names of the players in game.asm. Although we won't go through it instruction by instruction, due to the size of the routine we will implement it in blocks.

```
GetPlayersName:
ld    hl, Name_p1
ld    de, Name_p1+$01
ld    bc, LENNAME*2-$01
ld    (hl), " "
ldir
```

We have cleared the names of the players.

```
ld    e, $01
getPlayersName_loop:
ld    a, INK4
call  INK
ld    b, INI_TOP-$0f
ld    c, INI_LEFT-$01
call  CLL
call  AT

ld    hl, TitlePlayerNumber
ld    (hl), "1"
ld    a, $01
cp    e
jr    z, getPlayersName_cont
ld    (hl), "2"
getPlayersName_cont:
ld    hl, TitlePlayerName
call  PrintString

ld    hl, Name_p1
ld    a, $01
cp    e
```

```
jr   z, getPlayersName_cont2
ld   hl, Name_p2
```

We make a loop of at most two iterations, one per player, change the colour, delete the line where the names are requested, position the cursor, prepare the title depending on the player, and point HL to the player's name.

```
getPlayersName_cont2:
ld   d, $00
ld   a, INK3
call INK
call getPlayersName_getName

ld   a, (MaxPlayers)
cp   $02
jr   nz, getPlayersName_onlyOne
inc  e
cp   e
jr   z, getPlayersName_loop
ret
```

We use D to control the length of the name, change the ink and ask for the player's name. We get the players, see if there are two players, and if not, default the name to two. If there are two players, we check if the name entered is the name of player two, and if not, we loop to ask for it.

```
getPlayersName_onlyOne:
ld   hl, Name_p2Default
ld   de, Name_p2
ld   bc, LENNAME
ldir
ret
```

If it is a single player, give the second player the default name.

```
getPlayersName_getName:
push hl
call WaitKeyAlpha
pop  hl

cp   KEYDEL
jr   z, getPlayersName_delete
cp   KEYENT
jr   z, getPlayersName_enter
push de
ld   e, a
ld   a, LENNAME
cp   d
ld   a, e
pop  de
jr   z, getPlayersName_getName

ld   (hl), a
inc  hl
rst  $10
inc  d
jr   getPlayersName_getName
```

We wait for a valid key to be pressed, check if it is Delete and if so, we jump to its operation. We check if it is enter and if it is, we jump to its operation.

If it is neither delete nor enter, we check if we have reached the maximum length and if not, we add the character to the name and draw it.

```
getPlayersName_delete:
ld    a, $00
cp    d
jr    z, getPlayersName_getName

dec   d
dec   hl
ld    a, ' '
ld    (hl), a
ld    bc, (CURSOR)
inc   c
call  AT
rst   $10
call  AT
jr    getPlayersName_getName
```

If the key pressed is delete and the length of the name is not zero, we delete the previous character of the name and the display.

```
getPlayersName_enter:
ld    a, 0
cp    d
jr    z, getPlayersName_getName
ret
```

If the key pressed is enter and the length of the name is not zero, the name request is terminated.

The final aspect of the routine is as follows:

```
; ------------------------------------------------------------------
; Ask for the names of the players.
;
; Alters the value of the AF, BC, DE and HL registers.
; ------------------------------------------------------------------
GetPlayersName:
ld    hl, Name_p1           ; HL = address player name 1
ld    de, Name_p1+$01       ; DE = HL+1
ld    bc, LENNAME*2-$01     ; BC = length names - 1
ld    (hl), " "             ; Clears first position
ldir                        ; Clean up the rest

ld    e, $01                ; E = 1
getPlayersName_loop:
ld    a, INK4               ; A = ink 4
call  INK                   ; Change ink
ld    b, INI_TOP-$0f        ; B = coord Y
ld    c, INI_LEFT-$01       ; X = coord X
call  CLL                   ; Delete the line
call  AT                    ; Position cursor

ld    hl, TitlePlayerNumber ; HL = player number
ld    (hl), "1"             ; Player 1
```

```
ld    a, $01              ; A = 1
cp    e                   ; Player 1?
jr    z, getPlayersName_cont; Yes, skip
ld    (hl), "2"           ; Player 2
getPlayersName_cont:
ld    hl, TitlePlayerName ; HL = title player name
call  PrintString         ; Paints it

ld    hl, Name_p1         ; HL = address player name 1
ld    a, $01              ; A = 1
cp    e                   ; Player 1?
jr    z, getPlayersName_cont2 ; Yes, skip
ld    hl, Name_p2         ; HL = address player name 2
getPlayersName_cont2:
ld    d, $00              ; D = counter length name
ld    a, INK3             ; A = ink 3
call  INK                 ; Change ink
call  getPlayersName_getName; Request player name

ld    a, (MaxPlayers)     ; A = players
cp    $02                 ; Two players?
jr    nz, getPlayersName_onlyOne ; One player, default name
inc   e                   ; E+=1
cp    e                   ; Compare with players
jr    z, getPlayersName_loop; Equals, jumps
ret

; Single player
; Copies the default name of player 2
getPlayersName_onlyOne:
ld    hl, Name_p2Default  ; HL = default player name 2
ld    de, Name_p2         ; DE = name player 2
ld    bc, LENNAME         ; Length name
ldir                      ; Copy default name
ret                       ; Sale

; Requests the player's name
getPlayersName_getName:
push  hl                  ; Preserve HL
call  WaitKeyAlpha        ; Wait for valid key
pop   hl                  ; Retrieve HL

cp    KEYDEL              ; Delete?
jr    z, getPlayersName_delete ; Yes, skip
cp    KEYENT              ; Enter?
jr    z, getPlayersName_enter ; Yes, skip
push  de                  ; Preserves DE
ld    e, a                ; E = code Ascii
ld    a, LENNAME          ; A = maximum length name
cp    d                   ; D = maximum length?
ld    a, e                ; A = code Ascii
pop   de                  ; Retrieve DE
jr    z, getPlayersName_getName ; D = maximum length
                          ; other character
                          ; Enter or Delete

ld    (hl), a             ; Append character to name
inc   hl                  ; HL = next position
rst   $10                 ; Print character
```

```
inc  d                       ; D+=1
jr   getPlayersName_getName; Request another character

getPlayersName_delete:
ld   a, $00                  ; A = 0
cp   d                       ; Length 0?
jr   z, getPlayersName_getName ; Yes, another character

dec  d                       ; D-=1
dec  hl                      ; HL-=1, previous character
ld   a, ' '                  ; A = space
ld   (hl), a                 ; Clear previous character
ld   bc, (CURSOR)            ; BC = cursor position
inc  c                       ; BC = previous column for AT
call AT                      ; Position cursor
rst  $10                     ; Delete the display character
call AT                      ; Position cursor
jr   getPlayersName_getName; Other character

getPlayersName_enter:
ld   a, 0                    ; A = 0
cp   d                       ; Length 0?
jr   z, getPlayersName_getName ; Yes, another character
ret                          ; End name
```

Let's see if it works. In main.asm we find Init, and under CALL CLS we add the call to the name request, and another call to CLS.

```
call GetPlayersName          ; Request player names
call CLS                     ; Clear screen
```

We compile, load into the emulator and see the results. We can now enter the names of the players and they will appear in the game information. If it is a single player game, we are playing against ZX Spectrum.

Shift time

One of the options is the number of seconds each player has to make their move. If the move has not been made within these seconds, the player loses the turn and it passes to the other player.

We will use interrupts to control the time. We create the file int.asm.

At the top of main.asm, just below ORG $5E88, we add the following lines (we already did this in Space Battle):

```
; ------------------------------------------------------------------
; Flags
; bit 0 -> Reset countdown
; bit 1 -> Lose turn
; bit 2 -> Paint countdown
; bit 3 -> Warning sound, countdown ends
; ------------------------------------------------------------------
flags:      db $00
; Value countdown
countdown: db $00
; Seconds per shift
seconds:    db $00
```

Seconds is used to tell the interrupts how many seconds per turn the players have chosen. With seconds, the MaxSeconds variable is no longer needed, so we will remove it.

Locate Main and after the CALL OPENCHAN line, initialise seconds:

```
ld   a, $10            ; A = $10 BCD
ld   (seconds), a      ; Update seconds
ld   (countdown), a    ; Update countdown
```

Locate menu_Time and after JR NZ, menu_op modify the line LD A, (MaxSeconds), as follows:

```
ld   a, (seconds)      ; A = seconds
```

Locate menu_TimeDo, delete LD, (MaxSecond), A and add the following lines instead:

```
ld   (seconds), a      ; Update seconds
ld   (countdown), a    ; Update countdown
```

In screen.asm, at the end of the PrintOptions routine, we replace LD HL, MaxSeconds with:

```
ld   hl, seconds       ; HL = time value
```

Finally, we delete the MaxSeconds definition in var.asm.

The interrupt routine will change the value of the flags and the countdown, we need to take this into account in the main loop.

For the interrupt routine to run fifty times per second (in PAL, sixty in NTSC), mode two of the interrupts must be enabled. Locate Loop in main.asm and add over it:

```
di                     ; Disables interrupts
ld   a, $28            ; A = $28
ld   i, a              ; I = A (interruptions in $7e5c)
im   $02               ; Interruptions = mode 2
ei                     ; Activates interruptions
```

We disable the interrupts, load $28 into the interrupt register, set it to mode two and enable it.

We look for loop_key and just below it we implement the flag handling logic.

```
ld   a, (flags)         ; A = Flags
bit  $02, a             ; Bit 2 active?
res  $02, a             ; Disables bit 2
jr   z, loop_warning    ; Not active, skips
push af                 ; Preserve AF
call PrintCountDown     ; Paint countdown
pop  af                 ; Retrieve AF
```

We load the flags in A and evaluate if bit two is active and deactivate it. If it is not active, we jump, if it is, we draw the countdown.

```
loop_warning:
bit  $03, a             ; Bit 3 active?
res  $03, a             ; Disable bit 3
jr   z, loop_lostMov    ; Not active, skip
ld   bc, SoundCountDown ; BC = sound direction
call PlayMusic          ; Outputs sound
```

We evaluate whether bit three is active and deactivate it. If it is active, we jump, if it is not, we give the warning sound.

```
loop_lostMov:
bit  $01, a             ; Bit 1 active?
res  $01, a             ; Disables bit 1
ld   (flags), a         ; Update in memory
halt                    ; Synchronise with interrupts
jr   z, loop_keyCont    ; Not active, skip
ld   hl, TitleLostMovement ; HL = address mov lost
ld   de, TitleLostMov_name ; DE = address name
call DoMsg              ; Paint message
ld   bc, SoundLostMovement ; BC = sound direction
call PlayMusic          ; Outputs sound
jr   loop_cont          ; Jump
loop_keyCont:
```

We check if bit one is active, disable it, update the flags and synchronise with the interrupts. If it is, we draw the lost motion message and play the sound. The loop_keyCont tag is above the CALL WaitKeyBoard.

Finally, locate loop_cont, delete JR Loop and add the following lines in its place:

```
ld   a, $01             ; A = restart countdown
ld   (flags), a         ; Update flags
jp   Loop               ; Main loop
```

We have updated the flags so that the interrupt routine restarts the countdown. We also replaced JR with JP because the lines we added make JR out of range.

In screen.asm we will implement the routine that draws the countdown.

```
; ------------------------------------------------------------------
; Paint the countdown.
;
; Alters the value of the AF, BC and HL registers.
```

```
; ------------------------------------------------------------------
PrintCountDown:
ld    a, INK3               ; A = ink 3
call INK                    ; Change ink
ld    b, INI_TOP-$0c        ; B = coord Y
ld    c, INI_LEFT           ; C = coord X
call AT                     ; Position cursor
ld    hl, countdown         ; HL = direction countdown
call PrintBCD               ; Paint countdown left
ld    c, INI_LEFT-$1e       ; C = coord X
call AT                     ; Position cursor
jp    PrintBCD              ; Paints countdown right and exits
```

We paint the countdown in two positions, on the left and right of the board. We set the ink to magenta, move the cursor to the left, draw the countdown, move the cursor to the right and draw the countdown.

The interrupt handling routine is implemented in int.asm (do not include this file in main.asm). We will also look at this implementation in blocks.

```
; ------------------------------------------------------------------
; int.asm
;
; Mode 2 Interrupt Handling
; ------------------------------------------------------------------
org $7e5c

; ------------------------------------------------------------------
; Indicators
; bit 0 -> Reset countdown
; bit 1 -> Lose turn
; bit 2 -> Paint countdown
; bit 3 -> Warning sound, countdown ends
; ------------------------------------------------------------------
FLAGS:      equ $5e88

COUNTDOWN: equ FLAGS+$01    ; Countdown Value
SECONDS:   equ FLAGS+$02    ; Seconds per turn
```

The interrupt routine is loaded at address $7E5C. Then we add the constants with the memory addresses we will use for the information exchange between main.asm and int.asm.

```
CountDownISR:
push af
push bc
push de
push hl
push ix                     ; Preserves records
```

The first step of the routine is to preserve the value of the registers.

```
countDown_flags:
ld    a, (FLAGS)            ; A = flags
and   $01                   ; Reset countdown?
jr    z, countDown_cont     ; No, skip
ld    a, (SECONDS)          ; A = SECONDS
ld    (COUNTDOWN), a        ; Refreshes in memory
```

```
ld   a, $04               ; A = paint countdown
ld   (FLAGS), a           ; Update in memory
jr   countDownISR_end     ; End
```

We check if main.asm indicates that the countdown should be restarted (shift change) and jump if it does not. If there is a shift, it restarts the countdown at the value specified in the menu, indicates in flags that the countdown should be painted, and jumps to exit the routine.

```
countDown_cont:
ld   hl, countDownTicks   ; HL = ticks counter
inc  (hl)                 ; Counter ticks+=1
ld   a, $32               ; A = 50
cp   (hl)                 ; Counter ticks = 50?
jr   nz, countDownISR_end ; No, skip
xor  a                    ; A = 0, Z = 1, Carry = 0
ld   (hl), a              ; Counter ticks = 0
```

In countDownTicks we add one at each pause, and when we reach fifty it is a sign that a second has passed, which we check in this block. If it has not reached fifty, it jumps to exit the routine, if it has, we set the ticks counter to zero and continue with the routine.

```
; It's reached 50, it's been a second
ld   a, (COUNTDOWN)       ; A = countdown value
dec  a                    ; A-=1
daa                       ; Decimal setting
ld   (COUNTDOWN), a       ; Update in memory
ld   b, $04               ; B = paint countdown / 4 sec
cp   b                    ; Less than 4 seconds?
jr   nc, countDownISR_reset; A >= 4, skip
set  $03, b               ; Warning sound
or   a                    ; A = 0?
jr   nz, countDownISR_reset; No, skip
set  $01, b               ; Misses turn
```

If one second has passed, we calculate what kind of information to pass to main.asm. We subtract one second from the countdown, see if it is below four (it also communicates to main.asm that the countdown has to be painted), and jump if it is not. If it is, we set the bit for the warning sound, evaluate whether the countdown has reached zero, and jump if it has not. Turn on the shift loss bit if it has reached zero.

```
countDownISR_reset:
ld   a, b                 ; A = B
ld   (FLAGS), a           ; Updates in memory
```

Update the value of flags with the information you want to pass to main.asm.

```
countDownISR_end:
pop  ix
pop  hl
pop  de
pop  bc
pop  af                   ; Retrieves records

```

```
ei                          ; Activates interruptions
reti                        ; Exits

countDownTicks: db $00      ; Ticks (50*sec)
```

We get the value of the registers, enable interrupts and exit. Finally we declare the tick counter.

Remember that we now need to compile two separate .tap's and make our own loader.

The basic loader looks like this:

```
10 CLEAR 24200
20 LOAD ""CODE 24200
30 LOAD ""CODE 32348
40 RANDOMIZE USR 24200
```

The script to compile on Windows looks like this:

```
echo off
cls
echo Compiling oxo
pasmo --name OXO --tap main.asm oxo.tap oxo.log
echo Compiling int
pasmo --name INT --tap int.asm int.tap int.log
echo Generating Tic-tac-toe
copy /y /b loader.tap+oxo.tap+int.tap TicTacToe.tap
echo Process completed
```

The Linux version looks like this:

```
clear
echo Compiling oxo
pasmo --name OXO --tap main.asm oxo.tap oxo.log
echo Compiling int
pasmo --name INT --tap int.asm int.tap int.log
echo Generating Tic-tac-toe
cat loader.tap oxo.tap int.tap > TicTacToe.tap
echo Process completed
```

We compile it, load it into the emulator and check that the countdown is painted, that an alarm goes off if it goes under four seconds and that it loses the turn if it goes to zero. We also see the missed turn message.

End of game

At the end of this chapter we will implement the end of the game, which occurs when one of the players reaches the points defined in the menu, or when the maximum number of tables is reached.

At the end of the game we are asked if we want another game; we add the keys of the answer as constants in var.asm. We also add the maximum number of tables.

```
KEYN:      equ $4e      ; N key
KEYn:      equ $6e      ; Key n
KEYS:      equ $53      ; S key
KEYs:      equ $73      ; Key s
MAXTIES:   equ $05      ; Maximum number of tables
```

Depending on whether you want to play another game or not, you will jump to one place or another in main.asm. We locate the Init tag, and after CALL GetPlayersName we add the following tag:

```
Start:
```

We locate the loop_reset tag and just below it we will implement the check to see if someone has won the game.

```
call PrintPoints            ; Paint the dots
ld    a, (MaxPoints)        ; A = maximum points
ld    b, a                  ; B = A
ld    a, (Points_p1)        ; A = points player 1
cp    b                     ; Player 1 wins?
jr    z, EndPlay            ; Yes, skip
ld    a, (Points_p2)        ; A = points player 2
cp    b                     ; Player 2 wins?
jr    z, EndPlay            ; Yes, skip
ld    b, MAXTIES            ; B = maximum tables
ld    a, (Points_tie)       ; A = points tables
cp    b                     ; A = B?
jr    z, EndPlay            ; Yes, skip
```

We draw the points and compare the players' scores with the set maximum score. If one of the players has the required number of points, they win the game.

At the end of main.asm, before the includes, we add the split end routine.

```
EndPlay:
di                          ; Disables interrupts
im    $01                   ; Mode 1 interrupts
ei                          ; Activates interruptions
ld    hl, TitleGameOver     ; HL = title game over
call PrintMsg               ; Paints the message
endPlay_waitKey:
call WaitKeyAlpha           ; Wait key
cp    KEYN                  ; Pressed N?
jp    z, Menu               ; Yes, menu
cp    KEYn                  ; Pushed n?
jp    z, Menu               ; Yes, menu
```

```
cp   KEYS              ; Pulsed S?
jp   z, Start          ; Yes, start
cp   KEYs              ; Pushed s?
jp   z, Start          ; Yes, start
jr   endPlay_waitKey   ; Not pressed, loop
```

We deactivate interruptions, switch to mode one, activate interruptions, wait for the question to be answered and, depending on the answer, we jump to one place or another.

- Menu: return to the main menu. We can select the different options and enter new player names.
- Start: is the label we have added. It clears the screen, paints the screen, resets the game data and switches interrupts to mode two.

If none of the expected keys have been pressed, it will loop until one is.

If you go to the Menu tag, you will see that the first three lines are for switching to interrupt mode one, which is what we do in EndPlay. Delete the three lines below the Menu tag.

We compile, load into the emulator and see the results. Everything seems to work fine, but at the end of the game the score is flashing. This is something we inherited from the beginning, although we didn't notice it until now.

To change the behaviour, locate PrintPoints in screen.asm and add the lines needed to disable the flickering just below it.

```
ld   a,(ATTR_T)        ; A = temporary attributes
and  $7f               ; Removes flicker
ld   (ATTR_T), a       ; Update in memory
```

At this point, we can play the first full two-player games.

Want to play against the Spectrum and beat it? We will implement this in the next chapter.

Download the source code from here

https://tinyurl.com/28bdpg8p

Step 5: Me versus the Spectrum

Once we can play against friends and family, the possibility remains that we may not have anyone to play with, hence the need to be able to play against the Spectrum.

We wrote the bulk of this implementation in game.asm, starting with a routine that generates semi-random numbers between one and nine, so that when the Spectrum starts the game, it does so in a different way.

```
; --------------------------------------------------------------
; Gets a semi-random number between 1 and 9.
;
; Return: A -> Number obtained.
; --------------------------------------------------------------
GetRandomN:
ld    a, r              ; A = R
and   $0f               ; Leave bits 0 to 3
inc   a                 ; A+=1
cp    $0a               ; A > 9?
ret   c                 ; No, exit
rra                     ; A/=2, because Carry = 0, otherwise SRL A
ret                     ; Exits
```

GetRandomN gets a semi-random number between one and nine, using register R. In the RRA line, as seen in the comments, we divide A by two because the carry is zero and because we only do it once, otherwise we would have to do it with SRL A. RRA is one byte and takes four clock cycles, SRL A is only twice as long. It is only divided by two if the number obtained is greater than 9.

The part that carries out the movements of the spectrum is very long, as there are several combinations that are evaluated, so we will see it in blocks. However, as there are many similarities between the different blocks, we will only explain the most important ones.

```
; --------------------------------------------------------------
; Moves ZX Spectrum.
;
; Alters the value of the AF, BC and IX registers.
; --------------------------------------------------------------
ZxMove:
ld    a, (MoveCounter)  ; A = moves
or    a                 ; Movements = 0?
jr    nz, zxMove_center ; No, skip
call GetRandomN         ; A = number between 1 and 9
add   a, '0'            ; A = ascii code
ld    c, a              ; C = A
call ToMove             ; Move to cell
ret                     ; Exits
zxMove_center:
cp    $01               ; Moves > 1?
jr    nz, zxMove_cont   ; Yes, skip
ld    c, KEY5           ; C = key 5
call ToMove             ; Move to cell 5
ret   z                 ; If correct, exits
```

In this first part we decide if it is the first move of the game, and if so we take a random number between one and nine and move to that cell. If it is the second move, we try to move to cell five (middle). If these conditions are not met, we continue with the checks to see if the spectrum can win or lose.

```
zxMove_cont:
ld   ix, Grid-$01           ; IX = dir Grid-1
ld   b, $20                 ; B = Spectrum value can earn
call zxMoveToWin_123        ; Move to gain Spectrum
ret  z                      ; If valid, exits
ld   b, $02                 ; B = value player 1 can win
call zxMoveToWin_123        ; Move to avoid it
ret  z                      ; If valid, exits
jp   zxMoveDefence_diagonally ; Defensive movements
```

Remember that the moves of player two, in this case the Spectrum, are signalled in bit four of the cells, so we load $20 into B, which would be the value if there were two cells occupied by the Spectrum in a row.

We call zxMoveToWin_123 so that if Spectrum wins, it makes the move.

If the Spectrum has not won, we load two into B to check if player one has the move to win. We call zxMoveToWin_123 a second time to prevent it from winning.

If none of the above has happened, we go on the defensive.

```
; --------------------------------------------------------------
; Evaluates whether the Spectrum has the movement to win.
; --------------------------------------------------------------
zxMoveToWin_123:
ld   a, (ix+$01)            ; A = cell value 1
add  a, (ix+$02)            ; A+= cell value 2
add  a, (ix+$03)            ; A+= cell value 3
cp   b                      ; A = B?
jp   nz, zxMoveToWin_456    ; No, skip
; Spectrum can win
ld   c, KEY1                ; C = key 1
call ToMove                 ; Move to cell 1
ret  z                      ; If correct, exits
inc  c                      ; C = key 2
call ToMove                 ; Move to cell 2
ret  z                      ; If correct, exits
inc  c                      ; C = key 3
call ToMove                 ; Move to cell 3
ret                         ; Exits
```

If the Spectrum occupies two squares, we try to move to square one, if not, to square two and if not, to square three. To go from one square to the next, we increment C, numerically they are contiguous.

The checks for the combinations four, five, six and seven, eight, nine are the same as above.

```
zxMoveToWin_456:
ld   a, (ix+$04)            ; A = cell value 4
add  a, (ix+$05)            ; A+= cell value 5
```

```
add   a, (ix+$06)              ; A+= cell value 6
cp    b                        ; A = B?
jr    nz, zxMoveToWin_789      ; No, skip
; Spectrum can win
ld    c, KEY4                  ; C = key 4
call ToMove                    ; Move to cell 4
ret   z                        ; If correct, exits
inc   c                        ; C = key 5
call ToMove                    ; Move to cell 5
ret   z                        ; If correct, exits
inc   c                        ; C = key 6
call ToMove                    ; Move to cell 6
ret                            ; Sale

zxMoveToWin_789:
ld    a, (ix+$07)              ; A = cell value 7
add   a, (ix+$08)              ; A+= cell value 8
add   a, (ix+$09)              ; A+= cell value 9
cp    b                        ; A = B?
jr    nz, zxMoveToWin_147      ; No, skip
; Spectrum can win
ld    c, KEY7                  ; C = key 7
call ToMove                    ; Move to cell 7
ret   z                        ; If correct, exits
inc   c                        ; C = key 8
call ToMove                    ; Move to cell 8
ret   z                        ; If correct, exits
inc   c                        ; C = key 9
call ToMove                    ; Move to cell 9
ret                            ; Exits
```

The rest of the tests change slightly.

```
zxMoveToWin_147:
ld    a, (ix+$01)              ; A = cell value 1
add   a, (ix+$04)              ; A+= cell value 4
add   a, (ix+$07)              ; A+= cell value 7
cp    b                        ; A=B?
jr    nz, zxMoveToWin_258      ; No, skip
ld    c, KEY1                  ; C = key 1
call ToMove                    ; Move to cell 1
ret   z                        ; If correct, exits
ld    c, KEY4                  ; C = key 4
call ToMove                    ; Move to cell 4
ret   z                        ; If correct, exits
ld    c, KEY7                  ; C = key 7
call ToMove                    ; Move to cell 7
ret                            ; Exits
```

As the squares are not numerically contiguous, at the end we load each key instead of incrementing C. From here on, all the checks to see if the Spectrum can win or lose are the same.

```
zxMoveToWin_258:
ld    a, (ix+$02)              ; A = cell value 2
add   a, (ix+$05)              ; A+= cell value 5
add   a, (ix+$08)              ; A+= cell value 8
cp    b                        ; A=B?
jr    nz, zxMoveToWin_369      ; No, skip
```

```
ld   c, KEY2              ; C = key 2
call ToMove               ; Move to cell 2
ret  z                    ; If correct, exits
ld   c, KEY5              ; C = key 5
call ToMove               ; Move to cell 5
ret  z                    ; If correct, exits
ld   c, KEY8              ; C = key 8
call ToMove               ; Move to cell 8
ret                       ; Exits

zxMoveToWin_369:
ld   a, (ix+$03)          ; A = cell value 3
add  a, (ix+$06)          ; A+= cell value 6
add  a, (ix+$09)          ; A+= cell value 9
cp   b                    ; A=B?
jr   nz, zxMoveToWin_159  ; No, skip
ld   c, KEY3              ; C = key 3
call ToMove               ; Move to cell 3
ret  z                    ; If correct, exits
ld   c, KEY6              ; C = key 6
call ToMove               ; Move to cell 6
ret  z                    ; If correct, exits
ld   c, KEY9              ; C = key 9
call ToMove               ; Move to cell 9
ret                       ; Exits

zxMoveToWin_159:
ld   a, (ix+$01)          ; A = cell value 1
add  a, (ix+$05)          ; A+= cell value 5
add  a, (ix+$09)          ; A+= cell value 9
cp   b                    ; A=B?
jr   nz, zxMoveToWin_357  ; No, skip
ld   c, KEY1              ; C = key 1
call ToMove               ; Move to cell 1
ret  z                    ; If correct, exits
ld   c, KEY5              ; C = key 5
call ToMove               ; Move to cell 5
ret  z                    ; If correct, exits
ld   c, KEY9              ; C = key 9
call ToMove               ; Move to cell 9
ret                       ; Exits

zxMoveToWin_357:
ld   a, (ix+$03)          ; A = cell value 3
add  a, (ix+$05)          ; A+= cell value 5
add  a, (ix+$07)          ; A+= cell value 7
cp   b                    ; A = B?
ret  nz
ld   c, KEY3              ; C = key 3
call ToMove               ; Move to cell 3
ret  z                    ; If correct, exits
ld   c, KEY5              ; C = key 5
call ToMove               ; Move to cell 5
ret  z                    ; If correct, exits
ld   c, KEY7              ; C = key 7
call ToMove               ; Move to cell 7
ret                       ; Exits
```

The set of routines zxMoveToWin is used both to know if Spectrum can win and make the move to do so, and to know if Spectrum can lose and make the move to avoid it.

If both player one and Spectrum have no chance of winning, we try to anticipate player one's move. First we check if the player makes a diagonal move that occupies both vertices, and if so we make a cross block.

```
; ------------------------------------------------------------------
; Diagonal defensive movement.
; ------------------------------------------------------------------
zxMoveDefence_diagonally:
; Checks if player 1 has diagonal checkers
ld   a, (ix+$01)        ; A = cell value 1
add  a, (ix+$09)        ; A+= cell value 9
cp   b                  ; A = B?
jr   z, zxMoveDefence_crossBlock ; Yes, mov diagonal, skip
ld   a, (ix+$03)        ; A = cell value 3
add  a, (ix+$07)        ; A+= cell value 7
cp   b                  ; A = B?
jr   nz, zxMoveDefence_crossBlock1 ; No, skip

zxMoveDefence_crossBlock:
; Cross locking
ld   c, KEY4            ; C = key 4
call ToMove             ; Move to cell 4
ret  z                  ; If correct, exits
ld   c, KEY6            ; C = key 6
call ToMove             ; Move to cell 6
ret  z                  ; If correct, exits
ld   c, KEY2            ; C = key 2
call ToMove             ; Move to cell 2
ret  z                  ; If correct, exits
ld   c, KEY8            ; C = key 8
call ToMove             ; Move to cell 8
ret  z                  ; If correct, exits
```

Then we check if he has tried a diagonal move with the centre occupied, and if so, depending on which vertex is occupied, we block the vertical.

```
; ------------------------------------------------------------------
; Defensive diagonal movement with the centre occupied.
; ------------------------------------------------------------------
zxMoveDefence_crossBlock1:
ld   a, (ix+$05)        ; A = cell value 5
and  $0f               ; A = player value 1
jr   z, zxMoveDefence_cornerBlock16 ; Z = not occupied, skip
ld   a, (ix+$01)        ; A = cell value 1
and  $0f               ; A = player value 1
jr   z, zxMoveDefence_crossBlock3 ; Z = not occupied, skip
ld   c, KEY7            ; C = key 7
call ToMove             ; Move to cell 7
ret  z                  ; If correct, exits

zxMoveDefence_crossBlock3:
ld   a, (ix+$03)        ; A = cell value 3
and  $0f               ; A = player value 1
jr   z, zxMoveDefence_crossBlock7 ; Z = not occupied, skip
```

```
ld    c, KEY9            ; C = key 9
call  ToMove             ; Move to cell 9
ret   z                  ; If correct, exits

zxMoveDefence_crossBlock7:
ld    a, (ix+$07)        ; A = cell value 7
and   $0f                ; A = player value 1
jr    z, zxMoveDefence_crossBlock9 ; Z = not occupied, skip
ld    c, KEY1            ; C = key 1
call  ToMove             ; Move to cell 1
ret   z                  ; If correct, exits

zxMoveDefence_crossBlock9:
ld    a, (ix+$09)        ; A = cell value 9
and   $0f                ; A = player value 1
jr    z, zxMoveDefence_cornerBlock16 ; Z = not occupied, skip
ld    c, KEY3            ; C = key 3
call  ToMove             ; Move to cell 3
ret   z                  ; If correct, exits
```

If player one has not attempted a diagonal move, we will see if he has attempted a cross move and try to block it.

```
; -------------------------------------------------------------------
; Defensive cross movement.
; -------------------------------------------------------------------
zxMoveDefence_cornerBlock16:
ld    a, (ix+$01)        ; A = cell value 1
add   a, (ix+$06)        ; A+= cell value 6
cp    b                  ; A = B?
jr    nz, zxMoveDefence_cornerBlock34 ; No, no mov cross, skip
ld    c, KEY3            ; C = key 3
call  ToMove             ; Move to cell 3
ret   z                  ; If correct, exits

zxMoveDefence_cornerBlock34:
ld    a, (ix+$03)        ; A = cell value 3
add   a, (ix+$04)        ; A+= cell value 4
cp    b                  ; A = B?
jr    nz, zxMoveDefence_cornerBlock67 ; No, no mov cross, skip
ld    c, KEY1            ; C = key 1
call  ToMove             ; Move to cell 1
ret   z                  ; If correct, exits

zxMoveDefence_cornerBlock67:
ld    a, (ix+$06)        ; A = cell value 6
add   a, (ix+$07)        ; A+= cell value 7
cp    b                  ; A = B?
jr    nz, zxMoveDefence_cornerBlock49 ; No, no mov cross, skip
ld    c, KEY9            ; C = key 9
call  ToMove             ; Move to cell 9
ret   z                  ; If correct, exits

zxMoveDefence_cornerBlock49:
ld    a, (ix+$04)        ; A = cell value 4
add   a, (ix+$09)        ; A+= cell value 9
cp    b                  ; A = B?
jr    nz, zxMoveDefence_cornerBlock1827 ; No, no mov cross, skip
ld    c, KEY7            ; C = key 7
```

```
call  ToMove              ; Move to cell 7
ret   z                   ; If correct, exits

zxMoveDefence_cornerBlock1827:
ld    a, (ix+$01)         ; A = cell value 1
add   a, (ix+$08)         ; A+= cell value 8
cp    b                   ; A = B?
jr    z, zxMoveDefence_cornerBlock1827Cont ; Yes, mov cross, block
ld    a, (ix+$02)         ; A = cell value 2
add   a, (ix+$07)         ; A+= Value cell 7
cp    b                   ; A = B?
jr    nz, zxMoveDefence_cornerBlock2938 ; No, no mov cross, skip

zxMoveDefence_cornerBlock1827Cont:
ld    c, KEY4             ; C = key 4
call  ToMove              ; Move to cell 4
ret   z                   ; If correct, exits

zxMoveDefence_cornerBlock2938:
ld    a, (ix+$02)         ; A = cell value 2
add   a, (ix+$09)         ; A+= cell value 9
cp    b                   ; A = B?
jr    z, zxMoveDefence_cornerBlock2938Cont ; Yes, mov cross, block
ld    a, (ix+$03)         ; A = cell value 3
add   a, (ix+$08)         ; A+= cell value 8
cp    b                   ; A = B?
jr    nz, zxMoveAttack_123 ; No, no mov cross, skip

zxMoveDefence_cornerBlock2938Cont:
ld    c, KEY6             ; C = key 6
call  ToMove              ; Move to cell 6
ret   z                   ; If correct, exits
```

If we've got this far, we've established that Spectrum has no move to win, that player one has no move to win, that player one is in no danger from player one's diagonal or cross moves; it's time for Spectrum to go on the attack.

This last part will only be done in the first few moves, as the board fills up we will be more concerned with defending than attacking.

```
; --------------------------------------------------------------
; Horizontal, vertical and diagonal offensive movement.
; --------------------------------------------------------------
zxMoveAttack_123:
ld    b, $20             ; B = Spectrum value with two boxes
ld    a, (ix+$01)        ; A = cell value 1
add   a, (ix+$02)        ; A+= cell value 2
add   a, (ix+$03)        ; A+= cell value 3
ld    c, a               ; Preserve A in C
and   $03                ; A = player 1 cells
jr    nz, zxMoveAttack_456 ; Any? Yes, jump
ld    a, c               ; Retrieves A
and   $30                ; A = Spectrum boxes
cp    b                  ; Two busy?
jr    z, zxMoveAttack_456 ; Yes, jumps
ld    c, KEY1            ; C = key 1
call  ToMove             ; Move to cell 1
ret   z                  ; If correct, exits
```

```
inc  c                    ; C = key 2
call ToMove               ; Move to cell 2
ret  z                    ; If correct, exits
inc  c                    ; C = key 3
call ToMove               ; Move to cell 3
ret  z                    ; If correct, exits
```

For the attack, we look for combinations where player one has no cells occupied and the Spectrum has only one.

The rest of the checks are very similar to the previous one.

```
zxMoveAttack_456:
ld   a, (ix+$04)          ; A = cell value 4
add  a, (ix+$05)          ; A+= cell value 5
add  a, (ix+$06)          ; A+= cell value 6
ld   c, a                 ; Preserve A in C
and  $03                  ; A = player 1 cells
jr   nz, zxMoveAttack_789 ; Any? Yes, jump
ld   a, c                 ; Retrieves A
and  $30                  ; A = Spectrum boxes
cp   b                    ; Two busy?
jr   z, zxMoveAttack_789  ; Yes, jumps
ld   c, KEY4              ; C = key 4
call ToMove               ; Move to cell 4
ret  z                    ; If correct, exits
inc  c                    ; C = key 5
call ToMove               ; Move to cell 5
ret  z                    ; If correct, exits
inc  c                    ; C = key 6
call ToMove               ; Move to cell 6
ret  z                    ; If correct, exits

zxMoveAttack_789:
ld   a, (ix+$07)          ; A = cell value 7
add  a, (ix+$08)          ; A+= cell value 8
add  a, (ix+$09)          ; A+= cell value 9
ld   c, a                 ; Preserve A in C
and  $03                  ; A = player 1 cells
jr   nz, zxMoveAttack_147 ; Any? Yes, jump
ld   a, c                 ; Retrieves A
and  $30                  ; A = Spectrum boxes
cp   b                    ; Two busy?
jr   z, zxMoveAttack_147  ; Yes, jumps
ld   c, KEY7              ; C = key 7
call ToMove               ; Move to cell 7
ret  z                    ; If correct, exits
inc  c                    ; C = key 8
call ToMove               ; Move to cell 8
ret  z                    ; If correct, exits
inc  c                    ; C = key 9
call ToMove               ; Move to cell 9
ret  z                    ; If correct, exits

zxMoveAttack_147:
ld   a, (ix+$01)          ; A = cell value 1
add  a, (ix+$04)          ; A+= cell value 4
add  a, (ix+$07)          ; A+= cell value 7
ld   c, a                 ; Preserve A in C
```

```
and    $03                 ; A = player 1 boxes
jr     nz, zxMoveAttack_258 ; Any? Yes, jump
ld     a, c                ; Retrieves A
and    $30                 ; A = Spectrum boxes
cp     b                   ; Two busy?
jr     z, zxMoveAttack_258 ; Yes, jumps
ld     c, KEY1             ; C = key 1
call   ToMove              ; Move to cell 1
ret    z                   ; If correct, exits
ld     c, KEY4             ; C = key 4
call   ToMove              ; Move to cell 4
ret    z                   ; If correct, exits
ld     c, KEY7             ; C = key 7
call   ToMove              ; Move to cell 7
ret    z                   ; If correct, exits

zxMoveAttack_258:
ld     a, (ix+$02)         ; A = cell value 2
add    a, (ix+$05)         ; A+= cell value 5
add    a, (ix+$08)         ; A+= cell value 8
ld     c, a                ; Preserve A in C
and    $03                 ; A = player 1 cells
jr     nz, zxMoveAttack_369 ; Any? Yes, jump
ld     a, c                ; Retrieves A
and    $30                 ; A = Spectrum boxes
cp     b                   ; Two busy?
jr     z, zxMoveAttack_369 ; Yes, jumps
ld     c, KEY2             ; C = key 2
call   ToMove              ; Move to cell 2
ret    z                   ; If correct, exits
ld     c, KEY5             ; C = key 5
call   ToMove              ; Move to cell 5
ret    z                   ; If correct, exits
ld     c, KEY8             ; C = key 8
call   ToMove              ; Move to cell 8
ret    z                   ; If correct, exits

zxMoveAttack_369:
ld     a, (ix+$03)         ; A = cell value 3
add    a, (ix+$06)         ; A+= cell value 6
add    a, (ix+$09)         ; A+= cell value 9
ld     c, a                ; Preserve A in C
and    $03                 ; A = player 1 cells
jr     nz, zxMoveAttack_159 ; Any? Yes, jump
ld     a, c                ; Retrieves A
and    $30                 ; A = Spectrum boxes
cp     b                   ; Two busy?
jr     z, zxMoveAttack_159 ; Yes, jumps
ld     c, KEY3             ; C = key 3
call   ToMove              ; Move to cell 3
ret    z                   ; If correct, exits
ld     c, KEY6             ; C = key 6
call   ToMove              ; Move to cell 6
ret    z                   ; If correct, exits
ld     c, KEY9             ; C = key 9
call   ToMove              ; Move to cell 9
ret    z                   ; If correct, exits

zxMoveAttack_159:
```

```
ld    a, (ix+$01)         ; A = cell value 1
add   a, (ix+$05)         ; A+= cell value 5
add   a, (ix+$09)         ; A+= cell value 9
ld    c, a                ; Preserve A in C
and   $03                 ; A = player 1 cells
jr    nz, zxMoveAttack_357 ; Any? Yes, jump
ld    a, c                ; Retrieves A
and   $30                 ; A = Spectrum boxes
cp    b                   ; Two busy?
jr    z, zxMoveAttack_357 ; Yes, jumps
ld    c, KEY1             ; C = key 1
call  ToMove              ; Move to cell 1
ret   z                   ; If correct, exits
ld    c, KEY5             ; C = key 5
call  ToMove              ; Move to cell 5
ret   z                   ; If correct, exits
ld    c, KEY9             ; C = key 9
call  ToMove              ; Move to cell 9
ret   z                   ; If correct, exits

zxMoveAttack_357:
ld    a, (ix+$03)         ; A = cell value 3
add   a, (ix+$05)         ; A+= cell value 5
add   a, (ix+$07)         ; A+= cell value 7
ld    c, a                ; Preserve A in C
and   $03                 ; A = player 1 cells
jr    nz, zxMoveGeneric   ; Any? Yes, jump
ld    a, c                ; Retrieves A
and   $30                 ; A = Spectrum boxes
cp    b                   ; Two busy?
jr    z, zxMoveGeneric    ; Yes, skip
ld    c, KEY3             ; C = key 3
call  ToMove              ; Move to cell 3
ret   z                   ; If correct, exits
ld    c, KEY5             ; C = key 5
call  ToMove              ; Move to cell 5
ret   z                   ; If correct, exits
ld    c, KEY7             ; C = key 7
call  ToMove              ; Move to cell 7
ret   z                   ; If correct, exits
```

When we arrive here, the Spectrum has not found a place to go and will move to the first free cell.

```
; -------------------------------------------------------------------
; Generic movement.
; If with all of the above, you have not made any movement
; moves to the first free cell.
; -------------------------------------------------------------------
zxMoveGeneric:
ld    c, '1'              ; C = ascii 1 (cell 1)
ld    b, $09              ; B = total cells
ld    a, $00              ; A = empty cell
ld    hl, Grid            ; HL = address 1st cell

zxMoveGeneric_loop:
cp    (hl)                ; Free cell?
jr    z, zxMoveGeneric_end ; Yes, skip
inc   c                   ; C = ascii next cell
```

```
inc  hl                          ; HL = next cell
djnz zxMoveGeneric_loop          ; Loop until B = 0

zxMoveGeneric_end:
call ToMove                      ; Move to free cell
ret                              ; Exits
```

We have already implemented the way the Spectrum behaves in single player games. It's not perfect, it has some loopholes and sometimes the Spectrum makes some erratic moves. That's fine, if we made it perfect we could never beat the Spectrum and nobody likes that.

Now we need to integrate what we have implemented inside the main loop into main.asm.

Find the loop_lostMov tag, and five lines down replace JR Z, loop_keyCont with:

```
jr   z, loop_players        ; Not active, skip
```

Locate the loop_keyCont tag and replace the line above it, JR loop_cont, with:

```
jp   loop_cont              ; Jump
```

Between this line and loop_keyCont we add the Spectrum movement for single player games, this causes JR to give an out of range error, so we have replaced it with JP.

Finally, between this line and loop_keyCont, we add the following lines:

```
loop_players:
ld    a, (PlayerMoves)      ; A = player who moves
or    a                     ; Player 1?
jr    z, loop_keyCont       ; Yes, skip
ld    a, (MaxPlayers)       ; A = players
cp    $02                   ; 2 players?
jr    z, loop_keyCont       ; Yes, skip
call  ZxMove                ; Move Spectrum
jr    nz, loop_players      ; NZ = incorrect, loop
push  bc                    ; Preserve BC
ld    bc, SoundSpectrum     ; BC = sound address
call  PlayMusic             ; Outputs sound
pop   bc                    ; Retrieves BC
jr    loop_print            ; Paints movement
```

We get which player is moving, if it is two we get how many players there are and if it is one it moves the spectrum.

Compile, load into the emulator and see the result. If all went well, we can now play against the Spectrum. If you think it is too easy, you can tweak the Spectrum's movements, which we will do in the next chapter.

Download the source code from here

https://tinyurl.com/227mah88

Step 6: Final adjustments

We have reached the last chapter. We are going to make a couple of tweaks that, while not entirely necessary, I think might be of interest.

We will add an option in the menu to allow players to select the maximum number of tables they can have.

As for the tables, currently it is necessary to make all possible moves (occupy all the cells) to complete the point, although sometimes we already know that it is not possible to win and it is a table. We are going to implement the detection of tables to detect when it is no longer possible to win and end the point.

We will propose some modifications that can save some bytes and clock cycles.

We will modify the Spectrum's moves to make it harder to beat.

Finally, we'll add the loading screen.

Tables menu

Currently, the maximum number of tables is declared in the MAXTIES constant in var.asm; we delete it.

Locate MaxPoints and add the new variable for the tables below it:

```
MaxTies:      db $05           ; Maximum tables
```

Locate TitleEspamatica and add the Tables menu option just above it:

```
TitleOptionTies:    db $10, INK7, $16, $10, $08, "4. ", $10, INK6
                    defm "Tables"
```

To make it more symmetrical, we locate Title3InStripe and replace $16, $02, $09 at the end of the line with $16, $04, $09.

In Main.asm, let's add the handling of the new menu item. Locate menu_Time and replace JR NZ, menu_op two lines down:

```
jr    nz, menu_Ties       ; No, skip
```

Locate menu_TimeDo and three lines down, after JR menu_op, add the handling of the new menu item:

```
menu_Ties:
cp    KEY4                 ; Pushed 4?
jr    nz, menu_op          ; No, loop
ld    a, (MaxTies)         ; A = tables
add   a, $02               ; A += 2
cp    $0a                  ; A < 10?
jr    c, menu_TiesDo       ; Yes, skip
ld    a, $03               ; A = 3
menu_TiesDo:
ld    (MaxTies), a         ; Update tables
jr    menu_op              ; Loop
```

If the four key has been pressed, the maximum number of tables is increased by two, if it is greater than nine, it is reduced to three and loaded into memory.

Both this range of values and the difference between one value and the other can be modified as required. You can also change it in points and time.

Once we have the maximum number of tables in memory, we need to use them. Find the loop_reset tag, the LD B, MAXTIES line and replace it with the following:

```
ld   a, (MaxTies)       ; A = maximum tables
ld   b, a               ; B = A
```

All that remains is to print the selected value. In screen.asm, locate PrintOptions and add the following lines just above JP PrintBCD:

```
call PrintBCD           ; Paints it
ld   b, INI_TOP-$10     ; B = coord Y
call AT                 ; Position cursor
ld   hl, MaxTies        ; HL = time value
```

We compile, load the emulator and check that we can now define the number of tables and that the game ends when the number of tables is reached.

Table detection

Currently, in order for boards to be detected, all cells must be occupied and there must be no tic-tac-toe. In reality, it is possible to know if the point will end in a board before the board is full.

We go to game.asm and implement table detection.

To know if there is a possibility of a move, we just need to know if there is any combination left in which the cells are occupied by only one player or by no player at all.

```
; ----------------------------------------------------------------
; Check for tables.
; In order to check if there are tables.
;
; Output: Z  -> No tables.
;         NZ -> There are tables.
```

```
;
; Alters the value of the AF, BC, DE, HL and IX registers.
; -------------------------------------------------------------
CheckTies:
ld    b, $f0              ; B = single-player cell mask
ld    c, $0f              ; B = cell mask another player
```

We load in B the mask to keep the cells occupied by one player, and in C the mask for the other player.

```
checkTies_check123:
ld    hl, Grid           ; HL = grid address
ld    a, (hl)            ; A = cell value 1
inc   hl                 ; HL = cell address 2
add   a, (hl)            ; A+= cell value 2
inc   hl                 ; HL = cell address 3
add   a, (hl)            ; A+= cell value 2
ld    d, a               ; Preserve A in D
and   b                  ; A = cells occupied by a player
ret   z                  ; None, exits
ld    a, d               ; Retrieves A from D
and   c                  ; A = cells occupied by another player
ret   z                  ; None, exits
```

We place HL on the grid, add the value of the three cells in A and increment HL to move from one cell to another. We check if there are any cells occupied by a player, and if not, we leave. If so, we check if there are any cells occupied by the other player, and if not, we leave.

The next two checks have the same structure.

```
checkTies_check456:
inc   hl                 ; A = cell address 4
ld    a, (hl)            ; A = cell value 4
inc   hl                 ; HL = cell address 5
add   a, (hl)            ; A+= cell value 5
inc   hl                 ; HL = cell address 6
add   a, (hl)            ; A+= cell value 6
ld    d, a               ; Preserve A in D
and   b                  ; A = cells occupied by a player
ret   z                  ; None, exits
ld    a, d               ; Retrieves A from D
and   c                  ; A = cells occupied by another player
ret   z                  ; None, exits

checkTies_check789:
inc   hl                 ; A = cell address 7
ld    a, (hl)            ; A = cell value 7
inc   hl                 ; HL = cell address 8
add   a, (hl)            ; A+= cell value 8
inc   hl                 ; HL = cell address 9
add   a, (hl)            ; A+= cell value 9
ld    d, a               ; Preserve A in D
and   b                  ; A = cells occupied by a player
ret   z                  ; None, exits
ld    a, d               ; Retrieves A from D
and   c                  ; A = cells occupied by another player
ret   z                  ; None, exits
```

Look closely at how we go through the cells with HL, this helps us to save a few bytes in an implementation we did earlier.

The following checks cannot be done by changing cells with HL, as they are not numerically contiguous; we use IX.

```
checkTies_check147:
ld   ix, Grid-$01        ; IX = address Grid - 1
ld   a, (ix+$01)         ; A = cell value 1
add  a, (ix+$04)         ; A+= cell value 4
add  a, (ix+$07)         ; A+= cell value 7
ld   d, a                ; Preserve A in D
and  b                   ; A = cells occupied by a player
ret  z                   ; None, exits
ld   a, d                ; Retrieves A from D
and  c                   ; A = cells occupied by another player
ret  z                   ; None, exits
```

The rest of the checks follow the same structure.

```
checkTies_check258:
ld   a, (ix+$02)         ; A = cell value 2
add  a, (ix+$05)         ; A+= cell value 5
add  a, (ix+$08)         ; A+= cell value 8
ld   d, a                ; Preserve A in D
and  b                   ; A = cells occupied by a player
ret  z                   ; None, exits
ld   a, d                ; Retrieves A from D
and  c                   ; A = cells occupied by another player
ret  z                   ; None, exits


checkTies_check369:
ld   a, (ix+$03)         ; A = cell value 3
add  a, (ix+$06)         ; A+= cell value 6
add  a, (ix+$09)         ; A+= cell value 9
ld   d, a                ; Preserve A in D
and  b                   ; A = cells occupied by a player
ret  z                   ; None, exits
ld   a, d                ; Retrieves A from D
and  c                   ; A = cells occupied by another player
ret  z                   ; None, exits


checkTies_check159:
ld   a, (ix+$01)         ; A = cell value 1
add  a, (ix+$05)         ; A+= cell value 5
add  a, (ix+$09)         ; A+= cell value 9
ld   d, a                ; Preserve A in D
and  b                   ; A = cells occupied by a player
ret  z                   ; None, exits
ld   a, d                ; Retrieves A from D
and  c                   ; A = cells occupied by another player
ret  z                   ; None, exits


checkTies_check357:
ld   a, (ix+$03)         ; A = cell value 3
add  a, (ix+$05)         ; A+= cell value 5
add  a, (ix+$07)         ; A+= cell value 7
ld   d, a                ; Preserve A in D
and  b                   ; A = cells occupied by a player
```

```
ret  z                       ; None, exits
ld   a, d                    ; Retrieves A from D
and  c                       ; A = cells occupied by another player
ret                          ; Exits with Z in correct state
```

With this we now have the prediction of whether there will be tables, all that remains is to go to main.asm and use it.

Find loop_tie and three lines down substitute:

```
ld   a, $09                  ; A = 9
cp   (hl)                    ; Counter = 9?
jr   nz, loop_cont           ; No, skip
```

By:

```
call CheckTies               ; Any possible movement?
jr   z, loop_cont            ; No, skip
```

We no longer have to wait until the board is full to know if there are checkers or not. We call CheckTies and if there are no boards we continue with the point.

We compile, load the emulator and see the results.

You may see some behaviour that makes you think something is wrong. You see rows one, two, three free, but you know that the Spectrum will occupy one cell, then you another, and so it should mark tables.

The system is predicting, not guessing. Imagine that there are two free cells in a row and it is the turn of the player whose cell is not occupied to move. Well, he will occupy one of the cells, so we already know it is a draw, but imagine that the player rests on his laurels and loses his turn, the other player occupies another cell and there is only one free cell, and it is still not possible to predict draws, if the other player falls asleep again, he loses his turn again and the first player gets three in a row.

We save bytes and clock cycles

We will implement several modifications to save bytes and clock cycles.

The first of these will be in game.asm, on the set of CheckWinner and ZxMove routines, applying the way we have implemented CheckTies to the horizontal lines, the numerically contiguous ones.

Go to the CheckWinner_check tag and find the following lines:

```
ld    a, (ix+1)          ; A = cell 1
add   a, (ix+2)          ; A+= cell 2
add   a, (ix+3)          ; A+= cell 3
```

And we replace them with:

```
ld    hl, Grid           ; HL = cell address 1
ld    a, (hl)            ; A = cell value 1
inc   hl                 ; HL = cell address 2
add   a, (hl)            ; A+= cell value 2
inc   hl                 ; HL = cell address 3
add   a, (hl)            ; A+= cell value 3
```

We locate the lines:

```
ld    a, (ix+4)          ; A = cell 4
add   a, (ix+5)          ; A+= cell 5
add   a, (ix+6)          ; A+= cell 6
```

And we replace them with:

```
inc   hl                 ; HL = cell address 4
ld    a, (hl)            ; A = cell value 4
inc   hl                 ; HL = cell address 5
add   a, (hl)            ; A+= cell value 5
inc   hl                 ; HL = cell address 6
add   a, (hl)            ; A+= cell value 6
```

We locate the lines:

```
ld    a, (ix+7)          ; A = cell 7
add   a, (ix+8)          ; A+= cell 8
add   a, (ix+9)          ; A+= cell 9
```

And we replace them with:

```
inc   hl                 ; HL = cell address 7
ld    a, (hl)            ; A = cell value 7
inc   hl                 ; HL = cell address 8
add   a, (hl)            ; A+= cell value 8
inc   hl                 ; HL = cell address 9
add   a, (hl)            ; A+= cell value 9
```

This part is ready, add the comments of the routine to HL as the affected register.

This is the comparison between the two versions:

Version	Cycles	Bytes
1	688/641	118
2	638/591	111

As you can see, we save fifty clock cycles and seven bytes. We compile, load into the emulator and see that it still works.

We continue to modify ZxMove, specifically two parts of this routine set. We locate zxMoveToWin_123 and replace it:

```
ld   a, (ix+$01)        ; A = cell value 1
add  a, (ix+$02)        ; A+= cell value 2
add  a, (ix+$03)        ; A+= cell value 3
```

By:

```
ld   hl, Grid           ; HL = cell address 1
ld   a, (hl)            ; A = cell value 1
inc  hl                 ; HL = cell address 2
add  a, (hl)            ; A+= cell value 2
inc  hl                 ; HL = cell address 3
add  a, (hl)            ; A+= cell value 3
```

Locate zxMoveToWin_456 and replace it:

```
ld   a, (ix+$04)        ; A = cell value 4
add  a, (ix+$05)        ; A+= cell value 5
add  a, (ix+$06)        ; A+= cell value 6
```

By:

```
ld   hl, Grid+$03       ; HL = cell address 4
ld   a, (hl)            ; A = cell value 4
inc  hl                 ; HL = cell address 5
add  a, (hl)            ; A+= cell value 5
inc  hl                 ; HL = cell address 6
add  a, (hl)            ; A+= cell value 6
```

Locate zxMoveToWin_789 and replace it:

```
ld   a, (ix+$07)        ; A = cell value 7
add  a, (ix+$08)        ; A+= cell value 8
add  a, (ix+$09)        ; A+= cell value 9
```

By:

```
ld   hl, Grid+$06       ; HL = cell address 7
ld   a, (hl)            ; A = cell value 7
inc  hl                 ; HL = cell address 8
add  a, (hl)            ; A+= cell value 8
inc  hl                 ; HL = cell address 9
add  a, (hl)            ; A+= cell value 9
```

We have now completed the first part. The main difference with CheckTies and CheckWinner is that although they are numerically contiguous cells, the move from cell three to cell four and from cell six to cell seven is not with INC HL, as ToMove changes the value of HL.

Locate zxMoveAttack_123 and replace it:

```
ld   a, (ix+$01)        ; A = cell value 1
add  a, (ix+$02)        ; A+= cell value 2
add  a, (ix+$03)        ; A+= cell value 3
```

By:

```
ld   hl, Grid           ; HL = cell address 1
ld   a, (hl)            ; A = cell value 1
inc  hl                 ; HL = cell address 2
add  a, (hl)            ; A+= cell value 2
inc  hl                 ; HL = cell address 3
add  a, (hl)            ; A+= cell value 3
```

Locate zxMoveAttack_456 and replace it:

```
ld   a, (ix+$04)       ; A = cell value 4
add  a, (ix+$05)       ; A+= cell value 5
add  a, (ix+$06)       ; A+= cell value 6
```

By:

```
ld   hl, Grid+$03      ; HL = cell address 4
ld   a, (hl)           ; A = cell value 4
inc  hl                ; HL = cell address 5
add  a, (hl)           ; A+= cell value 5
inc  hl                ; HL = cell address 6
add  a, (hl)           ; A+= cell value 6
```

Locate zxMoveAttack_789 and replace it:

```
ld   a, (ix+$07)       ; A = cell value 7
add  a, (ix+$08)       ; A+= cell value 8
add  a, (ix+$09)       ; A+= cell value 9
```

By:

```
ld   hl, Grid+$06      ; HL = cell address 7
ld   a, (hl)           ; A = cell value 7
inc  hl                ; HL = cell address 8
add  a, (hl)           ; A+= cell value 8
inc  hl                ; HL = cell address 9
add  a, (hl)           ; A+= cell value 9
```

We make another modification in zxMoveDefence_cornerBlock34 and zxMoveDefence_cornerBlock67 that saves clock cycles but no bytes.

Replacement in zxMoveDefence_cornerBlock34:

```
ld   a, (ix+$03)       ; A = cell value 3
add  a, (ix+$04)       ; A+= cell value 4
```

By:

```
ld   hl, Grid+$02      ; A = cell address 3
ld   a, (hl)           ; A = cell value 3
inc  hl                ; HL = cell address 4
add  a, (hl)           ; A+= cell value 4
```

In zxMoveDefence_cornerBlock67 we replace:

```
ld   a, (ix+$06)       ; A = cell value 6
add  a, (ix+$07)       ; A+= cell value 7
```

By:

```
ld   hl, Grid+$05      ; A = cell address 6
ld   a, (hl)           ; A = cell value 6
inc  hl                ; HL = cell address 7
add  a, (hl)           ; A+= cell value 7
```

The changes in game.asm are done. As I said, add HL as affected registry in the comments of the routine, we forgot it before because the HL registry was already affected by the zxMoveGeneric routine.

This is the comparison between the two versions of ZxMove:

Version	Cycles	Bytes
1	4632/4079	808
2	4532/3979	802

Version two occupies six bytes less and takes a hundred cycles less than version one, which seems small when we compare it with the bytes saved by CheckWinner with fewer modifications. Remember that there the transition from cell three to cell four and from cell six to cell seven is done with INC HL, which we cannot do here.

The difference between INC HL and LD HL, Grid is four clock cycles and two bytes, and that limits our savings.

Same tile for both players

If we have capacity problems, which we don't, we can save another handful of bytes by painting the same tile in a different colour for both players.

We go to sprite.asm, comment out the Sprite_P2 definition and put the Sprite_CROSS, Sprite_SLASH and Sprite_MINUS definitions at the top of the file, like this:

```
; --------------------------------------------------------------
; File: sprite.asm
;
; Definition of graphs.
; --------------------------------------------------------------
; Crosshead Sprite
Sprite_CROSS:
db $18, $18, $18, $ff, $ff, $18, $18, $18 ; $90

; Sprite of the vertical line
Sprite_SLASH:
db $18, $18, $18, $18, $18, $18, $18, $18 ; $91

; Sprite of the horizontal line
Sprite_MINUS:
db $00, $00, $00, $ff, $ff, $00, $00, $00 ; $92

; Player 1 Sprite
Sprite_P1:
db $c0, $e0, $70, $38, $1c, $0e, $07, $03 ; $93
db $03, $07, $0e, $1c, $38, $70, $e0, $c0 ; $94

; ; Player Sprite 2
; Sprite_P2:
; db $03, $0f, $1c, $30, $60, $60, $c0, $c0 ; $95 Up/Left
; db $c0, $f0, $38, $0c, $06, $06, $03, $03 ; $96 Top/Right
; db $c0, $c0, $60, $60, $30, $1c, $0f, $03 ; $97 Down/Left
; db $03, $03, $06, $06, $0c, $38, $f0, $c0 ; $98 Down/Right
```

Commenting on player two's sprite not only forces us to change the routine that paints the tiles, it also forces us to change the routine that paints the board as the UDGs change. We have uploaded the board sprites above so that we can only change the board painting routine once, and so that if we decide to repaint the two tiles later, it won't be affected.

By commenting out Sprite_P2, we save thirty-two bytes. It doesn't sound like much, but in certain situations it can save us.

We go to var.asm and change the definition of Board_1 and _2 and leave them as they are:

```
; Vertical lines of the board.
Board_1:
db $12, $00, $13, $00
db $20, $20, $20, $20, $91, $20, $20, $20, $20, $91, $20, $20, $20
db $20, $ff

; Horizontal lines of the board.
Board_2:
db $92, $92, $92, $92, $90, $92, $92, $92, $92, $90, $92, $92, $92
db $92, $ff
```

We compile, load into the emulator and see the result, which is the mess we made.

That player two's tile is painted wrong is to be expected, but what about the board? We have changed the position of the sprite definition, but UDG is still pointing to Sprite_P1.

We go to main.asm and under the Main tag we replace:

```
ld    hl, Sprite_P1          ; HL = address Sprite_P1
```

By:

```
ld    hl, Sprite_CROSS       ; HL = address Sprite_CROSS
```

Also change the comment in the line below.

We compile, load it into the emulator and see that the board looks good, but the parts don't. Don't worry, this is to be expected.

435

We are going to modify the routine that paints the tiles so that it does it well, or not, you can leave it as it is; three in a bloody line.

We locate printOXO_X in screen.asm and the lines where the UDG is loaded in A. We add three to the value it loads:

```
ld a, $90 becomes ld a, $93
ld a, $91 becomes ld a, $94
```

We locate printOXO_Y and the lines on which the UDG is loaded in A. We add three to the value it loads:

```
ld a, $92 becomes ld a, $95
ld a, $93 becomes ld a, $96
ld a, $94 becomes ld a, $97
ld a, $95 becomes ld a, $98
```

So if we decided to paint two different tiles, the circle would be painted.

As we are now in the situation of painting a single tile, we comment on the lines:

```
ld    a, $95                 ; A = 1st sprite
ld    a, $98                 ; A = 4th sprite
```

And below that we add the line:

```
ld    a, $93                 ; A = 1st sprite
```

We comment on the lines:

```
ld    a, $96                 ; A = 2nd sprite
ld    a, $97                 ; A = 3rd sprite
```

And below that we add the line:

```
ld    a, $94                 ; A = 2nd sprite
```

A bit of a mess, isn't it? Here's what it looks like:

```
printOXO_X:
ld    a, INKPLAYER1          ; A = ink player 1
call INK                     ; Change ink
ld    a, $93                 ; A = 1st sprite
rst  $10                     ; Paints it
ld    a, $94                 ; A = 2nd sprite
rst  $10                     ; Paints it
```

```
dec   b                        ; B = bottom line
call  AT                       ; Position cursor
ld    a, $94                   ; A = 2nd sprite
rst   $10                      ; Paints it
ld    a, $93                   ; A = 2nd sprite
rst   $10                      ; Paints it
ret                            ; Exits

printOXO_Y:
ld    a, INKPLAYER2            ; A = ink player 2
call  INK                      ; Change ink
; ld   a, $95                    ; A = 1st sprite
ld    a, $93                   ; A = 1st sprite
rst   $10                      ; Paints it
; ld   a, $96                    ; A = 2nd sprite
ld    a, $94                   ; A = 2nd sprite
rst   $10                      ; Paints it
dec   b                        ; B = bottom line
call  AT                       ; Position cursor
; ld   a, $97                    ; A = 3rd sprite
ld    a, $94                   ; A = 2nd sprite
rst   $10                      ; Paints it
; ld   a, $98                    ; A = 4th sprite
ld    a, $93                   ; A = 1st sprite
rst   $10                      ; Paints it
ret                            ; Exits
```

So, if we want to redraw the two pieces, in sprite.asm we uncomment Sprite_P2, and in printOXO_Y we alternate the comments on the LD A, ... lines.

This will paint the pieces on the board, but not in the information part of the game.

We go back to var.asm and modify player1_figure to look like this:

```
player1_figure:    db $16, $04, $00, $90, $91, $0d, $91, $90
```

And we leave it at that:

```
player1_figure:    db $16, $04, $00, $93, $94, $0d, $94, $93
```

We modify player2_figure so that it now looks like this:

```
player2_figure:    db $16, $04, $1b, $92, $93, $16, $05, $1b
                   db $94, $95, $ff
```

And we leave it at that:

```
player2_figure:    db $16, $04, $1b, $93, $94, $16, $05, $1b
                   db $94, $93, $ff
```

Finally, we add the annotated definition for painting different tiles.

```
; player2_figure:    db $16, $04, $1b, $95, $96, $16, $05, $1b
;                    db $97, $98, $ff
```

We compile, load in the emulator and see the results.

You can paint the same tile in a different colour for both players, or you can paint a different colour for each player. If we were using a black and white TV, there would be no doubt.

If you keep all the changes, we have saved forty-five bytes and one hundred and fifty clock cycles. If you decide to paint different tiles for each player, the byte saving is thirteen bytes.

Spectrum movement

If you have played several games against the Spectrum, you will have worked out how to beat it every time you start the game, because there is at least one move that the Spectrum does not know how to defend, we have not programmed it.

The specific move is to occupy two corner cells: two and six or six and eight. If we occupy cell two, the Spectrum occupies cell five, we move to cell six and the Spectrum moves to cell seven, we move to cell three and we have two tic-tac-toe moves: cells one, two and three and cells three, six and nine.

In game.asm we locate zxMoveAttack_123 and above it we implement the lines that make it impossible to beat the Spectrum with this move.

```
; --------------------------------------------------------------------
; Defensive corner movement.
; --------------------------------------------------------------------
zxMoveDefence_corner24:
ld   a, (ix+$02)          ; A = cell value 2
add  a, (ix+$04)          ; A+= cell value 4
cp   b                    ; A = B?
jr   nz, zxMoveDefence_corner26 ; No, skip
ld   c, KEY1              ; C = key 1
call ToMove               ; Move to cell 1
ret  z                    ; If correct, exits
```

We check if player one has occupied squares two and four, in which case we move to square one if possible.

The rest of the checks follow the same structure.

```
zxMoveDefence_corner26:
ld   a, (ix+$02)          ; A = cell value 2
add  a, (ix+$06)          ; A+= cell value 6
```

438

```
cp   b                        ; A = B?
jr   nz, zxMoveDefence_corner84 ; No, skip
ld   c, KEY3                   ; C = key 3
call ToMove                    ; Move to cell 3
ret  z                         ; If correct, exits
zxMoveDefence_corner84:
ld   a, (ix+$08)               ; A = cell value 8
add  a, (ix+$04)               ; A+= cell value 4
cp   b                         ; A = B?
jr   nz, zxMoveDefence_corner86 ; No, skip
ld   c, KEY7                   ; C = key 7
call ToMove                    ; Move to cell 3
ret  z                         ; If correct, exits
zxMoveDefence_corner86:
ld   a, (ix+$08)               ; A = cell value 8
add  a, (ix+$06)               ; A+= cell value 6
cp   b                         ; A = B?
jr   nz, zxMoveAttack_123      ; No, skip
ld   c, KEY9                   ; C = key 9
call ToMove                    ; Move to cell nine
ret  z                         ; If correct, exits
```

Although the play is in two corners, we cover all four.

Just above zxMoveDefence_cornerBlock2938Cont is the JR NZ line, zxMoveAttack_123, we modify it and leave it as it is:

```
jr   nz, zxMoveDefence_corner24 ; No, no mov cross, skip
```

If you compile and play some games against Spectrum, you will see that it is no longer possible to beat him with this move, but it is still possible to beat him, there are still moves that he does not know how to defend.

Difficulty

Now it is more difficult to beat the Spectrum, we have to wait for him to start the game and depending on the move he makes, we can beat him.

We will add another option to the menu to be able to choose the level of difficulty: one to not cover the play in the corner, two to cover the play in the corner.

In var.asm, after MaxTies, we add the variable for the level of difficulty:

```
Level:      db $02          ; Difficulty level
```

When a new menu item is added, it is appended to the Spamatica line. We move all the menu items up one line, like this:

```
TitleOptionStart:  db $10, INK1, $13, $01, $16, $07, $08, "0. "
                   db $10, INK5
                   defm "Start"
TitleOptionPlayer: db $10, INK7, $13, $01, $16, $09, $08, "1. "
                   db $10, INK6
                   defm "Players"
TitleOptionPoint:  db $10, INK7, $16, $0b, $08, "2. ", $10, INK6
                   defm "Points"
TitleOptionTime:   db $10, INK7, $16, $0d, $08, "3. ", $10, INK6
                   defm "Time"
TitleOptionTies:   db $10, INK7, $16, $0f, $08, "4. ", $10, INK6
                   defm "Tables"
```

After the definition of TitleOptionTies, we add the definition of Difficulty:

```
TitleOptionLevel:  db $10, INK7, $16, $11, $08, "5. ", $10, INK6
                   defm "Difficulty"
```

In screen.asm we find PrintOptions and subtract one from all Y coordinate assignments:

```
LD B, INI_TOP-$0A go to LD B,INI_TOP-$09
LD B, INI_TOP-$0C go to LD B,INI_TOP-$0B
LD B, INI_TOP-$0E go to LD B,INI_TOP-$0D
LD B, INI_TOP-$10 go to LD B,INI_TOP-$0F
```

Above JP PrintBCD we add the following lines:

```
call PrintBCD         ; Paints it
ld   b, INI_TOP-$11   ; B = coord Y
call AT               ; Position cursor
ld   hl, Level        ; HL = difficulty value
```

The final aspect of the routine is as follows:

```
; -----------------------------------------------------------------
; Paint the values of the options.
;
; Alters the value of the AF, BC and HL registers.
; -----------------------------------------------------------------
PrintOptions:
ld   a, INK4          ; A = green ink
call INK              ; Change ink
ld   b, INI_TOP-$09   ; B = coord Y
ld   c, INI_LEFT-$15  ; C = coord X
call AT               ; Position cursor
ld   hl, MaxPlayers   ; HL = value players
call PrintBCD         ; Paints it
ld   b, INI_TOP-$0b   ; B = coord Y
call AT               ; Position cursor
ld   hl, MaxPoints    ; HL = points value
```

```
call PrintBCD          ; Paints it
ld   b, INI_TOP-$0d    ; B = coord Y
call AT                ; Position cursor
ld   hl, seconds       ; HL = time value
call PrintBCD          ; Paints it
ld   b, INI_TOP-$0f    ; B = coord Y
call AT                ; Position cursor
ld   hl, MaxTies       ; HL = time value
call PrintBCD          ; Paints it
ld   b, INI_TOP-$11    ; B = coord Y
call AT                ; Position cursor
ld   hl, Level         ; HL = difficulty value
jp   PrintBCD          ; Paints it in and exits
```

In main.asm find menu_Ties and then the line CP KEY4. After this line, replace JR NZ, menu_op with:

```
jr   nz, menu_Level    ; No, skip
```

After menu_TiesDo, after the JR line menu_op, we add the processing lines of the new menu item:

```
menu_Level:
cp   KEY5              ; Pushed 5?
jr   nz, menu_op       ; No, loop
ld   a, (Level)        ; A = difficulty
xor  $03               ; Alternates between 1 and 2
ld   (Level), a        ; Refresh in memory
jr   menu_op           ; Loop
```

Finally, in game.asm we locate zxMoveDefence_corner24, and just below it we add:

```
ld   a, (Level)        ; A = difficulty
cp   $01               ; Difficulty = 1?
jr   z, zxMoveAttack_123  ; Yes, jumps
```

These lines do not check for corner play when the difficulty level is one. Compile and test.

Loading screen

Finally, we're going to add the loading screen, but what's the difference when we've already seen how it's done in ZX-Pong and Space Battle? Well, this time we're going to do it differently, because we're not going to load the screen into VideoRAM, we're going to load it into a different memory address and then make it appear all at once.

This is the loading screen you can download from here:

https://tinyurl.com/2qe2txpz

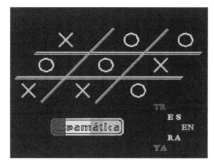

Please be kind, art has never been my thing. I will be happy if you design your own loading screen, which I am sure will be better than this one; it shouldn't be difficult.

In order to load the loading screen into a memory area and then dump it all at once into VideoRAM, we need to implement the routine to do this in a separate file and compile it separately.

The loading process will do the following:

- Load the loader.
- Load the routine that dumps the loading screen into memory address 24200.
- Load the loading screen at address 24250.
- Runs the routine that dumps the loading screen into VideoRAM.
- Load the tic-tac-toe routine at address 24200.
- Load the interrupt routine at address 32348.
- Run the tic-tac-toe program.

The first thing we are going to look at is the loader we developed in Basic to do all of the above.

```
 10 CLEAR 24200
 20 INK 0: PAPER 4: BORDER 4: CLS
 30 POKE 23610,255: POKE 23739,111
 40 LOAD ""CODE 24200
 50 LOAD ""CODE 24250
 60 RANDOMIZE USR 24200
 70 LOAD ""CODE 24200
 80 LOAD ""CODE 32348
 90 CLS
100 RANDOMIZE USR 24200
```

Don't forget to save it with SAVE "OXO" LINE 10.

The next step is to implement the routine that dumps the loading screen into the VideoRAM. We create the file loadScr.asm and add the following lines:

```
; -----------------------------------------------------------------
; LoadScr.asm
;
; The loading screen will be loaded in $5eba, and this routine will
; be passed by the VideoRAM to appear all at once and will then
; clear the area.
```

```
; Where it was initially loaded.
; The cleaning of this memory area is not necessary, but we do it.
; in case we need to debug, not to find code that actually are
; remnants of the loading screen.
; ------------------------------------------------------------------
org $5e88                   ; Loading address

ld    hl, $5eba             ; HL = address where the screen is located
ld    de, $4000             ; DE = VideoRAM address
ld    bc, $1b00             ; Screen length
ldir                        ; Flip the screen

ld    hl, $5eba             ; HL = address where the screen is located
ld    de, $5ebb             ; Next address
ld    bc, $1aff             ; Screen length - 1
ld    (hl), $00             ; Clear the first position
ldir                        ; Clean up the rest

ret
```

The loading screen is loaded at $5eba. This routine copies $1B00 positions (6912 bytes), the entire area of pixels and attributes, from this address into VideoRAM.

Once copied, we clean up the memory area where the screen was loaded; it is not necessary, but if we have to debug, we will avoid residual code that could confuse us.

Now we just need to modify the script we need to compile and generate the final .tap. The Windows version looks like this:

```
echo off
cls
echo Compiling oxo
pasmo --name OXO --tap main.asm oxo.tap oxo.log
echo Compiling int
pasmo --name INT --tap int.asm int.tap int.log
echo Compiling loadscr
pasmo --name LoadScr --tap loadScr.asm loadscr.tap loadscr.log
echo Generating Tic-Tac-Toe
copy /b /y loader.tap+loadscr.tap+TresEnRayaScr.tap+oxo.tap+int.tap
TicTacToe.tap
```

The Linux version would look like this:

```
clear
echo Compiling oxo
pasmo --name OXO --tap main.asm oxo.tap oxo.log
echo Compiling int
pasmo --name INT --tap int.asm int.tap int.log
echo Compiling loadscr
pasmo --name LoadScr --tap loadScr.asm loadscr.tap loadscr.log
echo Generating Tic-Tac-Toe
cat loader.tap loadscr.tap TresEnRayaScr.Tap oxo.tap int.tap >
TicTacToe.tap
```

And that is it. Thank you very much for joining me on this journey, I hope this is just the beginning, that it has helped you to learn and become passionate about assembly programming for the ZX Spectrum. I will continue to study and learn, and if I can gather more material in the future, I may write another book.

You can download the source code from here

https://tinyurl.com/2bwwwsjw

Appendix 1: Frequencies and notes

The values for the frequencies and notes of eight different scales are shown below. The smaller the scale, the lower the pitch, and the higher the scale, the higher the pitch.

The frequency values are taken from the Dilwyn Jones Sinclair QL Pages.

https://dilwyn.qlforum.co.uk/docs/articles/beeps.pdf

These frequencies indicate the duration of the note: one second. Each note is calculated using the following formula:

```
(437500/frequency)-30.125      ; . is decimal point
```

This formula is taken from the book "Advanced ZX Spectrum Programming" by Steve Kramer, page 18.

Below is a table of frequencies and values, in decimal and hexadecimal.

		Frequency, 1 second, DE		Note, HL	
		Decimal	**Hexadecimal**	**Decimal**	**Hexadecimal**
C	**0**	16.35	0010	26728.28	6868
Cs	**0**	17.32	0011	25229.69	628D
D	**0**	18.35	0012	23811.84	5D03
Ds	**0**	19.45	0013	22463.45	57BF
E	**0**	20.60	0014	21207.74	52D7
F	**0**	21.83	0015	20011.10	4E2B
Fs	**0**	23.12	0017	18892.89	49CC
G	**0**	24.50	0018	17827.02	45A3
Gs	**0**	25.96	0019	16822.73	41B6
A	**0**	27.50	001B	15878.97	3E06

As	0	29.14	001D	14983.60	3A87
B	0	30.87	001E	14142.21	373E
C	1	32.70	0020	13349.08	3425
Cs	1	34.65	0022	12596.14	3134
D	1	36.71	0024	11887.61	2E6F
Ds	1	38.89	0026	11219.55	2BD3
E	1	41.20	0029	10588.81	295C
F	1	43.65	002B	9992.78	2708
Fs	1	46.25	002E	9429.33	24D5
G	1	49.00	0031	8898.45	22C2
Gs	1	51.91	0033	8397.92	20CD
A	1	55.00	0037	7924.42	1EF4
As	1	58.27	003A	7478.03	1D36
B	1	61.74	003D	7056.04	1B90
C	2	65.41	0041	6658.45	1A02
Cs	2	69.30	0045	6283.01	188B
D	2	73.42	0049	5928.74	1728
Ds	2	77.78	004D	5594.71	15DA
E	2	82.41	0052	5278.70	149E
F	2	87.31	0057	4980.76	1374
Fs	2	92.50	005C	4699.60	125B
G	2	98.00	0062	4434.16	1152
Gs	2	103.80	0067	4184.71	1058
A	2	110.00	006E	3947.15	0F6B
As	2	116.00	0074	3741.43	0E9D
B	2	123.50	007B	3512.39	0DB8
C	3	130.80	0082	3314.68	0CF2

Cs	3	138.60	008A	3126.44	0C36
D	3	146.80	0092	2950.12	0B86
Ds	3	155.60	009B	2781.57	0ADD
E	3	164.80	00A4	2624.61	0A40
F	3	174.60	00AEU	2475.60	09AB
Fs	3	185.00	00B9	2334.74	091E
G	3	196.00	00C4	2202.02	089A
Gs	3	207.70	00CF	2076.28	081C
A	3	220.00	00DC	1958.51	07A6
As	3	233.10	00E9	1846.75	0736
B	3	246.90	00F6	1741.85	06CD
C	4	261.60	0105	1642.28	066A
Cs	4	277.20	0115	1548.16	060C
D	4	293.70	0125	1459.49	05B3
Ds	4	311.10	0137	1376.18	0560
E	4	329.60	0149	1297.24	0511
F	4	349.20	015D	1222.74	04C6
Fs	4	370.00	0172	1152.31	0480
G	4	392.00	0188	1085.95	043D
Gs	4	415.30	019F	1023.33	03FF
A	4	440.00	01B8	964.19	03C4
As	4	466.20	01D2	908.31	038C
B	4	493.90	01ED	855.68	0357
C	5	523.30	020B	805.92	0325
Cs	5	554.40	022A	759.02	02F7
D	5	587.30	024B	714.81	02CA
Ds	5	622.30	026E	672.91	02A0

E	5	659.30	0293	633.46	0279
F	5	698.50	02BA	596.22	0254
Fs	5	740.00	02E4	561.09	0231
G	5	784.00	0310	527.91	020F
Gs	5	830.00	033E	496.98	01F0
A	5	880.00	0370	467.03	01D3
As	5	932.30	03A4	439.14	01B7
B	5	987.80	03DB	412.78	019C
C	6	1047.00	0417	387.74	0183
Cs	6	1109.00	0455	364.37	016C
D	6	1175.00	0497	342.22	0156
Ds	6	1245.00	04DD	321.28	0141
E	6	1319.00	0527	301.57	012D
F	6	1397.00	0575	283.05	011B
Fs	6	1480.00	05C8	265.48	0109
G	6	1568.00	0620	248.89	00F8
Gs	6	1661.00	067D	233.27	00E9
A	6	1760.00	06E0	218.45	00DA
As	6	1865.00	0749	204.46	00CC
B	6	1976.00	07B8	191.28	00BF
C	7	2093.00	082D	178.91	00B2
Cs	7	2217.00	08A9	167.21	00A7
D	7	2349.00	092D	156.12	009C
Ds	7	2489.00	09B9	145.65	0091
E	7	2637.00	0A4D	135.78	0087
F	7	2794.00	0AEA	126.46	007E
Fs	7	2960.00	0B90	117.68	0075

G	7	3136.00	0C40	109.38	006D
Gs	7	3322.00	0CFA	101.57	0065
A	7	3520.00	0DC0	94.16	005E
As	7	3729.00	0E91	87.20	0057
B	7	3951.00	0F6F	80.61	0050
C	8	4186.00	105A	74.39	004A
Cs	8	4435.00	1153	68.52	0044
D	8	4699.00	125B	62.98	003E
Ds	8	4978.00	1372	57.76	0039
E	8	5274.00	149A	52.83	0034
F	8	5588.00	15D4	48.17	0030
Fs	8	5920.00	1720	43.78	002B
G	8	6272.00	1880	39.63	0027
Gs	8	6645.00	19F5	35.71	0023
A	8	7040.00	1B80	32.02	0020
As	8	7459.00	1D23	28.53	001C
B	8	7902.00	1EDE	25.24	0019

This table, together with the assembly code, can be downloaded from here.

https://tinyurl.com/25qdso64

Appendix 2: ZEsarUX

Throughout this book I have used ZEsarUX, an emulator developed by César Hernández Bañó, which you can get for free at https://github.com/chernandezba/zesarux. César is constantly adding new features and making improvements.

We have used ZEsarUX as a ZX Spectrum emulator, but it is capable of emulating many machines and doing many other things.

In this chapter we will not be creating folders, copying files or generating code. In this chapter we will go deeper into the use of ZEsarUX.

The first step is to set up ZEsarUX to suit your needs. ZEsarUX has many options that can be configured, but we are going to focus on the ones that I think are most interesting for the use we are going to make of it in this book. I encourage you to do your own research.

Personalisation

To customise ZEsarUX, press F5 to access the menu and then click on Preferences.

The first thing we need to do is configure a function key to restart the machine and another to enter debugging. Go to Settings and select the Function Keys option.

Once in the Function Keys, select the F11 key by either clicking or pressing Enter.

Once the key has been selected, we are shown the options available to us; we choose DebugCPU. We repeat the operation for the F12 key, but in this case we select Reset.

We need to test the buttons. Leave the menu by pressing Esc until it closes completely, or press F5 to go to the main menu and then Esc.

Once the menu is closed, check that pressing F11 opens the debug window and that pressing F12 restarts the machine.

There are many functions that can be associated with a function key, in fact I have defined several keys.

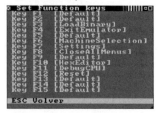

I do not define F5 or F9 as one opens the menu and the other gives direct access to file upload.

When debugging, I keep the debug window and the memory window visible, so it can be inferred that I am running out of space.

Next we go to Settings, select ZX Desktop and then the first option, **Enabled**. When you select it, more options are displayed, the first of which we are interested in, **width**. Click on it until the value is 512 (or another value that suits you). We can also set the value directly if we select **custom Width**.

To open the menu on the desktop, select the **Open Menu on ZX Desktop** option. On the other hand, if you don't want the menu to open when you click on it, I find it more convenient to go to Preferences/General and uncheck the **Clicking mouse open menu** option.

Now we have space to open other windows so that they don't share space with the screen of our beloved ZX Spectrum.

As I mentioned before, I like to have both the debug and memory windows visible while debugging. We need to change some options to be able to see how the memory is being updated while the program is running, and to be able to stop execution when the menu is open.

Go to Settings/ZX Vision and almost at the end, select the options **Stop emulation on menu** and **Background Windows**. Once the second option is activated, you will see another option to activate **Even when menu closed**.

We have already set up the environment. All we need to do is open the debug windows and the hexadecimal editor from the Debug menu and place them where we want them; press F11 to open the debug window.

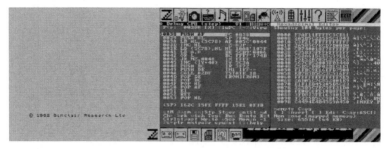

Under Settings/General we can change the language, although at the time of writing not all terms have been translated.

If at any time the windows do not respond, press F5.

Debugging

Let's say we have a program and we load it at address $8000; make sure you don't have the 16K machine selected or it won't work.

```
org    $8000

Start:
ld     hl, $4000
ld     de, $8100
ld     a, $ff

Loop:
ld     (hl), a
ld     (de), a
dec    a
jr     nz, Loop

Exit:
jr     Start

end    $8000
```

In this programme we point HL to the start of the VideoRAM, DE to position $8100 and load 255 ($FF) into A. Then we go through a loop in which we load the value of A into the positions pointed to by HL and DE and decrement A. At the end of the loop we go back to the start and continue in an infinite loop.

The programme is very simple, but it is enough to show what I want to show you.

The first thing we do is go into **Debug** and set a breakpoint at memory address $8000 so that execution stops at the start of the programme.

The different options are accessed by pressing the key corresponding to the highlighted letter.

In the central part of the screen, on the left, we see the disassembled code and the address where each instruction is assembled. On the right, we see mainly the value of the different registers and the state of the flags. Just below this we see the values of the stack.

At the top and bottom we see the different options; we will only see the ones we need to start debugging our programs.

On the top right we see **1-7**: **View**. Clicking from one to seven will show different views of this window; by default view one is shown.

At the top left we see **m**ptr. Pressing the M key opens a window where we can enter the address we want to go to. If we are entering hexadecimal values, the suffix H must be used.

Once we have entered the address, we press Enter and the disassembly from that address is displayed.

As we haven't loaded any programs yet, the only disassembly we see is NOP ($00).

We set a breakpoint at address $8000. If we look at the fourth option in the second line of options, at the bottom of the window, we see **Togl**; by pressing the L key we set or remove a breakpoint on the selected line.

We already have a breakpoint set at address $8000. When the program is loaded it will stop at this address and we will enter debugging mode. Press the N (**Run**) key to continue and return to Basic.

ZEsarUX displays a window warning us that there is a breakpoint, we have to press a key to enter the **Debug** window. We can prevent this window from appearing in the debug properties.

We load the program and debug it.

To follow the programme, we can run it in two ways: **en**: Stp and St**o**vr. In other environments, these are known as Step-by-instruction and Step-by-procedure.

Step by step by instructions (Enter) executes the instructions one by one, and when we are faced with a **CALL** to a routine, either ours or from the ROM, we enter it, with the possibility of executing it step by step and seeing its code.

In step by step procedures (O key), the execution is done instruction by instruction, but when we are faced with a **CALL** to a routine, either ours or from the ROM, it is executed and the PC (program counter) is passed to the instruction following the **CALL**; this must be taken into account in the loops.

In our programme, when PC is at instruction **JR NZ, 8008**, if we press Enter and A is not zero, it will jump to address $8008. Conversely, pressing O will execute the whole loop (all iterations) and point PC to the next instruction, **JR 8000**. Try it and see how it works.

At each iteration of the loop, it loads the value of A into the addresses pointed to by HL and DE. We can only see the different values loaded at the address pointed to by HL because it points to VideoRAM.

To see how the value of address $8100 changes, press F5, select the Hexadecimal Editor window, press M (memptr), type in address 8100H and press Enter.

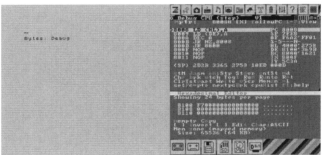

If we remove the breakpoint and press N (Ru**n**) we will see that the position $8100 is updated.

With this you should be able to debug programs, although ZEsarUX offers much more power, but it's up to you to discover it, but let's talk about one last thing: adding or modifying code directly in the debugger.

In the first line of options at the bottom, pressing the S (stM) key will display other options. Pressing the A (assemble) key allows us to modify the instruction at the selected address. To leave the Assemble window, press the Esc key.

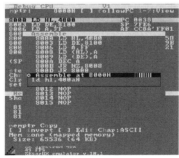

In our case, we will change the VideoRAM address where we load the value of A to column ten.

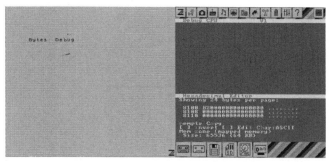

As you can see in the picture, the value of A is painted in column ten.

We have adapted ZEsarUX and acquired the necessary knowledge to debug our programs, but ZEsarUX is very powerful and there is still a lot to discover.

Download the source code of the example here.

https://tinyurl.com/27lvln2y

Let´s make a game?

Bibliography

Compiler Software's Z80 Assembly Course

https://wiki.speccy.org/cursos/ensamblador/indice

Santiago Romero

Dilwyn Jones Sinclair QL Pages

https://dilwyn.qlforum.co.uk/index.html

https://dilwyn.qlforum.co.uk/docs/articles/beeps.pdf

Advanced ZX Spectrum Programming, ROM Routines and Operating System

© Steve Kramer, 1984

© Ediciones Anaya Multimedia, S.A., 1985

ZX Spectrum Game Programming Club

© Gary Plowman, 2015

Printed in Great Britain
by Amazon

53007721R00256